Revolution and Tradition in
People's Poland

BY JOSEPH R. FISZMAN

Revolution and Tradition in People's Poland

Education and Socialization

PRINCETON UNIVERSITY PRESS

LC: 70-166369
ISBN: 0-691-05194-1

This book has been set in Linotype Caledonia

Printed in the United States of America by
Princeton University Press

To Gale and Sula

In compensation for all the time they missed their father and all the promises made but rarely kept

Contents

Tables

Tables

Tables

Acknowledgments

THIS WORK was undertaken with aid from the Inter-University Committee on Travel Grants and the Office of Education, U.S. Department of Health, Education, and Welfare, and I wish to thank them here for their generosity.

Many Polish colleagues were of enormous assistance in my work. Professor Jan Szczepański, presently Director of the Institute of Philosophy and Sociology of the Polish Academy of Sciences, was of great help to me. Professor Szczepański served as President of the International Sociological Association (1966-1970) and in early 1971 was appointed by the new Polish political leadership to head a special Committee of Experts whose task it is to study the current state of Polish education and to formulate recommendations for the future. It is my hope that this study will indeed (as he thinks it will) assist him in his present work thus repaying him in small measure for all the aid he has given me. Dr. Mikołaj Kozakiewicz of the Section for Research on Problems of Youth, Center for the Study of Industrializing Regions, Polish Academy of Sciences, one of the foremost theorists of Polish education, a prolific writer, a man of great personal warmth and charm; Dr. Dyzma Gałaj, Director of the Center and in 1971 elected as Marshal (speaker) of the Polish Parliament (*Sejm*); M. Szarras of the Research Department, Polish Teachers' Union; Adam Sarapata, Director of the Section for Sociology of Work, Institute of Philosophy and Sociology; Zygmunt Skórzyński, a sociologist presently associated with the Institute of Geography of the Polish Academy of Sciences; and Professor Wiktor Golde of the Warsaw *Politechnika* went out of their way to be helpful. There were, of course, many others.

Among my American and Canadian colleagues, I must acknowledge the help of Professor Robert E. Agger of the Department of Political Science, McMaster University, who has traveled repeatedly to Poland to help me with my work

Acknowledgments

and to offer his seasoned counsel; Professor Joseph Fashing of the Department of Sociology, University of New Mexico, whose aid was most valuable in preparing this report; Anita Chavan and Benson Bronfman of the Institute for Comparative Experimental Research in Behavioral Systems, University of Oregon. Special thanks are due to Marjorie Sherwood and Sanford Thatcher of Princeton University Press for their patient editorial assistance and advice, and last, but by no means least, Rachele Noto Fiszman whose counsel and selfless devotion I came to rely upon both in the field in East Europe, as well as at home, in the preparation of this manuscript.

None of these should bear any responsibility for this work, especially for its possible shortcomings.

JRF

Eugene, Oregon
November 1971

Preface

THERE ARE those who believe that ideology and programmatic statements are the true inspiration for political behavior and that such statements contain the blueprints for political action. There are also those who see in ideology only an attractive and thus convenient fig leaf that serves to camouflage political actions rooted in more prosaic interests and considerations. What, indeed, might be the relationship between ideological beliefs and norms and the behavior of actors on the sociopolitical scene of daily life?

Since the countries of Eastern Europe are officially committed to a formal and well-developed ideological system, one could reasonably expect that behavior in these countries would be directly and consciously related to ideological norms. We also assume that the ideological impact would be more clearly discernible there in areas of human activities which, although traditionally thought of as nonpolitical, are politically relevant nevertheless, inasmuch as they have an immediate bearing on people's attitudes, perceptions, social values, and styles. In this sense, all activities in the public realm could be legitimately considered as "political," and such a view indeed coincides with the theoretical and philosophical assumptions upon which the political systems of Eastern Europe are formally based. If this is the case, education as well as art, literature, music, and other disciplines perform a political function, and those engaged in these activities are political actors no less than formal political officeholders or citizens in the process of making formal political choices through the act of voting or through some similar political act, and that ideology has an impact on these.

Ironically, however, although East Europeans do relate politics to most social and public activities, they still tend to be more apprehensive about answering questions that touch directly upon formal and traditionally acknowledged areas of politics (e.g., questions about lines of command, power structures, interests, etc.) than they are about areas conventionally seen as nonpolitical. The social scientist, therefore, finds easier access to educators, musicians, writers, and others than he does to formal political actors, and he finds it more convenient to concentrate on the politics of education, for example, than he does on the command structure of the Party organizations or on the link between the Party and the formal agencies of government.

Also, since questions of obvious political character are not easy to ask under the circumstances, the social scientist in Eastern Europe usually must take the roundabout way and ask questions that are not of clear political significance but nevertheless reflect deep-seated political views, values, and norms (e.g., questions touching on religious beliefs, moral styles, attitudes toward science, technological progress, tastes in music and art, etc.).

Although in recent years Eastern Europe has become more accessible to the empirical social scientist, he is still faced with many problems. This, however, does not diminish the political character of the present study which is concerned with the role of education in Poland in a period of rapid and radical sociopolitical change and industrial development, and with how those in the field of education are prepared to meet their tasks—some of which are stated in ideological terms. It does so by ascertaining the attitudes of teachers with regard to a number of social, moral, or philosophical issues on which the Party as well as the Church have conflicting positions.

Western social scientists find it easier now to enter Eastern Europe and to establish contacts with colleagues in Poland, Czechoslovakia, Hungary, Rumania, Bulgaria, and East Germany, not to mention Yugoslavia. As a result, scholarly studies have appeared in the last few years in the United States and Canada which veer dramatically from the purely ideological approach (based on the assumption that if one is to learn what Communists think one must turn to the ideological scripts) but, instead, are based upon the

Preface

analysis of available and increasingly more accessible statistical data, published empirical research findings, biographical sketches of leaders and other members of the elite, patterns of succession, etc. Most of these studies while ingenious and useful are, however, in most cases in the nature of secondary analyses or reinterpretations of findings brought out by East European social scientists (and thus somewhat suspect as to reliability in some circles in the West). This book is the result of research in which a Western social scientist was actually and directly involved in almost all phases of the field work.

The field work for this study began late in 1965. Work continued throughout 1966 and during various periods of 1967 and 1968. Some of the supplemental data were incorporated as late as September 1969.

The year 1966 turned out to be particularly difficult for serious field research in Poland, especially in the area of education. The very fact that the initiative for the study came from an American citizen, affiliated with an American academic institution, sponsored in his research by an agency of the American government (i.e., the Office of Education) compounded the problem. The fact that the nature of the research endeavor necessitated a great deal of travel in Poland, including provincial cities and towns, did not help. In 1966 the press in the United States featured allegations of the connection between U.S. academic institutions and various agencies of American intelligence (and of U.S. social scientists serving such agencies under the guise of legitimate field research). These stories found their way prominently into the pages of the Polish press. Such reports rendered suspect, at least in certain circles, any American scholar engaged in serious field research in a Socialist country.

Coupled with this disclosure were two other developments that characterized 1966. The campaign against the war in Vietnam reached its zenith in Poland at that time. Antiwar and anti-U.S. slogans were strung across Polish city streets. There were periodic demonstrations in front of the U.S. Embassy in Warsaw. Most important, though, was the fact that 1966 was the year commemorating the Millennium of Polish statehood and Christian nationhood. This celebration highlighted claims of contending forces to that heritage—the secular state and the dominant Party, on the one hand, and the Church and religion, on the other. Since my research dealt precisely with questions of religion and secularism, Church and political socialization, and the attitudes toward these, I was treading in an area of particular sensitivity. Precisely because of these conditions, however, the responses obtained merit, I believe, additional attention.

Regardless of these special difficulties, research on problems of education is always wrought with difficulties in a country such as Poland. Although the Main Statistical Bureau (*Główny Urząd Statystyczny*) periodically publishes statistical data pertinent to education and in 1967 issued a special educational "Yearbook" covering the period 1944-1945 to 1966-1967, precise statistics are not easy to obtain. There are, for example, no exact figures for persons fully employed as teachers, as distinguished from teachers who are employed in education only part of the time. There are no readily available statistics on teachers with respect to social background (e.g., father's occupation), or to precise subject-matter specialization, not to speak of such vital background data as religious affiliation, party affiliation, etc. The Polish Teachers' Union is divided with respect to the level of education in which members are employed (e.g., higher, secondary, etc.), but there are no distinctions on its membership rolls at each level as to those engaged in actual classroom teaching, in school administration, or in custodial work. Even a precise distribution of ages among teachers is hard to obtain. Consequently, my research strategy had to reckon with these difficulties in addition to the sensitivity of the period.

The state/Party-Church friction of 1966 was replaced by frictions of another kind in 1968. The new problems were a result, in part, of the political situation in Poland, and in part related to the situation in neighboring Czechoslovakia. In order to proceed with the project, formal and informal arrangements had to be made with colleagues in Poland and with their institutions.

An initial questionnaire, which was designed for independent administration, had to undergo several revisions and finally had to be incorporated into a research instrument adopted by a Polish research unit interested in similar research problems for reasons of its own. Only in this way could answers to some of the questions be obtained. Conditions attendant to research in Europe, particularly Eastern Europe, are simply very different from those to which an American social scientist is accustomed and certain adjustments were required.

This study then is based upon the following:

1. Careful analysis of the available literature (books, monographs, statistical data, official laws, circulars, directives and orders, press releases, articles in the daily and periodic press, both professional and general)

2. In-depth interviews conducted with teachers, school administrators, and others involved in education

3. Observations derived from attendance at several local and regional conferences sponsored by (a) school district administrations, and (b) the Polish Teachers' Union

4. Visits to schools and focused interviews conducted with student groups

5. Analysis of secondary schools graduating examinations administered in five different school districts

6. Analysis of responses to a structured questionnaire administered to 416 students (including 68 student-teachers) of teachers' training colleges (*Studium Nauczycielskie*) located in five distinctively different localities

7. Analysis of responses to a structured questionnaire administered to 276 secondary school teachers drawn from the Union roster in five different school districts.

Despite difficulties, I was fortunate enough to be invited to staff seminars, research planning conferences, and to enjoy the cooperation (both informal and formal) of the personnel of the Research Department of the Polish Teachers' Union (this unit does not itself undertake research projects but, instead, sponsors or "farms out" projects it is interested in to other cooperating research units), the Institute of Philosophy and Sociology of the Polish Academy of Sciences which initially invited me to Poland, the Commission for Industrializing Regions of the Polish Academy of Sciences, and the personnel of various school district *kuratoria*.

This book is a report on the research just described. It proceeds from a brief analysis of the roles of education and of the teacher in a period of deep sociopolitical and economic transformation—an analysis which incorporates some of the basic philosophical assumptions underlying the present Polish educational system—to a description of the patterns of recruitment and training of teachers who would fill the anticipated roles and perform the expected functions. The study moves on to discuss the status of the teaching profession in the light of the *overall* social structure and the kind of life the newly certified teacher may expect within the community as well as within his professional milieu. At this point an attempt is made to critically analyze the level of preparedness of the new teacher in terms of the system's official expectations when these are confronted with the entrenched cultural norms and styles, perpetuated through the Church by focusing on the conflict between the two in the area of sexual morality—an area which highlights not only the young teacher's and would-be teacher's own internalization of conflicting points of view but also his professional preparedness to teach such a crucial and sensitive subject. The next step is to analyze in the same way the conflict of values and norms experienced by established teachers and to determine whether there are discernible differences in the respective handling of the conflict between tradition and systemic expectations among teachers of varying social background, professional identification, age, and tenure. Finally, the book deals with the product of the total educational effort by concentrating on secondary schools and their students. The purpose is to try to determine

Preface

whether the existing political system lives up to its own stated intentions with respect to education and whether the student graduating from the new "Socialist school" reflects in his knowledge, interests, and general thinking the announced ideal—the stated aspirations that the new "Socialist" teacher is to help mold and bring about. In other words, this study strives to ascertain whether the schools and the teachers, are successful in meeting official expectations and to what extent the political system itself is committed to encouraging the conditions that would realize these expectations. The book spotlights the nature of the gap, if any, between intent and performance, promise and reality, between the normative order (linked to the official ideology) and the empirical order of things. The schism between the normative and the real and the problems related to this discrepancy are, of course, among the foremost moral and political issues facing society in well-established as well as in newly developing political systems, and the resultant traumas may very well be at the root of much of the prevalent frustration and discontent that is particularly marked among the young. One would assume that these issues would confront more sharply those systems which are committed to a single ideology and belief system precisely because the latter tend to spell out lofty ideals and normative conditions with relative precision and conviction. Visions of the future aid such systems in their mobilization efforts.

This book was written before the Polish workers in the cities along the Baltic coast expressed their unrest in December 1970. This unrest which came on the heels of economic reform measures calling for a general wage freeze as well as an increase in the prices of services and food (while decreasing the prices of some hard consumer goods) took on clearly political dimensions resulting in riots and strikes which spread from the coastal cities to some inland urban centers and caused a change in both the government and the Party leadership. The altered status of some of the political leaders mentioned is acknowledged wherever appropriate. Although this study was written prior to the 1970 riots and the formal leadership changes, it still reflects cor-

Preface

rectly, I believe, the general state of sociopolitical flux. Periodic crisis situations would seem to be endemic to a system in which institutions old and new, some projecting deep-rooted values and traditional styles and others representing radically different norms, are thrown into uneasy coexistence. Occasional confrontations become inevitable. "Legal consciousness" alone is usually not sufficient to bind together a society that lacks deeply internalized and cementing fibers. Confrontations, however, usually resolve in new patterns of coexistence, a new modus vivendi, and in new coalitions of social forces. Hostilities which flare up from time to time have a way of receding into the background, of becoming sublimated for the sake of finding some working solution to a difficult situation. Each contending force strives to perpetuate its own authority and physical existence but at the same time must reach some accommodation with the other lest that which they hold commonly dear—the very survival of the country will be threatened. In the case of Poland, deep within Eastern Europe and bordered by the Soviet Union—a traditional enemy of past Polish political systems—whose armed forces maintain bases in the country, the threat or the perception of it is acute and ever-present.

The research instruments utilized in Poland—those used among students at the teachers' training colleges and among secondary school teachers—were subsequently applied in similar research in Yugoslavia and in the United States (in a West Coast community and in a large multiethnic metropolitan center in the Midwest). Comparative references to these studies are occasionally made in this book which, however, deals only with the Polish experience. It is an experience which bears implications for education generally in an age of rapid social and technological change, but has particular bearing on problems of education and socialization in societies in transition from traditionalism to modernity, regardless of the ideological coloration that the direction toward the latter assumes.

Revolution and Tradition in
People's Poland

The part played by make-believe, sublimation, hermetics, codes, in this culture, was not confined to poetry; they replaced reality; it is arguable that, next to the Jews, the Poles are the most literary nation in the world—not in the sense of having produced the greatest works, but because no other people has led a substitute existence for so long, or wallowed so deep in symbols.

—Kazimierz Brandys

Chapter 1: Introduction

Education in the Context of Revolution

EDUCATION has traditionally commanded the attention of political philosophers. Most of them perceive education as the primary medium for the dissemination and propagation of desirable values. Plato, for example, maintained that the ultimate aim of education is the development of insights into and understanding of the harmonious order of the world.[1] To Aristotle the goal of education should be the development of good citizenship, the ability to choose the "right" ends, and the corresponding "right" means for the achievement of these ends.[2] Even Rousseau's theory of natural education, antiestablishmentarian though it sounded, served only to augment his plea for a "naturalized" society which he viewed as ideal.[3]

Karl Marx did not develop a specific educational theory of his own. He viewed the institutions of education as components of the larger sociocultural and political superstructure which is basically conditioned by the level of economic development of the society and its class structure, which in turn is the result of the place of various groups in relationship to the dominant means of production. Nonetheless, he frequently expressed the view that the purpose of education is to integrate the individual into the larger collectivity by way of transforming his consciousness so that he may be able to rise above his atomized self and sublimate his narrow, private interest for the sake of a higher, universal interest

[1] See Plato, *The Republic of Plato*, Francis MacDonald Cornford, trans. (New York and London: Oxford University Press, 1945), especially Chapter IX.

[2] Aristotle, *The Politics of Aristotle*, Ernest Barker, trans. (New York and London: Oxford University Press, 1958), especially Book VII (Chapters XIII-XVII) and Book VIII.

[3] See Jean Jacques Rousseau, *The Social Contract and Discourses*, G.D.H. Cole, trans. (New York: E. P. Dutton and Company, Inc., 1950). See also *Emile or Treatise on Education*, William H. Payne, trans. (New York: D. Appleton and Company, 1908).

3

Introduction

and purpose.[4] And Lenin, the founder and foremost theorist of modern Communism, after pointing to the underlying link between education and politics, went on to view the institutions of education as important weapons in the revolutionary struggle. After the revolution he demanded the adaptation of the educational system to the needs of the new socioeconomic order and the construction of a Socialist society.[5] Lenin often referred to the process of education as an aspect of political propaganda.[6]

From a Marxist-Leninist perspective the values fostered by the schools (of whatever level) reflect the values and beliefs, the norms, goals, and interests of those in control of society's economic and political machinery. Those in control of the economic and political system assume that assimilation of these values will result in the development of desirable (from their point of view) behavior patterns. However, all theorists, ancient as well as modern, Marxist as well as non-Marxist, who have advanced a normative social vision maintained in addition that it should indeed be education's purpose to socialize the members of the ideal society into total identification with the perfect order.

Eastern Europe is presently in a process of massive value transition. In spite of this, however, institutions, belief systems, and styles of the old order continue to exist alongside those representative of the new political system; new political and social organizations dominate the formal stage, but must compete or share their influence with such deep-rooted institutions as the family and the Church.

Eastern Europe, especially Poland, has also undergone profound recent changes due to industrialization and urbani-

[4] See especially Marx's "Leading Article in No. 170 of the *Kölnische Zeitung*: Religion, Free Press, and Philosophy," his "Critical Battle Against French Materialism" and "Theses on Feuerbach" in *Writings of the Young Marx on Philosophy and Society*, Loyd D. Easton and Kurt H. Guddat, eds. and trans. (Garden City: Doubleday and Company, Inc., Anchor Books, 1967).

[5] Łukasz Kurdybacha, *Idee oświatowe i wychowawcze W. I. Lenina* (Warsaw: Państwowe Wydawnictwo Naukowe, 1970).

[6] Alfred G. Meyer, *Leninism* (Cambridge: Harvard University Press, 1957), pp. 49-56.

4

zation. In 1931, for example, only 27.2 percent of Poland's population resided in the cities. The ratio of city dwellers increased by over 10 percent (to 39.0) by 1950[7]—despite the extermination by the Nazis during World War II of 3 million Polish Jews (most of them lived in cities and towns), and in spite of the deliberate decimation of the Polish urban intelligentsia during the same period. Industrialization and urbanization were in part brought about by the political revolution and its goals. Another important contributing factor was the alteration of geographic boundaries after World War II—alterations which placed under Polish jurisdiction urbanized and relatively highly industrialized areas in the West and North which had been under German administration prior to the defeat of the Third Reich; at the same time Poland lost its Eastern provinces, areas of rich agricultural lands and forests. The latter were ceded to the USSR. While these provinces in the East (and Northeast) had large non-Polish populations (e.g., Ukrainians, Belo-Russians, Lithuanians, Jews, etc.) ethnic Poles also lived there in substantial numbers. These Poles were given the option of repatriation into a reestablished Poland whose boundaries had shifted dramatically westward. Once they availed themselves of this option they were settled for the most part in the cities of the newly gained western territories from which ethnic Germans were removed.

The trend toward industrialization and urbanization was accelerated by the impact of similar global trends. Whatever the reasons, by 1960 the percentage of urban residents rose to 46.0, and by 1970 to encompass over half of the Polish population (52.2 percent).[8]

To meet the demands of the revolution and of changing socioeconomic conditions, school authorities all over Eastern Europe have initiated a number of educational reforms. Educational reform began in Poland in 1962. The reform move-

[7] Główny Urząd Statystyczny, *Rocznik Statystyczny: 1966* (Warsaw, Vol. xxvi, 1966), Part i, Section ii, Table 5 (24), p. 24.

[8] According to preliminary results of December 1970 general census. See *Contemporary Poland*, Warsaw, Vol. v, No. 2 (February 1971), 30.

ment continued through the sixties and further changes are constantly discussed and contemplated. With varying success these reforms have attempted to bring the schools "into line" with the realities of changing sociopolitical conditions and the requirements of a new industrial economy. East European educators and educational theorists feel that corrective changes are imperative since, in the words of one veteran of Polish progressive education, "the traditional concept of education is crumbling under the pressure of new ideas and the demands of the age."

Fulfillment of such demands, however, is not without its problems. The schools are supposed to turn out citizens capable of being active and "cooperative" members of the new technological-industrial and Socialist community. Obstacles are encountered: an entrenched traditional culture perpetuated by the family, Church, and other established formal and informal institutions; educational traditions of a classical and humanistic character and elitist in nature; a scarcity of personnel equipped to meet the new system's technological goals and its ideological objectives; and a host of vested interests—functional, economic, and ideological— that may oppose the realization of the larger goals related to education. Even the educators are often reluctant—they fear the effect of radical alterations in the existing school system. A central issue is the conflict, not unfamiliar in the West, between demands imposed upon the educational process by the specialists, on the one hand, and by the ideologues, on the other. This is a conflict between science and Marxism, between secularism and the beliefs born of religious faith, between what is described in the official language as "approximate knowledge" ("the needs of the broad masses") and "selective knowledge."

The process of transformation will continue for a long time as even the most optimistic and most impatient among the leaders and planners realize. In the course of change, some school reforms will be discarded and new ones will emerge. The final outcome is hardly assured. What develops in the future may not be quite what the leaders of the system

Introduction

envision or desire nor what the traditionalists hope to salvage from the past. More likely, perhaps, is a synthesis of the new, the old, and the transitional itself, jelled into a pattern of its own. It would appear, however, that whatever the future of East European and particularly Polish education may hold, it will include an emphasis on vocationalism and "practicality" unknown in the past.

From the vantage point of the present political system, the ideal would be to develop future generations of citizens having not only the technical skills needed by the new economy but also a thorough commitment to the values and norms of a Socialist order and to the more traditional virtues of patriotism and love of Fatherland. Ideally, political leaders would hope to achieve a total identification of the young with the system. This identification would merge Socialist ideology and the concept of Fatherland so that there could be no divisive loyalties or doubts. When socialization is achieved, the acceptance of a lasting alliance between People's Poland and the Soviet Union would presumably follow. This alliance is not merely a feature of the current regime's foreign policy, but a cardinal principle of Poland's existence. In order to establish this principle, traditional hostilities toward the Soviet Union must be successfully stamped out.

Critical to the success of the new socialization efforts and the development of new economy related skills is the availability of a competent teaching cadre. Competence is here determined, of course, in terms of the system's goals. The objective of this study, therefore, is to determine how well those engaged in the process of socialization through education (i.e., Poland's teachers and student-teachers) are themselves socialized and thus, presumably, equipped to meet the system's educational goals.

Many of the teachers presently engaged in the educational enterprise were themselves educated under the new political system and under the conditions of the new economy. In this respect, the study will yield some insight into the general effectiveness of Polish education in meeting the expectations and goals the system has imposed. While exploring the various mechanisms for inculcating relevant sociopolitical values in the school organization, the study aims at identifying factors impinging upon or, conversely, fostering the process of value socialization, especially with respect to the teacher as a socialization agent.

Theoretical Orientation

Five closely related working hypotheses emerged from initial theoretical considerations of the problem of education in a period of radical sociopolitical and economic change. These hypotheses were used without any a priori intellectual commitment as to their inevitable correctness, but rather as guides to help sharpen the focus and facilitate the research. The hypotheses are:

1. As commitment to professional group norms (including disciplinary specialization) increases, a teacher's ability to internalize the system's ideological values is reduced thus rendering him less efficient in the ideological socialization of students.

2. Older teachers, and teachers of long tenure, are more amenable to accepting demands, values, and expectations imposed by the political system than younger teachers or teachers of shorter tenure. This was expected even though the latter were educated wholly under the new system while the former were educated predominantly in a prerevolutionary era. It is assumed here that age and professional tenure are factors accelerating socialization into the system and encouraging accommodation to existing conditions and demands.

3. Factors of social background (i.e., class origin, urban or rural residence, church affiliation, etc.) impede or facilitate the teacher's internalization of the ideological values and the ability to transmit these to students.

4. Among teachers of comparably advanced age (e.g., 46 years and over), those trained after World War II would manifest a higher commitment to the official educational

8

values than those trained prior to World War II. The underlying assumption is that older teachers feel a sense of gratitude toward the system for having enabled them to enter a profession at this advanced stage in life. This would be especially true where these are persons of working-class or peasant background whose chances under the old order were minimal, and whose previous education, if any, would have been interrupted by war and occupation.

5. Among teachers trained after World War II, the younger teachers would be less committed to the official educational values than older teachers. This hypothesis was prompted by considerations of an apparently growing "youth culture" and the concomitant rebellion against existing norms and expectations. This phenomenon, of course, is not limited to Eastern Europe generally or Poland in particular, but is characteristic of overall conditions in the sixties and seventies, induced perhaps by political uncertainties, technological change, and related conditions of cultural and social flux.

The book will concentrate on seeking answers to questions related to the kind of factors which may impede or facilitate the "harmonization" of values and beliefs, as officially espoused, and behavior, including teaching behavior. It will attempt to probe into the various dilemmas and conflicts that confront diverse groups of teachers (e.g., the young, the old, the prewar or post-World War II educated, the specialists, the scientists, the generalists, the humanists, the religiously oriented, the urban, the rural, etc.) which might hinder their own socialization and, thus, their occupational efficiency. What are the major difficulties encountered by educators in Poland, both in the community as well as in pursuit of their occupational activities? How, if at all, are difficulties overcome? And further, what organizational, institutional, general societal and cultural forces work toward conformity or nonconformity? The study attempts to explore the conditions contributing to generational differences among members of the teaching profession and the implications of these conditions for the system's future. Are these differences related solely to age or to the specific period of the teacher's own education and training, or to both? Are these difficulties perhaps related to larger social forces that influence certain groups of teachers more than others?

In addition, the study focuses on the nature of the various "corrective changes" made in the organization and content of Polish education in order to determine whether they are useful in the process of goal achievement. Have these changes affected established traditions? Conversely, do such traditions neutralize or cancel out the effects of planned change? How are the needs induced by technological change, industrialization, and urbanization being imposed upon the educational system, and how are such needs being met by a system which has been traditionally oriented toward the humanities and general social sciences?

Poland is, as indicated, a country undergoing both modernization and ideological and economic socialization. This raises an important question of how a system committed formally to such ends deals with the possible conflicts between those committed to a traditional humanistic educational curriculum and those who opt for a technical scientific emphasis. It also raises the question of how a country committed by virtue of its official ideology to social egalitarianism and classlessness deals with traditional social inequities and an educational system that was traditionally elitist. Could such traditions be adequately overcome, or must ideological intentions succumb to established, time-honored ways? How, indeed, do values and norms born of socialist ideology fare in the soil of a traditional national culture in which religion figured so prominently and, conversely, how are elements of traditional culture which may be viewed as impeding the achievement of the officially stated goals of the system dealt with? The range of problems and questions which suggest themselves are so numerous and of such importance that all of them obviously cannot be treated in this book with similar adequacy. Some are explored in greater depth and with greater precision than others. In spite of such limitations and in spite of the concentration on the experi-

Introduction

ence in a single country, it would appear nevertheless that the general conclusions of this book may very well be valid in considering other, especially newly developing, political systems, particularly those where broadly conceived social plans and goals, in the process of implementation, face deep-rooted cultural traditions and norms.

Chapter 2: Poland in the
Revolutionary Era

A System in Transition

WORLD War II and its aftermath brought about radical changes in almost all parts of the world. These changes are especially marked in Eastern Europe. Yet, concomitant with the transformation, many of the traditional prewar political, social, and cultural patterns have persisted (frequently in a modified form).

Poland has been affected by these changes to a greater extent perhaps than other East European countries. At the same time, the older, traditional behavior patterns have manifested a greater resiliency in Poland than elsewhere. Industrialization and urbanization have reached a country which prior to World War II was, by Western standards, backward. Often imposed upon old habits and styles, postwar changes could not but induce some degree of psychological strain. At the same time, advances in industrial and scientific technology, urbanization, and the spread of mass communication have given rise to economic, social, and political aspirations among segments of the population which in the past were (or felt) disenfranchised. Since the latter were primarily peasants and workers, the system of social relations in Poland was altered substantially.

The process of change was accelerated and made more radical by post-World War II border adjustments, mass migrations, and, as in other East European countries, by the introduction of a governing ideology which posits radical change as its goal.

The official ideology of present day Poland sets industrialization and technological development as a primary goal and as a precondition for the fulfillment of larger ideals. The new ideology was, however, introduced into a society which was almost feudal in structure and style. The tradi-

12

tional Polish intelligentsia had been recruited from a gentry class which had become impoverished due to repeated partitions of the country by foreign powers, socioeconomic and political repercussions which have followed periodic uprisings against the foreign authorities—uprisings in which some members of the gentry played leading roles—as well as to general economic depressions, crises, and shifting patterns of economic activity. However, although great segments of the gentry have lost economic ground, it has remained, as a class, the dominant social and cultural model in Poland. Even those who joined the ranks of the intelligentsia later and whose roots were in an emerging middle class, patterned themselves after their socially dominant peers. Consequently, the impoverished gentry has placed at least some mark on the other classes of Polish society and, through the leadership provided by the intelligentsia, on the various political movements, including the revolutionary Left.

In times of stress, when threatened by an external enemy, reliance on traditional symbols and values was synonymous with national patriotic resistance. Even those who were opposed to the old order found themselves upholding that order's institutions and goals. Thus, the comparatively radical leadership of the underground school movement in Poland during World War II, for example, considered itself duty bound to perpetuate the traditions of the old school system.[1]

The school system has since undergone significant structural and institutional changes. Within it, however, as within the larger society, many of the old prewar patterns remain. It is part of the complex revolutionary picture that these patterns continue alongside new norms and styles. A good example is the high regard for learning which, while fostered by the revolutionary regime, is a carryover of the old value system in Poland. It is noteworthy that young people in Po-

[1] Jan Woskowski, *O pozycji społecznej nauczyciela* (Lodz: Państwowe Wydawnictwo Naukowe for the Center for Sociological Research, Institute of Philosophy and Sociology, Polish Academy of Sciences, 1964), p. 172.

land clamor for entrance into overcrowded universities. Indeed, they often choose courses which not only do not prepare them in the technological skills needed in the new Polish economy but are also, in terms of future remuneration, less rewarding than more specialized and technical training would be. They tend to prefer courses and academic programs which are socially prestigious precisely because of past association of such study with the intelligentsia and its particular educational orientation (i.e., knowledge of languages, including Latin, the humanities, the arts, etc.).

The coexistence of old and new values is manifest in a number of other apparent anomalies in a revolutionary nation. New attitudes toward birth control and divorce are in vogue, but the woman is still accorded her traditional place in society. Although abortion is free and available upon request, women desirous of this service would rather turn to a private physician than to the public health clinic where she would have to place her problem on record and perhaps speak about it to a nurse or receptionist within earshot of other patients waiting in line. For the same reasons, medical doctors specializing in veneral disease advertise their private practice in newspapers. Similarly, the drive for efficiency, organization, and work is mingled with a relaxed attitude toward time and its proper utilization. Horse-drawn carts still amble on muddy streets in the shadows of the giant modern steel works named after Lenin and its surrounding workers' settlement, Nowa Huta, in the vicinity of Cracow. While "houses of culture" have been erected in cities, small towns, and even in some villages, so have street corner booths dispensing beer, and people in various stages of intoxication hinder traffic on city streets and country roads. For example, in 1965 the expenditure on alcoholic beverages, mainly the traditional vodka, constituted 15 percent of the total expenditure on food, and the per capita annual expenditure on these items approximated that year the average gross monthly salary of an employee in the public sector of the economy.

New interpersonal relations coexist with old status, re-

14

ligious, and ethnic prejudices, as well as with old courtesies. Although the once substantial Jewish population was destroyed during the Nazi occupation and most of those who survived left the country in the postwar years, although their old cemeteries presently lie in ruins and many of their ancient houses of worship have been converted into warehouses or cinemas, jokes of various degrees of subtlety focusing on Jews persist in the national folklore. Foreign films and television shows imported from abroad, transistor radios, and tourism have introduced the Poles, especially the youth, to foreign fads and styles—they are, however, viewed with suspicion precisely because of their non-Polish origin. While the guardians of both traditional and socialist morality stress the educational value of folksongs extolling traditional styles and longings, and of patriotic tunes celebrating heroism and self-sacrifice, the youth dances to the rhythm of "big beat" and rock and roll. Madame Mira Zimińska who heads the famous Polish folk song and dance ensemble *Mazowsze* complained that she finds recruiting fresh talent from among the village youth a discouraging matter nowadays.[2] Young girls seeking temporary employment abroad, often as domestics, ostensibly in order to learn foreign languages, are often looked upon with suspicion, and if such a girl should fall in love and marry a foreigner, especially of middle class, nonaristocratic background, she and her family would be criticized in terms of traditional and parochial nationalism, socialist morality, as well as in terms of gentry-rooted snobbism. For example:

> We could say much about those who pay verbal homage to the Fatherland and to Socialism but are engaged in shameful treason. They are the apostles of things alien and Western but live quite well in what they call "this country" on the sweat of the workingman. . . . We know people who mouth noble phrases here but when traveling abroad behave like beggars, rush after gadgets and trivia, void of self-respect and dignity. Some of them would talk

[2] *Kultura*, Warsaw (May 28, 1966).

15

to just anybody, defame their own country and the authorities believing that such behavior only testifies to their liberalism and broad intellectual horizons. I know personally of the family of a highly placed official of the People's Republic which is proud because their daughter married a Frenchman. The fact that the Frenchman turned out to be the son of an ordinary shopkeeper in Paris did not seem to bother this high socialist official. . . . Ordinary folk must be embarrassed by the current fashion of sending abroad during vacations Polish youth, mainly girls, to serve as domestics in the homes of foreign bourgeois families and storekeepers. Among those who leave for such employment are often the children of highly placed persons who enjoy a great deal of respect in our socialist country. Such travel, allegedly to learn a foreign language, is further being justified and rationalized with arguments that work, any kind of work, is virtuous and does not bring shame to the individual performing it.[3]

On the superficial, yet symbolic side, the coexistence of the old and the new is further and most vividly manifest in the increasing number of motorized vehicles competing for space and right of way with horse-drawn carts on old gravel or cobblestone roads as well as on new highways. Conversely, broad boulevards and squares which sprang up in cities devastated by the war are still empty of traffic as well as people. In Warsaw, the capital city, the multistoried Palace of Culture and Science—a postwar gift from the Soviet Union—rises within sight of war-torn but still occupied houses and ruins. Experimental films and music (both symphonic and jazz), a poetry of sensitivity, a graphic art of bold imagination have emerged and blossomed amidst a rather low level of sanitation. Men kiss the hands of ladies in traditional fashion and bow from the waist while the press reports churlishness and hooliganism, especially among the young. Pride in progress toward near eradication of il-

[3] Leszek Wysznacki, "O godności," *Stolica*, Warsaw, Vol. XXIII, No. 18, 1065 (May 5, 1968), 11.

16

literacy is dimmed by frequent complaints on the lack or low level of personal culture and hygiene.

Although the content of authority symbols is new, the respect accorded them is traditional. The house janitor, who before the war reported on his tenants to the "reactionary" police, now reports to the Citizens' Militia. Yet on city streets overhung with banners and slogans extolling the "eternal teaching of Marx-Engels-Lenin" or condemning the American presence in Vietnam, traffic is halted to allow the slow passing of a hymn-singing religious procession, and funerals of revolutionary veterans are accompanied by orchestras playing medleys of old revolutionary tunes as well as by priests fingering beads and whispering prayers. The former are there assigned by the deceased's organization, the latter at the request of the family. Indeed, a new "Socialist patriotism" conflicts and coexists with the Church.

Although the Church in Poland was often in conflict with the prewar secular authorities, it now remains as an organized reminder of the old order. Relations between the regime and the Church have passed through periods of hostility, coexistence and, at times, uneasy cooperation. Usually, when a new leadership takes over command of the political system and the Party, its seeks acquiescence from the Church hierarchy in return for certain concessions. This is precisely what occurred in October 1956 when Władysław Gomułka replaced the pro-Stalinist leadership and, again, in December 1970 when Gomułka, in turn, was replaced by Edward Gierek. Similarly, Church and Party may be drawn closer to each other when the latter, for whatever reason, decides to assume an active nationalistic stance—as happened in the aftermath of the March 1968 riots when blame for many of the system's ills was placed at the feet of "ethnically and culturally alien" cadres, in the main of Jewish descent, and stress was given to the quality of national purity and Polonism. On the other hand, in 1965-1966, at the time of the celebrations of the Millennium of Polish Statehood and Nationhood, relations between the regime and the Church reached a particularly high point of aggravation

17

because the Polish hierarchy assumed at the time (as it always did) to speak on behalf of all Poles since Poland is a Catholic nation. Indeed, the very emergence of the state coincided with the conversion to Christianity (in A.D. 966) of the once disunited Slavic tribes of the region.[4] However, the government and the Party claim the same right.

To be sure, such competing claims have brought the Church into conflict with secular authorities in the past, prior to the emergence of People's Poland, but never were they such a comparable source of real or potential tension. In the past neither the Church nor the state started out from philosophical assumptions and frames of reference so basically antagonistic. In the period of monarchic rule, for example, the Church felt subordinated to Rome rather than to the weak Polish kings, but the kings themselves assumed the role of defender of the faith. Periodically the king allied with the hierarchy to ward off a hostile gentry or other competing sociopolitical interests. It was also under the banner of the Church and the cross that the Polish monarchy expanded its boundaries and influence, eventually bringing the pagans of vast Lithuania into the Roman fold in the fourteenth century and into a mighty commonwealth extending from the Baltic to the Black Sea. Yet, though cemented by bonds of marriage between Polish and Lithuanian nobility, for all practical purposes the union dissolved in less than 100 years, a victim of competing socioeconomic and status conflicts, its grand designs often frustrated by the Church. However, the loss of union with Lithuania was soon compensated by the ascendancy of the Polish king, Władysław III, to the throne of Hungary—elected to that throne by the Hungarian lords themselves in the hope that he might save them from the threatening Turks. He gave his life in the battle at Varna.

Generations of Poles have been taught that they have a special mission in this world due, in part, to the geographic position of Poland in Europe. They fancied themselves the

[4] See *Orędzie biskupów polskich do biskupów niemieckich: Materiały i dokumenty* (Warsaw: Wydawnictwo Polonia, 1966), p. 121.

last outpost of a Western Catholic Europe in the East, and thus the defenders of Western civilization. As is sometimes the case with frontier residents, their attachment to what they were to defend was fanatical and unyielding. When Russia, Poland's non-Catholic neighbor on the east, emerged as a power surpassing Poland, and, in alliance with Poland's non-Catholic neighbors on the west who were once vassals of Polish kings, managed to help bring about the disintegration of that country, aided in the task by factionalism within the ranks of the Polish nobility, the notion of Pole and Catholic came to be equated. The good Pole was a Catholic Pole. The convert to Russian Orthodoxy was viewed as a traitor to the nation and was virtually excluded from the life of the community. During the long period of partition in Poland, as in the case of the Jews, nation and religious faith became identified with each other. Rousseau viewed Catholicism in Poland as a contributing factor to a sense of solidarity and cohesion. During the 150 years of national and political subjugation, the Church fostered allegiance in the faithful to the collective bodies of nation and Church rather than to religion alone as a road to redemption. Thus the loyal Catholic Pole did not necessarily feel compelled to internalize principles of piety and to practice them in daily life. His Catholicism, as the Church, was perceived in broad social, political, and symbolic terms, and the Church saw its role in like manner. As such it became generally conservative, traditionalist, and highly politicized.

With the establishment of People's Poland after World War II, state-Church relations became further complicated by the fact that the Polish clergy, unlike elsewhere in Eastern Europe, generally assumed an anti-Nazi position during the occupation thereby neutralizing possible future sources of opposition. Indeed, a measure of goodwill toward the Church remains from those years even among some strata of the current political elite. Such feelings toward the Church and the clergy may serve as a restraint on government action against the institution of religion, but it does not contribute to a complete resolution of existing state-

Church tensions. Official animosity is easily aggravated by the fact that a representative of the Polish emigré government is still accredited at the Vatican whereas the Holy See does not formally recognize the existing government in Warsaw, although its attitude toward that government has undergone certain modifications during 1970-1971. Tensions were particularly aggravated by the Vatican's official references until very recently to former German territories presently under Polish jurisdiction as "territories under temporary Polish Church administration," naming members of the German Church hierarchy residing in West Germany as "capitular vicars" of the dioceses in these territories. Conversely, Poles of all political shades view control over the former German territories not only as a matter of historical justice fulfilling an ancient claim, but also as a compensation for war losses. To the Poles, control over former German territories is one of the few symbols of having been the first to fight on the side of the victorious alliance. Moreover, many Poles displaced from the eastern areas ceded to the Soviet Union have settled in the cities and villages of the former German territories in the west and north. By now a generation of young Poles, native to the new locale, has established itself. Yet, it was not until 1970—that is, 25 years after the end of World War II—that official papal annals ceased mentioning names of German Church dignitaries when referring to the dioceses east of the Odra (Oder) and Nysa (Neisse) Rivers, and it was not until the beginning of 1971 that an official spokesman of the Holy See announced an initial step toward the normalization of the legal status of the Church in the area.[5] In the spirit of reciprocation, the government granted the Polish Church title deeds to the enemy Church properties in the former German regions.[6]

Much of the official governmental and Party animosity is directed against the person of Cardinal Stefan Wyszyński who symbolizes resistance against secularization. Yet it was Wyszyński who backed Gomułka's return to power at the

[5] *Contemporary Poland*, Warsaw, Vol. v, No. 2 (February 1971), 27.
[6] *Ibid.*, 34.

time of the "Polish October" in 1956. At that time Wyszyński saw in Gomułka the only possible alternative acceptable to both the Soviet Union and to those in Poland who sought greater independence from their powerful neighbor to the east. It did not take long for both Wyszyński and Gomułka to fall back on the rigid positions of their respective ortho-doxies, that of the Church for the former and the Party for the latter. And when the Gomułka leadership was forced to relinquish its position in the face of the unrest of De-cember 1970, Cardinal Wyszyński and his fellow Church dignitaries, confronted once more with a difficult situation, aware of past disappointments but with renewed hope, of-fered their "reasonable" assistance to Gomułka's successors, as well as their prayers for those who "are responsible today for order, peace, and justice."[7] And as did Gomułka in 1956, the new Party and government leadership under Edward Gierek accepted the offer.

Regardless of the periodic ups and downs in state-Church relations, however, the Church remains in opposition to the regime, offering the masses a competing value and belief system replete with a set of metaphysical, idealistic, and patriotic symbols. Buttressing this competing system is the Church's assumption that it represents a perfect society, and thus has the right and duty to "watch over the education of her children in *all* institutions, public or private."[8]

The open conflicts between the belief systems of Church and state have forced people, particularly those charged with the task of value socialization, to choose sides. Even if the choice were not explicitly forced upon them, the entire atmosphere would render even a wavering attitude untena-

[7] A statement offering "reasonable" (*rzeczowa*) collaboration to the new Gierek leadership was adopted at a Conference of Polish Bishops (January 27-28, 1971) and was signed by both cardinals. It was ordered that prayers be offered in all churches in memory of the victims of the December 1970 events as well as for the authorities. See entry of 14-2-71 in Section "Wydarzenia miesiąca" ("Events of the Months") in *Kultura* (Paris), N. 3/282 (March 1971), 148.

[8] Pope Pius XI, "The Christian Education of Youth," *Secondary Education: Origins and Directions*, Robert G. Hahn and David B. Bidna, eds. (New York: Macmillan Company, 1965), p. 144.

21

ble for very long. A deeply felt religious commitment is not compatible with the new national ideology just as a Socialist consciousness, as Marx conceived it, is contradictory to religion. In spite of such incompatibilities, the realities of present-day Poland are such that there are persons who consider themselves believing Catholics and, at the same time, are sympathetic toward the regime, just as there are those who declare themselves atheists yet are far from de-Christianized.[9] Within our theoretical framework, however, it is assumed that a person's proreligious attitudes virtually expunge his potential as an effective agent of socialization into a Communist-Socialist value and belief system—provided, of course, that serious weight is attached to such a system by those in charge.

Education in a Period of Transition

Those in control of the educational system in any society hope to instill in their charges an ability to synthesize the "right" ends with correspondingly "correct" means of social action. In Poland, education is not merely a mechanical process of introducing the student to a "scientific outlook or an acceptance of Marxist theory," it is a struggle for the totality of the student's personality.[10] Understanding is obviously not enough in itself. One can learn Marxism just as one learns physics or chemistry without necessarily having accepted an altered frame of reference and behavior. As one observer of modern Polish education states the problem:

[9] Both of these outcomes emerge as behavioral possibilities from studies conducted in Warsaw by the Center for Research on Public Opinion of the Warsaw Radio, by Father Wileński, on rural youth by Konstanty Judenko, and by J. Legowski among workers in the Wola District of Warsaw. See Tadeusz M. Jaroszewski, "Dynamika praktyk religijnych i podstaw światopoglądowych w Polsce w świetle badań socjologicznych," in *Kultura i Społeczeństwo*, Warsaw, Vol. x, No. 1 (January-March 1966), 133-49.

[10] Mikołaj Kozakiewicz, *O światopoglądzie i wychowaniu* (Warsaw: Państwowe Zakłady Wydawnictw Szkolnych, 1965), p. 21.

22

The Revolutionary Era

Many theologians learned Marxism, understood it, and even recognized its validity in many respects—yet after finishing their studies their general position is one of denial of Marxism. The pedagogue and educator must understand that the world outlook he must mold in his pupils cannot be achieved through books but through the mind and heart of the student; that it is not printed but felt and professed, lived and thought. . . . Thus, when one speaks of forming a scientific Marxist world outlook what is meant is the formation of a state of affairs in which the person thinks Marxist, lives Marxist, acts Marxist.[11]

It would appear, however, that before the pedagogue and educator can achieve the desired results he himself must possess the appropriate Marxist instincts.

Some Party ideologues rationalize imperfect conditions of socialization, theorizing that one can be both Catholic and pro-Socialist, and would settle for half the individual—one who is acquiescent if not fully committed. Yet most assume that nothing but full commitment on the part of the population, especially the younger generation, can assure the long-range security of the new sociopolitical system. The child must assimilate the values of the new system and absorb the symbols which express these values. The adult born and educated under the prerevolutionary regime must be retooled or resocialized. He is like the immigrant who must learn to adapt himself to a new value system and to new behavior patterns. Such problems are not limited to nations with revolutionary regimes. Many adults in the United States, for instance, refuse to face rapidly changing conditions or are unable, because of previous conditioning, to take full advantage of emerging opportunities. Such problems, however, are much more difficult in countries with revolutionary regimes that must contend with institutions and behavior patterns which are carryovers from the old order. It is said that the Puerto Rican in New York has diffi-

[11] *Ibid.*, pp. 21-22.

culty learning English because he lives within the compact mass of Spanish-speaking people and because Puerto Rico is nearby and relatively accessible. For the "immigrants" from the pre-Socialist system in Poland, the Church is their San Juan, and readily accessible.

The problem of transition in Poland is further compounded by the fact that relatively few migrated from the old system into the new voluntarily. Certainly the citizens of Poland did not develop, during the country's capitalist period, a personality suitable for entry into the higher Marxist developmental stage. Socialism in Poland did not evolve out of capitalism in the same gradual manner as capitalism evolved out of feudalism. As elsewhere in Eastern Europe, in Poland Socialism has emerged as the official ideology as a result of the upheaval brought about by World War II and its aftermath. Moreover, the political conditions which existed prior to the establishment of the new system were not hospitable to the kind of institutions—in the form of legal mass parties with subcultures of their own—which would have enabled the Pole to be schooled and prepared for the demands of the coming order. Only the Jewish Socialist movement in Poland managed to develop, prior to World War II, a substantial subculture of its own, complete with a wide network of secular schools, libraries, social organizations, trade unions, and parties, with a life style of its own—but then the Jewish Socialist subculture functioned only within the limited confines of minority existence, within the boundaries of particular neighborhoods and provincial settlements. As far as the larger Polish population is concerned, the impact of the Socialists and Communists while rich in tradition, was diffused primarily because their number was proportionately smaller than the number of Socialists and Communists within the Jewish minority and because they faced a tradition-oriented peasantry—the bulk of the Polish population in the interwar period—as well as a politically fragmented working class and a nationalistic urban middle class which hoped to benefit, and did indeed benefit, from the existing sociopolitical and economic order.

24

In this respect, it has been argued that the Socialist personality type clashes with traditional Polish personality types.[12]

The road to the new personality is further obstructed by demoralization left in the wake of the brutal occupation of World War II. Although more than 20 years have passed, the memory of that period lingers with most. Unsettled conditions of the postwar years and continuing change have further aggravated the situation. Present-day cynicism, juvenile delinquency, escape into alcohol, and the quick acceptance of current foreign fads can be attributed, in part at least, to these factors. Moreover, the relative well being of the masses resulting from industrialization and urbanization, instead of bringing people closer to the desired socialist perspective, seems to have induced a heightened yearning for material goods and gadgets, rather than for more idealistic values.

Even if it is true, as some Western observers maintain, that the political elite in Eastern Europe, faced with the necessity of making daily policies, is becoming deradicalized, and even if some of these policies have the effect of reorienting the population away from ideologically inspired values, official commitment to that ideology remains just as strong. As the Polish social scientist, Jerzy Wiatr, remarks in his critique of those who see the approaching end of ideology:

> . . . deideologization or even the weakening of the role of ideology would have been tantamount to putting on the brakes on socialist transformation . . . the educational ideal of Socialism is of fundamental importance. Only those who believe that conditions in our country are perfect can agree to the decline of the ideology or even to postulate deideologization.[13]

[12] Jan Szczepański, "Osobowość ludzka w procesie powstania społeczeństwa socjalistycznego," *Kultura i Społeczeństwo*. Warsaw, Vol. VIII, No. 4 (1964), 3-25.

[13] Jerzy Wiatr, *Czy zmierzch ery ideologii? Problemy polityki i ideologii w świecie współczesnym* (Warsaw: Książka i Wiedza, 1966), p. 194.

The Revolutionary Era

The Socialist educational model, as other educational models, is designed to build mass support for the existing system. This, of course, does not mean that the process may not backfire. Those introduced to the normative values of the system may be led to expect more than the system can deliver, given current sociopolitical and economic realities. Consequently, many may be appalled by the gap. The gap between official ideals and everyday realities may very well be at the root of student unrest in Poland as well as in many other parts of the world. One of the many difficult dilemmas facing contemporary Polish education is the problem of reconciling expectations induced by the new ideology with empirical conditions.

Bohdan Suchodolski, perhaps the foremost philosopher of education in Poland, describes education as a "process of social activity, deeply rooted in historical conditions and problems of our times, as well as historical aims of our nation."[14] To those directly involved with the task of education in Poland, the "historical conditions and problems of our times" boil down to a "process which is supposed to create in the student's mind a Communist consciousness, to guide them into Communistic behavior as well as to develop their scientific and creative abilities and talents."[15] The system, moreover, is in need of citizens who show a high degree of active involvement.

The school system of Poland attempts to inject into traditional patriotic education a new Socialist-Communist content, and to implant in the minds of the pupils the idea that the concepts of Fatherland, patriotism, and Socialism are inseparably associated. As the then First Secretary of the Katowice *Województwo* Committee of the Polish United Workers' Party and Politburo member (and since December 1970 the First Secretary of the Central Committee of the PUWP), Edward Gierek, indicated at the time of the Millennium celebrations in 1966:

[14] Gusta Singer, *Teacher Education in a Communist State: Poland 1956-1961* (New York: Bookman Associates, 1965), p. 11.
[15] Janina Filipczak, *ibid.*, p. 109.

The Revolutionary Era

Many of the interesting forms of patriotic education which are being developed during the present important period as we celebrate the Thousand Year Anniversary of Polish statehood should be permanently incorporated into educational activity. While kindling in the youth a pride in the accomplishments of the country and a love for Fatherland, the idea should also be implanted and strengthened in their consciousness that there is an unbreakable unity between the concepts of "Poland" and "Socialism." Patriotic education must be imbued with a Socialist content.[16]

Yet, the school system is only one of the socializing agencies, often in competition with other socializing agencies such as the family or Church. Even children of high Party officials are brought up in a religious tradition by their devout mothers and grandparents, often without the father's awareness. The latter situation often poses peculiar problems inasmuch as a major strategy for reaching the adult members of the society is through their socialized children educated in the new schools.[17]

The necessity of rearing deeply committed generations of citizens is prompted not only by the desire to build and

[16] Report of talk by Edward Gierek, at the time Politburo member and First Secretary of the Katowice *Województwo* Committee of the Polish United Workers' Party, at Plenum Meeting of that Committee at the City of Katowice. *Trybuna Ludu*, Warsaw (April 17, 1966). The 7th Plenum of the Central Committee of the PUWP meeting on December 20, 1970, following the workers' riots earlier that month, elected Gierek to the post of First Secretary of the C. C. of the PUWP, the position previously held by Władysław Gomułka. In addition to Gomułka, the 7th Plenum also released Gomułka's closest associates from membership in the Politburo and/or Central Committee Secretariat—namely, Bolesław Jaczczuk, Zenon Kliszko, Ryszard Strzelecki, Marian Spychalski. Three days later a special plenary session of parliament (*Sejm*) affected similar changes in the Council of Ministers. Piotr Jaroszewicz was named Chairman of the Council of Ministers (premier) while the previous long-time prime minister, Józef Cyrankiewicz, assumed for a while the largely ceremonial post of President of the Council of State.

[17] See report on Mokotów District Committee plenum of the Polish United Workers' Party, *ibid.*, April 16, 1966. Mokotów is a district in Warsaw.

strengthen the system but also by the need to defend it. As two authors of a prize-winning Polish military text explain:

> Discipline based on conscience replaces discipline based on terror. . . . No one can stand behind (the soldier's) back at all times to see how he executes an order. He will have to act alone, of his own free will, of his own initiative. . . . This can be achieved only if the man in the field is deeply committed, unswervingly convinced that the cause for which he fights is just—that is, a man of severe inner discipline, fully responsible for his own acts.[18]

The New Poland

As indicated earlier, profound changes of industrialization and urbanization have accompanied Poland's political revolution. While a primitive economy may have no need for an elaborate school system to train cadres for its purposes, an industrial nation needs an educational system which is attuned to its current needs and further development. As Clark Kerr and his associates point out, education in modern society becomes the "handmaiden" of industrialism.[19]

In 1931, 29.7 percent of the labor force in Poland was employed in nonagricultural work and by 1960 it was 52.9 percent.[20] The enormous growth of the nonagriculturally employed population in Poland, as already indicated, may be attributed in part at least to that country's loss of the industrially backward areas in the east after World War II. Yet, it is also the result of a conscious and deliberate effort on the part of the government. Poles like to compare their present state of technological and industrial development with that of Turkey which did not suffer from war devastation and

[18] Marian Jurek and Edward Skrzypkowski, *Konfrontacje: Tradycjonalizm a współczesność w wychowaniu wojskowym* (Warsaw: MON, 1965), pp. 23-24.

[19] Clark Kerr et al., *Industrialism and Industrial Man: The Problems of Labor and Management in Economic Growth* (Cambridge: Harvard University Press, 1960), p. 36.

[20] *Rocznik Statystyczny 1966* (Warsaw: Główny Urząd Statystyczny, 1966), p. 598.

whose nonagricultural labor force during the same period (1931-1960) rose only 6.8 percent. Most people attribute the Polish industrial advance to the regime's policies.

For Poland, as for any nation where Socialism has been officially established during the infancy of its capitalist development, the problem of adjustment to a technological age and the ability to compete in the international marketplace takes on special urgency. This is not merely a matter of catching up for the sake of prestige or even economic competition and profit. The vision of a Marxist future is closely linked with the ability to supersede semifeudal styles and values with technologically and scientifically oriented skills and value patterns. As Henryk Golański, a former Minister of Higher Education in Poland, stated it: "The general prospects of contemporary civilization lie in the welding of the twin factors of scientific and social progress and social revolution."[21] And it was Lenin who saw a symbolic link between a country's level of electrification and the conditions necessary for the establishment of the new order. It was also Lenin, however, who warned that "illiterate people cannot tackle electrification, and . . . mere literacy is not enough either."[22] The burden then, is on the school system and on those active in it, to prepare the youth for life in an industrial-technological society just as much as it is to socialize them into the sociopolitical values of the system.

In the United States the expectations attached to the school system in connection with the growth of industry began in the wake of the Civil War, almost 100 years before this became a serious problem in Poland. Nevertheless, even at the present, some critics of the existing school programs in the United States complain that the schools are behind the growing needs of industry, that there is too much emphasis on booklearning, or upon the development of pleasant

[21] Henryk Golański, "Planning for the Future," *Polish Perspectives.* English language edn., Warsaw, Vol. IX, No. 12 (December 1966), 26.

[22] *Marx: Engels: Marxism* (Moscow: Foreign Languages Publishing House, 1951), 4th English edn., p. 534.

manners, at the expense of shop-oriented skills.[23] Similarly, critics of the existing school system in Poland complain about the inability of graduates of the general educational (academic) secondary schools to "erect a decent, simple pig stall."[24] In Poland the drive to assimilate school youth into the patterns of the economic marketplace takes on, among others, the form of patronage links between certain large industrial enterprises and/or trade unions, and the schools of their area. Stress is increasingly given to the concept of polytechnic education which, in theory at least, entails the development of both a "proper" personality and economically useful skills.

In spite of efforts to date, however, entrenched traditional value patterns and styles clash with attempts at socialization into a technological-industrial culture. Thus, for example, the continued prestige enjoyed by nontechnological disciplines, the lack of eagerness among girls to enter technical-vocational schools, or the hesitation of women to give up their traditional roles in the family for industrial jobs. However, the push for the purely vocational aspects of polytechnization—prompted, no doubt, by current economic needs and by past educational neglect—awakens concern among some humanistically oriented educational theorists, and among those outside the school system who feel themselves responsible for maintaining traditional national values. Such concerns are further aggravated by the open tendency of some bureaucrats to measure the value of investments in education generally by education's ability to produce quick, visible, and measurable returns. Consequently, some fear and with good reason that vocational and technological training has a larger payoff value in the eyes of governmental administrators and planners than does the pursuit of basic science or learning for its own sake.[25]

[23] See, for example, criticism voiced by the Harvard Report and by Admiral H. G. Rickover in Hahn and Bidna, *op.cit.*, pp. 18-22, 202-09.

[24] Jurek and Skrzypkowski, *op.cit.*, p. 85.

[25] See, for example, Kazimiera Muszalówna's report on the plenary session of the Polish Academy of Sciences in *Życie Warszawy* (May

The Revolutionary Era

In addition to the divergence as to the means of goal achievement (assuming agreement on the goals) politicians, administrators, and educators assess the reality around them quite differently. Empirical sociological studies dealing with that reality are often viewed with suspicion by the political leadership. Such studies are seen as products of erroneous (because academic) perception, or worse yet, as influenced by "bourgeois" social science in both methodology and concern. The periodic difficulties experienced by social scientists in Poland led Jan Szczepański to remark that "every politician is deeply convinced that he has a firm grasp of the reality he is transforming and is not always inclined to agree with the sociologists' explanation."[26]

Much as a consequence of these conditions, discussions of the relationship between the two cultures, the humanistic and the technological-scientific, which was current in the United States in the early sixties, is presently in vogue throughout Eastern Europe. Underlying such discussions is an attempt to find a common ground between the presumably different value systems characteristic of each of these cultures. The search for such a synthesis actually began in the United States with John Dewey, but in Poland it has become a meaningful issue only recently.[27] The goal of such a synthesis would be to educate future generations of technologues who would also be humanists and ideologues. Members of these generations would assume command of the total society, including the economy. In the meantime, on the level of the public school system, the search for a

27, 1966), as well as Konstanty Grzybowski, "Place in Society," *Polish Perspectives*, English language edn., Warsaw, Vol. IX, No. 12 (December 1966), 43-49.

[26] Jan Szczepański. "Sociology 1968." *Polish Perspectives*, English language edn., Warsaw, Vol. XII, No. 3 (March 1969), 30.

[27] For Polish voices in the debate, see Jarosław Iwaszkiewicz's talk at the Congress of Polish Culture, as reported in *Życie Warszawy* (October 8, 1966); Bohdan Suchodolski, *Społeczeństwo i kultura doby współczesnej a wychowanie: Zarys pedagogiki*. (Warsaw: Państwowe Zakłady Wydawnictw Szkolnych, 1958), Vol. I, 320-23; Jan Szczepański, "The State and the Planning of Higher Education," *Poland*, Warsaw (January 1969), 32-33, 50-51.

synthesis is to take on the form of a dual emphasis on both "moral-political education in the socialist spirit" and training in the "acquisition of skills, practical and productive habits, a polytechnic education."[28]

Teachers as Agents of Socialization

Despite difficulties related primarily to economic causes and manpower shortages, secondary education has become popularized in Poland. Increasingly, the level of one's education, rather than his politics, determines his position in society. Traditionally, the level of one's education was more important in terms of status and prestige than income level. Unlike the status patterns in bourgeois France, for example, a proper social background in Poland was not necessarily related to economics. The prewar Polish elite was, as indicated, recruited largely from an impoverished gentry whose sons staffed the officers' corps and the professions, and who served as a model to be emulated by the other classes. It was a class which disdained wage earning as somehow below a man's dignity. It was a class which lived on in a heroic and romantic past, and whose life style left an imprint on the current Polish elite.

Secondary education in Poland may be of a general or a vocational character. It was traditionally the former, however, which perpetuated the gentry educational orientations and which served as training ground for the newer urban intelligentsia, in itself by and large a product of impoverished gentry background. To members of the intelligentsia lacking a gentry past, a diploma (a Certificate of Maturity or *Matura*) from a secondary school of general education— or, as it was known traditionally, a *gimnazjum* (and in the late thirties modified as a *gimnazjum* followed by a two-year lyceum)—served, in the words of one Polish sociologist, as the "equivalent of the gentry coat of arms" because

[28] Wojciech Polak, *Organizacja pracy domowej ucznia: Zagadnienia obciążania* (Warsaw: Nasza Księgarnia, 1965), p. 18.

it was proof not only of education but more importantly of gentlemanliness as well.[29] This secondary school of general education (presently known only as *lyceum*) is still the only type of secondary education which provides opportunities for entry into academic institutions and, subsequently, the more prestigious professions.

The selection of candidates for academic institutions and the professions begins, in reality, at the time when the pupil graduates from grade 7 of elementary school. Although the teacher is not wholly responsible for the process of selection, the institution of education is so closely knit with the individual's future and career that the teacher is an important object of concern to students, parents, and society. Many expectations are associated with the teacher. Comparatively rigid conceptions develop as to what kind of person he should be and the type of relationships he should have with children and their parents. Perceptions also develop as to the appropriate relationships between teacher and school authorities, and toward his role in the community.

The teacher is seen as the carrier of crucial values, both within the school and outside of it. The school and the teacher are public property, and a teacher is, as Willard Waller points out with respect to the American context, but applicable no less to Poland, "a paid agent of cultural diffusion . . . the teacher's position in the community is much affected by the fact that he is supposed to represent those ideals for which the schools serve as repositories."[30] Even so, the formal guidelines for teachers in the areas of professional morality are less precisely drawn than those concerning his professional duties.[31] Professional-morality guide-

[29] Aleksander Gella, "The Life and Death of the Old Polish Intelligentsia," *Slavic Review*, Vol. 30, No. 1 (March 1971), 15.

[30] Willard Waller, *The Sociology of Teaching* (New York: John Wiley & Sons, Inc., 1965), p. 40.

[31] See Mikołaj Kozakiewicz, *Niezbadane ścieżki wychowania* (Warsaw: Nasza Księgarnia, 1964), p. 185; Jan Woskowski, *Nauczyciele*

lines often are formed on the basis of unstated anticipations, vague notions frequently growing out of conflicting demands made on the school system. However, it is precisely this professional morality which is instrumental in how the teacher infuses in his students the expected spirit of patriotism, including that of the Socialist variety.

Educational literature in Eastern Europe, classic as well as modern, assumes that teaching is not merely a job but a lofty calling which should appeal to and attract idealists. Emphasis is placed on the moral-ideological qualities of the teacher while his subject matter qualifications are sometimes relegated to a secondary position or taken for granted.

The list of qualities expected in the average teacher is staggering, yet there seems to be general agreement among educational theorists on the minima. For example, a small sample would include such personal characteristics as intelligence, maturity, a high sense of responsibility, discretion, loyalty, etc., and he should be serious. A sense of humor might be misconstrued as frivolity, or worse yet, cynicism. In addition to expertise in his particular field, the teacher is expected to be a savant, local political leader, and lifetime student; to relate well to parents and organizational acquaintances; to be unwavering in his political views while avoiding "sensitive" questions in the classroom which might "confuse" students relative to established authority symbols; and to be imbued with the right spirit—generally enthusiastic. As if this weren't beyond the capacity of most men (perhaps *any* man), he is to treat his profession, not merely as a job but as a calling. In this regard, of course, he would feel it unbecoming to bargain for higher wages. Instead he should be satisfied with whatever the community can afford. The disdain for the pecuniary aspects of the profession are, though, quite compatible with the tradi-

---

szkół podstawowych z wyższym wykształceniem w szkole i poza szkołą (Warsaw: Państwowe Wydawnictwo Naukowe for the Inter-Institutional Center for Research on Higher Education, 1965), p. 100; Józef Kozłowski, *Nauczyciel a zawód* (Warsaw: Nasza Księgarnia, 1966), p. 187.

The Revolutionary Era

tion of the Polish gentry which, though impoverished, finds discussion of money matters beneath its dignity and honor. While the causes may vary, however, such expectations of the teaching profession are similar to those in many, if not most, other countries including the United States.

What distinguishes the Polish Communist educational system from other (especially non-Communist) systems, is the expectation that the teacher should consider himself a member of the "working-class intelligentsia" and, as such, feel a sense of solidarity with the working class as a whole. This expectation is not necessarily inconsistent with gentry prestige models. What constitutes a departure from the gentry tradition is the expectation that the teacher in contemporary Poland should strive to develop in his students a respect for work, particularly manual labor. That this expectation clashes with the aristocratically oriented style of the new political elite (many of whose members are of non-aristocratic origin), and that because of the prevailing prestige models manual work continues to be perceived as inferior to professional or white-collar work, is beside the point.

As vague and unstated as the moral and political guidelines often are, Józef Kozłowski, on the basis of normative expectations held by formal school authorities relative to "ideal" teacher behavior, was able to draw up a statement of "do's" and "don'ts." Thus, the ideal teacher *should not*

> . . . lack in culture or demonstrate an ambivalent ideological and political posture. He should not show a negative attitude toward Socialism and the people's authority. He should not be a person without clear perspective or without specific life goals. He should not be ambiguous with regard to the officially proclaimed world outlook nor should he be backward in his own social views, nor religiously devout or intolerant.[32]

On the other hand, the teacher should, according to Kozłowski, manifest the following positive characteristics:

[32] Kozłowski, *op.cit.*, p. 175.

He should be generally cultured and mature, possess a proper ideological and scientific world outlook, display a positive attitude toward prevailing sociopolitical reality, and deep conviction as to the correctness of the Socialist idea. He should be ever ready for self-sacrifice and be unselfish. His moral posture should grow out of his inner convictions; he should be honest both in word and deed; his behavior should at all times be in accord with the officially proclaimed slogans and principles. He should possess civil courage and personal dignity. He should be altruistic and at the same time down-to-earth; he should be guided by objectivism.[33]

The Polish teacher is expected to participate in the Pedagogic Council of his school. Actual school administration, however, remains in the hands of a principal or director who, in turn, is subordinate to a Department of Culture and Education of the local National Council. The latter, in its own turn, is subordinate to the respective culture and education departments of National Councils of higher administrative levels. The principal or director is simultaneously responsible to the *curatoria* or local education organs of the central Ministry of Education. These elected and administrative agencies work closely with the parallel existing culture-education committees of the appropriate leading Party organs at each governmental level (that is, the conglomerate of rural villages known as *gromada*; the town; the *powiat*, the county; the *województwo*, country district or the metropolitan area; national).

Along with the several demands imposed on teachers, there are in theory at least, reciprocal obligations imposed on the community at large. More often than not, however, the community views the teacher with a mixture of admiration and hostility. Especially in communities removed from large metropolitan centers, where the teacher is often one of the very few professionals in the locality, he is looked upon with a mixture of respect and resentment. On the one

[33] *Ibid.*

36

hand his learning is admired but on the other it is considered a manifestation of snobbism. His activism is expected and relied upon, but it is also resented. He is seen as an outsider, frequently as a transient, a meddling agent of city based authorities.[34] Because many organizations see him as a natural candidate for their activities, usually unrelated to teaching, others in the community perceive him as too eager to become involved, and often consider him an imposition. At the same time, the teacher's education often creates ill feeling among the leaders of the very organizations seeking his involvement, and even among his administrative superiors, who themselves were chosen not infrequently on the basis of their organizational abilities and/or loyalties, rather than for the level of their education.[35]

Feelings of resentment are often strengthened by the fact that changes induced by the school system are not always welcomed or appreciated by the community.[36] Religious elements, especially in rural areas, see in the school a threat to the Church and in the teacher a challenge to the parish priest. Zbigniew Kwiatkowski, an astute but friendly observer of the current Polish scene, reports on a visit to a village in which a new Church structure is being erected (the third one for the *gromada*) while only three classrooms are being added to an overcrowded, old, and dilapidated school building. The new Church is being built by volunteers—peasant women who, Kwiatkowski notes, carry the brick with expressions of "pious concentration." The new Church is to serve four adjoining villages, the residents of which are contributing not only their free labor but funds and material

[34] See Barnard Tejkowski, "Społeczność małego miasteczka Pomorza Zachodniego," *Studia Socjologiczne*, Warsaw, No. 4 (1965), 103-17; Zbigniew Kwiatkowski, *Byłem niemilczącym świadkiem* (Warsaw: Iskry, 1965), pp. 237-53; there are many other testimonies as to the actual existence of these conditions, including those I gathered from in-depth interviews.

[35] See Tadeusz Jackowski, "Miejsce młodej inteligencji: Pod milionowym dębem," *Życie Warszawy* (May 29-30, 1966), and Tejkowski, *op.cit.*, p. 110.

[36] Kwiatkowski, *op.cit.*, p. 245; see also, for example, letter to the editor. "Głosiciel linii politycznej," in *Polityka*, Warsaw, Vol. v, No. 46 (506) (November 12, 1966), 1.

as well. In addition to the school, other structures in the village are in need of repair but the brick destined for the new Church is safe, no one would dare to steal it. Even the poorest among the villagers find enough spare cash to contribute to the parish building fund—cash, Kwiatkowski maintains, they did not possess prior to the establishment of a Socialist Poland. The school, unlike the Church, must pay for every piece of material, for every hour of labor. Even the chairman of the local *gromada* National Council is active on the Church building committee. There is a great deal of social pressure on the village residents to become involved in the parish project while the pressures, if any, in support of the school are official and pro forma and thus less effective. Kwiatkowski complains:

> The construction of the new Church has drained the village of its energy and funds. . . . The priest demands that the villagers donate to the Church the first penny (*grosz*) they have left after meeting the most essential expenses—yet the Church as an institution did not provide them with these pennies nor with the source of their income. . . . I do not ask by what right does the priest make his demands; I merely ask, in the name of what? In whose authority? Does the priest really believe that the Church should have priority over the school and the several hundred children who attend classes under the most deplorable conditions? . . .
> . . . You ask in the name of what? In the name of faith, blind faith if you will . . . .[37]

The teacher's morals, especially in the case of young unmarried females, are always suspect, but especially in small localities.[38] The male teacher generally, but especially one living in the big city and employed at the elementary school level, is seen as an occupational-economic failure. The "feminization" of the profession is both the cause and the effect of such attitude. On the other hand, teachers of work-

[37] Kwiatkowski, *op.cit.*, p. 184.
[38] *Ibid.*, p. 245.

ing-class or peasant background are considered to be social climbers, ambitious, and career oriented, and as having deserted their class. It is the popular impression, often incorrect, that they feel best, and most at ease, only in the company of other members of the intelligentsia.[39] At the same time, teaching is generally perceived as the most convenient and accessible vehicle for entry into the professions by youth of working-class and rural background.

To boost teacher morale and prestige within the community, the Polish government instituted a special Teacher's Day and the title of "Meritorious Teacher of the Polish People's Republic." In addition, teachers are usually recognized on the various occasions when medals and crosses of merit are awarded. Such rewards also serve as bases for additional material benefits to supplement a rather modest income. Also, the Party in certain areas give out monetary prizes to teacher-activists.[40]

As is true of the members of any other occupation or pro-

[39] Woskowski, *Nauczyciele szkół podstawowych z wyższym wykształceniem*, pp. 80-85. Dr. Woskowski's findings, based upon a questionnaire administered to 184 elementary school teachers with academic education, indicate that teachers select their social associations, aside from family contacts, on the basis of common interests held rather than on the basis of the formal educational level of the associates. His findings show further that close to half of the teachers of working-class or peasant backgrounds continue to maintain contacts with persons still belonging to these classes, with females favoring such "old class" ties to a greater extent than males. Continuation of such ties is reduced among teachers of self-employed artisan milieu. On the other hand, 50 percent among the female teachers of working-class background do not maintain any contacts with persons outside of the intelligentsia and 76.5 percent of male teachers whose fathers were teachers themselves do not maintain contacts with nonintelligentsia persons. Unlike the United States, career orientation in Eastern Europe is generally not viewed as a positive personal characteristic since it implies in popular perception singlemindedness toward the pursuit of career goals at the exclusion of other values and interests; persons to whom such characteristics are ascribed are perceived as climbers, opportunists, and termed "careerists."

[40] See speech by Edward Gierek at Regional Conference of Polish Teachers Union at Katowice, June 17-18, 1966, as reported in *Głos Nauczycielski*, organ of PTU (Warsaw), June 26, 1966, 5-6. Gierek informed the gathering that the *Województwo* authorities allocated 2,500,000 złotys worth of prizes to teacher-activists.

fession, teachers develop an image of themselves and of their role in society. In part the teachers' image of themselves reflects what society thinks of them. Such images are, in some respects, defense mechanisms countering what teachers consider erroneous conceptions of the profession.

Thus, the teacher in Poland considers himself a victim, a martyr to the cause of cultural diffusion, better than, and misunderstood by, his community. He sees himself as a person in need of cultural and academic opportunities, largely because of the requirement imposed by superiors for professional advancement, and in smaller measure because of a natural hunger for these. He sees himself as underpaid, and is always concerned about problems of proper housing, health, and retirement prospects. He is a good family man, attached to his children, and therefore concerned about their education and future career opportunities. He resents administrative-political interference in school matters, and feels himself intellectually superior to those who would interfere on the strength of their administrative and political positions. He resents the parents of his students and considers required association with them an imposition on his time. Status and prestige, both in the community and vis-à-vis other educators, are matters of great concern. Consequently, he is resentful of laymen who, in private or in public, criticize the school. Such criticism is interpreted as a threat to professional status and prestige. Polish teachers even went so far as to adopt resolutions demanding that their union intervene against frequent press criticism of the schools and of the profession by what they considered "uninformed laymen."[41] Polish teachers are sensitive to authority—their own as well as that of others. They are resentful of too many nonschool related impositions on their time. They view themselves as professionals and resent being utilized for other purposes. They see themselves as being moderately idealistic as well as cynical but also loyal toward the group.

[41] *Ibid.*

40

The Revolutionary Era

An important issue among Polish teachers appears to be a clearer definition of the yardsticks applied to their professional competence. They are concerned that although they are pressed into community service which takes them away from school work, the authorities are ambiguous as to which, school work or community service, is evaluated more highly in giving promotions and rewards. Some among them feel that nonschool related activities make them objects of controversy in the community, thus affecting their status. Others see in community activity an excuse for poor work as educators, as well as an avenue whereby they may advance on the administrative and political ladder. There is talk of the need for a larger measure of teacher solidarity, feeling that teachers are faced with a hostile united front of the community and the authorities.

In Poland teachers feel that it is improper to openly criticize a colleague, to deliberately seek popularity among students and their parents, or to seek direct personal favors from superiors. They further feel that a teacher should avoid conflict situations or singlehandedly challenge authority. Similarly, they believe that the individual teacher ought to be careful about his classroom conduct lest he invite repercussions. A rule of thumb for teachers is to avoid jobs in the provinces as this may place one in a visible position. The provinces also offer fewer opportunities for cultural expression and professional advancement. In the big city there is the advantage of potential anonymity and greater opportunities. Therefore, a job in a big city is considered superior to a job in the provinces, even at increased remuneration, material benefits, greater responsibility, and at a higher educational level.

Although less is being said in the available literature in Poland about the perceptions held by students of their teachers, one can nevertheless glean from scattered evidence, including literary memoirs, a picture of an educational bureaucrat, seldom inspiring, whose primary concern is fulfilling assigned tasks without too much friction. The student seems to perceive his teacher as a sort of operative,

The Revolutionary Era

a bit timid and generally loyal to the system who, in order to gain favor in the eyes of superiors, tends to discriminate in the classroom in favor of students of working-class or peasant background, or in favor of children whose parents hold high administrative or political posts.[42]

[42] See, for example, Henryk Grynberg, "Pochodzenie społeczne czyli Łapa," *Kultura*, Paris, Nr. 4/259 (1969), 45-57, a fragment of his literary memoirs *Życie ideologiczne* (*Ideological Life*).

Chapter 3: Educating the Teacher

The Road to a Teacher's Education

THE POLISH Higher Education Act adopted in 1958 states:

> Universities and professional colleges participate actively in the building of socialism in People's Poland through training and education of professional intelligentsia cadres, the conduct of scientific research, the development and cultivation of national culture, and collaboration in advance of technical progress.[1]

The stress is on the ethical and moral ideological values of the system, as well as on the need to transmit accumulated knowledge and to keep abreast of new knowledge. The teacher is an important agent of socialization into the values of both cultures, the ethical and the technological-scientific. The government and the Party, although wishing to transform the society, find their own position insecure, however. As a result, both seem to place greater emphasis on the need for loyalty among teachers than on expertise. The latter is usually taken for granted or becomes an issue only if the individual fails or is otherwise suspect in his loyalty, or if his professional qualifications are of such low caliber that his incompetence is difficult to ignore. Ryszard Strzelecki, at the time a member of the Politburo of the Polish United Workers' Party, suggested following the student riots of 1968 that "people should be judged (in order) according to class, political, and professional criteria."[2]

As persons of working-class or peasant background are successful in entering the professions or become established in higher political or administrative posts, their children can no longer properly be considered of "desirable" class background. The terms "working-class intelligentsia" or "work-

[1] Zygmunt Ratuszniak, "The System," *Polish Perspectives*, English language edn., Warsaw, Vol. IX, No. 12 (December 1966), 6.
[2] *The Polish Review*, New York, Vol. XIV, No. 1 (Winter 1969), 95.

43

Educating the Teacher

ing intelligentsia" are officially employed to categorize such persons, that is, those who are active in the professions but stem from a proletarian background, however distant. These terms are also used to describe those members of the traditional intelligentsia who profess to an emotional or ideological identification with the working class. As Aleksander Gella correctly points out, however, the friendly intelligentsia occupies third rank, after workers and peasants, in official Communist rhetoric as well as on application forms for jobs and schools.[3] Nevertheless, the whole concept of class background, in terms of desirability or undesirability, becomes increasingly ambiguous as the system grows older and matures. Instead, the criterion of political loyalty becomes, in fact, the most important one. Political loyalty does not necessarily mean membership in the Party. Of basic importance is behavior which meets the accepted social requirements and expectations. As Heliodor Muszyński describes it:

> . . . [What counts] is the conduct of the individual in the light of the established moral requirements of society relative to individual behavior. For an individual to be able to assimilate and recognize the social role expected of him he must have a positive attitude toward the system which sets these expectations. . . . The individual who does not have before him a specific model of moral behavior to emulate cannot very well judge and, subsequently, react to his own deviations from the model, nor is he able to consider his own behavior relative to the system in whose terms models are to be established.[4]

Ideally, the teacher is to serve as such a model of behavior. Yet the teacher is a product of his home and of the larger social environment, of which institutions predating

[3] Aleksander Gella, "The Life and Death of the Old Polish Intelligentsia," *Slavic Review.* Vol. 30, No. 1 (March 1971), 2.
[4] Heliodor Muszyński, *Teoretyczne problemy wychowania moralnego* (Warsaw: Państwowe Zakłady Wydawnictw Szkolnych, 1965), p. 54.

the present system are a part as well as the postrevolutionary institutions.

The school reforms of 1966 established the end of grade 7 of elementary school as the first point of selection for possible professional training. The reforms of that year added grade 8 to the elementary school structure, but only for those students whose grades, economic-social conditions, or other considerations are such that they are destined to enter the secondary schools (lyceums) of general education. From there, they may continue toward a university or other academic education or terminate their education with a general secondary school diploma (*Matura*).

If a student ceases his elementary schooling with the traditional grade 7 he must either join the labor force or continue his education in a secondary school of specialized or vocational training. It is the lyceum of general education alone which normally would lead one into higher education. The new system was designed to channel more students into specialized vocational training. The practice of opting for the prestigious secondary school of general education, even where later attendance at a university was impossible, made such reforms necessary. When given a choice the popular preference for general education was, of course, a carryover of the gentry tradition and of the gentry-oriented values associated with the *Matura*. Such tradition and orientation found institutional reinforcement during the interwar period when only *Matura*-holders were eligible (in terms of the revised Constitution of the late thirties) to serve in or to vote for the upper chamber of parliament and when only graduates of the classical-humanistic or mathematical-scientific *gimnazjum* could qualify for officers' rank in the armed forces. In turn they could marry girls of at least similar educational background. Thus many students opted for this type of education although the job market, with its increasing demand for technical skills, could not absorb the many graduates. The reform of 1966 was designed to encourage as many as possible to remain in grade school until completion of grade 7, and then to enter into specialized training. Students destined neither for higher education nor vocational training were to be encouraged to finish at least grade 6, designated officially as incomplete elementary education. Due to shortages in manpower and school buildings, and other economic problems, however, many rural schools contained six grades or less, making them de-facto incomplete. To remedy the situation, incomplete schools were organized into districts attached to at least one complete elementary school—containing grade 8 or at least an intermediate grade 7. In many rural areas though, economic pressures (e.g., the need for labor on the small family farm, etc.) and lack of dormitories and school buses serve to discriminate against local youth who are forced to terminate their schooling at the incomplete elementary level.

The reforms were also conceived in order to alleviate an acute teacher shortage on the elementary school level. Qualifications of teachers underwent scrutiny and many found themselves transferred, together with grade 8, from the secondary school level to the lower elementary one. Teachers were told that these transfers would result in more space and generally better working conditions for those retained by the secondary schools of general education.[5] Still, the academic year 1966-1967 saw 30 percent student vacancies in the vocational secondary schools while those of general education were, as always, oversubscribed.

The reforms of 1966 foreshadow the gradual liquidation of special secondary schools for pedagogic training whose graduates qualified for teaching on the preschool (kindergarten) level. However, shortage of teaching personnel also on that level of the educational pyramid made the temporary continuation of the pedagogic lyceums a necessity. Yet, the pedagogic lyceums, although presumably preparing their graduates for a profession, do not enjoy the prestige accorded the lyceums of general education because of their

[5] Editorial, *Głos Nauczycielski*. Official weekly organ of Polish Teachers' Union, Warsaw (June 26, 1966), 1, 3.

vocational classification. It is assumed that brighter students, or students of some social status, continue at the secondary school of general education. In 1966 only 70 percent of those enrolled in the pedagogic secondary school completed the four years required there.[6]

The low status attached to preschool or lower elementary teaching leads to a critical dilemma. In many respects, those who are teaching at this level see themselves as failures. Most, if not all, would have opted for the general studies program and later study at a university. In a very real sense, they have been failed by the system which they are expected to support with all their energies. Such circumstances may engender a certain amount of ambivalence on the part of teachers at the lower levels regarding both their position and the system which led them there. While they play a crucial role in the formation of the child's attitudes toward the new Poland, inasmuch as they are the first to have him in the educational setting, their commitment is often undermined by their own failure. The depth of feeling in this respect is underscored by the fact that many will seek admission to the general studies program illegally rather than accept the route which leads toward consignment to lower elementary teaching. Rumors abound about the use of pull involving highly placed politicians, bureaucrats, and even clergy with connections in local school administrations. A provincial school official complained:

Such rumors hurt the schools and the prestige of teachers. Parents who feel that their children were unjustly not admitted to a given school write letters to the editor and the editors print such letters. The problem is that there are more candidates for secondary education than there are vacancies. Students are required to pass an entrance examination and it is the Examination Commission which decides who is to be admitted and who not. An Examination Commission may consist of a dozen persons and it makes its decisions usually in colleagial fash-

6 *Ibid.*

ion. Yet, it is true that parents find out who the members of the Commission are and often try to bribe us. I am a member of such a Commission and I know. I was offered chickens, eggs, a few hundred *złotys* at times, invitations to parties and so on. Many of those making these offers do not even realize how embarrassing it can be.[7]

Residents of rural areas feel discriminated against not only with respect to admissions to secondary schools of general education but even with respect to admissions to vocational secondary schools and *technikums*. They suffer not only from lack of educational facilities in the immediate vicinity but also from lack of contacts and lack of knowledge as to proper procedure, including examination dates, etc. It also appears that many admission officers who interview prospective candidates are discriminatory and discourage sons and daughters of peasants by curt responses. Perhaps, too, being shy and timid, children of peasants find the bureaucratic manner of busy admission officers discouraging. Moreover, students from rural areas fare less well than urban students in the examinations largely because of inferior school preparation. Many peasants cannot understand why their children sparkled in the village elementary school but failed to gain admission to the school of higher level in the neighboring town.[8] As a result of these and other conditions, most of the unskilled labor force in Poland is recruited from the villages where many of the youth fail to complete even the first six grades. It was estimated that in 1963, for example, 30 percent of the youth from the State Farms (*Państwowe Gospodarstwa Rolnicze*, PGR) joined the labor force with only a six-year education or less.[9] A survey conducted among the youth of 133 State Farms in 11

[7] Personal interview with a vice-director of an agricultural *technikum* in K., Warsaw *Województwo*, November 1966.

[8] Błażej. "Rozmowy z czytelnikami," *Fakty i Myśli*. Organ of Executive Board of Association of Atheists and Freethinkers, Bydgoszcz (November 1-15, 1966), 7.

[9] Jerzy Bońkowicz-Sittauer, "Dlaczego się uczą?" *Polityka*, Warsaw, x, 1, No. 46 (506) (November 12, 1966), 4.

48

counties as well as among sons and daughters of independent (i.e., private) farmers in 19 counties of the Kielce *województwo* indicates that the chances of a peasant child fulfilling his ambitions for further education are more likely to be frustrated than not, regardless of the type of postelementary school aspired to. Ironically, only those students of peasant background who do not desire to continue any education past the elementary level stand the best chance of having their goal, as it were, attained. Thus, in the sample of 5,576 peasant students, 29 percent did not intend to continue past their basic education but 39 percent actually could not continue, whereas though 34 percent hoped to attend a general education lyceum or some other nonagricultural secondary school, only 24 percent could do so.[10]

The youngster of rural background, therefore, who could go to a pedagogic lyceum (not to speak of a lyceum of general education) may well consider himself fortunate even though teacher training institutions of nonuniversity level are looked upon as inferior in status and prestige by the more gifted or more sophisticated students from urban centers. As a consequence in the lyceums of general education, the road to the university (or the university-level higher school of pedagogy), the intelligentsia is dramatically overrepresented (see Table 3-1). This is true everywhere, but it is especially true in major urban centers. Thus, for example, youth of intelligentsia background represent 72.2 percent of the secondary general education school population in Warsaw, 61.6 percent in Cracow, 60.5 percent in Poznań, and 58.2 percent in Wrocław. Children of peasant background, while still a minority, are represented in larger numbers only in the lyceums of general education in cities and towns located in predominantly agricultural districts (e.g., Lublin, 45.1 percent; Rzeszów, 31.3 percent; Kielce, 33.1 percent; Białystok, 40.1 percent). Similarly, youth of working-class background form a substantial part of the student population only in the secondary schools of general education in predominantly industrial cities and regions

[10] *Ibid.*

Educating the Teacher

TABLE 3-1

SOCIOECONOMIC CLASS BACKGROUND OF STUDENTS IN LYCEES
OF GENERAL EDUCATION, 1964-1965

Class Background	No. of Students	Percent
Intelligentsia	174,555	43.1
Working Class	106,515	26.3
Peasantry	74,115	18.3
Other Agricultural Workers (Agronomers, etc.)	4,455	1.1
Independent Artisans/Craftsmen	28,350	7.0
Other	17,010	4.2
TOTAL	405,000	100.0

SOURCE: Główny Urząd Statystyczny (GUS), *Statystyka Szkolnictwa: Szkolnictwo Ogólnokształcące: Opieka nad dziećmi i młodzieżą, 1964/ 65*, Warsaw, No. 4.

with major working-class populations (i.e., Lodz, 42.7 percent; the coalmining district of Katowice, 40.5 percent). In fact, in spite of the officially proclaimed policy of preferential treatment for youth of working-class and peasant background (manifested on and off by the application of several credit points for background on the entrance examination scores), the number of youth of working-class background, especially in secondary schools of general education, has actually declined somewhat over the years. Moreover, even when such youth is admitted to the lyceums of general education, their success there is far more problematic than for children of elite background.

Because of the limited educational resources of the country, the schools at every level (but especially on the secondary and higher education levels), impose relatively demanding performance standards. Poor work is usually dealt with quickly and decisively. Students who do not meet the high standards of the school are dismissed with little opportunity for recovery. Here again, peasant and working-class youth are at a disadvantage in that their preparation has usually been inferior to that of those with whom they are forced to compete. Students of peasant background are

50

known to work harder in order to achieve grades comparable to those obtained by students of intelligentsia background. On the other hand, students of working-class background, especially in the provinces, are reported to take their studies less seriously with corresponding effects on their grade cards.[11]

In addition to the rigid academic demands, moral deviance is not tolerated. What constitutes a moral offense is an ambiguous question, however, and given the demand for educational opportunities, school officials are able to behave quite arbitrarily in their judgments and actions. Moral offenses are met with swift dismissal and it is rural and working-class youth, whose ways are often offensive to the school authorities, who are the most frequent victims.[12] Such factors progressively reduce and block the representations of the lower classes as one goes up the educational ladder.

Once past secondary school, the scramble for entry into institutions of higher level is repeated. In a society in which higher education is a vehicle for social advancement and in which a degree is a symbol of status very much akin to the traditional aristocratic title, there are more candidates for admission to degree granting institutions than the system is actually able to absorb. The pressure for admission is the highest in those institutions whose fields of specialization offer the graduate the highest social status and prestige, although not necessarily the promise of higher income. The values of a new industrial-technological culture, although widely propagated, have as yet not taken root in the popular consciousness but instead, the older, traditional, and humanistically oriented values still prevail. Schools of art or music could not accommodate all comers while institutions specializing in the physical and technical sciences

[11] Konstanty Grzybowski, "Refleksje sceptyczne: Czy istnieje młodzież robotnicza i chłopska?" *Życie Literackie*, Cracow, Vol. xv, No. 45 (719) (November 7, 1965), 3.

[12] Janina Borowska, "Miejsce w internacie," *Trybuna Ludu*, Official organ of Central Committee of Polish United Workers' Party, Warsaw (July 26, 1966), 4.

51

Educating the Teacher

usually still have vacancies in midsummer. Moreover, due to the general and traditional stress on the humanities, great numbers of candidates for higher education fail during examinations in the sciences as well as in mathematics.

Although the number of students of working-class and peasant origins continuing their education beyond the secondary school level has increased in the postwar era despite the still existing odds, the bulk of the student body in institutions of higher education continues to consist of sons and daughters of the intelligentsia, many of whom are descendants of the prewar impoverished gentry. At the universities, the institutions of highest prestige, the socioeconomic class backgrounds of the student body during the academic year 1965-1966 is shown in Table 3-2.

TABLE 3-2

SOCIAL CLASS OF UNIVERSITY STUDENTS IN POLAND, 1965-1966

Class Background	Number	Percent
Working Class	10,470	26.1
Peasantry	5,631	14.1
Intelligentsia	21,347	53.3
Self-Employed Artisans	2,028	5.1
Other	578	1.4
TOTAL	40,054	100.0

SOURCE: Główny Urząd Statystyczny, *Rocznik Statystyczny Szkolnictwa: 1944/45-1966/67*, Warsaw, 1967, p. 434.

At institutions for teacher training the representation of the lower socioeconomic classes increases as one moves down on the scales of prestige and educational level. In the higher schools of pedagogy, equivalent to schools of education at the university level in the United States, children of the intelligentsia still predominate although the percentage of workers and peasants is higher there than in university departments of humanistic or scientific studies.

52

Educating the Teacher

TABLE 3-3

SOCIAL CLASS OF STUDENTS AT HIGHER PEDAGOGICAL SCHOOLS
ACADEMIC YEAR 1965-1966

Class Background	Number	Percent
Working Class	2,575	35.6
Peasantry	1,512	20.9
Intelligentsia	2,784	38.3
Self-Employed Artisans	309	4.3
Other	55	0.7
TOTAL	7,235	100.0

SOURCE: Główny Urząd Statystyczny, *Rocznik Statystyczny Szkolnictwa: 1944/45-1966/67*, Warsaw, 1967, p. 435.

In other university-level professional schools (e.g., medical, art, etc.), youth of intelligentsia background also predominate, with the sole exception of theological academies (see Table 3-4).

TABLE 3-4

ENROLLMENT IN UNIVERSITY LEVEL PROFESSIONAL SCHOOLS
BY SOCIAL CLASS
(percentages)

School	Intelli-gentsia	Working Class	Peasant	Self-Employed Artisan	Other
Agricultural Engineering	40.3	20.5	33.9	4.5	.8
Art	65.5	20.9	7.6	5.9	.1
Economics	43.2	33.6	18.3	3.9	1.0
Medicine	55.9	23.7	14.4	4.7	1.3
Physical Education	50.9	32.4	10.7	5.4	.6
Technical-Scientific	51.0	29.7	15.0	3.5	.8
Theology	20.1	27.8	45.6	5.0	1.5

SOURCE: Główny Urząd Statystyczny, *Rocznik Statystyczny Szkolnictwa: 1944/45-1966/67*. Occupational Yearbooks Series No. 7, Warsaw, 1967, pp. 434-35.

In order to rationalize their overrepresentation in higher education, the intelligentsia, as already indicated, is described in ideological terms as a working-class or a working intelligentsia. In terms of prevailing ideology it is precisely this strata, because of its identification with the working masses—an identification which transcends economic self-interest and is the result of the dialectic of ideas—which is to be considered the real carrier of proletarian consciousness.[13] This is after all the strata which produced Lenin and many of the other leaders of the Russian Revolution as well as the founders of Polish Socialism and Communism. However, it is the working class first and, second, an emancipated peasantry, which serve as the backbone of the new social order and on whose behalf the Party claims to rule. The working class is ostensibly the most forward looking segment of society and, presumably, efforts are being made to facilitate the advancement of their children. The predominance of children of working-class and peasant background in theological seminaries and academies suggests, however, that a new socialist-oriented consciousness has not yet fully sifted down to the level of these classes. Indeed, the institution representing a competing social value system, the Church, still has a foothold among the masses. Suffice it to point out that the 24 theological seminaries currently existing in Poland had an enrollment of 3,327 in 1969 alone and many of the seminarians are graduates of the prestigious lyceums of general education located in the provinces. Furthermore, that year the Church ordained 406 new priests,[14] and the figures for the preceding years were only slightly higher. In fact, in 1970 Poland had 5,445 more priests than it had in 1937—i.e., prior to the establishment of the new order (16,839 as against 11,394)—thus making a ratio of one priest per 1,337 residents (as compared to one priest per 1,897 residents before World War II). Half of the Polish clergy is under 40 years of age—i.e., persons who were in their teens when Socialism became the formal ideology and secularism an official policy. In addition, 58 percent of the newly ordained priests are of peasant background, 31 percent of working-class background, and only 11 percent

[13] Alfred G. Meyer, *Leninism* (Cambridge: Harvard University Press, 1957), p. 31.
[14] *Contemporary Poland*, Warsaw, Vol. v., No. 2 (February 1971), 31-32.

Educating the Teacher

claim intelligentsia origin. Apparently, next to teaching, the priesthood is considered an avenue for relatively easy upward mobility for youth of lower-class background in addition to reflecting patterns of deep-seated religiosity among these classes.

Graduates of secondary schools of general education may not learn until October whether they will be accepted into the institution of higher learning to which they have applied. Generally, every third candidate's application is approved. The ratio of acceptance is less favorable at the most prestigious universities. Only every fifth applicant to the Department of Pedagogy of Warsaw University may expect to be admitted.[15] About 40,000 secondary school graduate-applicants are annually rejected. Graduates subsequently turn to institutions of their second choice or to other institutions of higher learning regardless of type or specialization.

But even the least discriminating establishments cannot admit all comers. Initial vacancies are promptly filled from among those who pass entrance examinations administered in June. If any vacancies for the freshman year should be left after the first round, a secondary school graduate seeking admission may have another chance in August when a second round of examinations is administered.

Just as the scramble for admission into secondary school repeats itself at the higher level, so too the pressures on admissions officers, recruitment and examination commissions are repeated at the higher level. As in the case of admissions to secondary schools, officials and teachers find it awkward and sometimes even difficult to resist pressures to admit certain individuals who have failed to qualify. It is especially awkward when such pressures come from highly placed persons, particularly in smaller communities. Future repercussions may be in store for the uncooperative school official or teacher. Although members of the examination commissions are required to report each call for special

[15] Anna Kornacka, "Matura i . . . co po maturze?," *Express Wieczorny*, Warsaw (July 13, 1966), 3.

favor this may not always be a pragmatic course of action. The result is that while the examinations are administered in an impersonal manner and the student being tested remains anonymous, the atmosphere surrounding the procedure is fraught with anxiety both for the examinees and their families as well as for the examiners. Too much is at stake.[16]

Once admitted, the question of support while in school arises. Although education at all levels is technically free, the problem of subsistence remains. Various unions and economic enterprises award assistance stipends or scholarships, usually to children of members or employees, or to students studying for careers in a given area. The future teacher has fewer opportunities. If he cannot support himself, he must rely on limited state or community aid, or on the assistance of political, civic, or professional organizations as well as grants-in-aid or loans given by the Student Association. Some aid programs may be limited to meals without cost at the student cafeteria or free lodging at the student house. While special allowances are available to families whose children attend school, these expire when the children reach the age of twenty and thus have little effect on the economic status of the student in higher education.

Youth of worker and peasant backgrounds are clearly favored in the competition for fellowships and stipends. The student of rural or working-class background, although at a competitive disadvantage when seeking admission, stands a far better chance of obtaining financial support than the youth of intelligentsia background who find admission a less formidable problem. This advantage is offset considerably, however, by the fact that there are more and better scholarships available for the more prestigious academic and scientific-technological areas. To the extent that these areas

[16] That examinations generate feelings of uneasiness was told to me in many in-depth interviews conducted with teachers and officials of all school levels as well as with the students and parents concerned. See also *Kurier Polski*, Organ of Democratic Alliance SD, Warsaw (June 22, 1966); and *Trybuna Ludu*, Organ of Central Committee of the Polish United Workers' Party, Warsaw (June 22, 1966).

are dominated by the traditionally privileged classes, the advantage enjoyed by working-class and peasant youth is diminished. Also, the scarcity and size of scholarships in the area of education are an early indicator of the future marginal status of teachers which, despite their officially hallowed position, is a constant concern.

The Organization of Education

Education in Poland has undergone enormous expansion since the end of World War II. Prior to World War II there were relatively few vocational training institutions, and only in the last few years before the outbreak of the war were attempts made to establish secondary schools (lyceums) for teacher education. Secondary general education was divided into a public (state or municipally supported) and a private sector: the first was by and large limited to children of government officials and it quite consciously practiced a policy of discrimination in terms of admission with respect to youth of minority backgrounds. The second was expensive and thus economically prohibitive to most. Before the war, there were in Poland only 32 institutions of higher learning, but by 1947-1948, despite devastation and dislocation of large segments of the population, and despite a deliberate policy on the part of the German occupation forces to eliminate the Polish intelligentsia, the number of institutions had grown to 56. By 1963-1964 the number of institutions of higher learning had increased to 74.

The institutions of higher education also engaged in restrictive admission policies prior to World War II. Some of these institutions adopted admission quotas (*numerus clausus*) with respect to certain minority groups (e.g., Jews); others practiced, especially toward the end of the interwar period, actual policies of exclusion (*numerus nullius*) with respect to such candidates. The latter policy was favored by institutions training for prestigious and traditionally remunerative professions, such as medicine and law.

In 1967, the hitherto separate ministries of Education and of Higher Education merged. Before the merger the social

Educating the Teacher

status and prestige of a particular institution were dictated largely by whether it came under one or the other of the two ministries. Schools of teacher education of various types, although of postsecondary education level, were under the jurisdiction of the Ministry of Education.*

UNIVERSITIES AND HIGHER SCHOOLS OF PEDAGOGY

Highest in terms of prestige among the institutions of higher learning are the universities. Prior to World War II there were 6 universities in Poland, including the still existing Church-supported Catholic University of Lublin. The organizational structure and curriculum offerings at these institutions followed the patterns established during the 19th century. Although the changes following World War II and the establishment of the People's Republic have imposed a different set of demands, the universities have been rather slow in meeting these demands. It is hoped, however, that separation of previously joined departments or the establishment of semi-autonomous schools and colleges within the university structure, will facilitate closer coordination between the work of the higher institutions of learning and the needs of the economy.

While the war was still going on, but after the liberation of the Eastern part of present day Poland, a new university (named after Maria Curie-Skłodowska) was established in Lublin which served at that time as the provisional seat of Polish authority. In 1945 a university was created in the industrial city of Lodz and one in Toruń (named after Mikołaj Kopernik [Copernicus]). The Bolesław Bierut University was founded in Wrocław (Breslau) after that German city came under Polish jurisdiction.

A new university opened before the end of 1970 in the former Free City of Danzig (Gdańsk) utilizing the existing plants and faculties of the Higher School of Pedagogy

* The post-Gomułka leadership reconstituted separate ministries, significantly naming one as the Ministry of Science, Higher Education and Technology and the other as the Ministry of Education and Training.

and the School of Economics in the neighboring resort town of Sopot. Some of the universities contain specialized pedagogic programs within different academic departments. Jagiello University in Cracow as well as the University of Lodz, the Adam Mickiewicz University in Poznań, and Bolesław Bierut University in Wrocław offer a program in education within their respective departments of philosophy and history. Maria Curie-Skłodowska University in Lublin offers pedagogy within the Department of Humanities. The Mikołaj Kopernik University in Toruń maintains a special program on art education within its Department of Fine Arts. Warsaw University encompasses a separate Pedagogic Department which also specializes in psychology.

In addition, the higher schools of economics in Cracow, Poznań, and Wrocław, which exist apart from the universities in these locations, as well as the Main School for Planning and Statistics in Warsaw maintain special programs of pedagogic studies (*Studium Pedagogiczne*). Work in this field within these schools of higher learning requires at least two semesters of intensive concentration and encompasses such subjects as psychology, general pedagogy, history of theories of education, methods of teaching economics, and field work practice in economic education. Similarly, the higher schools of the plastic arts in Gdańsk, Cracow, Poznań, Warsaw, and Wrocław incorporate special pedagogic studies which include such subjects as foundations of education and current problems of education, principles of didactics, and teaching methods, especially in the area of the plastic arts, as well as art education, school organization, and problems of mass culture, with special emphasis on the propagation of "plastic art culture."[17]

The universities prepare their graduates majoring in education for work in the secondary schools of general education with special emphasis on their particular major. The specialized schools of higher education offering pedagogic

[17] Ministerstwo Szkolnictwa Wyższego (Ministry of Higher Education), *Informator dla kandydatów do szkół wyższych i średnich szkół zawodowych dla maturzystów na rok szkolny 1966/67* (Warsaw, 1966), p. 277.

training (i.e., economics and art) prepare teacher-specialists for secondary vocational schools within particular areas of specialization. Nevertheless, because of the shortage of secondary schools, many teacher-graduates of higher institutions of learning are ultimately compelled to seek or to accept employment on the elementary school level. Although within the total population of teachers working at the elementary level the percentage of those with a university education is not exceedingly high, their number is on the increase largely because the program of constructing secondary school facilities is lagging behind the production of graduates from institutions of higher learning qualified to teach on that level. Thus in 1957-1958 the percentage of higher education graduates teaching on the lower school level was 3.6 of all teachers employed on that level. By 1960-1961, however, the percentage of such teachers had almost doubled to 6.0.[18]

At the university, the education major is exposed to a curriculum which encompasses theories of education, history, and psychology. The student must also do some practice teaching in the field. Teacher training at the university (referred to as pedagogic education) is designed to take up five years. At the completion of their studies graduates are entitled to the degree of *Magister Pedagogiki*. At the university the prospective teacher is generally exposed to two programs: one dealing with various aspects of pedagogy and another devoted to a specific subject matter. Theories of education, history of education, courses in psychology (general psychology, developmental and educational psychology), in addition to training in teaching methodology, didactics, elements of basic education and of teaching education, comparative education, special pedagogy, and social pedagogy come under the pedagogy phase of the university student's education. The advanced student is further

---

[18] Jan Woskowski, *Nauczyciele szkół podstawowych z wyższym wykształceniem w szkole i poza szkołą*, Monographs and Studies for the Inter-Institutional Center for Research on Higher Education of the Ministry of Higher Education (Warsaw: Państwowe Wydawnictwo Naukowe, 1965), p. 12.

exposed to specialized seminars in problems of education and school organization, problems of adult education, problems in dealing with retardation and/or social deviation. The university student majoring in education is also required to master and pass examinations in two foreign languages during his first two years.

Practice teaching included in the pedagogic phase of university training lasts six months. During that period the student may be assigned to work in a school, a correctional institution for children or youth, in some special institution, an orphanage, a prison, or in a variety of other educational or reform institutions. The university student aiming for a teaching career is expected to manifest active social and political concerns, especially as these affect youth and youth organizations. Graduates of these programs qualify for eventual high level professional work—in a sense they are to become in time future teachers' teachers. In the meantime, they may be employed at schools of various levels as organizers and administrators of various educational and cultural activities both for youth and adults, as education directors in special institutions, including prisons, organizations, clubs, houses of culture, on the staffs of the educational press, publishing houses, educational radio programs, etc.

In addition to the universities, a major source of supply of teachers for the secondary schools of all types (i.e., general education, pedagogic lyceums, vocational) are the higher schools of pedagogy (*Wyższe Szkoły Pedagogiczne*). In terms of prestige, the higher schools of pedagogy fall somewhere between universities and schools of teacher education (*Studium Nauczycielskie*, SN). The latter provides the main pool of future elementary school teachers. Nevertheless, entrance to the higher schools of pedagogy may sometimes be as stringent as to a university.

The higher schools of pedagogy contain subject-matter departments, but their main stress is on teaching methods and, generally, on social studies. All of them contain departments of philology (which invariably offer courses in Polish

61

and Russian philology), history, mathematics, and physics, but some also maintain specialized branches in biology (Cracow), geography (Gdańsk and Cracow), and chemistry (Gdańsk and Katowice). In fact, the schools in Rzeszów, Katowice, and Opole specialize in technological education, i.e., in training teachers specifically for employment in secondary vocational schools and *technikums*. The Higher School of Pedagogy in Opole narrows down its specialization even further to the training of teachers in the areas of mechanical and electrical engineering at a secondary vocational school level. Since polytechnic education was recently introduced into schools of general education, graduates of higher schools of pedagogy are being prepared to fill the personnel needs in this area. That is, although they are primarily trained for teaching at secondary schools of general education, they are also beginning to gird themselves to meet the anticipated demands for teaching cadres in the field of polytechnic education both in vocational and general education schools. However, due to the inability of the system to absorb all those trained to teach on the postelementary school level, close to 40 percent of the graduates of the higher schools of pedagogy (and of the education programs associated with universities) eventually teach in elementary schools, the level of education in which their training is not fully utilized and for which they are less well prepared.[19]

There were 5 higher schools of pedagogy in the country until 1970, located in Gdańsk, Cracow, Katowice, Opole, and Rzeszów—none in Warsaw since Warsaw University features a special education department of its own. The capital city, however, is the home of the State Institute of Special Pedagogy (named since 1970 in memory of Maria Grzęgorzewska, its former director). As indicated previously, the premises and staff of the Higher School of Pedagogy

[19] Karol Dziduszko, *Uniwersyteckie kształcenie nauczycieli* (Warsaw: Państwowe Zakłady Wydawnictw Szkolnych, 1963), p. 95. As indicated, teachers with higher education still constitute a small minority among all teachers working at the elementary school level.

in Gdańsk were taken over in 1970 by the newly formed university there.

Although normally designed for regular daytime students, the higher schools of pedagogy maintain a system of correspondence courses and a network of extensions to enable working teachers to complete their education and certification for secondary school teaching without having to take time off. As at the universities, the normal duration of study at the higher schools of pedagogy is designed to cover five years. Majors in mathematics and physics, however, may complete their course work in four years. During the period of residence, students at higher schools of pedagogy must participate in physical education programs and, if male, in military studies as well. Upon graduation (involving completion of a written thesis and required examinations, including one indicating proficiency in two foreign languages) the student is awarded a *Magister* degree (equivalent to a Masters degree in the United States) in his chosen major which entitles him to teach in his field of specialization.

The student at the higher school of pedagogy, as the university student, may go on to broaden his subject-matter knowledge so as to further perfect his credentials for specialized teaching at the secondary school level. He may also concentrate further on general teaching theory and practice or on the philosophical and economic aspects of education in order to be able to:

discern and solve problems of his professional competence and work in the light of the general needs of the nation's economy and culture, to understand the relationship of his field of work with the goals of social, political, and economic development, and to order his own life aspirations in accordance with social interests.[20]

The higher schools of pedagogy are thus essentially not only training grounds for secondary school teaching—al-

[20] Ministerstwo Szkolnictwa Wyższego, *op.cit.*, p. 304.

though this remains their stated primary objective—but also for posts in the broad area of administration in the fields of education and cultural organization. Whereas the universities train higher echelon professional cadres, prepared to work in posts requiring a higher degree of intellectual refinement, the higher schools of pedagogy provide a pool of middle-level administrative technicians who may eventually rise in the hierarchy of the educational and cultural organization structure on the strength of their expertise and political loyalty. Eventually also they may fully replace those who came to fill these positions—especially in the earlier stages of the system's development—on the strength of political loyalty and Party activity alone.

Accordingly, the practice teaching of the student at the higher schools of pedagogy may involve field work in secondary schools of differing type, in organized nonschool activities for young people (e.g., clubs, political organizations, etc.), summer camps, vocational training, and the like.

Facilities at the disposal of students at the higher schools of pedagogy and at the universities are superior to those available at the less prestigious schools of teacher education of the SN type which train cadres for the elementary schools. Students have access to methodology laboratories and modern teaching aids and equipment, yet less stress is placed on practice teaching than at the SN schools.

Not only is little weight given to teaching experience as part of the training offered future teachers at these higher levels of education, but what is available is apparently rather poorly organized. The student-teacher is met with indifference in the field. He is often seen more as a hindrance than a help. He is not present in any one place long enough either to become accustomed to the particular environment or to be fully utilized by the teachers and students of the institution. The problem of practice teaching apparently reached such gravity that it demanded the attention and intervention of the Party. The 11th Plenum of the Central Committee of the Polish United Workers' Party (PZPR) adopted decisions stressing the need for practice teaching for students at the universities and higher schools of pedagogy.

SCHOOLS OF TEACHER EDUCATION: STUDIUM NAUCZYCIELSKIE (SN)

Although consigned to eventual liquidation, the schools of teacher education (*Studium Nauczycielski,* SN) constitute, as indicated, the main source of teachers for the elementary schools in Poland. Training in these schools was designed to extend two years beyond secondary school until 1966; then a three-year training program was begun. The teacher education schools are especially attractive to graduates of pedagogic lyceums which themselves require the completion of a five-year program. They also attract graduates of the lyceums of general education, usually those who could not gain entrance to a university or some other institution of higher education. Of all the postsecondary educational institutions, the schools of teacher education (popularly referred to as SNs) enjoy the least prestige. They are heavily feminized—foreshadowing the feminization of the teaching profession, especially on the lower levels of the educational system. A 1966 report from a school of teacher education (SN) in Ciechanów shows an enrollment of 370 females as against 131 males, a fairly typical ratio. For many of the men, acceptance at that institution constituted a last chance for higher education and an alternative to their primary choice, which in some cases was even a higher school of agriculture or a *technikum.* Most SN recruits are either intellectually not on par with those entering the universities or the higher schools of pedagogy, or they come from backgrounds where poverty or lack of connections is mixed with hope and aspiration for the children's advancement. As a result of these factors one encounters a certain sense of resignation and fatalism permeating the atmosphere at an SN. One student at the Ciechanów school said: "No one in our town treats a SN education seriously."[21] Such feelings

[21] Janusz Rolicki, "Prestiż nauczyciela: Coraz lepsi," *Polityka,* Warsaw, Vol. x, No. 45 (505) (November 5, 1966), 6.

are not limited to the students at the Ciechanów SN. A working teacher confided in the course of an interview: "When I was told by my secondary school advisor to apply to an SN I felt my eyes filling with tears. The teacher always used to tell the weaker students, 'Nothing will come of you anyway—you will probably land at an SN.'" Nevertheless despite complaints and memories of derogation, it is the school of teacher education of the SN type that serves as a realistic "possibility" to many of ever being able to enter the professions and the ranks of the intelligentsia. As a consequence, the number of teachers at the elementary school level who have graduated from SNs has increased over the years. While the secondary schools are not capable of absorbing all graduates from institutions of higher learning trained for work on that educational level, the elementary schools are facing the opposite problem, a manpower shortage. Thus, the elementary schools not only can pick up the surplus of teachers originally destined for the secondary schools as well as all graduates of the schools of teacher education, but they also must resort to the employment of those who did not continue past the secondary pedagogic lyceum and who are officially qualified to teach only on the kindergarten level. The elementary school also must resort to the assistance of part time teachers and teachers who are still studying to complete their various degree requirements.

As in the case of the other schools of higher education, the schools of teacher education have a surplus of students specializing in the humanities and a shortage of candidates capable or willing to combine teaching with majors in the physical sciences. Some SNs also have vacancies in the departments of Russian philology (language and literature) and music education. The same situation prevails among students taking SN courses via correspondence or through the various extension divisions.

Formally, the schools of teacher education aim to train personnel for elementary school teaching, teaching of practical subjects in basic (elementary) vocational schools as well as arts and crafts, vocational teaching in agricultural schools or in schools of agricultural preparedness, preschool education, and work in children's homes, dormitories, vacation resorts for children, orphanages, and child care centers.[22]

Depending upon the student's occupational goal within the teaching profession, his program of study will vary. Thus, the candidate for elementary school teaching will be exposed to courses in Polish language and literature, Russian language and literature, history and civics, geography, physical education, biology, chemistry, physics, mathematics, music education, art education, polytechnic education, and principles of elementary education. The student may specialize in any of these subjects or in a combination of subjects. The most frequently encountered combinations are history and civics, geography and physical education, geography and polytechnic education, biology and chemistry, biology and physical education, physics and mathematics, physics and chemistry, art and polytechnic education, general elementary education and physical education, general elementary education and music. The range of specialty combinations is rather wide since no real in-depth subject specialization is expected from teachers at this level. On the other hand, SN students aiming at careers in elementary vocational school teaching are expected to function as teachers in particular areas of specialization, e.g., agriculture, business-trade, mechanical, electrical, textiles, telecommunications, vehicular (drivers' education and automobile repair), etc.

For teachers preparing for careers on the general elementary school level, the program will also differ according to the grade level for which they are being trained. There is greater subject-matter emphasis for those aiming to teach at the higher elementary school grades (i.e., grades 5-8). For candidates intending to teach at the lower elementary grade level (1-4), the emphasis will be more on methods of teaching than on subject matter. Some, though, may choose to prepare themselves for teaching at the general elementary

[22] Ministerstwo Szkolnictwa Wyższego, op.cit., p. 304.

school level without any particular grade level emphasis. Their education will include work on some select sociological and philosophical problems, psychology, pedagogy, and the history of education, seminars on school organization, school hygiene, teaching methods, and practice teaching. Partly due to the acute manpower shortage at the elementary school level, the SN student is exposed to more extensive (and more rigidly supervised) practice teaching than the student at a higher school of pedagogy or the education major at a university.

In addition, regardless of specialization, students at the SNs are encouraged to learn two foreign languages. A lesser degree in foreign languages proficiency is expected, however, from SN students than from students at universities or higher schools of pedagogy since mastery of foreign languages does not appear to be a specific requirement for graduation. Greater stress in the SN seems to be on semivoluntary participation in extracurricular activities which would attune the future teachers to problems of contemporary culture. One aspect of such participation involves activity in an educational circle or a more formally organized specialization club. Special hours are set aside each week for these informal-formal activities. Male students who have not yet completed their military training are required to participate in a program of military preparation, equivalent to the programs of Reserve Officers' Training in the colleges and universities of the United States. Participants in these programs are entitled, upon entering the armed forces, to have their military obligation reduced by one year. Although again not formally required, the student is also expected to show his civic awareness through involvement in the various social and political organizations operating within the school.

The successful applicant for regular (daytime) admission to a school of teacher education whose intention is eventually to teach on the general elementary school level, must submit his certificate of completion of a general education lyceum (the *Matura*), submit a medical certificate testifying to his physical fitness, possess the necessary ideological-moral qualifications, not be above 23 years of age, and successfully pass his entrance examination. The age restriction does not apply to students pursuing their studies via correspondence or extension, nor does it apply to future teachers who are able to receive their education through a university or higher school of pedagogy. Ideological-moral fitness is ascertained by a recruitment commission at the time of application for admission to the SN when the candidate is still a lyceum student. The entrance examination is judged and certified by an examination commission of the institution to which the candidate has applied for admission.

In addition to graduates of secondary schools of general education, the SN will also accommodate graduates of the music and plastic arts lyceums, but only if the latter agree to continue their specialized studies and subsequently teach these subjects on the elementary school level. On the other hand, graduates of vocational secondary schools and *technikums* may be admitted only if suitable candidates from the general education lyceums are not available. In addition to meeting the regular requirements for admission, the regional school *kuratorium* must approve their application.

Graduates of secondary pedagogic schools, for whom the SNs hold a special attraction, are in a category by themselves. Less privileged than their colleagues from the secondary schools of general education, but more than those who graduated from vocational secondary schools, they may be admitted to the SN at the regular entrance period, but only if they choose to specialize in any of the following: Russian philology, music education, art education, or vocational teachers' training. This requirement is designed to meet the shortage of teaching manpower in these subjects on the elementary school level. Such admission is not automatic though. Graduates of the pedagogic lyceums must be recommended by their respective secondary schools as being exceptionally able and their individual applications must be approved by the regional school *kuratorium.*

Policies of restrictive admission allow the school system

69

to perpetuate traditional patterns of stratification. Consequently, even the least prestigious of the institutions of higher learning, the schools of teacher education of the SN category, tend to favor graduates of the higher status secondary schools of general education, the heirs to the traditional *gimnazjum*. The SN school, carrying less prestige than other postsecondary educational institutions, attracts the least able or least socially fortunate among the graduates of the general education lyceums. Yet these schools would rather admit such graduates in the normal process than perhaps more gifted (or late-blooming) graduates of secondary schools of some other type. The latter, in order to reach the portals of even the SN, must overcome additional obstacles.

Partly as a result of such experience the SN graduate, regardless of his individual social background, carries a stigma of failure even within the field of education, both in terms of prestige and career opportunities. Both, but especially the latter, have repercussions also in terms of future income. Janusz Rolicki characterizes SN graduates as "somewhat disoriented, lacking in self-confidence, in faith in themselves, but not in goodwill."[23]

THE SPECIAL INSTITUTES

Set aside, but within the general framework of the teacher training system, is the network of artistic-cultural education institutions, including those preparing librarians. Before the ministerial mergers, these schools were under the jurisdiction of the Ministry of Culture and Art. These special artistic-cultural institutes operate at the elementary, secondary, and postsecondary levels. Each of the schools trains students for a special area in the arts or educational-cultural activity, e.g., music, fine arts, dance, theater, and film, etc. There are two secondary schools which train librarians for educational and cultural institutions. In addition to their specialty, these schools also encompass a program of general education. They generally enjoy a great deal of prestige and admission

[23] Rolicki, *op.cit.*, p. 7.

70

is highly selective. Enrollment in schools of this type at all levels has more than doubled since the prewar period. Until then, many of the schools were operated by private interests.

The Organization of the Teacher-Trainee's Life

Upon admission to a university, higher school of pedagogy, or school of teacher education, a student must submit to the *rektor's* (president) office a signed pledge which is kept in the student's file. The pledge (*ślubowanie*) reads as follows:

> I solemnly swear that I will study systematically and with diligence. I will meet all demands and orders issued by my academic institution and by superior authorities. I will accord proper respect to the authorities of the academic institution, its professors and workers, and I will scrupulously adhere to the principles of collegiality in my association with fellow students and will use school property with proper care. I will in my entire conduct be careful to maintain a posture worthy of a student in the Polish People's Republic. With a full sense of responsibility I will strive to achieve the best preparation possible for future labor in the cause of a socialist Poland.[24]

Failure to sign or to submit the pledge by a designated date is officially taken to mean that the student has resigned from further studies at the institution. On the other hand, disciplinary infractions in the course of residence at the institution, especially of a political nature, are considered to be "breaches" of the solemn pledge.

Much of the student's social life is centered around the student house which serves as a place of rest, independent work and study, recreation, and as a dormitory for students beyond commuting distance. The student house is administered by a manager who is assisted in policy matters and in the development of appropriate programs by a resident council (*Rada Mieszkańców*). A student loses residence privileges at the house if he fails in his course work, violates

[24] Ministerstwo Szkolnictwa Wyższego, *op.cit.*, p. 19.

71

the code and regulations, if his parents live within commuting distance, or if expelled from school.

The student is faced with an array of organizations operating at the institution and its adjuncts. These organizations are political, civic, social-recreational, and cultural, as well as professional-educational. Among the most important and strongest are: the Union of Socialist Youth (*Związek Młodzieży Socjalistycznej, ZMS*), the Union of Rural Youth (*Związek Młodzieży Wiejskiej, ZMW*), and the Association of Polish Students (*Zrzeszenie Studentów Polskich, ZSP*).

The Union of Socialist Youth (ZMS) operates on all school levels and is structurally, ideologically, and politically, subordinated to the Polish United Workers' Party, although technically autonomous. The statutes of the Union, particularly Articles 1 and 2, posit as its goals the propagation of the Party program, assistance in the realization of Party objectives and policies, and preparation of youth cadres for eventual membership in the Party. Organized in 1957, ZMS claims to continue in the tradition of prewar Communist, Socialist and progressive-liberal youth organizations. Its branches and cells in industrial enterprises aid management in fulfilling production goals, plant maintenance, and care of equipment. In the schools it cooperates closely with the corresponding institutional authorities. Its main objective, however, is in the area of political education. It organizes discussion circles (*Studenckie Ośrodki Dyskusyjne, SOD*), attempts to acquaint the student with institutions of possible future employment, and is active in military preparedness programs. It organizes and mobilizes cadres for work at Workers' Universities and offers evening courses for working youth. In the course of the academic year, each member is given a specific work assignment which actively involves him in the organization's programs and activities. In 1964, 36,000 teachers belonged to the Union of Socialist Youth.

The Union of Rural Youth (ZMW) was also founded in 1957. It too is ideologically linked with the Polish United Workers' Party as well as with the United People's Movement (*Zjednoczone Stronnictwo Ludowe*). The latter, organized in 1949, is a peasant party committed to the "building of Socialism" although its leaders allege that it is a continuation of the traditional prewar peasant movements and parties, including the powerful opposition party, *Stronnictwo Ludowe*. Along with the Polish United Workers' Party and the Democratic Alliance (*Stronnictwo Demokratyczne*)— the formal political organ of the traditionally independent professional intelligentsia, private sector entrepreneurs, and urban middle class—the United People's Movement belongs to the Front of National Unity (*Front Jedności Narodu*), the tripartite coalition which officially governs the country and in which the Polish United Workers' Party is constitutionally assigned a dominant role. At the village level the working teacher is frequently involved in the operation of the local ZMW; 13,000 rural teachers belonged to the organization in 1963. The primary goal of the Union of Rural Youth, aside from political activism, is to assist rural youth in overcoming difficulties encountered in their studies and/or adjustment to an urban environment. It cooperates closely with the Union of Socialist Youth. Broadly speaking, it is designed to develop a new rural intelligentsia and its activities—as those of the Union of Socialist Youth—extend to all levels of the educational enterprise.

The Association of Polish Students (ZSP), on the other hand, limits its activities and membership to the postsecondary educational setting. In fact, one of its major objectives is to facilitate the transition from secondary to higher education which many students find difficult. Although the atmosphere in Polish institutions of higher education is more highly structured and student discipline is stricter, for example, than that prevailing at most American universities since the mid-sixties, incoming students may still find it difficult to cope with the relative freedom they encounter. Structured as the atmosphere may be, it is one of laxity if compared to that of the secondary school from which the freshman student has just graduated.

As far as the student in a Polish institution of higher

learning is concerned, therefore, the Association of Polish Students is broader in scope than the openly partisan Union of Socialist Youth or the Union of Rural Youth. It also deals with matters of his immediate interests and concerns. Formally non-Party oriented, the ZSP was founded in 1950 to replace prewar "bourgeois" student associations. The latter had been organized primarily along ethnic-religious lines and were generally conservative and nationalistic in outlook.

Service oriented, the ZSP appeals to a wide student membership. In 1962, for example, it counted over 103,000 student members. While the total membership of either the ZMS or the ZMW is many times larger than that of the ZSP (and includes nonstudents, pupils of the lower levels of the educational structure, teachers, etc.), the comparative postsecondary student membership for the same year was about 30,000 for the Union of Socialist Youth (ZMS) and about 10,000 for the Union of Rural Youth (ZMW).[25]

The Association at each institution of higher learning monitors student progress, sees to it that they meet requirements on schedule, organizes tutorials for students falling behind in their course work and, in order to facilitate adjustment to student life, assigns to each incoming freshman a patron or guardian from among the senior students. It further organizes counseling service during the usually traumatic examination periods as well as postexamination evaluation sessions. It is instrumental in establishing and operating preprofessional and scientific clubs, hobby groups, sport activities, student cabarets (some of which enjoy broad community popularity and from time to time encounter censorship difficulties with authorities), theater groups, choral and dance ensembles, festivals, competitions and contests, practice teaching, and trips into the country and abroad. Of greater import as far as the individual is concerned is the Association's activity in the area of student health and financial assistance. This includes assistance with housing, cafeteria service, etc. Although officially nonparti-

[25] *Polska Ludowa: Słownik encyklopedyczny* (Warsaw: Wiedza Powszechna, 1965), pp. 474-77.

san, the Association nevertheless strives quite consciously for ideological involvement. Its primary goals, in fact, are "educational activity whose aim is to develop cadres of socialist intelligentsia," to generate scientific, cultural, socio-political interests and involvements, and to activate students in "fulfillment of their basic obligations toward the institution of higher learning, the organization, and society."[26]

Many of the activities in which the Association is engaged are of the same general type in which junior chambers of commerce or community booster clubs are involved in the United States. Thus, it helps organize celebrations and parades on holidays, it gets out the vote during elections, participates in various civic projects (e.g., collecting money for the School Fund, city beautification, mobilizing aid to areas in distress, Sunday outings—so-called "White Sundays" to assist villages with the harvest, etc.).

In the realm of ideological and political activity the Association has voluntarily subordinated itself to the Union of Socialist Youth. The ZSP also works closely within the various educational institutions with the Secular School Association (*Towarzystwo Szkół Świeckich, TSS*) and the Association of Atheists and Freethinkers (*Stowarzyszenie Ateistów i Wolnomyślicieli, SAiW*). Both of these organizations were formed in 1957 for the purpose of achieving greater secularization through "the development and propagation of a scientific and materialistic world outlook; struggle for realization of the principles of tolerance and Socialist coexistence; to combat the designs of the clergy."[27] In 1969 the two associations merged formally as the Association for the Promotion of Secular Culture (*Towarzystwo Krzewienia Kultury Świeckiej, TKKS*).

The Secular School Association (TSS) in particular has centered its work among students in institutions of higher education, especially those training teachers. Teachers form a high proportion of its membership, approximately 35 per-

[26] *Ibid.*, pp. 474-75; see also Ministerstwo Szkolnictwa Wyższego, *op.cit.*, p. 32.
[27] *Polska Ludowa: Słownik encyklopedyczny*, p. 351.

cent. The goal of this Association is to bring about complete secularization of the school system through the creation and mobilization of mass support for that goal. Student branches of TSS organize lectures, conduct special seminars, counseling centers, and vacation courses for teachers, prepare educational materials, and sponsor special research projects. Since 1958 the Secular School Association (jointly with SAiW), has operated a Free Pedagogic Studium, later renamed Center for the Perfection of Lay Cadres, which offers long and short term courses in ethics, problems of education, and religion.

Limited only to secondary schools before World War II, military training has since been introduced into institutions of higher learning. Male students (and in medical academies female students as well) above the age of 18, physically fit for service but not having met their military obligation prior to entering a school of higher learning, are obliged to participate in a military training program. A person removed from academic status may be enlisted into the armed services at any time. Conversely, an enlisted man accepted for higher study may appeal to the Military District Commander and gain release from the services. Upon completion of the military training program, the student is transferred to a regular military unit for a prescribed period of further training at the end of which he must pass a set of tests and, if successful, is transferred to the reserves with the rank of reserve ensign which later entitles him to an officer's commission. The process of differentiation thus begun at the last grades of elementary school continues and extends further and deeper to encompass the military services where many of the children of the social elite meet with those left on the side in a traditional command-giving/command-receiving relationship.

Before the war, given the relatively small number of secondary school graduates, the person with a *Matura* was either called into the services with the ensign rank, or was never called to active duty. Once called he had to be given his rank. As a result, members of minority groups (e.g.,

Jews, Ukrainians, Belo-Russians, Lithuanians, etc.) or members of the Polish ethnic core group suspect of political deviation were never called into the services if they were secondary school graduates and thus entitled to a commission. This tradition persists for students involved in unorthodox political activities. If such students are expelled, however, and thus not entitled to a commission, they may be called into the armed forces to serve as privates. This process, in fact, usually follows expulsion for whatever reason, and is looked upon, if not as punishment, as the system's opportunity to "retool" the malcontent.

The student riots in the spring 1968 were followed by demands from school administrators and politicians that formal courses in Marxism-Leninism be reintroduced as required subjects. But even without such obligatory courses, the future teacher has many opportunities to absorb and assimilate the principles of the official ideology. These include both extracurricular indoctrination and the regular learning process, especially in the humanities and social sciences. Since many prospective teachers tend to major in these areas and once working, teach these or related subjects, it is presumed that they will transmit the values of the ideology to their own charges.

History is taught from a Marxist-Leninist perspective. The history of Russia and the Ukraine, presented formerly in negative terms, is currently being offered in a rather sympathetic light. Thus stress is given to the growth of Russia as an international power and to the significance of the Ukrainian revolt of national liberation under the leadership of Bohdan Chmielnicki (1648) against Polish oppression. Polish history stresses the destructive role of the aristocracy, the reactionary character of the Church, peasant rebellions, the importance of the Eastern markets for Poland, national revolts, and the origins of the labor movement. Although the instructor at the institution of higher learning has a great deal of personal discretion in presenting his subject matter, he is also restricted by the demands of a curriculum outline and required reading, and by the possibility that his statements during a lecture may be reported. Emphasis is also placed on the emergence of the Socialist movement worldwide. Special attention is given the revolution in Russia. Events in interwar Poland are portrayed as leading the country toward increased "fascization." Treatment of the interwar period in Poland requires a great deal of political sensitivity and tact inasmuch as one must deal with strife between Socialists and Communists (presently merged), the liquidation of the Communist Party of Poland in the thirties by the order of the Third International (Comintern), factional struggles within the Party, etc. Courses in philosophy include dialectical materialism (ontology) and historical materialism (ethics).

Final examinations begin in June. Some students prefer to postpone these until fall. Nevertheless, the beginning of summer is a hectic period for all during which warm weather, sports, romance, and social life compete with school pressures. Many student-teachers prepare themselves for field work at youth camps and vacation resorts. After the fourth year at an institution of higher learning, male students are obligated to attend military camp, a prerequisite toward successful completion of their military training. The official end of the academic year (June 27) is accompanied by festivities and brief outings. Some leave for their practice teaching or military camp, others continue their training in special summer camps (for language training, science education, etc.). In 1966 some 10,000 higher education students served as volunteers on state farms, worked in the forests, on road construction, and similar projects. Even more of them traveled abroad, mainly to other Socialist countries to participate in special foreign language seminars and school organized scientific expeditions.[28] Some go back home to wait for the beginning of next academic year, or vacation privately at some sea or mountain resort, or go to one of the retreats maintained by youth organizations. These retreats operated by the Union of Socialist Youth,

[28] *Kurier Polski*, Organ of Democratic Alliance SD, *Stronnictwo Demokratyczne*, Warsaw (June 22, 1966).

Union of Rural Youth, and the Association of Polish Students, combine rest and recreation with education. Highly placed political personalities often leave their desks in steaming Warsaw to visit and lecture at these retreats. Thus, for example, General Mieczysław Moczar, the powerful ex-Minister of Internal Affairs (security) and former partisan leader, is a frequent visitor and lecturer on problems of patriotic education or on current events. The Minister or Vice-Minister of Agriculture will visit an academic retreat operated by the Union of Rural Youth (ZMW), and generals or veterans of the partisan movement will recall exploits of the War of Resistance.[29]

The community may understand and forgive a certain amount of student frolic, mischief, or even what some interpret as immoral behavior. They may even sympathize with student political dissidence since students in Poland have been traditionally politicized, except for an approximate ten-year period after World War II when apathy and antiheroism were in vogue. The apathy, so foreign to the Polish student character, came to an abrupt end in October 1956 when Gomułka was returned to power. Traditional national sentiments, less spirited perhaps than in the past, reemerged and sometimes became mingled with libertarian and humanistic interpretations of the official ideology. The events of spring 1968 brought students back again into politics—dissident politics for many.

Their Czech neighbors to the South—both admired for their superior technological and industrial development and despised for their ability to adjust to external circumstances and to survive physically intact with their ancient cities and national treasures—had launched a new policy of "Socialism with a new face," something reminiscent of the promise held out for many by the events of the "Polish October" of 1956. The moves in Czechoslovakia both inspired and aroused the envy of many students in Poland. In addition, the Jews, who (until their mass extermination in World War II) lived for centuries on Polish soil and

[29] *Życie Warszawy*, Warsaw (July 20, 1966).

79

were bound with Poles through a complex web of mutual hate and love, who were traditionally thought of by many Poles as being clever but physically weak and lacking in heroic qualities—the romantic élan so admired by Poles—fought a surprisingly successful war in the Middle East the year before against overwhelming odds. The fact that the Soviet Union, a traditional but powerful and feared enemy, sided openly with the anti-Israeli forces evoked strange feelings among many Poles who otherwise still harbored deep-seated animosities toward the Jews—a residue of a long nationalistic and religiously parochial educational tradition. The negative attitude of the Polish government—sensitive in matters of foreign policy to the cues from Moscow—to both of these events (i.e., the Dubček reform movement in Czechoslovakia and the Israeli victory in the 1967 war) served to intensify student dissent to an almost anarchic surge of abandon. The banning of a theater presentation of the classic romantic drama by the Polish national poet Adam Mickiewicz, *Dziady* (*Forefathers*), because of the anti-Moscow lines it contains—lines aimed against Czarist Russia's overlordship of a century ago of Polish land and culture but presumably open for reinterpretation and applicable to current conditions—served as the spark which ignited the incendiary situation.

Student politicization while in keeping with Polish traditions, arouses ambivalent sentiments in the community, however. Such sentiments, if properly played upon, may serve the regime in mobilizing mass support for its repressive measures against student dissidents and offers a convenient target for popular frustrations in times of crises. In 1968 rioting Polish students were accused of being influenced by Czechoslovak reformists and led and manipulated by "alien" elements, i.e., Zionist Jews and "cosmopolitans." Thus, while many could sympathize with subsequent student demands (many of which were essentially economic in character—dealing with living and housing conditions, support for education, etc.), their deviant political behavior is often viewed negatively by the community which is prone to see students as a privileged elite, exempt from the day-to-day problems of the working class and peasantry. Such community attitudes toward student discontent are also discernible elsewhere—as, for example, in France (during the May 1968 riots there) or in the United States (following the student unrest of 1970 and 1971). Related community sentiments also color attitudes toward the educational enterprise generally and frequently express themselves adversely in popular votes on school budgets, especially during times of economic uncertainty and in systems where the population is afforded the opportunity to vote freely on such matters. In Poland, where the masses are relatively poor (by Western standards), incomes modest, and housing conditions inadequate, resentments borne of economic frustration and status anxieties are easily aggravated and could be turned against those who are *perceived* to be privileged or "better off." In the past such feelings were released in hostility toward Jews and the fact that most of those who suffered from such hostility were of low income (most visible in their compact ghetto neighborhoods) only underlined the ills of the system. Presently, in the absence of Jews, resentments borne of economic hardship and social frustration may turn against the class of industrial managers and Party bureaucrats (sometimes popularly referred to as the Red Bourgeoisie)—as evidenced in the workers' riots of December 1970 during which Party and trade union headquarters on the Baltic Sea Coast were put to the torch. The fact that the rioting Polish workers of 1970 addressed themselves to some of the same material and sociopolitical grievances as the rioting Polish students in 1968 points only to the lack of coordination and organization among the protestors. The workers were by and large bitter over interrupted routine and traffic jams caused by the student riots in 1968, and the students were absorbed in examinations and preparations for Christmas-New Year celebrations when the workers acted. It is also significant that it was the workers' riots which initiated some alterations in the composition of the Party and governmental leadership as well as in some stated public policies, whereas the riots of the students two years earlier served only to stiffen the back of the regime, as it were. Students seem to be more vulnerable to systemic counterpressures and their discontent is more easily dealt with, especially in a system which looks for ideological legitimization in the working class.

Moreover, because of their generally favored position, students are expected to behave with conformity to accepted standards and, if anything, to set a model of correctness for others to emulate. These expectations are especially imposing for students training for the teaching profession.

The First Job

The first job for the graduate is, in a sense, an extension of his student life. Job assignment is conditioned by his original professional-occupational choice and the manpower needs within the profession. Because education is at the expense of the state, the first job assignment is formally regulated and codified.[30] It is hoped that the graduate will have as much freedom in job selection as possible and that he will be given all the incentives on his first job to make him wish to remain permanently in the assigned position. In addition to the conditions of work, these incentives would include assistance in securing suitable housing. Such assistance may involve a loan for the purchase of an apartment in a cooperative housing unit—a loan usually not exceeding 80 percent of the employee's own financial resources toward such purchase and repayable within five years.

Housing remains a problem, however. One of the most frequently voiced complaints relates to the inability to find housing, especially for teachers with families. One hears about teachers forced to camp out on school premises or to live with colleagues due to a paucity of housing facilities,

[30] *Statute on the Employment of Graduates of Higher Institutions of Learning,* published in *Dziennik Ustaw,* No. 8, para. 48 (February 25, 1964).

either upon arrival at the location of the first job or immediately afterwards. Moreover, the purchase of an apartment in a cooperative housing project exceeds the resources of any teacher (loans notwithstanding) who lacks independent funds or outside assistance. In fact, cooperative houses built by unions for their members (such as the Teachers' Cooperative Housing Project on Wiejska Street in Warsaw) had to place vacant apartments on the open market since the union members who had priority for them lacked the necessary funds.

The new teacher who for some reason is dissatisfied with his first job assignment or any of its conditions may bargain or appeal the assignment. As long as there is a shortage of teachers his efforts to change the assignment are likely to be successful. It is during such bargaining that the young teacher with a degree from a higher school of pedagogy or even a university often decides to settle in a less prestigious elementary school position. His first job assignment may have been to a secondary school—the level for which he was trained—and it also may have been within the area of his specialization, but matters of a nonprofessional nature (such as difficulties in securing proper housing, the size of the locale, family pressures, etc.) or concern over the availability within the vicinity of assignment of cultural or future career opportunities, may compel the beginning teacher to trade off even a choice professional post for a job more desirable in terms of personal comfort or other considerations.

Once he has accepted a job, the teacher signs an agreement which must be verified by the proper authorities. Once on the job he is normally obligated to remain for at least three years.

During the first three years after graduation the graduate cannot leave the profession for which he was trained at public expense. This rule is very explicit and applies to all graduates of institutions of higher education. Only those who enter the armed forces, invalids with certain physical incapacities, and those retained by the universities or scientific institutes as teaching or research assistants, are exempt from this rule. Should the graduate decide to renege on his 3-year obligation there are severe financial penalties. The state must be paid back half the cost accrued in his education plus the full cost of whatever assistantship, fellowships, or stipends he received over the years. Such sums of money are prohibitive to most (somewhere from 30,000 to 50,000 *złotys*) and few leave during the prescribed period. If one does leave before the prescribed 3-year period, it is usually (in addition to the contingencies foreseen by the formal rules) because of sociopolitical pressures from above to have him elevated to some other activity (usually political organization) or expelled and purged for some real or imagined infraction. Cases of elevation from teaching ranks during the first three years occur rather rarely. Political and administrative authorities usually want to observe an individual's performance in a job situation and, in the case of teachers, the need for politically active, conscious, and loyal members of the profession is considered vitally important to the future of the system.

On the other hand, termination of one's 3-year obligation by virtue of expulsion or purge is seldom welcomed by the individual affected. Following the riots in the spring of 1968 a number of graduates of institutions of higher learning were expelled from their original job assignments, from their profession, and some (e.g., persons of Jewish descent who were seen as not completely attuned to the national culture) were encouraged and enabled to leave the country. Once these persons agreed to leave the country they automatically renounced their citizenship and with it their jobs, privileges, and also, obligations.

The Teaching Graduate: Assessments and Reactions

Foremost among the demands on the new teacher is that he be a conscious bearer of Socialist ideas and that he effectively inculcate a similar Socialist consciousness in his

84

students.[31] Polish educational literature rates graduating teachers low in this respect. Such failures are not limited to the area of ideological education, however. In other areas where cultural traditions impinge on potential success, there are similar problems.[32] Such problems are compounded, according to some observers, by the fact that prospective teachers are ill prepared by their own education to deal with the classroom situations which they encounter. University graduates feel shortchanged in the area of educational methodology, while the graduates of schools of teacher education are deficient in subject-matter preparation.[33] In the latter case, there is a kind of stifling effect on the classroom atmosphere as teachers who are embarrassed by their own inadequacies rigidly confine discussion and study. The intellectual curiosity of the students often suffers immeasurably under such circumstances. One critic of Polish education asks:

> What can one really expect from an elementary school teacher who received his own education in a two-year *Studium Nauczycielskie* (SN) where in a record short time (shorter than, for example, in the self-respecting *Technikum* for Hotel Management or for Pharmacology which require three years of training) an attempt is made to stuff the future teacher with pedagogic knowledge as well as with a bit of psychology and ideology and philosophy and with at least two subject matter specialties? To be sure, they have to deal as teachers with young children only, but these children of *anno* 1966 have their little heads ordered and furnished entirely differently than was the case when teachers' training seminaries were thought to be sufficient to do the job. These children have

[31] Maria Żytomirska and Zbigniew Radwan, *Praca dydaktyczna w Studium Naucycielskim* (Warsaw: Państwowe Zakłady Wydawnictw Szkolnych, 1965), especially pp. 25, 75.

[32] Mikołaj Kozakiewicz. "Co myślą kończąc Studium Nauczycielskie?" (Warsaw: Secular School Association, mimeographed research report for internal cadre use, 1967).

[33] See, for example, Dziduszko, *op.cit.*, p. 192.

85

undergone an undisputable acceleration in physical and mental development. Moreover, the school reform has added to the elementary school an eighth grade consisting of youth age 15 or 16. . . . These are children who from age two are exposed to television.[34]

Despite widespread criticism of this sort, the *Sejm* Commission on Education and Science debated the question of extending the period of training at the schools of teacher education (SN) from two to three years for the first time as recently as 1966. It was pointed out then how difficult it is to find faculty to adequately educate future teachers even during the 2-year training period, and how acute the shortage of educational manpower is generally, but especially on the elementary school level. Fear was expressed that if the SNs were to extend their training period to three years (as they finally did), it would be harder to staff the extra faculty positions. What is more important, delaying graduation from the SNs by one full year would reduce even further the already short supply of elementary school teachers.[35]

The reforms of 1966-1967 were intended to help remedy the existing situation. With the eventual liquidation of the pedagogic lyceums all prospective teachers would, at the very least, be expected to hold a *Matura*. Effort would be made under the reform provisions to increase the number of higher schools of pedagogy and to place greater stress on these rather than on the universities as training centers for future secondary school teachers. Schools of teacher education (SNs) would eventually be phased out, but in the meantime should be staffed with holders of doctoral degrees. Given the problems of staffing higher level institutions, especially in the field of teacher training including the higher schools of pedagogy, however, such goals were simply untenable. In addition to such unrealistic training

[34] Mikołaj Kozakiewicz. "Alergia nauczycielskiego zawodu," *Fakty i Myśli*, Organ of Executive Board of Association of Atheists and Freethinkers, Bydgoszcz, Vol. IX, No. 21 (193) (November 1-15, 1966), 6.

[35] *Życie Warszawy*, Warsaw (May 27, 1966).

goals, the reforms failed to define clearly the nature of other training improvements, such as increased specialization, on the one hand, and the meaning of general education, on the other.

Potential reform is indeed hampered by a continuing indecision about where to place the emphasis—on ideological development or technical expertise. The resolution of conflicts between demands in these two areas remains problematic. At one time or another either may be dominant, but the titillating question is what happens when demands are being posed from both sectors. The issue is a particularly sensitive one. The desire seems to be to move in the direction of training teachers who would be at once both generalists as well as subject-matter specialists. What is ideally expected is a teacher who is knowledgeable as well as naturally gifted, enthusiastic, devoted, committed to the goals of the system and liked by all, especially by the students. At the same time, however, an expanding industry is pressing for greater (and narrower) specialization, often at the expense of well roundedness. Moreover, the economic and technical skill demands are spelled out with much more clarity and precision than the ideologically oriented expectations.

On the level of the individual's relationship to the system, one would suspect that given the need for the skill and service of the more technically specialized person, his political and ideological deficiencies might be overlooked as long as these do not posit a major threat to the political order. On the other hand, should the political system feel threatened, the needs of the economy would ultimately have to be relegated to an inferior position. However, for many individuals, narrow technical specialization offers an escape from political-ideological pressures. Significant in this connection is the following statement made in an interview by a teacher who was trained both in a humanistic discipline as well as in a technical subject but who chose to teach only in the latter: "To teach modern poetry I have to be very good as well as careful. *They* read poetry and *they* have their judgments on the merits of a given poet. If my judgment should conflict with theirs I am in trouble. But organic chemistry—*they* do not even understand the language much less what I am doing in the laboratory." Indeed, specialists in the sciences suffered much less from the repercussions following the riots of 1968 than did those working in the areas of the humanities or the social sciences. While the language of the former remains largely obscure to the leading members of the political elite, they do think of themselves as knowledgeable in the latter.

In addition to the problems relating directly to the teacher's professional preparation, effectiveness is hampered in many cases by a cynicism born out of a continuing sense of failure. This is true in many cases of youth from the urban intelligentsia who view teaching, especially on the elementary level, as a second rate profession of questionable status.

Assessments in the existing educational literature, the constant soul-searching and continuous dialogue of criticism and self-criticism in the press, and organizational and structural reforms are all meant to develop new tools, and new and hopefully more effective forms of communication within the educational system. Yet, at the same time, while new values and criteria are being established, old patterns persist. Whether the new, revised, or modified educational forms constitute real departures from the anachronism of the past and, more importantly, whether they are capable of producing effective teachers in terms of new needs remains to be seen.

Chapter 4: Life and Status of the Polish Teacher

The Place of the Teacher in the Social Structure: Social Status and Material Conditions

THE STRESS on education as a vehicle for social advancement and the time and intellect required to become a professionally functioning part of the educational enterprise, together with the gentry tradition, have combined to produce a social esteem scale in which teachers rate extremely high. University professors and teachers, despite their own frequently voiced dissatisfaction with the status of their respective professions, occupy similarly high positions on the prestige scale among residents of large urban centers as among Poles living in rural areas (see Tables 4-1 and 4-2).

These tables would indicate that, generally, popular esteem in Polish society is related to the length of time required to train for a particular profession. At the same time, it also seems to be related to the traditional class structure of that society. Thus, for example, while the army officer's prestige position is relatively low for a country which historically has honored dash and valor and the romanticism associated with patriotic service and heroic death, it should be borne in mind that the professional officer of the contemporary Polish army—unlike the gentleman-officer of the prewar Polish army—is often of working-class or peasant background (or is perceived to be of such background). In a sense, he carries with him into a traditionally highly regarded occupation the stigma of his lower-class background.

Sociologists in Eastern Europe frequently maintain that the prestige hierarchy in Socialist society is less related to factors of income than in countries with a capitalist economy. This contention is in some ways borne out by comparative occupational prestige studies which indicate that in such countries as the United States, West Germany, Eng-

89

Life and Status of the Teacher

TABLE 4-1

ESTEEM RATINGS OF OCCUPATIONS AND POSITIONS BY WARSAW RESIDENTS

Sequence	Occupation	Scale Value[a]
1	University professor	1.22
2	Physician	1.44
3	Teacher	1.71
4	Mechanical engineer	1.78
5	Airman	1.83
6	Lawyer	1.97
7	Agronomist	1.97
8	Minister of government cabinet	2.07
9	Journalist	2.13
10	Skilled steel worker	2.18
11	Skilled lathe operator	2.27
12	Priest	2.35
13	Nurse	2.38
14	Factory foreman	2.53
15	Bookkeeper/Accountant	2.54
16	Self-employed tailor	2.70
17	Self-employed locksmith/steamfitter	2.73
18	Office supervisor	2.77
19	Private farmer	2.78
20	Commissioned officer	2.79
21	Private storekeeper	3.01
22	Railway conductor	3.18
23	Militiaman (policeman)	3.21
24	Office clerk	3.43
25	Office secretary	3.50
26	Store clerk	3.59
27	Unskilled building worker	3.95
28	Charwoman in office	4.08
29	Unskilled worker on state farm	4.16

SOURCE: Adam Sarapata, "Stratification and Social Mobility in Poland," *Empirical Sociology in Poland*, Institute of Philosophy and Sociology, Polish Academy of Sciences, Warsaw, PWN, Polish Scientific Publishers, 1966, p. 41.

[a] Scale: 1–very high esteem; 2–high; 3–average; 4–low; 5–very low.

land, New Zealand, and Japan, corporate and industrial directors and managers score rather high.[1] On the other hand, physicians are rated extremely high in both Socialist and capitalist societies while less lucrative occupations (relative

[1] Alex Inkeles and Peter H. Rossi, "National Comparisons of Occupational Prestige," *American Journal of Sociology*. Vol. 61 (1956), 329-

Life and Status of the Teacher

TABLE 4-2

ESTEEM RATINGS OF OCCUPATIONS AND POSITIONS BY
AGRICULTURALLY EMPLOYED RESIDENTS OF
RURAL AREAS IN POLAND

Occupation/Position	Median Point[a]
University professor	1.51
Minister of government cabinet	1.81
Teacher	1.94
Physician	2.03
Industrial engineer	2.08
Priest	2.14
Skilled miner	2.20
Agronomist	2.25
Commissioned army officer	2.37
Skilled lathe operator	2.63
Office supervisor	2.65
Factory foreman	2.69
Private middle-range farmer	2.82
State farm director	2.90
Self-employed locksmith	2.97
Self-employed tailor	3.02
Office clerk	3.21
Private storekeeper	3.22
Office secretary	3.32
Unskilled building worker	3.63
Unskilled worker on state farm	3.79

SOURCE: Adam Sarapata, "Stratification and Social Mobility in Poland," *Empirical Sociology in Poland*, Institute of Philosophy and
Sociology, Polish Academy of Sciences, Warsaw, PWN, Polish Scientific Publishers, 1966, p. 42.

[a] Scale: 1–very high; 2–high; 3–medium; 4–low; 5–very low.

to industrial manager incomes) such as university professor
or scientist rate high in esteem regardless of the ideological
orientation of the particular system. In the Soviet Union the
esteem enjoyed by factory managers, functional equivalents
to corporate directors in the United States or factory directors in West Germany or Great Britain, is higher than
that enjoyed by other occupations including engineers, army
officers, and teachers. This might indicate a lesser relation-

39. Reprinted in Seymour Martin Lipset and Neil J. Smelser, eds.,
Sociology: The Progress of a Decade (Englewood Cliffs, N.J.: Prentice-Hall, Inc., 1961), pp. 506-16.

Life and Status of the Teacher

ship between ideology, occupational ranking, and income.[2] Certain occupations rank high in every system irrespective of income. On the basis of such observations Alex Inkeles and Peter H. Rossi suggest that perhaps differences in prestige rankings are related to levels of industrialization and industrial maturity rather than to ideology or socioeconomic system.[3] As far as teachers are concerned (other than university professors) their relative prestige might indeed be related to the level of industrialization and technological sophistication and to the concomitant level of their knowledge monopoly. Thus, the prestige of teaching would decrease as the level of industrialization and technology increases (see Table 4-3). The apparent decrease in teacher prestige in the face of industrialization may explain the cynicism toward their professional status that one often en-

TABLE 4-3

COMPARATIVE PRESTIGE POSITION OF TEACHERS IN
SELECTED NATIONS

Country	Sequence Position of Teachers	Occupation Immediately Preceding	Occupation Immediately Following
United States	16	Building contractor	Farmer
West Germany	9	Army Major	Farmer
Great Britain	9	Builder	Farmer
New Zealand	9	Builder	Farmer
Japan	10	Office clerk	Small Farmer
USSR	7	Army officer	Chairman of Collective Farm
Poland	3	Physician	Mechanical Engineer

SOURCES: Alex Inkeles and Peter H. Rossi, "National Comparisons of Occupational Prestige" in *Sociology: The Progress of a Decade*, Seymour Martin Lipset and Neil J. Smelser, eds., Englewood Cliffs, N.J.: Prentice Hall, Inc., 1961, pp. 513-14; Adam Sarapata, "Stratification and Social Mobility in Poland," *Empirical Sociology in Poland*, Institute of Philosophy and Sociology, Polish Academy of Sciences, Warsaw, PWN, Polish Scientific Publishers, 1966, pp. 41-42.

[2] *Ibid.*, in Lipset and Smelser, p. 513.
[3] *Ibid.*, pp. 515-16.

92

counters in speaking to Polish teachers. They may indeed sense decreasing prestige as Polish industrialization accelerates. However, the continuous exceedingly high prestige level of Polish teachers in spite of industrialization— as evidenced by various surveys undertaken at different times and places—suggests that the relative prestige of occupations is also substantially influenced by the character of the particular political culture, including traditional patterns of prestige. The latter conclusion is reinforced by the relative rating similarly given to the prestige of teaching by residents of Warsaw and by village dwellers (with the latter rating the teacher's prestige only slightly higher than the former). It is further borne out by the similarity in the esteem accorded teachers in Great Britain and New Zealand —countries more akin to each other in terms of political culture than in levels of industrialization. Thus, while he may be economically deprived, especially in terms of his relative prestige (see Table 4-3), the status anxieties of the Polish teacher are probably (at least for the time being) unwarranted.

As a rule, those working in the private sector of the economy (e.g., self-employed tailors, locksmiths, small farmers, hothouse cultivators, small storekeepers) rate above those employed in the public sector in terms of income. However, only in rural areas of Poland do certain private economy occupations (especially private farming) rate higher on the prestige scale than certain occupations related to the public economic sector. Generally, private entrepreneurs live on a visibly higher consumption level than the rest of the population, as a result generating a great deal of envy and animosity, and making the group as a whole a convenient political target, especially in times of crisis. The rest home, for example, of the Association of Self-Employed Artisans in the mountain resort of Zakopane is an imposing facility, featuring a kidney-shaped swimming pool, a bar, and a parking lot which is always filled with expensive, foreign automobiles. It is not surprising, therefore, that the unrest of the spring 1968 brought in its wake a campaign not only against "disloyal" intellectuals, restive students, "culturally alien, incompletely Polonized" persons of Jewish origin, but also against the socalled privateers (*priwaciarze*) of the nonagricultural segment of the economy.

That income levels have generally little relationship to prestige levels in Poland is further evidenced by the salary distribution among employees in the public economic sector (Table 4-4). Although there are no great differences in the salaries obtainable in that sector of the economy—they are all rather low, especially in relation to consumer prices— teachers' incomes (except for those in higher education) are far from a reflection of their relatively high prestige. Within the general field of education itself those employed on the level of higher education do constitute both an economic as well as a social elite and in this particular case prestige and income do indeed coincide. The economically as well as socially favored university professor also has greater opportunities than the elementary or secondary school teacher to further increase his income—sometimes quite substantially —through involvement in professionally related activities, such as research, the authorship of texts, scholarly books and articles, lectures, travel abroad on foreign scholarships or on government-sponsored semiofficial missions, etc. If of sufficient prominence to be elected to the Academy of Sciences, he receives additional supplementary remuneration.

Others, too, within the public sector of the economy may have an opportunity to boost their incomes substantially, especially if their skills are in high demand or if their jobs necessitate travel abroad (which means, in addition to a per diem paid in foreign currency, the possibility of selling to foreigners highly sought after Polish goods, such as vodka, amber necklaces, sheepskin-lined leather coats, and/ or importing foreign items which could be traded domestically). Pilfering on the job seems to be a widespread practice among those employed in some branches of industry as is manipulation with scarce goods among those working in consumer services and distribution.

The life of a rank and file teacher, on the other hand, is

Life and Status of the Teacher

TABLE 4-4

AVERAGE MONTHLY GROSS SALARIES RECEIVED IN 1966 BY
FULL-TIME EMPLOYEES OF PUBLIC SECTOR OF THE ECONOMY

Rank	Branch of Economy/Occupation	Average Monthly Gross Salary (in złotys)	Total Employed at Each Educational Level and Type
1	Building Construction	2,356.00	
2	Public Administration, including Justice	2,178.00	
3	Industry	2,176.00	
4	Communal-Municipal Housing	1,830.00	
5	Finance and Insurance	1,829.00	
6	*Education, Science and Culture*	1,780.00	
	a) Higher Education	3,202.00	29,522
	b) Teachers' Training	2,999.00	4,346
	c) Vocational Education	2,603.00	41,832
	d) Secondary General Education	2,376.00	15,973
	e) Art Education	2,346.00	2,365
	f) Elementary General Education	1,730.00	173,128
	g) Preschool Education	1,393.00	21,789
7	Trade	1,699.00	
8	Agriculture	1,618.00	
9	Health, Welfare, and Physical Culture	1,543.00	
10	Forestry	1,471.00	

SOURCES: Główny Urząd Statystyczany, *1966 Rocznik Statystyczny*, Vol. XXVI (1966), p. 495; Główny Urząd Statystyczny Polskiej Rzeczpospolitej Ludowej, *Rocznik Statystyczny Szkolnictwa 1944/45-1966/67*, Series "Occupational Yearbooks," No. 7, Warsaw, 1967, p. 39.

much harder. Among employees in the public sector, the salaries of teachers, as well as of medical doctors, rate average or below. While doctors, like so many others, have opportunities to supplement their incomes substantially through private practice (especially in the lucrative fields of venereal and skin disease treatment), teachers of elementary and secondary school levels have few supplemental income sources, and those available are not enough to increase total earnings appreciably. To be sure, teachers are entitled to certain extra monetary rewards and premiums which are distributed either on a selective basis among deserving individuals (e.g., in recognition of teaching excel-

Life and Status of the Teacher

lence or some special services) or are given to a teaching *collective* in a particular school. In the latter case, the principal or director, in consultation with the Pedagogic Council, awards the extra bounty among the members of the staff, according to a scale of preference which may be based upon seniority, political, personal, professional or collegial considerations, or a combination of these. Teachers serving in the capacity of elementary school principals or secondary school directors receive additional monetary allowances. The additional pay for administrative duties varies according to the size and type of school but ranges from a minimum of 150 *złotys* per month for a principal in an incomplete 6-grade elementary school to a maximum of 600 *złotys* per month for a director in charge of a full secondary school.

As seen, within the field of education salary scales are geared to the educational level on which one is employed. Moreover, earnings of teachers in small towns and villages are lower than those of teachers in large metropolitan areas although rural teachers have possibilities, by living closer to the land, of aiding their budget by raising some of their own food or obtaining food from the parents of students and other sources, usually in return for services rendered. Generally, although lacking in cultural and educational opportunities, life in the rural areas is somewhat easier materially than in the cities. On the whole, however, limited financial resources prevent the teacher from enjoying many of the cultural opportunities to which he feels entitled, even if available. Yet, even though he may not be able to afford the theater, concerts, or an occasional evening out in a restaurant or night club, the provincial teacher is acutely sensitive to the lack of these activities in his community. He also feels restrained as to the type of recreation he may properly enjoy without courting criticism.

Vocational teachers seem to fare better than teachers of general education or those specializing in the humanities or social and theoretical sciences. Vocational and shop teachers have the option of entering higher paying industry or, after expiration of their initial employment agreement, they

96

may even seek work in the more remunerative small industry of the private economic sector.

Because the development of industrialization and technical skills are new, personnel with advanced technical skills are scarce. *Glos Nauczycielski,* the official weekly organ of the Polish Teachers' Union, regularly carries advertisements of mechanical *technikums,* basic vocational schools, or agricultural schools in the provinces soliciting applicants nationally for faculty positions. Such advertisements usually enumerate the material conditions attendant to employment and benefits, including guaranteed housing.

As for most Poles living in urban centers, housing for teachers is an acute problem. In 1957 a few hundred employees of the educational system in Warsaw organized themselves, through the Union, into the housing cooperative called "Education." The cooperative erected its first apartment building in a residential settlement along Washington Street in Warsaw and over the years has built a number of additional structures in the same area. "Education" is presently planning to build apartment houses in other Warsaw locations. Many of these are multistoried high-rise buildings but since they include within each building recreational facilities, offices, large lobbies, etc., the actual space allocated to tenants is rather limited. In 1966, for example, the existing buildings contained only 3,000 apartments while the waiting list contained 15,000 names. According to the chairman of the housing cooperative, the waiting period for a small apartment is at least two years and for a larger apartment three years. While imposing from the exterior, many of these buildings show serious interior defects. Residents complain of frequent breakdowns in the elevator system, power failure, poor soundproofing, weak water pressure, water leakage, etc. Because of the desperate need for housing some of the buildings are put into residential use before completion.

As inadequate as the new cooperative houses are, they are beyond the financial reach of most teachers. As a result only a minority of the residents in the cooperative houses designed for those working in the field of education are bona fide teachers. To recapture their capital investment the cooperatives are compelled to open the apartment vacancies and waiting lists to those who can afford the initial price regardless of their occupation or profession. The chairman (*prezes*) of the Polish Teachers' Union (ZNP) Committee of the Warsaw District, Stanisław Jeziorski, spoke of the housing problem facing teachers in all of the Mazowsze region. He discussed the need to regulate housing allocation and assignments, especially for newly employed teachers, in the cities of the area. The problem of housing for young teachers is of particular urgency because they are not even entitled to join a housing cooperative even if they possess the necessary funds. Only those with several years' tenure are eligible for membership in a teachers' housing cooperative. This limitation was necessary to stem the existing pressure for vacancies and new building construction.[4]

The question of building construction both for school plants and for teachers' housing, is a frequent topic of parliamentary (*Sejm*) discussion. Deputy Maria Augustyn of the Polish United Workers' Party (PZPR) and a member of the *Sejm* Commission for Education and Science said at the end of one such debate:

> Our discussion proved that the most important present problem facing us is that of securing some kind of material base for the reformed elementary school system. Of equal importance are the matters of building teachers' housing, of full realization of the financial resources mapped out in the plan for school investments, as well as the question of training and perfecting the teaching staffs.[5]

[4] *Głos Nauczycielski* (December 30, 1966), and *Życie Warszawy* (December 31, 1966–January 2, 1967), 6.
[5] A. W. Wys. "Postulates Relative to the 5-Year Plan," *Życie Warszawy* (October 15, 1966), 5.

Life and Status of the Teacher

As a rule, if married, both husband and wife work, contributing their combined salaries to the maintenance of the family. Some select teachers (both vocational as well as in general education) have occasional opportunities to earn additional income by undertaking extracurricular chores (e.g., program development, work in a summer camp, etc.) but most are forced to moonlight as best they can in order to make ends meet. Popular dailies carry long lists of advertisements in special columns on education inserted by teachers seeking off-hours work. They advertise tutorials in foreign languages, coaching for preparatory examinations, remedial work in mathematics and physics. They usually specify their qualifications: long experience, *Magister* (MA) degree, professional standing, etc. Some mention the price of their labor, usually rather moderate, about 10 *zlotys* an hour for individual tutorial work in preparation for the matriculation examinations on the secondary school level. Some may ask for meals in lieu of payment in cash and single teachers may request modest sleeping accommodations in return for their services. In the rural areas some teachers instead of, or in addition to, individual tutorials, will travel to remote villages during off-hours in order to lecture at schools of agricultural preparedness, usually for 15 *zlotys* an hour plus transportation.

As a result of existing income discrepancies in the general field of education, its lower levels (i.e., kindergarten, elementary, and secondary, but primarily the first two) tend to be feminized. The feminization of the teaching profession at the lower levels is already discernible at the institutions training teachers for these levels, such as the schools of teacher education of the SN type. As pointed out earlier, the graduate of a school of that type is inclined to consider the institution which provided him with his professional credentials as the stepchild of Polish education. His chance of an attractive job assignment after graduation is slim in comparison with graduates from other educational training institutions. Moreover, if as a student he had to work to supplement a meager stipend and allowance (as so many do), as a teacher he often must undertake extra jobs just to keep his head above the economic waters. Within the profession the graduate of a school of teacher education (SN), or even the graduate of a higher school of pedagogy who has passed his final course examinations but has not written his thesis, as a rule simply does not enjoy the status, privileges, or pay of a graduate of an institution of higher learning (especially a university) in possession of his Master's (*Magister*) degree.

To upgrade the SN graduate's prestige and self-esteem it was recommended that he be enabled to continue his education at the more prestigious higher schools of pedagogy while employed in the school system. This would at least constitute a breakthrough in the obstacles erected toward his professional advancement and higher status. Post-SN opportunities might well make elementary teaching more attractive. As it is, many feel blocked, caught in a web of inferior social background, inferior elementary and secondary educational opportunities, and a bad start with numerous negative career implications.

As a consequence of the many problems, real and imagined, with which the Polish teacher is faced, some 80,000 persons left the occupation between 1953 and 1963. Significantly, 77.1 percent of those who left the teaching profession were between the ages of 21 and 35, and three-fourths resigned somewhere between the first and ninth year of teaching. It is the younger teacher, raising a family, who is economically most affected and he leaves most frequently.

Most of those who left the teaching profession were employed in elementary schools, the lowest paying in the educational structure. Among the reasons given for leaving were low pay, lack of prospects for the future, bad relationships with administrative authorities, job difficulties, family considerations, etc.[6]

[6] Mikołaj Kozakiewicz. "Kilka słów o środowisku nauczycielskim." *Wieś Współczesna*, Warsaw, No. 6 (1967), 73-82.

Life and Status of the Teacher

Compounding the problems of the elementary teacher is the fact that his status in the community, as already indicated, is likely to be reduced as the general level of education in the society increases. In the past the teacher was not infrequently the only person in the small community aside from the priest who was able to read and write. By losing his monopoly on knowledge he is apt to lose some of his erstwhile prestige, even in the village. This may well be the reason for the comparatively low status of teachers in technologically advanced Western societies and Poland may move in this direction.

Consequently, although empirical studies conducted by Polish sociologists indicate that the teacher in Poland continues to enjoy high prestige and that status is not related to income, many Polish teachers feel slighted both in terms of prestige and income, and they apparently see a relationship between the two.

There is indeed a certain ambiguity associated with the status of the teacher and the ambiguity is particularly glaring in the case of the young teacher, especially the graduate of the school of teacher education (SN). On the one hand, he is a member of a profession which carries a great deal of prestige and much is expected of him. On the other, he is underpaid and perceived as being idealistically naive, or a failure. Because of his continuous high esteem rating, moreover, the gap between the teacher's income and prestige is indeed the highest among all occupations. His prestige, in fact, is far out of proportion to his low income. Among other occupations only nursing approximates—but not quite—that of teachers in terms of the extensiveness of the gap. The gap between prestige and income, with the gap weighted in favor of income, is strongest generally among those working in the private sector of the economy (see Table 4-5).

While the prestige patterns are determined by community values and traditional norms, incomes, especially in the public sector, are set by the political authority and governed

TABLE 4-5

RELATIONSHIP-GAP BETWEEN PRESTIGE AND INCOME
OF SELECTED OCCUPATIONS: WARSAW AREA

Rank Order of Gap Between Prestige and Income	Occupations Whose Income Exceeds Its Prestige	Occupations Whose Prestige Exceeds Its Income
	High Gap	
1		Teacher
2		
3		
4		Nurse
	Medium Gap	
5	Shopkeeper	
6		
7		
8	Private Tailor	
9		University Professor
10	Ministerial Member of Government Cabinet	
	Low Gap	
11	Private Locksmith Unskilled Construction Laborer	Medical Doctor Mechanical Engineer Agronomist Railway Conductor
12	Shop Assistant	Office Cleaner
13		Airline Pilot Accountant Office Clerk
14	Lawyer Policeman Army Officer	Factory Foreman Typist
15	Priest Office Supervisor Small Farmer	Journalist
	Occupations of Coinciding Prestige-Income Relationship Skilled Steelworker Machinist Unskilled Worker	

SOURCE: Based upon data supplied in Adam Sarapata, "Social Mobility," *Polish Perspectives*, English edn., Warsaw, Vol. IX, No. 1 (January 1966), 18-27.

Life and Status of the Teacher

by that authority's needs and perspectives. The economic market and its demands have only a limited impact on the results.

Yet, in spite of teachers' perceptions, their social status is, as indicated, still high in the sense that the profession is theoretically held in high esteem. This esteem is symbolized, if not by corresponding pay scales, by other rewards and public recognition. On the Day of Teachers on November 20, they find themselves the center of public attention and official praise. However, teachers are recognized and rewarded not only on special occasions, such as the Day of Teachers, but also at annual award granting ceremonies staged by the central government and local authorities, as well as by the Party and the Front of National Unity (*Front Jedsności Narodu*, FJN). Moreover, in addition to being given a variety of socio-organizational functions (not all of which are welcome) teachers are also drawn into membership of largely honorary (and thus prestigious) committees formed on the eve of festive occasions. Thus teachers' representatives will be included in local committees in preparation of the May Day celebration and will share such membership with other leading citizens. It was estimated in 1963 that 110,000 teachers held offices in various socio-political organizations and 16,000 of them were members of National Councils of various levels of administration.[7] Of a total of 460 deputies (one deputy per 60,000 population) in the Polish parliament (*Sejm*), 54 were teachers during the 1961-1965 term. They constituted the fourth largest occupational-economic group in that body, after workers (62 deputies), engineers and technicians (62), and farmers (59).[8]

[7] *Polska Ludowa: Słownik encyklopedyczny* (Warsaw: Wiedza Powszechna, 1965), pp. 167-68.

[8] *Ibid.*, pp. 329-32. The *Sejm* is formally the highest constitutional authority of People's Poland. The prewar Senate was liquidated because it was, as defined under the revised pre-World War II Constitution, a body to which only persons of position or education could elect or be elected. The prewar Senate was thus associated with social and economic privilege while elections to the prewar lower chamber

Life and Status of the Teacher

The reality of everyday life for the ordinary teacher is much less attractive and less glamorous, however. Subsequently, he worries about his prestige and feels his status threatened. He lives, after all, in a society in which prestige and status matter very much. Some teachers, on the other hand, are concerned lest their colleagues' worries and the continuous public debate over the prestige of the teacher that follows will have the adverse effect of creating doubts as to the teacher's proper position where none existed before. As one teacher in a provincial town told me:

> I am really concerned that the constant complaints of my colleagues regarding the diminishing status of teachers will have unforeseen effects and indeed contribute to a lowering of our prestige in the community.

Q. I take it then that you are not too worried over your present prestige.

A. No, that is not it. I am not an extreme optimist, but at present, from where I am sitting, I do not see what the worry is all about. Teachers are complainers it seems to me.

Q. You personally have no complaint?

A. That's not it either. I have some complaints but on the whole I have always encountered community sympathy and assistance from the local (*terenowe*) authorities. Here I am, with higher education, working in what others call the dead provinces (*zabita prowincja*) but I really have no regrets. You have to believe this. I have held various posts here, both in education as well as generally, I am well respected. Teaching gives me a great deal of satisfaction.

(*Sejm*) were boycotted by the opposition parties after the revised Constitution of the thirties abolished the system of party list voting. The present Polish parliament is thus unicameral and replaced the Land National Council (*Krajowa Rada Narodowa*) which existed between 1944 and 1946. The first postwar *Sejm* of 1947 consisted of 114 members of the Polish Workers' Party (Communists), 116 of the Polish Socialist Party, 109 of the People's Party, 41 of two other peasant groups, 41 of the Democratic Alliance, and 18 representatives of Catholic and Christian Democratic organizations. During the 1961-1965 term the Polish United Workers' Party (merger of Communists and Socialists) held 256 seats, the United Peoples or Peasant groups had 117 deputies, the Democratic Alliance 39, and 21 seats were allotted to formally "nonparty" groups, i.e., *Znak* (5), Christian (3), *Pax* (3), Union of Socialist Youth (5), Union of Rural Youth (6). The Catholic *Znak* representation was the most independent group in the 1961-1965 *Sejm*.

Life and Status of the Teacher

Q. Why do you think other teachers are dissatisfied?

A. Why? It is simple. You see, the teacher, by virtue of his occupation, is supposed to be the pronouncer of and commentator on the general political line of his government. If he does this job well and honestly and in accordance with his own conviction he will not, or at least should not, meet with disrespect in our country. When the line is correct and the results meet people's hopes and expectations the authority of the teacher and the school should be correspondingly high since it is the school that fires the hopes and defends the line.

Q. Is it all then a question of politics?

A. Not entirely. It is natural that the individual characteristics of the teacher should reflect on the profession in the eyes of the environment, locally I mean. However, one has to look at it from a global perspective and in terms of principle. The question really is: Do teachers manage to generate public confidence in themselves and in what they are supposed to stand for? This is the measure of the teachers' authority, confidence, trust. It would be tragic indeed if the position of the teacher under our system should be lower than it was. I don't think it is.

By placing the problem in a larger political context this teacher has perhaps pointed out another of the variables upon which teachers' prestige is based, and according to which it fluctuates. The teacher's status and standing in the community is, perhaps, not only a function of his knowledge vis-à-vis the community, but also of the popularity of the political system of which he is viewed as an agent. As an ex-officio agent of the system his future social status may very well rest upon community acceptance of that system, in addition to other variables related to skill and the value of education generally. In this respect the teacher's situation is similar to that of the army officer and the member of the government, activities traditionally held in high esteem. Their presently lowered prestige is due largely to the greater recruitment of traditionally lower-class persons into these positions, but also to their connection with a system which is not yet fully in tune with prevailing community sentiment. Like the army officer and cabinet minister, the teacher's prestige suffers by proxy.

Life and Status of the Teacher

The underlying philosophy of contemporary Polish educational theory might be subsumed in three general principles: (1) the educational system is an important instrument in the construction of a Socialist society; (2) the educator's task is to develop a generation which will continue with the work of building and perfecting a Socialist society; and, (3) the educational ideal is to develop a type of "new man," one who has internalized the moral values growing out of the Socialist belief system and, at the same time, continues the best of Polish traditional culture.

In addition to his vital revolutionary role, the Polish teacher remains, as always, an important agent in the cause of general cultural advancement in the community. In carrying out the demands imposed upon him in his social-missionary role, the teacher faces a difficult dilemma, however. He must, at the same time, manifest his superior knowledge and commitment while retaining community goodwill by showing that he is "of the people."

The bulk of the Polish gentry, having lost their landholdings and traditional economic base—as a result of mismanagement as well as of economic and sociopolitical developments long predating the present order—has assumed, in conjunction with the priesthood, the role of cultural prodder. They are, in effect, the "old" intelligentsia. While the priests' prodding was in the direction of Catholic religious and national values, the gentry prodding has been less parochial. For a time, propagation of religious values was a part of the gentry mission since these values were seen as part of a national cultural heritage. But the gentry was also the conveyor of social and scientific enlightenment and thus its cultural mission has been broader than that of the clergy. Traditionally then, members of the Polish gentry have occupied a missionary role roughly equivalent to that of the contemporary teacher. This tradition, because of its missionary character, incorporated a contempt for the lower classes (perceived as uncultured), for manual labor, and

106

Life and Status of the Teacher

for money making in general—activities which, in their perception, deprived a man of honor, dignity, as well as of the time and energy necessary for the pursuit of the loftier things in life. On the basis of their education, cultural refinement, and gentry heritage, the intelligentsia claimed political and social leadership but, at the same time, remained aloof from the masses. Often they took up the cause of social and political reform and joined radical revolutionary movements of direct benefit to the lower classes, but they remained apart nevertheless. This tradition remains true of the teaching profession in some circles.

The life of a member of the intelligentsia, regardless of his occupation, differs with the size of the community in which he resides. Intelligentsia interests are oriented toward big-city amenities. Thus, when faced with a choice between life in the city or a small town, they invariably choose the former. This preference often deprives the small community of the services of the intelligentsia. In addition, it induces in the small-town resident feelings of suspicion toward the intelligentsia who are seen as alien, transient, aloof, and snobbish. Such feelings make it easier for provincial bullies to throw their weight about, to display their anti-intellectualism and suspicion of the outsider, and in the process reaffirm, as it were, their own local loyalty. This behavior, in turn, may even be considered by some as being in defense of local (and parochial) values over those of the outsider whose origins are the big city and whose values are therefore perceived to be worldly, cosmopolitan, alien, and morally corrupting. Zbigniew Kwiatkowski reports instances of physical abuse against teachers committed by well-connected small-town hooligans whose acts are overlooked by timid (or intimidated) authorities, including the local militia.[9]

According to surveys by Bernard Tejkowski in two small towns in the maritime areas of western Poland, a negative attitude toward the intelligentsia is most frequently dis-

[9] Zbigniew Kwiatkowski, *Byłem niemilczącym świadkiem* (Warsaw: Iskry, 1965), pp. 237-46.

Life and Status of the Teacher

played by lower status white-collar employees (i.e., clerks, low government officials, etc.) and members of the working class.[10] In a country in which educational opportunities are still very much restricted despite reform efforts, anyone with a completed secondary education may be considered by small-town residents as a member of the intelligentsia. Furthermore, because the privilege of education was attained at public expense, the hardworking graduate of elementary school (not to speak of those with even less education) often sees the educated person as a parasite. The new teacher in a small provincial town frequently senses an underlying hostility that adds to his own consciousness of being a stranger the feeling of being unwanted as well. Such a reception can have a devastating effect—akin to the proverbial cold shower—on a young teacher on his first job, regardless of his initial enthusiasm and good faith.

Limited material resources, social indifference, and the suspicion surrounding them breed among small-town intelligentsia a sense of frustration and futility, often of cynicism. They envision themselves as martyrs on an altar of progress, as combatants in a battle they are doomed to lose. As a result, many of them lose whatever enthusiasm they had when coming to the small town. Often they turn to self-centered concerns such as promotions, a better standard of living, and gaining visibility with superiors in larger centers so they may eventually be transferred.

Tejkowski maintains that the period of the system's stabilization in the late 1950's has replaced the once common social-activist intelligentsia with the businessmen-intelligentsia. The latter are concerned primarily with their own professional status and income. They are marginal to the life and interests of the community. Consequently they are not considered by the people as natural leaders. Whatever leadership functions they fulfill are usually of an

[10] Bernard Tejkowski, "Społeczność małego miasteczka Pomorza Zachodniego," *Studia Socjologiczne.* Institute of Philosophy and Sociology, Polish Academy of Sciences, Warsaw, No. 4 (1965), 103-17.

Life and Status of the Teacher

ex-officio character. The ruling authority of the small town usually remains with local people, regardless of formal education, who have emerged because of their organizational abilities and activism.[11]

For the member of the intelligentsia to become an integral part of a small community, he must "go native," become culturally attuned. Once he takes the route of assimilation, however, he may lose standing among professional peers who are big-city oriented and generally look down at the small-town person as being provincial, backward, and boorish.

The teacher who willingly accepts an assignment in an area such as Podlasie where the soil is poor, tuberculosis common, and horse-drawn carts are still the accepted mode of transportation, is one who frequently is still working for his degree and who likes the big city, but could not afford the pleasures it has to offer. In the small town, television brings him in touch with the world and allows him to partake, at least from a distance, in the culture of the metropolis.

The teaching component of the Radzyń (one of the larger towns in Podlasie) intelligentsia consists of 100 persons. They keep to themselves since their lower earning potential sets them apart from other members of the intelligentsia in the community. Their housing is inferior to that of other professionals. Some must travel long distances to work. One female teacher lacking housing occupies the staff room at the lyceum. Some teachers supplement their income by tutoring individual students or by traveling to villages to lecture at the schools of agricultural preparedness for a modest remuneration.[12] A teacher-principal in a small town in the equally poor neighborhood of Białystok told me:

> Our world is very small and it is for the individual even further narrowed by a set living standard, by occupation, cultural and social interests, personal ambition, often selfishness.

[11] *Ibid.*, p. 110.
[12] Tadeusz Jackowski, "Miejsce młodej inteligencji: Pod milionowym dębem," *Życie Warszawy* (May 29-30, 1966), 3.

Life and Status of the Teacher

We lack some kind of integrative intellectual force, or maybe tradition. The sphere of our intellectual life is simply very limited and most of us know it.

Q. What about contacts with the larger world? With Warsaw? With Białystok?

A. Oh, we have organized group excursions to Warsaw or to Białystok or even to Lublin for the theater or a concert. Television, if one can afford the price, is our substitute for culture.

Q. Are there any material compensations?

A. Not many. I waited several years for a housing assignment although it was promised to me before I came here. If I hadn't taken the job of school principal I would probably still be waiting.

Q. So what hopes are there? I mean, personally?

A. Almost everybody is working for some advanced degree in the hope that it will get him to the big city. But it is hard.

Q. Why ?

A. Because you have to do it on your own time—especially if you have exceeded the time officially allowed for writing the thesis. Because townspeople view advanced degrees with suspicion and view anyone working for one as a person who does not like it here, despises it here. It has its effects. They want people who are already finished with their studies and who have made peace with life here.

The same teacher-principal who complained about life in his small town in the vicinity of Białystok tried to make it clear in the course of the interview that he is not only a member of the Party, but that he considers himself a good and loyal Communist and he enumerated the achievements of the Socialist system.

Local Party and administrative functionaries, although self-satisfied and suspicious of the cosmopolitan pulls to which local teachers are subject, are enrolled in evening courses in order to complete their own, often elementary, education. The teacher, while viewed with suspicion, is also silently admired. Yet, the institution of education, especially that above elementary level, is not an integral part of the provincial community. Kwiatkowski writes:

The lyceum in N., although in existence for eighteen years, is until today an alien body. It is simply an institution which has not found a place in the town's model. This model does not provide for a secondary school, a good one, with a well-deserved reputation, highly regarded professionally, one which can show concrete accomplishments. In the web of small-town personal relationships the teachers have no bonds.

Moreover, the school is constantly making demands upon the town. It demands a new building because the old palace in which it is located is simply not suited for its purposes. The school demands protection from the MO (Citizens' Militia, police). The dormitory, especially that for women, is a permanent center of interest to local youth; the barbed wire, partly broken, separating the school grounds from their surroundings is a sort of "no man's land" and very symbolic.[13]

In order to become a part of the community the small-town teacher is compelled to become socially and politically active in that community. By doing so, however, he must often alter his priorities. Educational superiors, although expecting him to be civically active, want him primarily in the school or, at least, they want his extracurricular activities to be an integral part of his educational role. On the other hand, the local political and administrative authorities would like to absorb as much as possible of the teacher-activist's time as long as he "knows his place" and agrees to a subordinate position. He can fill many needs for which there is a manpower shortage. There is always a need for a qualified secretary and keeper of minutes, social worker, recreation director, organizer, mobilizer, etc. There is, in fact, no limit to the tasks he may be asked to perform, from census taker to resource person in the establishment of a new cooperative enterprise. Jan Woskowski reports that in answer to a question, "What does a village teacher do?," it was found in 1959-1960 that, in addition to teaching, he is also involved in the following activities:

---

[13] Kwiatkowski, op.cit., p. 242.

111

Life and Status of the Teacher

1. He organizes the Women's Day festivities
2. He organizes celebrations for Mother's Day
3. He organizes celebrations for Children's Day
4. He organizes celebrations for the Day of the Forest
5. He commands the scouting troop
6. He leads the local circle of the Union of Rural Youth (ZMW)
7. He is in charge of the school of agricultural preparedness or the local Agricultural University
8. He organizes artistic amateur clubs
9. He is a councilman or otherwise involved in the work of the local National Council
10. He participates in the activities of the agricultural circles
11. He puts on and shuts off the street lights in the villages where electricity is available
12. He conducts the periodic livestock census
13. He participates in the collection of funds for the Millennium School Project[14]

Although less is expected of the nonvillage teacher (and much less of the teacher in the larger urban centers), he is seldom paid for the extra chores, for his service to the community not directly related to teaching. Yet, it is quite easy for a teacher to become totally absorbed and involved in these chores, and many teachers become, in effect, town bureaucrats.

To many teachers social activism serves as a legitimation for poor classroom performance. However, the tasks he is usually given to perform in the community are, as can be seen, the least desirable in terms of popular appreciation. Local political leaders, dependent upon local grass-roots support and periodic elections, tend to shy away from performing unpopular tasks themselves and relegate these instead to the teacher whom they see as the representative

[14] Jan Woskowski, *O pozycji społecznej nauczyciela* (Lodz: Państwowe Wydawnictwo Naukowe on behalf of Center for Sociological Research, Institute of Philosophy and Sociology, Polish Academy of Sciences, 1964), p. 181.

of the system. The teacher's activism thus becomes ex officio in character. Should he attempt to move beyond the limitations of his ex-officio role and become too deeply and too intimately involved in the town's affairs, should he try to exert his own will too openly, the local administrative and political hierarchy may begin to consider him a meddling intruder. While pleasing one faction in town he may alienate another and subsequently be accused of stifling local community and mass initiative. Yet, assigned unpopular tasks which generate public antipathy (e.g., community mobilizer, organizer, etc.), he and the school invariably become the natural objects of grass-roots grumbling. He and the school are often the first to be blamed for whatever goes wrong. From the standpoint of the educational enterprise the entire process is frequently self-defeating.

In America, there is a disparity of educational philosophy between teachers and the communities in which they live. With regard to education, teachers in every locale are more progressive than their fellow citizens. On sociopolitical issues, however, small-town American teachers tend to be more conservative than their community while big-city teachers tend to be more liberal.[15] It is rather difficult to translate the conservative-liberal dichotomy familiar to Americans into the Polish context. The disparity in value orientation between the Polish teacher and his small-town environment is related not so much to educational philosophy as it is to style, cultural interests, and an entire complex of ideological commitments. The Polish teacher is more involved in the community than his American counterpart, yet he is less a part of it. More frequently than the American teacher, he is cast, at least formally, in the role of an opinion leader. At the same time, he is subject to his neighbor's immediate direct and indirect pressures. In the small rural community, the Polish teacher, as pointed out elsewhere, is often viewed as the antithesis of the priest and the

[15] Harmon Zeigler, *The Political World of the High School Teacher.* (Eugene, Oregon: The Center for the Advanced Study of Educational Administration, 1966), pp. 136-37.

school as a challenge to the Church. Regardless of the teacher's personal views on religion or the place of the Church in Polish society, the parish priest will often view the incoming teacher as a natural enemy from the outset. His American counterpart, on the other hand, is expected, informally at least, to uphold conventional religious tradition. This is especially true of rural America. In Poland, the rural teacher faces the competing demands of the political regime and the peasant community. The situation is a relatively unhappy one for the rural or small-town teacher. Comments from one interview are relevant in this regard.

Q. How did you get to this town?

A. I came here immediately after I completed my course work at the university. When I came here I was only four years older than my lyceum students.

Q. Are you happy here?

A. I am here. At one point I had the opportunity to move but decided to stay. The administration and my older colleagues were nice to me. There is a greater in-group feeling among teachers here than in the big town. We are mutually dependent on each other. In the big city the teacher has many opportunities to leave his profession. I do not want to leave, really. My friends who graduated with me from the university are surprised that I stuck it out this long in teaching. They think me odd because of this. They say "a few years on the job, just to meet the obligation, should be enough for anybody."

Q. Why do they think so?

A. The teacher is generally seen as a person who has not succeeded in life. You know, all the discussions and research on the status and authority of the teacher do not help either because they make it appear as if the teacher is someone to be sorry for, that he is very sensitive with regard to status and authority.

Q. You maintain that this is not true? He isn't?

A. I think that most teachers in Poland want to be treated like normal people, not like some problem. I would like to be treated by the environment on a par with other university graduates, in other professions, both in pay and prestige. No more and no less. I don't think really that we receive what the energy we put into our work would command in some other occupation. I would also like to see the teacher judged by the effectiveness of his educational work, not by his po-

114

litical, organizational, or administrative abilities. Then all this talk about status and authority would not be necessary. It doesn't do us any good except to draw attention to us.

Q. Does the attention bother you?

A. Yes, it does because it does not always result in sympathy or understanding. Someone joked that teachers are sensitive to their authority which they think is undermined when they do not have a television set or an automobile while the big shot father of his student has both a television set and an automobile.

Q. Why do you think teachers are not being appreciated?

A. For one thing, most people do not even know all we do. Our work is not limited to the classroom alone and not only to work among youth. Take, for example, meetings with parents, conferences of one sort or another. Yes, in this town, I must teach the parents as well as their children.

Q. How do you mean?

A. My students are for the most part the first in their families to receive a secondary education. This generates conflicts, misunderstandings. I have parents who do not understand that their children need the minimum of facilities, both in school and at home, for learning. And then I have parents who treat their 18-year-old girl as they would some princess only because she goes to school—no demands are made on her, nothing. Then you have parents who think it is "coming to them." This is a special category. A bad grade, failure to promote their child, brings on the teacher's head a flood of suspicions, innuendo, and veiled threats. They write letters to the authorities. You will say this is nothing new but it is not very pleasant in a small town where everybody knows everybody and my weakest student's father is a big man and he drinks with the school inspector.

Q. Couldn't one appeal?

A. Yes, one could but it often only makes matters worse. One hand washes the other. The teacher is caught between hammer and anvil. On the one hand, there are the goals of the program and constant talk of the educational level and how to maintain proper standards, and, on the other, there is the school administration with its quota on failing grades, always worried how it will look statistically, worried over funds and savings and so on. Something has to give, one or the other. Either they want the commendation of the inspector (*wizytator*) because the school has so few 2's or they want quality education. [Grades range from 2 to 5, 2 being "unsatisfactory" and 5 "very good." Grade 3 or "satisfactory" is passing. Two 2's on the final annual report card is normally sufficient cause to keep the student on the same grade level for another year.]

Q. Aren't these matters discussed openly?

A. By whom? The union is in favor of the failing quota system because it supposedly helps children of working-class background. But this is not so. Most often those who benefit from the limit on failing grades are children of parents with connections in town. Among colleagues we often talk privately of how good it would be to meet face to face with those who set the curricula programs and assign hours for the realization of these programs.

Q. You think the speed set from above is not realistic?

A. Listen, how do they expect me to cover Polish literature from the Middle Ages to 1863 in one year when I have only 2 hours a week, and sometimes these 2 hours are "saved" for the purpose of extracurricular meetings. As a result, many an important book of Polish classical literature, even *Pan Tadeusz* by Mickiewicz, is not covered in class but is assigned to the students as elective. Imagine, they come out of a secondary school and know nothing! We do not teach, we are realizing a program of set subjects and hours.

Q. But education seems to be the acceptable vehicle for advancement.

A. *Pro forma.* Like the prestige of the teacher. Comes Teachers' Day and there will be speeches and articles in the papers, and rewards and flowers. But the teacher is a very lonely person, especially in a small town and especially if he is serious about what he is doing. He is unfortunately not assisted in the process of education by the environment. Some films are prohibited to those under 18 years of age but they see them in the cinemas anyway. They sell beer and wine to 15-year-olds because the gastronomical enterprise is eager to make a profit. Try to make an issue of it—they would only laugh at you. A colleague of mine caught one of his students smoking a cigarette—he was called into the director's office because the boy's father telephoned.

Q. Have you changed your mind about the small-town environment? About your job?

A. As to the job, I like teaching. But about the town: I think the pressures are less in a big city and also one can more easily forget the troubles of the day there. The teacher in a big city does not stick out, does not aggravate so many eyes as here.

116

Life and Status of the Teacher

What was less characteristic for the prevailing feeling among provincial teachers in the cited interview was this teacher's willingness to remain in the small community when he had a chance to leave. In a study of teachers who were university graduates, Woskowski found none employed in the provinces who were there entirely by choice. Even those of rural background who presumably would find adjustment to small-town life easy, viewed the teaching profession as an opportunity to escape from the provinces.[16]

Although small-town teachers complain of limited cultural opportunities, few of their big-city colleagues, as already indicated, actually utilize what is available, primarily for lack of money. While small-town teachers complain that they are socially dependent on each other, and envy big-city colleagues their opportunities for wider ranging social contacts, Woskowski finds that big-city teachers are also limited to their immediate peer group, to teachers in the same school. Lack of wider friendships and of utilization of cultural opportunities among big-city teachers is not due to finances alone, however. They appear to lack the will to join groups and organizations which would activate them culturally. They do not even read much outside of assigned and/or required readings.[17] On the other hand, there are teachers in the provinces who become voluntarily and enthusiastically involved in such activities as amateur theater groups which have nothing to do with politics. It seems, therefore, that what makes a provincial town less desirable for a teacher than a big city is not so much the inability to become involved in cultural activities as the fear of not being able to do so. Moreover, from a practical point of view, the big city is the place where the big decisions are made and promotions determined. This is also the place where former professors, fellow graduates who have made

[16] J. Woskowski, "Losy studentów pedagogiki Uniwersytetu Łódzkiego: Ich praca zawodowa, sytuacja materialna, zainteresowania," in *Wykształcenie a pozycja społeczna inteligencji,* Jan Szczepański, ed. (Lodz: 1960), p. 287.
[17] *Ibid.*, p. 291.

117

good, universities, research institutes, and libraries are located. Here one, especially the teacher with an advanced degree, could possibly become involved in research or bring himself to the attention of those well situated in academic and educational circles. Eventually perhaps, he might be able to leave elementary or secondary school teaching. The lack of cultural opportunities is not so important then as the lack of opportunities for professional advancement. Equally important is the fact that the big city provides opportunities of getting lost. The big-city teacher is not the object of so much public scrutiny nor is he subjected to comparable demands for community service.

Pay for the small-town or village teacher is, as mentioned previously, less than in the big city and one cannot always teach in his speciality. In the very small communities and villages, the teacher may have to teach combined grades. Small-town teachers, more frequently than their big-city colleagues, find they have difficulty keeping abreast of new developments in their specialty. They also have fewer opportunities to take periodic refresher courses. But most frequent is the complaint of the various extracurricular pressures both within the school and outside it in the small town. As one elementay school principal told me: "There is a lot of talk about broadening the teacher's intellectual horizons but in the same breadth demands of various kinds are made on his time leaving him little opportunity for self-enrichment. Bah, he even has little time to perform his professional job adequately. Meetings, conferences, reports, in addition to all other things."

Indeed, the sociopolitical activities into which the Polish teacher is drawn, coupled with his need to seek additional income (especially if he must support a family) affect the quality of his professional work. He is often unable to meet the high expectation imposed by the public. While the political authorities may prefer the teacher-activist, the general community (e.g., parents, students, others) may disapprove of the teacher who falls behind in his primary

118

educational function. Where poor quality work in other occupations is not necessarily associated with inferior personal qualities, the inferior teacher is often perceived by the community as an inferior person. Although the public is not always willing to pay for the education of its children, it views work of inadequate quality in this area as almost criminal. The poor shoemaker may only have damaged a pair of shoes but the poor teacher has damaged something precious in terms of the individuals concerned and in terms of the nation's future.

The Teacher's Immediate Occupational Environment

Polish educational guidelines emanate to the school through the Ministry of Education and Higher Learning and the Polish United Workers' Party. The latter's Department of Science and Education (headed during the period of this study by Andrzej Werblan and his deputies, Henryk Garbowski and Zenon Wróblewski) offers programmatic and policy guidance to the Ministry. (In the personnel reshuffle following the riots of December 1970, Andrzej Werblan was replaced by Romuald Jezierski as head of the Department of Science and Education of the Polish United Workers' Party. Werblan, in turn, became in February 1971 one of the three deputy speakers [Vice-Marshal] of the *Sejm*. While the Marshal of *Sejm* [Dyzma Gałaj] is of the United Peasant Movement, his deputies are one each from the UPWP, the Democratic Alliance, and the nonparty bloc.)

The lines of responsibility between the Party and the Ministry of Education are not sharply delineated. The Ministry may at times initiate educational policies and innovation while the Party may concern itself with matters of school construction, salaries, school and curricula administration, etc. What emerges is a joint form of management of the educational enterprise with parallel authority, but the voice of the Party takes precedence over that of the educational administration. The Ministry directs its school affairs through the local *kuratoria* and the Party through the

119

local Party committees, each of which contains a department or bureau of science and education. Although the central authorities, both Party and government, exercise minute supervision and guidance, much discretion is left to the local functionaries. The latter may not, however, contravene or contradict the intent of the central powers. In addition, local National Councils, through their own departments of education and culture, supervise, assist, and become generally involved in school affairs under their territorial jurisdiction. Local problems may involve adjustment of general policy, but on the whole, the job of the local authorities is to see to it that general guidelines are implemented and that schools meet certain standards, however vaguely defined.

The individual teacher is subject to the scrutiny and pressures of those concerned with matters of education both within the Party and the Ministry. A powerful Party functionary, a commandant of a local Citizens' Militia (MO), or the chairman of a local National Council—although not directly responsible for educational affairs—may at any time involve themselves in school matters and exercise a strong voice in a decision. Such a wide network of authority obviously creates jurisdictional disputes. Occasionally one may dampen the effect of the crosspressures by playing off one authority against the other. Generally, however, homage is paid to the wishes of the Party and the MO. Should any conflict arise, the school authorities and those in government would retreat in the face of demands from the Party and security organization. The teacher having difficulties with the Party or security authorities could hardly expect protection from the school authorities who are easily intimidated.

Formally the teacher may look for the protection of the school authorities and the Polish Teachers' Union. The union, however, though charged with guarding the teacher's welfare and security, would shy away from problems of political sensitivity as readily as the school authorities.

Polish society seems permeated by jealousies and competition for limited stakes. Thus, while the teacher in disfavor or on the brink of demotion finds himself alone and isolated, the teacher favored with promotion fares little better. One teacher commented:

> The person who is being advanced finds himself frequently in a very lonely position. Oh, on the surface his colleagues will be nice to him but behind his back they will say that he was promoted because of pull (*protekcja*) and so forth. Sometimes they will advance innuendos as reasons for the promotion, such as the person promoted is in the service of security and so on. In my own case, being a woman, my promotion was attributed to my friendship with a Party secretary although he honestly had nothing to do with it. Moreover, the Party Secretary at the time of my promotion was a woman.

In his daily professional life the teacher is normally subject to the supervision of the school principal (or director, in case of secondary schools). The principal is usually a teacher of senior status and, presumably, of political reliability. By choice or circumstance Polish education (of any level) has not encouraged the development of a professional school administration as such. The president (*rektor*) of a university, for example, is elected from among the faculty for a set period. He is expected to engage in teaching and research while in office and to return to the faculty ranks upon the expiration of his administrative term. Even the Minister of Education, as for example former Minister Wacław Tułodziecki, was a working teacher before assuming the cabinet post.

The teaching load of a principal in an elementary school depends upon his professional credentials and the size of the school. In any case, an elementary school principal teaches a minimum of six hours a week. Usually he teaches civics, sex education, or a similar subject. Many elementary school principals appear to come from a physical education background. A principal whose elementary school em-

121

ploys a staff of 6 teachers will teach, on the average, eleven hours a week if he is a graduate of higher education and sixteen hours a week if he lacks such credentials.[18]

Generally, the instructional program is set in advance and handed down to the school by the central administration. The individual teacher and his school are also given little discretion in the choice of textbooks or other educational aids. It is only in the area of general character education that the guidelines are vague and much discretion is left to those in the field. The teacher and principal try to make a good impression and meet the performance expectations of the school inspector no matter how ill-defined the standards. The inspector may visit the school at any time, announced or unannounced. The school inspectors, sent on periodic visitations by the locally based *kuratoria*, are professional educators with long standing in the system. Their primary concern seems to be with the quality of instruction in the traditional subject-matter fields rather than with civics, general morale building, etc. The tendency is also for more frequent inspections in the higher grades of education than in the lower, with special emphasis on classes in Polish language, mathematics, biology, geography, physics, vocational training, history, physical education, and Russian language instruction, in that order. While 104 hours of inspection were devoted in the Warsaw elementary schools during 1961-1962 to the teaching of the Polish language, only two hours were given to inspection of student government, clubroom activity, etc. Forty-four inspection hours were given to school festivities and ceremonies.[19] This might indicate that professional educators in the field continue to promote the traditional educational role of the school system to the neglect of the political function stressed by the Party and the political system. There might thereby be a conflict between the intent of the policy planners and the performers in the field.

[18] Józef Szymański, *Rola kierownika w doskonaleniu pracy szkoły podstawowej* (Warsaw: Państwowe Zakłady Wydawnictw Szkolnych, 1965), pp. 12-13.

[19] See table on average school inspection hours, *ibid.*, p. 71.

Life and Status of the Teacher

In spite of the apparent lack of emphasis by inspectors on "character education," the school principal is responsible for the standards of behavior and ideological position of his students and staff. While his own performance is subject to scrutiny and complaints from various quarters, he is also the first recipient of complaints and pressures concerning individual teachers and the school. In addition, complaints addressed to higher authority find their way eventually to the desk of the principal. The Department for Elementary Schooling of the Ministry of Education receives annually close to 2,000 complaints from parents, pupils, educators, and concerned adults dealing with the behavior of teachers, school principals, etc. (see Table 4-6).

The principal must also serve as liaison with the economic enterprises in the community. Some of these enterprises help the school by providing busses for outings, periodic financial assistance for needy students or special school projects, people with special talents, etc. In return, the school may provide the enterprise with entertainment programs during special festivities, voluntary work during vacations, etc. Sometimes, the collaboration with a community organization lacks material benefit but provides both parties with mutual moral support.

To the young teacher, however, the principal is the first person with whom he must reckon. If the first job brings him away from home he looks to the principal not only as an occupational superior but also as a parent surrogate and protector. In a sense, the principal is to the young teacher what the sergeant is to the young army recruit—a person to be feared, guided by, relied upon, and to treat with caution. The first meeting between the young teacher and his principal or director can be a traumatic experience. One female teacher described such a meeting in a letter to the editor of the official Teachers' Union organ, *Głos Nauczycielski*. It was cold and the principal, a fat woman, came out on the veranda of her house adjoining the school and told her that she could not expect the school to help her with housing and that she would have to find some on her

Life and Status of the Teacher

TABLE 4-6

COMPLAINTS ADDRESSED TO MINISTRY OF EDUCATION REGARDING
TEACHERS, PRINCIPALS AND ELEMENTARY SCHOOLS, 1960-1962

Subject of Complaint	Nature of Complaints	No. of Complaints		
		1960	1961	1962
School Principal	Conflict with parents, physical punishment of students, neglect of work, financial mismanagement, failure to adhere to code, conflict with teachers.	207	435	346
Teachers	Inadequate professional preparation, unjust grading, conflict with parents.	90	203	203
Teachers and Principals—Behavior Outside of School	Housing problems, misuse of public property, drunkenness, quarrelsomeness.	110	214	154
Pedagogic Councils	Mutual conflicts, conflicts with principal.	112	124	56
Parents' Committee	Conflicts with principal, conflicts with teachers, with parents, cooperating institutions—e.g., patrons, etc.	17	13	25
School	Unfair grading, forgery of documents, corruption, including bribery.	116	77	186
Treatment of Pupils	Transfers, dismissal, monetary fines.	130	174	162
School Administration	Appeals from principals and teachers, parental complaints.	36	31	17
Miscellaneous		1089	674	482
Total Complaints		1907	1945	1631
Total Elementary Schools		26179	26345	26367

SOURCE: Józef Szymański, *Rola kierownika w doskonaleniu pracy szkoły podstawowej* (Warsaw: Państwowe Zakłady Wydawnictw Szkolnych, 1965), pp. 82-83.

own. The principal did not invite her to enter the warm house nor the school office. The first conversation took place entirely on the veranda, in the cold, with passersby and neighbors looking on. It was a degrading experience, the teacher maintained, and she pleads for principals to be friends, advisers, and colleagues of younger teachers.[20]

[20] *Głos Nauczycielski* (June 16, 1966), 9.

124

Life and Status of the Teacher

Perhaps to compensate for such humiliations the teacher tends to assert his authority with pupils and to guard that authority jealously. Some teachers even take pleasure in humiliating the parents of their pupils for the child's misconduct or poor performance. Parent-teacher conferences often turn into ordeals for the parents. In time the teacher also learns to adjust to his immediate environment and how to handle the principal. Mikołaj Kozakiewicz writes:

> Another way of gaining authority and weight for oneself, in addition to bullying children, is to become a busybody in school and the community. Such teachers tend to denounce their colleagues to the principal, the principal to the inspector, they try to become active in all self-management authorities, social and political, they instigate one against another, participate in informal caucuses prior to elections to the council of the village cooperative, they assist in "finishing off" the existing chairman in order to replace him with their own candidate or to gain themselves a seat on the council, etc., etc. They are everywhere, dip their fingers into everything, nothing can occur without them in the village or the small town, but everywhere they appear they are accompanied by meddling, intrigue, and gossip. They become involved not because they want to see things run smoothly in the village or town but because they desire to broaden their own influence, to increase their own authority and weight, so that they would be reckoned with, feared.[21]

These kinds of activities often bring the teacher greater visibility thus exposing him to even more rigid behavioral expectations. Since the teacher demands perfection from his environment, perfection, in turn, is demanded of him. Having primary responsibility for the younger generation, he is expected to serve as the model of perfection. This consideration and the teacher's activism, in addition to the grievances occasioned by the ordinary performance of his

[21] Mikołaj Kozakiewicz, *Niezbadane ścieżki wychowania* (Warsaw: Nasza Księgarnia, 1964), p. 191.

job (grades, examinations, conflict with the parish, village work, etc.), make teachers an easy and convenient target for gossip, intrigue, defamation—and in one known case in Koszalin, the target of assassination. A teacher's innocent interest in a student of the opposite sex is easily misinterpreted by the youngsters, and parents may accept that interpretation as valid.

Kozakiewicz maintains that the files of the disciplinary commission of any *kuratorium* are full of denunciations against teachers related to misinterpretation of apparently normal, innocent behavior. He consequently advises teachers that if, for example, they must participate in periodic dances organized by the school, they should avoid a dancing style which might be appropriate for a big-city night club but might be misunderstood in a village or small town. He also cautions teachers not to pay too much attention to any one particular student of the opposite sex and, if dancing, to change partners as frequently as possible. Male gymnastic instructors are urged to avoid the habit of catching female students jumping over gymnastic equipment, especially on the secondary school level, but instead have a strong girl perform that chore.[22]

Generally, teachers are advised to avoid fraternization with particular parents lest they may be accused of favoritism toward the latter's children, and principals are urged to avoid any drinking and chumminess with select teachers under their jurisdiction.

While dangers related to misunderstood sex relations, to inflamed imaginations, fraternization with particular parents or students or teachers are limited largely to teachers working in small provincial towns and villages, the dangers inherent in classroom discussions on problems of politics, ideology, or current events are present everywhere. By promoting free discussion in order to maximize participation, the teacher knows that he may subsequently be blamed for tolerating the expression of a student's unorthodox political views. He must also be wary lest he deviate, even momen-

[22] *Ibid.*, pp. 198-203.

tarily or for didactic reasons, from the approved political line. Kozakiewicz writes:

> ... helplessness and apathy on the part of educators may generate in the older youth an attitude of hypocrisy which expresses itself in the rather prevalent phenomenon of "praising a certain program on the outside, and condemning the same program privately." This is a phenomenon created under the pressures of external and environmental conditions. A person hopes to derive certain benefits from publicly making certain declarations which he "privately" rejects. A person may try to avoid through such public declarations certain unpleasantnesses, such as barriers to his career, difficulties in admission to a higher level of education and in professional advancement, etc.
>
> Such behavior is clearly contradictory to the ideals of socialist education, and, in fact, does harm to society and causes demoralization.
>
> What are the remedies? How can such fatal effects of political education be avoided? What are the means whereby the dissonance in the views among students, and between students and teachers, can be discovered early and unloaded and balanced? There are remedies and these are quite simple. First, the educator and teacher must himself be wise, politically engaged, ideologically mature, knowledgeable in the psychology of youth. Second, there must be in the entire school an atmosphere of sincerity, of free and animated ideological debate where no one could possibly be afraid of future punishment and repercussions so that every teacher may know what each student thinks at any given moment about our country, our political system, our construction, what he likes in it as well as what he finds irritating or disturbing. Third, the whole of political education must be based upon far-reaching, theoretical premises and perspectives and goals of Socialism rather than on momentary policies and actions which may be only passing in nature, ephemeral.[23]

[23] *Ibid.*, p. 283.

Life and Status of the Teacher

What the latter means is that stress should be given to the long-range goals of Socialism, for example, rather than to "temporary" difficulties or political exigencies. Similarly, basic differences between sociopolitical systems should be emphasized, rather than momentary difficulties or temporary alliances between countries of diverse systems. The task is to lend broader perspective to current events so that the student may look beyond the current confusion to long-range and general objectives.

As in the case of miners, steelworkers, railroad employees, and maritime workers, the teacher's employment is formally regulated by an elaborate set of conditions contained in a special charter (*Karta Nauczyciela*). Only those employed in institutions of higher learning are exempt from the provisions of the *Karta*. The Teacher's Charter defines, in rather precise terms, the educator's rights and obligations:

1. The teacher is nominated to his post. Only in exceptional cases is his employment subject to a contractual agreement.
2. The termination of a teacher's services does not require notice of three months as in other kinds of employment; it occurs by special process.
3. The teacher is entitled to extra remuneration for additional workloads.
4. Teachers' retirement pensions are governed by special provision and by the highest pension norms.
5. The teacher's vacation time is to last as long normally as the school vacation but in any case should not be less than six weeks (in the case of teachers in special educational institutions). In addition, the teacher is entitled to time off with or without pay for reasons of health, continued education, etc.
6. Teachers of merit are to be given the special title of "Meritorious Teacher of People's Poland" (*Zasłużony Nauczyciel Polski Ludowej*).

Life and Status of the Teacher

7. The Polish Teachers' Union (ZNP) is to enjoy special statutory privileges.[24]

A special statute of April 27, 1956 further regulates the rights and duties of teachers as well as the terms of their employment. Thus, the teacher's individual record is open for examination at all times. Remuneration is to be commensurate with tenure in the profession and tenure itself is extended to include practice teaching. Teachers are to be given initial housing assistance, severance pay, and special favorable retirement provisions. The special statute reemphasizes that special rewards in the form of honorary titles be given to meritorious teachers and that special statutory rights be granted to the Teachers' Union. Many of these provisions (e.g., housing) are frequently bypassed because of local difficulties or are exercised arbitrarily in individual cases.

THE TEACHERS' UNION

The Teachers' Union is a powerful organ and speaks up for the interests of the teaching profession, if not for the rights of individual teachers in political difficulties. Theoretically, the highest policy organ of the union is the Land Congress of Delegates. Between congresses direction is exercised by the Executive Board. The union is divided into professional sections (including higher education) and geographic regions (*okręgi*), districts (*odziały*), and branches (*ogniwa*). On the central level the union is directed on a day to day basis by a professional staff, many of whom are former teachers or teachers temporarily on leave.

All persons employed in the field of education belong to the Teachers' Union regardless of whether or not their work is directly related to teaching. Generally, however, the union stresses its political-didactic functions in the larger society in addition to functions of a professional and occupational character.

In its daily activities the Teachers' Union collaborates

[24] *Polska Ludowa* . . . , p. 100.

129

with the formal school authorities and is concerned with the achievement of official educational goals. In this respect, the Polish Teachers' Union does not differ from other Polish trade unions which work closely with management for the achievement of given targets and enterprise programs. Union meetings are attended by representatives of the Department of Science and Education of the Party organ of appropriate level. Thus a meeting of the Executive Board of the Union would be attended by representatives of the Department of Science and Education of the Central Committee of the Polish United Workers' Party (PZPR). Local meetings are attended by local Party representatives.

The Teachers' Union organizes educational and recreational activities for its members on a regional basis. These may include outings, picnics, interschool or intercity contests, lectures, concerts, etc. At the end of June 1966 the Teachers' Union of the Kielce region, for example, staged a *spartakiada* for its members which involved a variety of competitive sporting events.

In their private and informal conversations teachers will address each other in the traditional forms of *Pan* and *Pani*, or *Panna* (Mr., Mrs., or Miss), but in official parlance it will be *"kolega"* or *"koleżanka"* (colleague), rather than *"towarzysz"* or *"towarzyszka"* (comrade) which is reserved for Party gatherings.

In the course of my field research, I attended several conferences of the Polish Teachers' Union: a countywide conference in a village in the Białystok *Województwo*, a citywide conference (Warsaw), and three regional conferences (one in Katowice which included teachers' representatives from Katowice, Częstochowa, Bielsk, Cieszyń, Sosnowce, Chorzów; one in Kraków [Cracow] which included representatives from Kraków, Nowy Sącz, Tarnów; one in Toruń which included teachers from Toruń, Bydgoszcz, Grudziądz, and the rest of the Pomerania region).

Except for the much smaller county conference which took place in a village setting, and in which a young-looking school inspector and regional and Warsaw-based union

Life and Status of the Teacher

leaders were actively participating—which, in addition to my own presence, served perhaps to intimidate the gathering of provincial teachers and school functionaries—I had the impression that teacher-delegates felt generally unrestrained and expressed themselves rather freely, both during the work sessions and in semiprivate gatherings in the corridors. Many complaints were voiced from the floor. At the rural conference especially, extensive discussion was devoted to the problem of state-Church relations and the need for increased secularization of the school system. Generally, in all these conferences, the stress was on a number of recurrent themes:

1. The ideological-political posture of members of the teaching profession
2. Inadequate school plants and facilities
3. Inadequate and poor housing for teachers
4. Continued educational opportunities for teachers in elementary and secondary schools
5. Organization of Teachers' Day celebrations
6. Relations between administrative authorities and the Teachers' Union (closer contacts were urged)
7. Activities in local branches (many branches were accused of being inactive or dormant)
8. The role of the union in the school reform program
9. Problems of teachers' welfare other than housing
10. Economic investment in education
11. Teachers' authority and status
12. Conditions of nonteaching staff
13. Need for popularization of scientific research findings and textbooks
14. The burden of extracurricular work
15. Coordinating educational theory with educational practices
16. Church-state relations and secularization.

Delegates demanded rewards commensurate with the expectations that society holds with regard to the profession.

Life and Status of the Teacher

It was pointed out that many National Councils, especially those in the rural areas, either lack concern about the material problems of teachers, or, if they act, they deduct the funds spent from the general educational budget (supply funds, etc.). As a result, it was pointed out, teachers must suffer either financial deprivation or inadequate work facilities.

It was pointed out that the union does not adequately safeguard the interests of the nonteaching staff (e.g., office clerks, custodians, cooks, school nurses, etc.) who are dues-paying members of the union; that the union fails to mobilize behind its demands the natural allies of the educational enterprise, e.g., parents, social organizations, industrial enterprises, etc.

During the discussions it was pointed out that teaching effectiveness in vocational schools is not what it is supposed to be and that there is a need to develop new educational principles and forms to accommodate vocation-bound youth. Delegates also pointed to a need for greater collaboration between professional scientists and university personnel and those in elementary and secondary education. They felt that persons in higher education bear a special responsibility because the system lavishes greater material rewards on it than on lower levels.

Finally, teachers spoke quite frankly about what some called "the poor atmosphere" surrounding education. They spoke of conflicts with school authorities, but when pressed for specific details, they again enumerated poor working conditions. Some speakers were bitter about the union's failure to defend individual teachers. There were complaints of frequent criticism in the media, especially the daily press, of teachers and the schools. It was felt that such criticism by "uninformed laymen," while playing up to community emotions, tends to lower the authority of the teaching profession and adversely affect its prestige. The union was urged to intervene with the proper authorities in order to curtail such "unjust" press coverage. The last demand was

132

Life and Status of the Teacher

incorporated in a formal resolution at the closing of the Katowice conference.[25]

Thus, within certain limits, teachers, especially teacher-activists, are free to criticize. They speak out, especially where their professional interests are perceived to be threatened. Teacher-activists, as insiders, apparently feel free to criticize certain aspects of the system's operation, while, at the same time, accepting its basic premises.

Teachers talk, but apparently there are distinctions with respect to repercussions for talk and criticism. The consequences of criticism vary with the form and style of such criticism, as well as with the target. The type of brutal persecution that took place against malcontents under Stalinism, however, is apparently no longer extant. More subtle forms of persecution exist, especially if someone high in the bureaucracy feels challenged by a malcontent's behavior. Attacks which would reflect on a higher level official, or, in general, criticism against the basic assumptions of the system or against the Soviet Union, are viewed with disfavor.

Teachers may manifest a sense of solidarity on issues of general concern to the profession—inadequate housing, working conditions, etc.—but when it comes to defending an individual threatened by authority, solidarity crumbles. All the affected individual may hope for is the sympathy of other individuals, usually expressed in various degrees of passivity or quietism. Usually, however, the teacher who runs afoul of authority senses immediately the tenuousness of his position not only from the attitude of his superiors but also from that of his colleagues and others. A teacher in a secondary school in a large city in western Poland said: "Some of my colleagues are like barometers. You can easily read from their behavior the state of pressure within the environment. Their attitude toward a colleague would change according to the ways by which this colleague is 'noted' (*notowany*) in the eyes of the authorities."

[25] *Głos Nauczycielski* (June 16, 1966), 5-6.

Life and Status of the Teacher

The front of the forces of repercussion against the "threatening" individual is much more solid and includes school authorities, the Party, the police, and the union bureaucracy. In this contest between individuals on the one hand, and authorities acting in concert on the other, the cards are obviously stacked in favor of the latter. The outcome is rigged in advance. The officeholder who perceives himself menaced by an individual responds as if the system of authority itself were threatened, and once put in such light, one authority enlists the support of other authorities who, in turn, act as if the very political system were at stake. The individual can appeal and he may plead, but the authority, now impersonal and united, has all the advantages. It can accuse without producing documents if rumor will suffice. It does not have to adhere to due process if it can cite support from the "community of public opinion." If some official should want to come to the defense of the individual under fire, he is restrained by organizational pressure. Moreover, there is the tacit assumption that no accusation is wholly groundless. The maxim that "where there is smoke there must be some fire," prevails. The authorities can hide behind formal rules, confidentiality, and the need for discipline, in order not to explain their behavior—they assume certain statutory prerogatives. As one administrative official put it, unable to suppress a smile: "The people's authority has rights and is not accountable to anyone but the people." There is no place to appeal in the face of such reasoning.

Many in Poland blame this state of affairs on the vestiges of Stalinism persisting in patterns of administrative behavior and procedure.[26] It would appear, however, that in this political culture, as in many others, authority assumes the mantle of omnipotence. A familiar argument advanced in this regard is, "Authority knows what it is doing because if it doesn't it would not be authority." This does not mean that people necessarily agree with what is happening, but

[26] Zbigniew Kwiatkowski, "Czwartego dnia po święcie nauczyciela," *Życie Literackie*, Cracow, Vol. xv, No. 49 (723) (December 5, 1965), 5-6.

134

Life and Status of the Teacher

that authorities have a right to act in terms of their interests. While the authority symbols have changed in People's Poland, the authorities command traditional allegiance nevertheless.

To the individual teacher whose behavior does not posit a challenge to the system, however, the Teachers' Union can be useful in overcoming various obstacles and hardships. It can help disentangle bureaucratic red tape, facilitate the administrative processing of sick benefits, claims for overtime pay, assignment to a sanatorium, a vacation resort, or to a retirement home. Union intervention can also be crucial in arranging the admission of a teacher's son or daughter to secondary school, or in some institution of higher learning, or in gaining a place in a school dormitory. The local union branch can be helpful to the teacher in many other ways as well. A retired female village teacher, in the course of an interview, shows how:

> I started in 1945 as a teacher without any formal credentials, unqualified really. I began in a little village school. The war was still going on in the West.
>
> Q. You are retired now, aren't you?
> A. Yes. I live here in town in the House of Teachers. It is a nice place to live in, especially when you are alone. Many other colleagues in my circumstances live in the House.
> Q. How do you get along otherwise?
> A. Financially, very poorly. The pension I receive is very low, about 1,000 *zlotys* a month. However, local colleagues help out if a real emergency should arise.
> Q. Like what?
> A. If I should need special medicine. The doctor advised that I need some foreign drug which could be obtained only through the PEKAO. [A network of foreign currency stores selling various import items or Polish export goods otherwise not available to the domestic consumer. Poles may purchase in these stores if in legal possession of foreign currency or of special coupons remitted to them from abroad.] Somehow the union arranged that I got it. The union also helped me in getting my daughter admitted first to the State Textile *Technikum* and then to the University in Wrocław. She studies chemistry there.
> Q. Are you the only one the Teachers' Union helped in this way?

Life and Status of the Teacher

A. Not so much the union as such but colleagues, local colleagues, of the union. Thanks to their help children of teachers are able to go to secondary schools and gain places in the dormitories (*internaty*). You see, this town is too small to support a secondary school and the children must go to secondary school away from here.

Q. What do you think of the younger generation of teachers?

A. Well, they give me worries. In our country career-mindedness was frowned upon. A careerist (*karierowicz*) meant a pusher, a person who would ruthlessly push ahead, even over dead bodies. But our young people speak unabashedly about making a career, about making money, security, and they see nothing wrong in it. They lack idealism, I tell you. Things have changed. In the past people would have these things in mind but it was not in good taste to speak of it.

Q. Don't other people speak of money?

A. Yes, they do, I did, with you. This is because things are so difficult, so hard here. But financial worries are not career worries. Maybe I am old fashioned.

Q. I heard teachers complaining about their prestige. How do you feel about it?

A. Prestige? Money I have none but prestige, homage, I get plenty. Even retired teachers like myself are honored and remembered. Former pupils of mine, now leading citizens in the community, remember me on my birthdays. On that score I have no complaints. The county (*powiat*) authorities are good to us, I think, so is the union. Even the school inspector drops in from time to time for a chat although there is nothing for him to inspect here. But, of course, we get little money with all this.

The Career Road

High administrative posts in the field of education, as in other areas, are still assigned with political considerations in mind rather than on the basis of professional competence. Moreover, such high posts are also assigned on the basis of a "key," with a given number of posts going to each of the political-organizational components of the Front of National Unity. This "key" (*klucz*) is weighted in favor of the dominant component of the Front, the Polish United Workers' Party. However, an ambitious person can build a power base for himself through active membership in one of the Front's

136

minor political groups (such as the United People's or Peasant Movement, the Democratic Alliance, etc.) since these groups must be given some representation.

The allotment of high administrative posts according to political considerations and organizational balancing frequently creates paradoxical situations and individual hardships. An example can be seen in the interview excerpt which follows:

Q. When did you begin your career in education?
A. Personally I started in 1947. At that time I was one of the youngest people in a leading post in the field of education. I was advanced from what we call "a social base" (*awans społeczny*). That is, my formal training or education did not really equip me for the post, but, instead, sociopolitical criteria were taken into consideration.
Q. How did you do?
A. I think I did rather well. But I thought that my subordinates resented my lack of professional qualifications and it hurt, frankly. I also came to the conclusion that energy and dedication alone are not enough—and believe me, I was both energetic and very dedicated. But I was afraid that there would come a moment when the problems would surpass my abilities and qualifications. I began to feel my lack of adequate higher education acutely, especially in formal child psychology, sociology, and so on. These feelings of inadequacy increased as new, young people entered the field and talked a language wholly unfamiliar to me. They kept on referring to studies and tests and methods I had never heard of. Frankly, although I accumulated through the years many diplomas of recognition, given to me at First of May celebrations, I felt that these are not a substitute for a real diploma. It became rather embarrassing.
Q. What did you do then?
A. Well, you may not believe it but I went back to school. I was not the only one to do so at the time. One of our leading Party secretaries went back to school for an advanced degree. He found that the education he obtained in the anti-Nazi underground or in jail during the interwar period was not enough to cope with the problems of today, especially with the rapid change in science and technology. Well, to make the story short: I went back to school, finished correspondence courses at an SN, gained entrance to the university. It took over nine years of murderous labor. I had a family to

137

feed, exams to pass. If not for my wife I never would have managed. Also, superiors and professors helped a lot. After graduation I was convinced that the road to further advancement was now really open for me.

Q. Was it?

A. Yes and no. Because of my new professional qualifications I was transferred to a new job but with considerably lower pay. Subsequently the living standard of my family became lower. I had to resort to seeking additional incomes, such as writing articles for journals, working on a book which is an outgrowth of my dissertation. But my pay is still less than that of older persons in my present capacity since they bring to their job greater expertise. Now I have to compete on professional expert grounds while before I belonged to a different category altogether. In my present position the only way I can substantially increase my salary is to move from job to job. If one stays in the same post too long his salary falls behind those newly hired on the same level of employment. Presently, after three job changes I have finally reached a more or less decent salary level and am making more than my colleagues here who lacked the courage to resign. My present job is, as you can see, concerned with curriculum development in vocational education and it is rather gratifying. I have contacts with people in industry. I enjoy the scope of my activities. But who knows, maybe I will soon have to change jobs again in order to satisfy my economic needs. In fact, I have a few prospects.

Q. What about commitment to one's work?

A. There would have been greater commitment if the pay that goes with it were more justly allocated. If I had stayed in my old post, before I went back to school, I would have done much better financially. I also would have had other benefits, such as an official car and so on.

The greater payoff accorded those who make their way politically rather than through the slow grind of professional advancement is a reflection of the preference given to politics over expertise.

Pull, *protekcja*, has also traditionally played an important role in this political culture. The correct personal and family connections and class mean a great deal. This reflects a condition in which the values of expertise and hard work have not yet become ingrained in the social consciousness, although verbal and symbolic tribute is paid to these values.

Life and Status of the Teacher

As long as the criteria of success are not measured in terms of productivity, but rather in terms of sociopolitical adjustability, acceptability, and survival, the tendency is for the organization to reward the person with political connections. Professional competence is relegated to a secondary role. These considerations affect persons employed in all branches of the economy—industry as well as education. The *kurator* is more likely to be politically well-connected than distinguished as an educational expert. This, of course, does not mean that he himself is guided solely by political incentives either in private life or in the performance of his duties. Often quite the contrary is the case as was seen in the pattern of school inspections conducted by *kuratorium* officials. On the other hand, the *kurator's* initial appointment to his post was more likely than not the result of a personnel process in which political factors were weighed quite heavily. This condition contrasts with another Socialist country, Yugoslavia, where enterprises must manifest independent survival capacity. There, an outside agency such as the government or Party do not come to their assistance and bail them out of difficulties, hence maintaining a political hack on the payroll is a luxury any enterprise can ill afford. Consequently, in Yugoslavia it is no longer enough to look good politically, one must be good professionally. Poland has not reached this stage of "apoliticization" although tendencies in that direction are already becoming discernible, especially since the replacement of Władysław Gomułka by Edward Gierek in the post of First Secretary of the Party following the workers' riots of December 1970. These riots were triggered by widespread discontent with economic mismanagement and planning. Gierek's ascendency to the top leadership position has lent greater prominence and sociopolitical legitimacy than was previously enjoyed to the new (and younger) cadres of managerial technocrats, often at the expense of the old Party veterans and ideologues. These technocrats are loyal to the existing political system but less rigid in their ideological orientation. Nevertheless, *protekcja*, whether in the form of

139

social pull or political connections, continues to count rather heavily as does good standing within the dominant Party. Moreover, the old pattern is more likely to continue in the field of education than in the fields of industry or agriculture within the public sector of the economy.

Useful political connections include not only positions in the Polish United Workers' Party or any of the constituent organizations of the Front of National Unity, but also with Church-related networks. Many persons interviewed, especially members of the Party, spoke bitterly of the "Catholic cabals" or cliques in the union and the administration that look out for their own (*swoje*). The person with such connections is allegedly favored in terms of promotion, vacation time, housing, etc. Many interviewees maintained that, in effect, these cabals and cliques (operating from within) work to subtly discriminate against Party activists. One interviewee, when questioned about this in greater depth, said: "Don't get me wrong. When the Party has its heart set on pushing ahead a certain person no amount of sabotage from the religionists could stop him. But without the explicit backing of the Party, especially when it concerns higher posts, the Party member is often at a disadvantage when competing for the same post against a person favored by the Catholic clique."

Thus, the problem of political favoritism may not be as simple as would appear at first glance. Party connections are, of course, most important for personal advancement. But Party connections are not the only ones useful to the individual. Given the traditional social structure and the persistence of traditional values, Church and parish connections can be useful, despite the official negativism toward the Church. Connections with the hierarchy could be of great importance, especially when one is competing against someone with no connections or without strong organizational links.

140

Chapter 5: The Teacher in the Mill of Change

Crosspressures

IN THE towns and cities of the western and northern territories acquired after World War II, the names of the former German shopkeepers are still visible through the dull paint. In cities throughout Poland, old buildings bear the scars of past battles. The Old Town Square in Warsaw, however, totally destroyed during the war was, like most other national monuments, meticulously restored; the facades of the ancient bourgeois homes and historical wine cellars were recreated so that today they resemble their prewar appearance. With some differences, however: at the entrances to some of the old buildings new plaques were put up—plaques commemorating some past events of patriotic or revolutionary significance connected with the given house, the given site, or the Square. Within the restored shells of the old buildings modern conveniences were installed.

These buildings on Old Town Square in Warsaw symbolize, in a sense, what is transpiring in Poland at the present time—but in reverse. More closely reminiscent of the storefronts in the former German territories, there is a facade of change, but with a substance which persists much as it was in the prerevolutionary era. While some of the symbols and emblems of authority have changed, the respect accorded them is traditional. The portraits of the new leaders (usually those of the First Secretary of the Central Committee of the Polish United Workers' Party, the Prime Minister, the Chairman of the Council of State) adorn the walls of offices and classrooms just as did in the past the portraits of the old leaders. If during the interwar period the exploits of Piłsudski's legionnaires were surrounded with an aura of romanticism, similar homage is paid today to the veterans of the Polish units formed on Russian soil during

141

The Teacher in the Mill of Change

World War II which fought their way westward, on to Berlin, alongside the Soviet Red Army. An eternal flame flickers, as it always did, at the grave of the unknown soldier, and military guards keep watch—but the tablets at that grave memorialize different battles from those remembered before the last war. If, then, these tablets commemorated the battles fought under Piłsudski against the young Red Army in 1920, they now recall the battles of the Spanish Civil War in which Polish Communists participated as volunteers. Passersby tip their hats when passing the grave, the flame, the tablets, and the guard. The Party, once small and illegal, is now in authority and is usually spoken of with the respect, if not admiration, traditionally accorded those in power in this political culture. Consequently, although the coexistence of new and old patterns, of change and traditionalism has already been stressed in this work, it merits repetition nevertheless, for failure to keep it constantly in mind is a failure to understand Poland today. On the other hand, realization of the existence of these conditions and an understanding of their significance, may help explain, at least in part, the continuing elusiveness of revolutionary goals in Poland.

In spite of continuing poverty and generally rather modest standards of living, especially in comparison with the West, the new system is able to claim a number of considerable successes in the area of material accomplishments. Thus, for example, the country has been greatly rebuilt since the war, whole cities and towns have been restored from the ashes of near total destruction, and in spite of difficulties, industrialization proceeds apace. Even the standard of living, and with it the level of material aspirations for the better things in life, has risen substantially for some segments of the population—primarily the independent (i.e., noncollectivized) peasantry and certain elements of the working class. Although by and large still in the realm of the unattainable, many, especially among the intelligentsia, the better paid professionals, and the middle strata, are now even dreaming of an automobile, either domestic, Soviet, Czecho-

142

The Teacher in the Mill of Change

slovak, or East German and relatively inexpensive. The post-Gomułka leadership which took over after the workers' riots of December 1970 is apparently making some effort to alleviate certain of the consumer difficulties.

In its nonmaterial aspects, however, the Polish revolution, like all revolutions it would seem, moves more slowly. The older generation retains a sense of nostalgia for the past. Old institutions, especially the Church, retain their influence and therefore inhibit progress in the battle for men's loyalties. While there is a verbal commitment to change, there is a lingering feeling among many that change will result in the loss of something unique and very precious in the national culture. The result has been the development of a type of morality shared by many Poles which represents a peculiar amalgam of traditional as well as Socialist values.

The teacher, as the chief socializing agent of the state, is a central figure in the attempt to get out of the existing ideological morass and set new generations on a "proper" course. But the teacher himself represents a problem in this regard. His commitment, given his roots, is tenuous at best. The Church, despite the official ideological position of the regime, retains a great deal of influence in Poland, especially among those classes from which many of the upwardly mobile, aspiring young teachers have emerged. In fact, despite their own ideological position, the Party and the government, in the face of the authority of the Church, must often retreat from their erstwhile expectations and assumptions, and frequently, for tactical purposes, attempt to reach some sort of accommodation with the hierarchy. As already indicated, this is particularly true in periods of political insecurity when, for example, a new set of leaders assumes the highest office within the system and is in need of broad social support.

The strength of the Church is especially potent in the small towns and villages, but it cannot be disregarded even in larger cities. Its power is reflected in a still substantial church attendance, maintenance of important traditional religious rituals (such as the first communion), extensive religious training in the home, and in a pervasive ambivalence among the young and an antagonism among the old toward practices traditionally frowned upon by the Church, i.e., sexual license, abortion, divorce, certain fashions, etc. But the Church is more than an agency of moral guidance in Poland: for many it is virtually synonymous with Polish nationhood. In this respect it served, as already mentioned, as the only form of national continuity, as a surrogate for the state, when Poland was destroyed in the past by the forces of non-Catholic Prussia and Russia. Thus, although officially out of favor, the Church remains a formidable force with which the state must reckon.

Adapting to Crosspressures

The existing conflicts between the Church and the state impose peculiar problems for the individual in Poland. The conflict is often carried over into the individual's personal experience in the form of competing demands from the home and Church, on the one hand, and the school, the official agency of the state, on the other. The school is formally charged, among other things, with responsibility for socializing youth in the new secular norms and values.

Although the competing demands of the two major institutional forces impinge on virtually everyone in Poland, the intensity differs, and response to such crosspressures appears to vary among generations. Among the older members of the population, the situation is frequently so conflict-ridden that a synthesis of competing ideologies and belief systems is often almost impossible. In such cases the individual may be forced to resort to the expedient of paying lip service to the demands of one or the other. Among youth, however, there is more likely to emerge a synthesis of competing elements out of which evolves an ideology and a life style that is peculiar in its own rights. The focal point of this synthesis is the child's and young person's peer group.

To the extent that they are more confusing from his perspective, the competing demands of Church and state are

The Teacher in the Mill of Change

likely to weigh more heavily on youth than on the adult. The adult, for whom the crosspressures are indeed real, may deal with the problem, as indicated, by verbal accommodation and external conformity. Such an option may not be apparent to the young person, especially the child, with little experience or little commitment to one or the other of the value systems. The result is that competing demands are often sorted out in the context of peer groups composed of individuals exposed to similar conflicts. It is precisely from such peer groups that a subculture is emerging—a subculture resting on a value synthesis which may, in time, become the source of the prevailing ideology and life style.

Meanwhile, however, the Polish school system is expected to deal with the Church and religion. This being a sensitive subject schools cannot launch an all-out assault, lest it reinforce existing proreligious sentiments or generate sympathy for a persecuted Church. The school somehow must meet the curiosity of the young about religion, the Church, and the conflict between the Church and the secular authorities. Mikołaj Kozakiewicz, a vice-chairman of the Association for the Propagation of Secular Culture, offers a sample of positive and desirable treatment of the subject of Church and religion from a secular-materialist point of view by demonstrating and reporting on his own conversation with a curious child:

CHILD: Uncle, where do all these people go?
UNCLE: To Church.
CHILD: What is a "Church?"
UNCLE: This is the red building you see, the one with spires on top of which are iron crosses. You see?
CHILD: This I know. But what do people do in Church?
UNCLE: They sing songs and read prayers.
CHILD: Why do they do that? Cannot they sing and read at home?
UNCLE: They could but here they gather to do it together. A Church is a kind of house in which nothing else is being done except singing songs and reading prayers.
CHILD: But why do they do that?
UNCLE: You see, they do this in memory of a certain man who

lived a long, long time ago. His name was Jesus and
he was killed, hung on a cross.

CHILD: Uncle, I have seen such a man. He was made from
iron.

UNCLE: Precisely. This was an image of Jesus.

CHILD: Why do they sing to him and read from books?

UNCLE: Because many people think that he was not just a man
but God.

CHILD: You also think so?

UNCLE: I think that Jesus was a man just as you and I. He was
a good and poor man but only a man.

CHILD: But I would like to see how it looks inside and how
people sing. Could we go in?

UNCLE: Of course. But it would be better if we go some other
time. When there is no Mass.

CHILD: And what is a "Mass?"

UNCLE: This is what the gathering of people is called, when
they sing and read prayers.

CHILD: Isn't it permitted to enter during Mass?

UNCLE: It is permitted. But I would like to show you many
things in Church and during the Mass there are many
people and we could not move around freely. It would
disturb them.

CHILD: All right, then, we will go some other time. But for now
I would only want to peek inside. Just for a second. . . .
I wouldn't move and wouldn't disturb anyone. All
right?

UNCLE: All right. We can look in for a minute. But when you
go in you must take off your cap.

CHILD: Why?

UNCLE: You always bare your head when you go into a house
or into kindergarten, right? Church is a big house.[1]

Although from an atheistic environment, the preschool
child participating in the conversation already knew of the
Church and could identify its building. The child's curiosity
was primarily centered on the mysteries locked behind the
heavy portals. It is a curiosity widespread among Polish
children and it must be dealt with. How to deal with it and
the personal dilemmas which it raises is a key issue in Polish
education. How are such dilemmas resolved on the indi-

[1] Mikołaj Kozakiewicz, *Niezbadane ścieżki wychowania* (Warsaw:
Nasza Księgarnia, 1964), pp. 130-31.

146

The Teacher in the Mill of Change

vidual level? How are they coped with and how does the educational system affect the individual pupil and student?

With its stress on mass dynamics and its accent on the analysis of broad social forces and movements, Marxist philosophy until recently has neglected the problem of the individual.[2] As a consequence, economic, social, and educational planners in Socialist countries were apt to think in broad social categories and evolve their blueprints accordingly. There was an assumption that the individual would adapt himself to the conditions thus created. The success or failure of revolutionary goals, however, may rest on the ability of the individual to adapt to rapid social change. In Poland, the primary obstacles to such adaptive capabilities are the Church and its primary agent, the family. The state expects the school to counter any negative influence from other institutions in the sphere. In this connection it is often recalled that it was Stanisław Staszic, one of the sages of Polish education, who wrote as early as the 18th Century: "Different governments use different means because they are in need of dissimilar citizens' skills. Therefore, in each country education must be adjusted to that country's type of government." The school is seen as the system's chance to salvage the young from possibly hostile or opposition influences and the teacher is perceived to be a vital cog in the machinery of socialization. The very definition of their roles places the school and the teacher in objective opposi-

[2] See Adam Schaff, *Marksizm a jednostka ludzka: Przyczynek do marksistowskiej filozofii człowieka* (Warsaw: Państwowe Wydawnictwo Naukowe, 1965), pp. 45, 140. The "discovery" of the problem of the individual and individuality has emerged in East European Marxist literature with the discovery of the writings of the "young" Marx (1835-1847). See *Writings of the Young Marx on Philosophy and Society*, Loyd D. Easton and Kurt H. Goddat, eds. and trans., (Garden City, N.Y.: Doubleday & Company, 1967). With few exceptions traditional Marxist literature was colored by the later and "major" works of Karl Marx. In addition to Adam Schaff, other Marxist theorists in Eastern Europe began to pay attention to the problem of the individual and individual alienation even within the socialist system— notably the late Gyorgy Lukács (Hungary), Marek Fritzhand and Leszek Kołakowski (Poland), Danilo Pejović and Predrag Vranicki (Yugoslavia), Ernst Bloch (East Germany), and others.

The Teacher in the Mill of Change

tion to the Church and the priest who in the past held a virtual monopoly over the Polish moral system.

However, because in the past the Church often served as a rallying point for those in defiance of state authority, it may continue to attract the youth which for one reason or another would become dissatisfied with the system. During the Millennium Celebrations of May 1966, students marched along the streets of Poznań shouting the slogan, "With God." The same or similar slogans appeared on many a wall. This does not necessarily mean that these students have no doubts about the Church or religion; the Church may merely serve them as a symbol, a rallying point, a cause projecting a multitude of grievances. These grievances may be totally unrelated to religion but, instead, may be rooted in existential difficulties such as poverty, inferior housing, a restricted educational system, the banning of a favorite play, etc. Placed in such a position, every statement issued by the Church hierarchy becomes fraught with political implications and attains the status of a challenge to the political authority. The government and Party, in turn, are forced to pick up the challenge and place further pressures on the educational system so that it may be forged into a more effective tool for the socialization of youth. If the Church has presented itself traditionally as the defender of patriotic values, the Party and the secular school system must deny it that monopoly.

Aside from the psychological problems to which such conflicting demands and pressures might subject the child, there is also a possibility of developing a widespread cynicism which may preclude genuine internalization of any of the traditional values, including those endorsed by both Church and Party. Thus many writers bemoan the lack of knowledge among the young of the events related to the nation's heroic past and the sense of boredom which permeates lectures on patriotism and morality.

In the confrontation with the Church the secular authorities must continue to rely on the schools and the teachers. Teachers, however, are torn between the demands of the

148

community (still very much governed by traditionalism) and those of the political authorities. The latter not only pay the teachers' salaries, but have enabled them to enter a profession and provided them with opportunities for work. But the advantage here accrues to the state and this is crucial for, as Kozakiewicz points out, the teacher is expected to: "watch over the formation in his pupils of a set of characteristics, the inculcation in their minds of views and convictions which taken together would eventually be decisive of the totality of the pupil's personality—that is, whether it would, in the final analysis, conform to Marxism or not."[3]

The Teacher's Dilemma

The Polish teacher, exposed and sometimes vulnerable to crosspressures, is expected to mold new generations loyal to the new system. The students themselves come to the institutions of learning having already assimilated some of the conflicting values, perhaps having already reconciled the various conflicts within themselves. Some students unprepared for a scheduled class topic (not having done their homework) have learned enough of the ideological jargon to steer the discussion into the area of generalities concerning the class struggle, the conditions of peasants under feudalism or of workers under capitalism, and the teacher is compelled to pick up the altered direction of the class hour. But as Henryk Grynberg recounts in his autobiography, most of the students in his lyceum simply fell silent when talk on ideology or related topics would begin in a history or literature class. When he, the secretary of the political youth organization cell in his school, wondered why this was so, one of his classmates, a youth of working-class background intimated:

> You repeat what they taught you and you think that you are terribly smart. . . . But you are stupid. . . . You are more stupid than the rest of the boys. I feel sorry for you.

[3] Mikołaj Kozakiewicz, *O światopoglądzie i wychowaniu* (Warsaw: Państwowe Zakłady Wydawnictw Szkolnych, 1965), pp. 28-29.

149

The Teacher in the Mill of Change

Do you really think that only you understand what they, the teachers, say? Everybody here understands all. Not worse than you do. In fact, better! But they feign stupidity. What can they do? They listen to what the teachers tell them and to what you tell them, you sucker! They listen because they must. That's why they do not respond when questioned, they keep silent. But the devil gnaws them inside, or they laugh to themselves. The thing is that they do not believe. They aren't such suckers as you are! You understand? They do not believe a single word.[4]

The teacher must compete with the student's peer group and family, with the Church or Church-related influences, and finally, with the mass media, especially the popular magazines and television (whose programs are often foreign in origin, e.g., "The Saint," "Dr. Kildare," "Bonanza," etc.). As in virtually all other modern societies, the student's relationship to his teacher is a tenuous one. The student is not in school by choice. Consequently, the teacher's influence is somewhat abridged. Moreover, the teacher's ability to sanction the inattentive student is limited. His most severe punishment is the low grade, but this may cause him to lose the pupil's interest altogether. If he threatens with a low grade, but does not actually give it, the teacher loses some of his credibility. If he is lavish with inferior grade marks he may court repercussions from influential parents and/or school administrators. Moreover, any failing grade above the customary 10 percent limit usually allowed for failures must be justified and explained.[5]

In addition to conflicts in broader social values, the teacher is further torn between conflicting role expectations. He is expected to be a friend of the student as well as a disciplinarian. More difficult is the demand that he be an integral part of the community and yet, at the same time,

[4] Henryk Grynberg, "Pochodzenie społeczne czyli Łapa." A fragment from his Życie ideologiczne (*Ideological Life*) in *Kultura*, Paris, No. 4/259 (April 1969), 55.
[5] Mikołaj Kozakiewicz, "Kilka słów o środowisku nauczycielskim," *Wieś Współczesna*, Warsaw, No. 6 (1967), 81.

The Teacher in the Mill of Change

a disseminator of values which the community may not be ready to absorb. As we pointed out earlier, he is expected to embody every conceivable intellectual virtue while retaining a working-class identification and an appropriate modesty. Of course, most fail. This makes the teacher's position particularly uncomfortable since any trouble, political or otherwise, may be used against him.

Every phase of the teacher's existence is fraught with competing, usually contradictory, demands. His problems are compounded by the lack of clarity which governs even official expectations. He is often forced to operate in a normative vacuum. It is interesting at this point to examine the ways in which the teacher, when himself a student still training for his profession, resolves the key value dilemma of religion and secular ideology.

THE STUDENT-TEACHER AND SEXUAL MORALITY: A TEST OF COMPETING VALUE SYSTEMS

As in other societies, the subject of sex and sexual relations, is surrounded in Poland with a veil of inhibitions and taboos growing out of the traditional value system. Religion, however, is not the only source of sexual repression. The romantic tradition which idealizes relations between the sexes, has caused even nonreligiously oriented Poles to view the physical aspect of sex relations as something necessary, but animalistic. If devoid of romantic love, sex is regarded as unclean, or at least degrading. The war and the uncertainties it created, the shifting population, urbanization, and, finally, the emergence of an official ideology which to some implied a sanctioning of liberalization from many of the traditional inhibitions and sentiments, have induced in this area, as in many others, conflicting patterns of behavior. Marxism's stress on historical materialism—a term viewed by many Marxists as both unfortunate and misleading—is frequently quite crudely interpreted as promulgating a style of realism and toughmindedness if not outright materialism even in interpersonal behavior. Conversely, sentimentality is seen as an indication of softness and is viewed as bourgeois

151

and, consequently, decadent. The cruel conditions of the past war, the sheer struggle for survival during that period and the upheaval which followed, provided fertile ground for the development of such attitudes and many took the official ideology as an intellectual legitimization of these.

Research conducted by Professor Hanna Malewska for the Institute of Physiology and Sociology of the Polish Academy of Sciences shows that only one-third of devoutly religious women in Poland are capable of attaining full pleasure and satisfaction in a sex act. Yet 65 percent of her sample of 861 women experienced sexual relations prior to marriage, and 50 percent had such relations with at least one male partner other than the future husband. One-third had engaged in intercourse with more than one male other than their future spouse. While 25 percent of the women in her sample became interested in the opposite sex before age 16, and 20 percent experimented with it prior to that age, one-quarter had little factual knowledge of matters related to sex. Perhaps due in part to taboos and traditional restraints, only 19 percent of the women in Malewska's study indicated that they enjoy their sex life fully. The majority experience joy and happiness in sex only rarely or partially and 80 percent of the married women in the sample, although enjoying sex relations with their partners, view their married life generally as unhappy. Of those who enjoy sex little or not at all, 53 percent engage in it two or three times a week, submitting themselves against their free will to the force of their husband, or out of a sense of duty or habit. Almost half of these would rather refrain from sex altogether.[6]

Surveys undertaken by the Bureau for Public Opinion Research in Poland project a great deal of confusion on the subject of sex and sex education, reflecting mixed emotions, attitudes, and values.

[6] Hanna Malewska, *Zachowania seksualne u ludzkiej samicy*. As reported by Agnieszka Romańska, "Intymna statystyka Polek: Raport Docent Malewskiej," *Kulisy* supplement of *Express Wieczorny*, Warsaw (December 24-31, 1967), 7.

The Teacher in the Mill of Change

It is interesting to explore how this conflict, containing in great measure the confrontation between religious and ideological values, between traditionalism and modernity, affects the young person preparing himself to become a teacher in a formally rationalistic, scientifically oriented, socialist system. The important question is how deeply, if at all, has the student-teacher internalized the outlook and the values of the official ideology and the new Socialist materialist morality? Just as it does in the school systems of the West, including that of the United States, the matter of sex education in the public schools presents a problem of dealing with local sensibilities as well as problems of adequate teacher preparation.[7]

[7] There is quite a substantial American literature, varying in quality and emphasis, dealing with problems of sex morality and sex education. Among the more interesting and relatively recent publications are: Frank D. Cox, *Youth, Marriage and the Seductive Society*, rev. edn. (Dubuque: William C. Brown Company, 1968); Hugo G. Beigel, *Sex from A to Z* (New York: Stephen Daye Press, Frederick Ungar Publishing Co., 1961), a paperbound dictionary of sex related terms; Mary Breasted, *Oh! Sex Education* (New York: Frederick A. Praeger, Inc., 1970); Urban T. Holmes, *The Sexual Person: The Church's Role in Human Sexual Development* (New York: The Seabury Press, 1970), moral theology discussed by a clergyman-educator; Robert K. Kelley, *Courtship, Marriage and the Family* (New York: Harcourt Brace, Jovanovich, Inc., 1969), college text; Donald S. Marshall and Robert C. Suggs, eds., *Human Sexual Behavior: Variations in the Ethnographic Spectrum* (New York: Basic Books, 1971); Panos D. Bardis, *The Family in Changing Civilization*, 2nd edn. (New York: Associated Educational Services Corp., 1969); Dorothy Walter Baruch, *New Ways in Sex Education* (New York: McGraw-Hill Book Company, 1959); John H. Gagnon and William Simon, eds., *Sexual Deviance* (New York: Harper and Row, 1967); Eric W. Johnson and Corinne B. Johnson, *Love and Sex and Growing Up* (Philadelphia: J. B. Lippincott Co., 1970); Eric W. Johnson, *Sex: Telling It Straight* (Philadelphia: J. B. Lippincott Co., 1970); Kate Millet, *Sexual Politics* (New York: Doubleday and Co., 1970), bestselling and somewhat controversial treatment of "sex exploitation" over the ages stressing the historical evolution of sexual attitudes; Donald L. Taylor, ed., *Human Sexual Development* (Philadelphia: F. A. Davis Co., 1970), resource book for educators. See also various pamphlets and reports issued by the U.S. Department of Health, Education, and Welfare, The American College of Obstetricians and Gynecologists, National Council on Family Relations, various state Departments of Health (e.g., Kansas State Department of Health, *Sex Education Issues*),

153

The Teacher in the Mill of Change

I was given access at various stages of its development to a research project undertaken jointly by the Polish Secular School Association and the Commission for Research on Industrializing Areas of the Polish Academy of Sciences. The research team was headed by Dr. Mikołaj Kozakiewicz. The project was conducted during April-June 1966 among second year (graduating) students enrolled at the schools of teachers' education (*Studium Nauczycielskie,* SN) in four communities: Ełk, Toruń, Przemyśl and Gdańsk (Danzig)-Oliwa. The four schools were chosen at random from the total of 27 teachers' education schools of this type in Poland and the results were primarily intended for internal use.[8] Of the four communities Gdańsk is the largest (about 310,000) and Ełk is the smallest (about 22,000). Each serves as the seat of the county (*powiat*) administration. Gdańsk, moreover, serves as the center of an administrative district (*województwo*). Przemyśl and Toruń belonged to Poland during the interwar period, while Ełk was part of Germany (Mazury Lake Area, East Prussia), and Oliwa, a residential resort district of Greater Gdańsk, was part of the Free City of Gdańsk (Danzig). Of the four cities, Ełk and Przemyśl are the least industrialized. Ełk has some lumber and woodworking enterprises, and industry (mainly machine tool factories) came to Przemyśl only after World War II. Przemyśl

---

National Education Association, American Medical Association, Family Forum, Planned Parenthood-World Population, American Social Health Association, American Association for Health, Physical Education, and Recreation, etc.

[8] The aspect of this study dealing with sex morality and attitudes toward sex education among teachers and student-teachers in Poland I am duplicating, with the assistance of a team of graduate students from Wayne State University, in a large midwestern metropolitan area. The same research instrument utilized in Poland was also applied in the replication which used a general sample of student-teachers (excluding persons of Polish descent) and a separate sample of American student-teachers of Polish ethnic origin. One of the objectives of the replication is to determine whether American teachers of Polish descent are in their response patterns closer to their Polish or to their "general American" colleagues. This study is in its final stage at this time.

154

The Teacher in the Mill of Change

though, served historically as a communication and administrative center.

Each of the communities in the SN sample boasts a cultural history all its own. Ełk claims to be the cultural center of the Mazury Lake region while Toruń is one of the oldest settlements in Poland and since 1945 has been the home of Mikołaj Kopernik (Copernicus) University, being the birthplace of the renowned astronomer. Ełk is located in the northeast, Przemyśl in the southeast (close to the border of the Ukrainian SSR, on the main highway to Lwow), Gdańsk-Oliwa on the Baltic Sea in the north, and Toruń, which before World War II was in the northwest of Poland, is in the northcentral area as a result of border changes at the end of the war.

Of a total of 442 second-year graduating students in the four schools of teacher education, 416 (94.1 percent) answered the questionnaire. The sample represents 3.2 percent of all second-year students (about 10,000) enrolled in the SNs. Of the respondents, 81.0 percent (337) were females and 19.0 percent (79) were males. The high proportion of females to males is indicative of the feminization of the elementary school teaching staffs as well as general SN student population. In 1965 female teachers on the elementary school level constituted 75 percent of the total, and 67 percent of all first and second year students at the SNs were female.

The average age of respondents was 23.2 years. The youngest group of student teachers was enrolled at the SN in Gdańsk-Oliwa (19.7 years of age). The oldest enrollees were found at the Toruń school (35.5 for the males, 32.3 for the females). The age difference is significant here: the older group at the Toruń SN (101 persons) are students not in regular residence. They are practicing teachers with an average of 13.5 years previous experience and are enrolled in off-campus course work in order to complete the requirements for teaching at the elementary school level. They are, in effect, the functional equivalent of American teachers

The Teacher in the Mill of Change

with a provisional certificate which allows them to teach because of existing manpower shortages.

It is noteworthy that the older respondents, among whom many are actually engaged in elementary school teaching, have a generally less romanticized view on love than the younger student teachers (see Table 5-1). The response of the older group may be due to a cynicism born of experience or to having adopted a simplified pseudo-scientific view of life. At the same time, the oldest students (over 28), along with the youngest respondents, appear less certain about the validity of their replies. However, while the oldest

TABLE 5-1

RESPONSES OF SN STUDENTS TO STATEMENTS ON THE NATURE OF
SEX AND LOVE: BY AGE OF RESPONDENTS
(percentages)

Age of Respond- ents	Human sex life is entirely directed by instinct			Love is nothing but the result of a biochemical process		
	Agree	Disagree	D.K.	Agree	Disagree	D.K.
18-19 (N=105)	49.5	44.8	5.7	28.6	62.8	8.6
20-22 (N=210)	43.3	56.7	–	20.0	80.0	–
23-28 (N=38)	48.8	55.2	–	31.6	68.4	–
Over 28 (N=63)	27.0	61.9	11.1	42.9	41.4	15.7

respondents have a less romanticized view of love, they do see sex in less vulgar biological terms than the younger ones. It may be that while the younger SN students long for some kind of romantic attachment they see the sex act as a mere physiological function devoid of lasting obligations or deeper bonds.

Of greater interest are the responses to statements related more directly to traditional Catholic ethics on matters of sex (Table 5-2). Although the declaration of the Second

TABLE 5-2

PERCENT OF STUDENT AGREEMENT WITH TRADITIONAL CATHOLIC
POSITION ON SEXUAL ISSUES: BY AGE

Statement	18-19[a]	20-22	23-28	Over 28
1. Premarital virginity is testimony to the moral purity of a girl, and certainly the most decisive factor in consideration for marriage.	30.2	36.4	21.7	17.4
2. Forced termination of pregnancy is synonymous with murder, regardless of the circumstances.	48.9	45.5	31.2	36.9
3. Marriage should be inviolate and even in the most difficult situations one should not resort to divorce.	38.5	35.0	46.7	32.6
4. In the ideal family the woman does not work but devotes all her time to the household and the upbringing of children.	31.2	35.6	43.8	45.6
	N=105	N=210	N=38	N=63

[a] All but six respondents indicated agreement or disagreement. The six (in 3 age groups) indicated uncertainty only on the issue of abortion.

Vatican Council has somewhat liberalized the traditional position of the Church on some types of sexual behavior, it did not radically alter a tradition which treats sex as something less than holy and views the question of secular sex education with suspicion.

In varying degrees, traditional principles related to sex and family morality have lost their impact among the young, probably due, in large part, to the political and economic revolution. At the same time, these principles wield considerable influence among those preparing to teach in Polish elementary schools. Age appears to have little effect in this regard.

Despite the liberalization of abortion laws and practices, the traditional view that termination of pregnancy is tantamount to murder seems to be the most persistent of the old beliefs. A substantial minority also retains the view that the

157

marriage contract is indissoluble despite a growing divorce rate, especially among members of the professions. Acceptance of the traditional view on the propriety of the hierarchical family structure is remarkably persistent despite the fact that most of the respondents are women, and the stigma attached to premarital sex, despite the prevalence of such sex relationships, remains widespread. In addition, the responses are quite uniform, showing no significant differences among the respective localities except on the issue of divorce. On this single item, students in the two largest cities were a little more liberal than their confreres.

It may be counted as something of a victory for the system and the new secular culture that none of the traditional statements was endorsed by a majority. Rejection of the traditional Catholic viewpoint is not sufficient, however. What is more important is the internalization of the components of the official ideology and new culture at more than a pseudo-scientific level. Without such acceptance and internalization, the teacher, facing a questioning audience of students and aware of parental misgivings and community hostility, may stray from the accepted position, if for no other reason than to avoid personal and social complications. From the point of view of the regime the fact that, with the exception of the item on the woman's role in the economy, younger respondents were more prone to accept traditional values may bring into question the reliability of the school system as an agency of socialization. After all, the younger students have gone through a school system which has had a better chance to become established and to develop the necessary tools of socialization. Disagreements with Catholic-rooted statements seem generally to increase with age. This may indicate that those already in the teaching profession or closer to entering have learned to conform to official expectations. It may be that the profession exercises a socializing influence of its own on its members and that the younger respondents are more influenced by the values and styles of their home environment. It may also be that the views of the more experienced reflect a pragmatic judgment involving adjustments to signals and demands of secular political authorities.

It should also be kept in mind that these questions do not deal with the actual behavior of the students. It might very well be that their own behavior in matters of sex and family relations are much more secularized and modernized than their opinions would indicate. This would reflect a not uncommon state of affairs in which behavioral change has simply outpaced attitudinal adjustment.

As indicated, teachers in Poland, as elsewhere, are currently expected to offer some aspects of sex education and hygiene and, indeed, the subject is being increasingly introduced on the elementary school level. It is important to the Polish school system that the teacher be not only free from the traditional and Catholic taboos and attitudes, but reasonably well informed on the subject. Knowledge is not synonymous, however, with modernity in the sense of open-mindedness with respect to sexual experimentation or promiscuity. The ideal Socialist Pole is almost puritanical in his sexual morality. He is shocked by sexual humor, pornography, exhibitionism in attire, prostitution, suggestiveness in visual arts, in dance, etc. Polish visitors in the West are curious about nightclubs featuring striptease acts and nude or scantily clothed dancers since these are generally frowned upon in his own country. Prior to 1968 only one major Warsaw nightclub, located in a hotel frequented by foreign tourists from capitalist countries, featured a mildly suggestive erotic dance act. Whether related or not in some ways to the student unrest of that year (1968)—an unrest which reverberated most strongly in literary and artistic circles since it was triggered by the banning of a popular and classic drama—certain prohibitions on the "morality front" were lifted while others were applied with increasing laxity. Significantly, pornographic literature also appeared on the newsstands in Czechoslovakia and striptease acts in the nightclubs of its larger cities following the invasion of the same year. Thus, while still limited to the capital city and usually to places frequented by foreigners, striptease made

159

its debut on the Polish scene in 1968. In addition, certain magazines of mass circulation, such as the monthly *Kino* (*Cinema*) and the weekly *Współczesność* (*Modernity*) began to feature photos of nude women. To be sure, these manifestations of moral relaxation are constantly being criticized and attacked by the more serious and ideologically or traditionally oriented press. The same press is also calling for greater moral vigilance on the part of educators, for on-site inspections by teachers of clubs favored by pupils and students during off-hours. Some secondary school directors, especially in the provinces, continue to issue periodic reminders on proper behavior, and to caution students on the eve of official school dances against dancing "too closely."

The ideal Socialist is a folkdance devotee rather than an admirer of modern social dancing which he views as intended to generate unhealthy sexual excitement without offering fulfillment. He prefers folk songs conveying images of folk longings, struggle, martyrdom, to those which glorify love or disappointment in love, which he views as socially and politically dysfunctional and serving no useful purpose. The latter are seen as manifestations of "bourgeois sentimentality," and emphasis on sex is generally indicative of "bourgeois cultural decadence." The love songs which the ideal Socialist does approve of have a folk quality to them and contain, at least by implication, a social message—such as the legend put to song about the young shepherd whose love for the fair village maiden remained tragically frustrated because she, having been seduced by the playboy son of the lord of the manor, committed suicide by drowning in the lake; the lake swallowed the young lover next, leaving the poor sheep forlorn and unattended.

Yet, unlike the religiously oriented puritan, the ideal Socialist believes in divorce if the marriage turns out to be destructive to the couple and thus, consequently, socially and economically unproductive. He also believes in birth control, again because of its socioeconomic utility. His peculiar view of sex is that it is a necessary social and physiological function bringing happiness, restfulness, and contentment which allows individuals enjoying it to devote the bulk of their physical and intellectual energies to useful and productive labor for the good of society. He suspects that in environments where there are repressive religious scruples, preoccupation with things sexual renders the individual otherwise useless.

Many who have superficially assimilated the tenets of Socialist sexual morality confuse it with a modernity and emancipation which is, from the Socialist point of view, a pseudo-modern, decadent, shallow imitation of foreign models camouflaging the selfish exploitation of one partner by the other (usually the male). To explore the extent of such confusion, students of the four SNs in the sample were asked to respond to statements usually associated with a modern and emancipated (but not Socialist) point of view (see Table 5-3).

Neither Socialist nor conventional contemporary sexual morality free sexual behavior from all moral restraints and fears. There is, for example, a persistent negative attitude toward infidelity or rape. A majority of the respondents disagreed with virtually all of the statements in Table 5-3 which largely reflect popular conceptions of modernity in its extreme. However, the statement that "modern love denies all fears, restraints, and taboos of traditional morality which treats sex as sin" obtained a much larger rate of agreement (45.1 percent) than the other statements. This could conceivably be interpreted as a departure from Socialist morality which stresses, among others, the value of self-restraint, of will power—applicable to matters of sex as to other activities. It is likely, however, that the phrase is ambiguous enough to allow for several alternate interpretations, i.e., modernity may be associated with a general rejection of fear or superstition, thus rendering agreement more compatible with current Socialist morality.

It should be recalled that the statement that "forced termination of pregnancy is synonymous with murder" received relatively high endorsement (43.5 percent). This matches the low level of agreement (36.8 percent) with the

161

The Teacher in the Mill of Change

TABLE 5-3

PERCENT OF STUDENT AGREEMENT WITH STATEMENTS
REFLECTING SEXUAL "MODERNITY": BY AGE

Statement	18-19[a]	20-22	23-28	Over 28	Total
1. Modern love denies all fears, restraints, and taboos of traditional morality which treats sex as sin.	48.7	42.9	60.5	35.0	45.1
2. Modern love rejects the prerequisites of sentimental romanticism (e.g., serenading, flowers, oath of fidelity, etc.) since these are obsolete to the busy men and women of the 20th Century.	20.9	20.5	23.7	27.0	22.3
3. If there were foolproof devices against pregnancies, there should be no reason why young unmarrieds should be restrained in their sex relations.	15.2	15.2	23.7	19.0	16.6
4. Termination of pregnancy is in itself a morally neutral act, provided it takes place with the free consent of the female.	32.3	38.0	44.8	35.0	36.8
	N=105	N=210	N=38	N=63	N=416

[a] No D.K.s.

statement regarding abortion as a "neutral act." Whether the relative acceptance of the first statement and the rejection of the second is indicative of Catholic morality or of a realization that even the modern outlook on sex is not without some restraints remains a moot question. Abortion is an issue which remains controversial even among many non-Catholics.

Responses to statements (Table 5-4) dealing with the moral obligations of the male in cases of unplanned pregnancy bring into focus the moral problems faced by youth in a period of transition. There is often a rejection of traditional morality with nothing to replace it. The young are therefore faced with a quest for a new moral code.

The first statement in Table 5-4 reflects a prevailing at-

162

The Teacher in the Mill of Change

PERCENT OF STUDENT AGREEMENT WITH STATEMENTS ON
MORAL OBLIGATIONS OF THE MALE IN CASE OF PREGNANCY: BY AGE

Statement	18-19	20-22	23-28	Over 28
1. An unmarried male who causes pregnancy in an unmarried female must feel obligated to marry her under all conditions.	25.7	27.1	23.7	31.7
2. A male who causes pregnancy in a female is obligated to marry her if she refuses to terminate pregnancy and desires to give birth to the child.	27.6	26.7	34.3	14.3
3. The only obligation a male who has caused pregnancy in a female has is to regularly pay for the support of the child.	41.1	48.1	39.5	25.4
	N=105	N=210	N=38	N=63

titude which assumes that the sin of sex may be repaired through the sanctified institution of marriage. The second statement is a milder variant of the first. It assumes that the legalized bonds between a male and female would legitimize their previously illicit affair. The third statement in the table represents a presumably rationalistic position since it assumes that the only obligation the male has toward the pregnant female is to support the child after its birth. From the standpoint of Socialist morality though, none of the statements in Table 5-4 are acceptable. None take into account a variety of possible mitigating circumstances. With its emphasis on rationalism, the Socialist moral attitude would vary with circumstances. The circumstances might conceivably absolve a young man who was seduced by a more mature woman of any moral obligation, including child support, although he might be held legally responsible. Moreover, the original (and pure) Socialist perception of money as a symbol of exploitation and evil would lead one to reject equating love with any kind of financial arrangement per se.

The Teacher in the Mill of Change

About one-quarter of the respondents seem to believe that the logical consequence of illicit love and resultant pregnancy is indeed legal marriage. On the other extreme, there is the much larger group of respondents which believes that the male has no obligations other than child support. This response is surprising because of the overwhelming majority of females among the respondents (39.0 percent of whom endorsed the statement). It also represents a departure from traditional morality, but it manifests again an acceptance of a simplified version of what is understood to be a modern attitude. It is only among the older students that the attitude limiting the male's obligation to a financial responsibility gains relatively little support. Younger students, as much as one can judge from their responses, tend to view sexual morality in a somewhat streamlined and uncomplicated fashion.

In exploring attitudes toward the institution of marriage, the study focused on issues which are especially sensitive to the impact of rapid change—divorce, sex-role differences, etc. (see Table 5-5). The first statement may imply a careless attitude toward marriage since it assumes that relaxed divorce laws minimize the chances one takes upon entering a marriage. It fails to address the social, economic, and psychic consequences a divorce may bring to either of the marriage partners whether or not children are involved. The way the statement is structured, although reflective of changing social conditions, agreement might be interpreted as an endorsement of easy divorce and a less serious assessment of the marital commitment.

Statement No. 4 (Table 5-5) acknowledges, in the sense that it does not condemn, premarital sex relations. From that standpoint it reflects conditions of emancipation and change. Yet, it includes traditional values and styles by granting greater privileges in premarital sex to the male than to the female. While Catholic morality would denounce this statement as legitimizing illicit sex, Socialist morality would condemn it for the use of double standards, therefore being in the bourgeois tradition and hypocritical. The

164

The Teacher in the Mill of Change

TABLE 5-5

PERCENT OF STUDENT AGREEMENT WITH STATEMENTS ON
MARRIAGE AND HUSBAND-WIFE RELATIONS: BY AGE

Statement	18-19	20-22	23-28	Over 28
1. The danger of error in the choice of a wife is far less in the 20th Century than it was in the past due to the availability of divorce.	43.9	32.4	47.3	47.6
2. The requirements of fidelity should always be more stringent for the wife than for the husband.	17.2	20.5	10.5	12.7
3. For harmonious family relations it is preferable that the wife have the same or lower level of education than the husband, that if employed she occupy a lower occupational level than her husband, and that she also earn less.	36.1	29.8	39.5	33.3
4. It is preferable that among newlyweds the husband be of greater experience in matters of sex.	24.6	17.2	28.9	30.2
	N=105	N=210	N=38	N=63

Socialist moral position would be that if premarital sex experimentation is at all useful and healthful, both male and female should enjoy the same rights.

Statements 2 and 3 in Table 5-5 represent conventional middle-class bourgeois morality. Statement No. 2 is like No. 4 in that it expects different patterns of sex behavior in females and males. Here, however, differing expectations are within the institution of marriage. While statement No. 4 expects (by implication) greater premarital chastity from the female than from the male, statement No. 2 expects greater postmarital loyalty from her than it does from him. In conventional bourgeois morality playing the field is frequently considered to be a mark of masculinity, youthfulness, and adventurism in the married male and he is sometimes admired by his peers for these qualities. He, sensing such admiration or at least approbation, may even boast of

165

his exploits. The married female, on the other hand, seldom dares to confide to her friends of her own extramarital affairs knowing well that what may be socially acceptable behavior for males is frowned upon with respect to women.

Statement No. 3 (Table 5-5) is in the traditional sociocultural pattern and serves to acknowledge the husband's position as the head of the family structure. Agreement with such a statement would indicate the extent to which the respondents—teachers and future teachers—are still anchored in the traditional value system.

Many more respondents accept the perhaps ambiguous statement regarding the decreased risks of marriage because of the availability of divorce than the similarly modern statement on premarital sex. Also, more endorse the statement in support of the superior role of the husband within the family structure than the statement expecting greater postmarital fidelity from the female. What emerges then, appears to be a greater inclination to grant the female equal freedom in sexual behavior than to accept her as an equal in social and organizational terms.

Since the wording of the statements (especially Nos. 2, 3, and 4) contained in Table 5-5 tend to affirm the traditionally accepted position of the male it might be expected that they would gain greater approbation among the male SN students than among the females. Table 5-6 views the same statements from a male/female perspective.

On matters relating to sexual freedom, males are more likely than females to hold to the traditional position which grants them greater license. On the other hand, women endorse male dominance in the family structure more generally than men. This response pattern suggests developments paralleling those in the West where the issue of sexual freedom for women has usually preceded attacks on traditional family authority structure. Underlying the relatively high rate of approval by the female SN students of the traditionally dominant role of the male in the family might also be a longing for material security, for someone stronger to lean on in an environment which is fraught with economic

166

TABLE 5-6

PERCENT OF STUDENT AGREEMENT WITH STATEMENTS ON
MARRIAGE AND HUSBAND-WIFE RELATIONS: BY SEX

Statement	Males	Females
1. The danger of error in the choice of a wife is far less in the 20th century than it was in the past due to the availability of divorce.	43.0	35.3
2. The requirements of fidelity should always be more stringent for the wife than for the husband.	31.6	14.2
3. For harmonious family relations it is preferable that the wife have the same or lower level of education than the husband, that if employed she occupy a lower occupational level than her husband, and that she also earn less.	39.2	45.4
4. It is preferable that among newlyweds the husband be of greater experience in matters of sex.	29.1	20.8
	N=79	N=337

hardship and competitiveness. Characteristic for such long-ings, however muted, are the reactions of some of the women who joined the alternative life-style movement in the United States during the late sixties, and after having experienced commune living began to view, in retrospect, the traditional nuclear family of the "straight" society more favorably since it at least guarantees women room and board in exchange for their labor and love.[9] Yet, while having second thoughts about the counterculture and having despaired over its own male supremacist ethos, they, like the female Polish SN students, are eager to retain the sexual freedoms which have come their way with emancipation and liberation. On the other hand, the Polish male SN student faced with the same conditions of economic hardship as his female colleague may begin to look to the woman he marries as an equal partner in an effort to overcome environmental odds while maintaining traditional jealousy

[9] See, for example, Lynn O'Connor, "Alternative Life Styles: A Monster in Disguise," *Women's Press*, Eugene, Oregon, Vol. I, No. 5 (May-June 1971), 7-10.

167

over the exclusive proprietary rights over "his" woman, especially in the area of sexual relations. At the same time he desires perpetuation of the traditional male prerogatives in sexual behavior.

Response patterns up to this point suggest the coexistence of values and behavior patterns rooted in tradition with others growing out of the general economic, sociopolitical, and technological revolutions. The former uphold the superior social and economic position of the male while the latter express themselves in a liberalized attitude toward sexual behavior in general and the previously accepted sanctity of the family and marriage. The patterns of response to the various statements do not suggest that the new and specifically Socialist secular moral code, at least where sex and the family are concerned, have become entrenched. Rather, they appear to be in a transitory phase, during which old values and behavior patterns mingle or coexist with an often warped perception of the values of the new creed.

Although the overwhelming majority of students in the sample were in their infancy or not yet born when Socialism was declared Poland's official ideology, the persistence of living reminders of the traditional order (clergymen, parents, grandparents, older and unreformed teachers) to whom these youngsters have been exposed make this a transitional generation. What may be more disturbing, from the point of view of the system, is that it is precisely the youngest group, born and educated under the new order, which appears to be more traditionally oriented than their elder counterparts.

In addition to the attitude tests, the aspiring teachers were given a battery of questions to test the extent of their factual knowledge of sex and hygiene. The questions dealt, for example, with the ability of modern medicine to determine the sex of an infant in its prenatal state, whether it is possible through blood and biochemical tests to conclude who is the father of a child, as well as questions derived from the rich lore of popular stereotypes and super-

168

stitions related to sexual potency, venereal disease and its consequences, deviation, etc. Since the respondents' ability to answer these questions correctly is not germane to this study, the results are not reported here in detail. It is worth mentioning, however, that younger student-teachers seem to be more susceptible to the popular myths regarding sexual problems than are their older colleagues. On the whole, Dr. Kozakiewicz indicates, their command of scientifically established data relative to sex is generally rather low and would point to a need for further learning.[10]

One of the factual questions had a direct relationship to the problem of valuation and conflicting moral systems. It was phrased in the form of a statement requiring, as did the others in this category, a "true" or "false" response. The statement, concerning homosexuality, was: "Homosexualism is a psychic disease and people suffering from it should be placed in institutions for the mentally ill."

Now, although some scientific research on homosexuality has sought a biochemical explanation for the phenomenon, suggesting the possibility of an association, but not necessarily a cause-and-effect relationship, between homosexual inclinations and some chemical imbalance in the sex hormone, prevailing contemporary psychological and psychiatric opinion maintains that the causes of homosexual behavior are rooted entirely in psychological and environmental conditions, free from any biochemical factors. However, neither endocrinologists and others seeking a biochemical explanation for homosexual behavior nor psychologists or psychiatrists suggest that aside from their deviation from conventional norms of sexual behavior, persons of homosexual tendencies are otherwise abnormal or threatening society's psychic order. In fact, those scientists who suggest some chemical hormone imbalance are careful to point out that similar conditions attend such physical disorders as thy-

[10] Mikołaj Kozakiewicz, "Co myślą studenci kończąc Studium Nauczyciekskie: Z badań wśród studentów SN." Unpublished monograph for internal use, cadre material, Research Series: Discussion Material (Warsaw: Towarzystwo Szkoły Świeckiej, 1968), pp. 39-45.

The Teacher in the Mill of Change

roid or diabetes in heterosexual persons while psychologists and psychiatrists emphasize that homosexuals are sometimes exceptionally gifted and probably no less socially useful than persons with less exotic sexual tastes. Yet nearly half of the students in the sample accepted the view that homosexualism is a psychic disease requiring isolation in a mental institution. Neither age nor locale affected the responses (Table 5-7). The responses on homosexualism thus not only betray a significant ignorance of contemporary scientific thought on the issue, they also reveal a measure of puritanism and prejudice.

TABLE 5-7

STUDENT RESPONSE TO STATEMENT ON HOMOSEXUALITY:
BY TEACHERS TRAINING INSTITUTIONS (SN) OF RESPONDENTS
(percentages)

Institution	True	False	N
SN Ełk	44.1	55.9	115
SN Gdańsk-Oliwa	44.9	55.1	98
SN Przemyśl	44.8	55.2	102
SN Toruń	43.6	56.4	101

To be sure, the fact that over half of the respondents disagreed with the statement damning homosexuals to isolation in institutions for the mentally ill might be viewed as an encouraging sign of enlightenment. It is also possible that responses to the same statement in a different sociopolitical system or from nonstudents and nonteachers within the same system would have indicated a greater degree of prejudice or ignorance. It should be remembered, however, that the respondents in this particular case are teachers and student-teachers, many of whom may be expected to teach sex education, laboring in a system whose official ideology emphasizes new forms of interpersonal relations, enlightenment, and rationality as well as a scientific outlook on the affairs of mankind and the world. These teachers and student-teachers, in addition to possibly having to teach sex education, are also expected to be the guardians of ideo-

170

logical consistency. It is perhaps worth recalling in this connection that it was Nazi Germany which officially incarcerated homosexuals as "socially dangerous and criminal" elements and that this was seen by the opponents of National Socialism, including Communists, as additional proof of that system's perversion. On the other hand, when zealots of the vigilante Committees for the Defense of the Revolution in Cuba proceeded in 1968 to round up thousands of known homosexuals, along with "loafers and other undesirables," and send them to farm labor camps, the so-called Military Units for Aid to Production, where they were also expected to undergo social and political indoctrination, Fidel Castro stepped in to intervene, disbanding the camps altogether. He said at that occasion: "The Revolution can survive any political or economic error, but not a moral one."[11]

How do these student-teachers, some of whom have been teaching for some time and others about to enter the profession, feel about teaching the subject of sex on the elementary school level? They were asked to respond to several statements which might reveal their attitudes toward sex education (see Table 5-8).

Statement No. 1 in Table 5-8 was deliberately worded so as to make the goal of sex education appear rather restricted. It places emphasis primarily on the development of practical wisdom in order to avoid future life complications rather than on attempts to generate, through sex education, a set of attitudes toward love, marital partnership, and related matters. Statement No. 2 in Table 5-8 refers to the tradition of Catholic education which assumes that the less said about sex, the less evil will result. This position conflicts not only with the premises of contemporary educational theory but also with the Declaration of the Vatican

[11] Jose Yglesias, *The Fist of the Revolution* (New York: Random House, 1969), p. 275. The Cuban "experience" in dealing with homosexuality is also detailed in Gregory Kafoury, "Moral Incentives in the Cuban Revolution," unpublished M.A. thesis, Department of Political Science, University of Oregon, Eugene, Oregon, 1971, pp. 57ff.

TABLE 5-8

PERCENT OF STUDENT AGREEMENT WITH STATEMENTS
RELATING TO SEX EDUCATION: BY AGE

Statement	18-19	20-22	23-28	Over 28
1. The main objective of sex education should be to teach youth how to order their sex lives skillfully, sensibly, and safely so as to avoid future complications as much as possible.	83.8	87.6	71.1	77.8
2. It is preferable not to tell young people anything about sex because all discussion of the subject only leads to heightened sexual curiosity, a factor sufficiently present anyway.	3.8	2.4	5.3	14.3
3. One should not begin discussing problems of sex with youth earlier than grades 10-11 of secondary school.[a]	22.9	24.2	44.1	38.1
4. Coeducation is harmful because it aggravates sexual instincts in youth and facilitates premarital relations between girls and boys.	15.2	12.4	18.4	23.8
	N=105	N=210	N=38	N=63

[a] Grades 10-11 of Polish secondary school equal in terms of years of schooling junior-senior grades in a 4-year American high school. Since first grade education in Poland begins generally one year later than in the United States, the ages of students of grades 10-11 of Polish secondary school is comparable to that of juniors-seniors in the 4-year American high school, i.e., 17-18 years old.

Council on the Christian Education of Youth. Statement No. 3, which stresses that the proper time for sex education might be when the pupil is already sexually mature, is counter to the thinking of virtually all modern educators who seem to believe that sex education ought to begin at a much earlier stage of development. The question of coeducation (No. 4), while still unresolved in some educational circles, has been traditionally opposed by the Church. Moreover, regardless of the merits or demerits of coeducation per se, the statement places on it the responsibility for aggravating sexual instincts of which this type of education

The Teacher in the Mill of Change

could possibly be only one of many contributing factors and perhaps not even the most important one.

The students seem to accept overwhelmingly the simplified and practical statement (No. 1) on the goal of sex education. To be sure, younger respondents seem to endorse the statement to a higher degree than older and more mature respondents, although not conclusively. The important point is that over 70 percent of all respondents accepted as valid, the view that the main objective of sex education should be to teach youth how to avoid future complications without qualifications which would lessen the implication of practicality inherent in the statement. It is further noteworthy that this view on the aim of sex education received greater approbation among the student-teachers of small-town Ełk than it did among those from big-city Gdańsk-Oliwa although the difference is not great. Of special interest here are the responses from the school of teacher education at Toruń which concentrates the working teachers of the sample—this being the SN which caters mainly to an off-campus student body (see Table 5-9).

More respondents from Toruń than from the other schools accept the statement that it is preferable not to tell young people anything about sex—but at the same time, this school also demonstrated the greatest opposition to the technical-practical concept of sex education. This is also the school which shows the most respondents opposed to coeducation. The explanation which suggests itself here is that older persons may be less inclined, at least for didactical purposes if nothing else, to deprive the subject of love and sex of its more romantic and sentimental aspects although they themselves harbor less romanticized notions about love, as was indicated by their responses to the statement on the nature of love in Table 5-1. Older persons may also be less inclined to divorce from any discussion of the subject the idea of individual responsibility as a condition of which one must be conscious before involving oneself in love or in sexual activities—an idea underlying both traditional as well as Socialist morality. That is, older student-teachers

TABLE 5-9

PERCENT OF STUDENT AGREEMENT WITH STATEMENTS
RELATING TO SEX EDUCATION: BY SCHOOL

Statement	Ełk	Gdańsk-Oliwa	Przemyśl	Toruń
1. The main objective of sex education should be to teach youth how to order their sex lives skillfully, sensibly, and safely so as to avoid future complications as much as possible.	87.8	84.7	85.3	74.9
2. It is preferable not to tell young people anything about sex because all discussion of the subject only leads to heightened sexual curiosity, a factor sufficiently present anyway.	5.9	1.0	0.9	9.2
3. One should not begin discussing problems of sex with youth earlier than grades 10-11 of secondary school.	26.1	21.4	22.4	37.5
4. Coeducation is harmful because it aggravates sexual instincts in youth and facilitates premarital relations between girls and boys.	15.6	7.1	15.4	20.8
	N=115	N=98	N=102	N=101

may be more anchored than younger student-teachers in the traditional culture and its taboos and feel safe about voicing these, especially since similar taboos attend the Socialist moral code. Moreover, the students at Toruń, themselves practicing teachers, some with considerable job experience, received their own preprofessional training at a time when sex education was not yet generally introduced into the curriculum of the elementary schools nor was it then the issue it later became. Once it becomes an issue the tendency among a number of older persons is to react to that issue in terms of traditional morality—a reaction which could be further legitimized if buttressed by arguments derived from the sources of Socialist moral indignation.

It is also clear that the notion that sex education should

174

begin in the last grades of secondary school generated (aside from the endorsement given to statement No. 1 in Tables 5-8 and 5-9) the least opposition from respondents. Being elementary school teachers (or future teachers) they may feel either inadequate to handle sex education or they may feel generally awkward about it, or both. They may wish also to avoid possible community reprisals by avoiding this extremely sensitive subject. Shifting the burden for such education to the secondary level relieves them of a potential problem.

It is rather characteristic for the still persisting and traditional taboos surrounding discussion on sex that respondents who expressed emancipated and modern opinions in response to questionnaire items were reported to have blushed and to have had difficulty suppressing a giggle when answering many questions, particularly those dealing with masturbation and its possible effects. Those in charge of one of the schools of teacher education initially objected to the administration of the questionnaire on the grounds that it contains "indecent questions and statements," and the director of that SN confided to Dr. Kozakiewicz that if he were to ask such questions he would be embarrassed to look into the students' eyes without blushing. While in certain respects the youngest of the teachers seem to look up to the authority of the Church in greater measure than older ones, in matters of sex and sex education older teachers seem to be more tradition-bound and conservative than their younger colleagues.

The other statement in Tables 5-8 and 5-9 which received relatively little opposition—aside from No. 1 which was overwhelmingly endorsed—that on coeducation, may again be explained not only in terms of deep-rooted tradition but also in terms of anticipated professional difficulties in situations of sexually mixed elementary classes. In analyzing the findings Dr. Kozakiewicz commented:

We are dealing here with a rather complex situation. Here we have the younger teachers who are quite willing to see the subject of sex included in the curriculum but are themselves, as we have seen, ill prepared to do an adequate job of teaching that subject. Also their moral posture and life experience makes their fitness to engage in sex education rather doubtful: on the one hand, they still adhere in many cases to obsolete concepts and theses and, on the other hand, they fall easy prey to vulgarized pseudo-modernity. Then we have the older teachers who for the most part possess a correct ethical outlook and have a good deal of knowledge about sex, marital life, etc., but who are, for their part, mistrustful and full of reservations and doubts as to the propriety of sex education.[12]

Part of the responsibility for the failure seems to fall on the system of teacher training which in some instances, as in the local institutions of the SN type, is sometimes directed by persons who themselves have not yet assimilated the blend of values generated by both Socialist morality and modernity. This failure and the subsequent feeling of inadequacy among the teachers, in addition to their caution resulting from the fear of anticipated difficulties both on the job and in the local communities, lead many teachers to attempt to shift responsibility. If they accept, in the final analysis, the concept that sex education should begin much earlier than the last two grades of secondary school, the majority of the respondents would still want to shift the burden of sex education to the shoulders of others. Rather than see members of their profession burdened with the task of sex education, the student-teachers would delegate that task first to parents (who may or may not know about sex or how to teach it), or second, to medical doctors (who may or may not individually possess the skill as educators but who certainly are not trained as such). Unfortunately, because it might be considered too provocative perhaps, the teachers were not given the option of the priest as a possible

12 Kozakiewicz, "Co myślą studenci kończąc Studium Nauczycielskie . . . ," p. 51.

The Teacher in the Mill of Change

source of sex education. Of the options they were given (i.e., parents, physicians, teachers) they rated their own profession as the least qualified. In fact, the older the student-teacher the less confidence he has in teachers' ability to do an adequate job of sex education, or the less he wants to assume the responsibility, or both (see Table 5-10).

TABLE 5-10

PERCENT OF STUDENT-TEACHER RESPONDENTS WHO THINK THAT TEACHERS ARE BEST QUALIFIED AS SEX EDUCATORS: BY AGE

Age	Percent	N
18-19	44.8	105
20-22	34.8	210
23-28	31.6	38
Over 28	27.0	63

Despite the reluctance of teachers to assume the responsibility, sex education on the elementary level is seen as an important aspect in the totality of Socialist education. Its aim is the development of a personality free from some of the old taboos and prejudices, immune to the influences of the external and superficial effects of modernity, but committed to a Socialist moral code. In addition, sex education on the elementary level is seen as a further step toward the secularization of the system—a way of socializing young generations to withstand the lures of the Church. Since, despite the modifications adopted by the Vatican Council, the Church is associated with the old taboos relative to sex, freeing the youth from these taboos might accelerate their liberation from the influence of the Church. The difficulty is that those freed from a traditional puritanical system are not quite willing or able to embrace or submit themselves to another puritanical system which, unlike the Church, has as yet not managed to make its own moral expectations known or to spell them out fully and clearly. Consequently, those emancipated from the old value system almost automatically drift into the physically comfortable and less de-

The Teacher in the Mill of Change

manding style and code of superficial modernity which is neither Catholic nor Socialist. The problem, from the point of view of the political system, is that if young teachers, trained in Socialist schools, are not ready to serve as agents of socialization into the new value system, who could or would do the job? Could it be that young teachers, although poorly prepared and trained, may in time acquire the necessary skills, either on the job or through some other formal or informal learning process? Perhaps the very process of professionalization to which the young teacher will be subject, once involved as a fullfledged member of the profession, will result in the kind of self-concept which would induce him to strive to meet the system's expectations. He then would himself be socialized and be able to serve as an adequate agent in the process of socializing others into the system.

Settling on a Modus Vivendi

In the absence of fully socialized teachers the system must compromise on teachers who have accepted the status quo but whose assimilation of Socialist values may not go beyond the symbolic level. Grzegorz Leopold Seidler, until recently the *Rektor* of the Maria Curie-Skłodowski University at Lublin, refers to the acceptance of the status quo within the population at large as a state of "legal consciousness."[13] He suggests that members of the society, although not necessarily identifying themselves with the particular political authority, accept that authority as legitimate, obeying its laws and conforming to its demands. The acceptance of that authority's laws and the obedience it commands is, in large measure, due to the system of material coercion, of reward for "good" behavior and punishment for "bad," which is at the authority's disposal. It is only when "legal consciousness" is converted into a generally prevailing "Marxist consciousness" (i.e., internalization of social norms) that the

[13] Grzegorz Leopold Seidler, "Marxist Legal Thought in Poland." *Slavic Review*, Vol. 26, No. 3 (1967), 382-94.

system of coercion could be done away with. When respect for law and for the demands of political authority arising out of fear or expectation of reward is transformed into a voluntary identification with the system and its values, the apparatus of coercion might be abolished and society might become fully Socialist. The self-policing individual would not have to be watched over to see that he does the right thing. It would only be necessary for authority to define "right" and explain it to the individual in terms of a common value system.

In the meantime, however, the statutory laws which Seidler views as "instruments of social reconstruction" may either lag behind or run ahead of realistic conditions and the readiness of the population to accept the new norms. The success of the system and of the political authority hinges upon its ability to strike a balance between those of its norms society is ready to accept and how far it can move ahead without inducing conditions of disturbance and thus lawbreaking. Consequently, the political system must keep abreast of the level of "socialist consciousness" existent within the larger political culture. If the political authority moves too swiftly toward its objectives, it may have to retrench and compromise. This is precisely what happened in the area of agriculture when the regime had to withdraw in 1956 from its goal of collectivization because the Polish peasant was unwilling to give up the gains he had personally derived from land reform. Similarly, in 1970, far-reaching economic plans and reforms backfired though they had been viewed by some Western economists as valid if they could but be implemented.[14] These reforms proposed to do away with some of the "anachronisms" of the period of Socialist economic experimentation—such as replacing a more or less egalitarian wage structure with a system of incentive bo-

[14] See, for example, article written almost a year before the riots of December 1970 by Michael Gamarnikow, "The Polish Economy in Transition." *Problems of Communism*, Washington, D.C., Vol. xix, No. 1 (January-February 1970), 40-47. Also, A. Ross Johnson, "The Polish Riots and Gomułka's Fall." The RAND Corporation, Santa Monica, Calif., March 1971, pp. 4ff. (Mimeo.)

The Teacher in the Mill of Change

nuses—but at the same time also called for a measure of consumer sacrifices and higher productivity at sometimes lower wages. The latter triggered workers' riots and the subsequent replacement of the top leadership, and, ultimately, resulted in a modification of the reform plans. A somewhat identical phenomenon is occurring in the area of culture and education. The regime feels compelled to compromise with existing sentiments, with traditional values, styles, and institutions, and sometimes even to resort to these in order to achieve particularly urgent and immediate objectives. But the very process of compromise is, in fact, delaying the eventual victory of Socialism in the mass consciousness.

Faced by a lack of totally committed and socialized teachers, Poland is forced to utilize only partially committed educators. How reliable are the teachers, themselves only superficially socialized, as agents of socialization into the new values and norms? Does the system really expect that as a result of the activities of such teachers future generations will be more ready than the present to voluntarily accept a "Marxist consciousness?"

The events of March 1968 and their aftermath emphasized the brittle state of the Party's position within the educational enterprise and the extent to which the authorities are willing to compromise with some of the traditional values and norms, e.g., nationalism and anti-Semitism, in order to further legitimize their standing in the public eye. At the 12th Plenary Meeting of the Central Committee of the Polish United Workers' Party, called after the student riots of that year, Andrzej Werblan, a Central Committee member and then head of the Central Committee's Department of Science and Education (and after the reshuffle following the workers' riots of December 1970, a Vice-Marshal or deputy speaker of *Sejm*), criticized past Party personnel policies which, according to him, were "particularistic," favored persons of Jewish origin, and thus "did not take into account the resonance it would have within society." He further maintained that by continuing the tradition of the

The Teacher in the Mill of Change

prewar Polish Communist Party whose intelligentsia and ideological leadership were primarily persons of ethnically and culturally non-Polish core/origin, the Party is in danger of losing touch with society and its basic and prevalent norms. He advocated that the Party free itself of the "heritage of Luxemburgism."[15]

In the course of his speech at this post-March 1968 Plenary Meeting of the Central Committee, Werblan also said: "The teaching of ideological subjects is poorly apportioned with respect to time, is centered on the last years of study rather than the first, is burdened with formalism, and suffers from a lack of properly prepared teaching cadres."[16]

Torn between consequential adherence to the values the system would ideally like to see inculcated and internalized, and the necessity to survive under conditions of persisting old values, styles and norms, compromise becomes in itself a value and a style of the system. Shortage of properly

---

[15] Speech by Andrzej Werblan at 12th Plenary Meeting of the Central Committee of the Polish United Workers' Party (KC PZPR), reported in full in *Trybuna Ludu*, Warsaw (July 11, 1968), 3. By "Luxemburgism," Werblan refers to Rosa Luxemburg, founder and leader of the Left-Wing of the Polish Social Democratic Party (SDKPiL) in the part of Poland and Lithuania then under Czarist domination. Later Polish revolutionary parties of the Left, including the Communist Party, were upshots of the factional strifes within the SDKPiL which, eventually, led to its demise. Rosa Luxemburg, of Polish-Jewish origin, left for Germany to become one of the leaders of the revolutionary movement in that country. Together with Karl Liebknecht, another German revolutionary leader, she was arrested by the *Junkers* and assassinated while in prison in 1919. During her life she frequently differed on both ideology and tactics with Lenin. While Lenin, from his position as a Russian revolutionary, viewed with sympathy the aspirations for independence from Czarist Russia of the Polish nationalistically oriented bourgeoisie, and in general favored self-determination for the various nationalities of the Czarist empire, hoping, thereby, to accelerate the radicalization of the Russian masses and the destruction of the system, Rosa Luxemburg, from her Polish perspective, considered the strivings of the Polish nationalistic bourgeoisie as retarding the process of Socialist consciousness formation and the development of revolutionary internationalism. Nevertheless, prewar Communists in Poland (as elsewhere) commemorated her by celebrating the Day of the Three L's (i.e., Lenin, Luxemburg, Liebknecht).

[16] *Ibid.*

trained and reliable socializing personnel further increases patterns of compromise producing a total picture that is a mixture of the new and the traditional, that projects images and symbols which are both of traditional and socialist origin but that are not deeply rooted in either of the two value systems and whose only justification seems to be the authority's survival and acceptance in the realm of "legal consciousness." The half-socialized teacher, drifting between traditional morality and Socialist morality, but settling on the comfortable and relatively easily assimilated values of modernity, is thus, in a sense, only mirroring the state of the system and the current political culture.

Nevertheless, the ideology offers the substance for a formal educational model. If successful it might perhaps eventually result in an ideological neutralization of the Church (so it would not compete with the formal socialist ideological system) and, at the same time, tolerate religion oriented values and styles as long as these persist. It was Lenin, after all, who maintained that it is foolish and naive (a manifestation of "bourgeois progressivist culturism") to fight religion per se as long as the masses themselves are not cognizant of religion's "evil" roots in the exploiting system.[17]

In the meantime, official compromise affects the youth who go through the paces of conforming to chosen aspects of tradition as well as chosen and symbolic aspects of Socialism while, at the same time, concerning themselves with consumption of whatever "modernity" and technology have to offer. As Jerzy Wiatr points out: "One can . . . speak of a discrepancy between the educational goals of Socialism and the actual level of consciousness formation of a part of the youth already educated in People's Poland."[18] Nevertheless, Wiatr is convinced that when the chips are down, when the youth is confronted with the dilemma of choos-

[17] V. I. Lenin, "The Attitude of the Workers' Party Towards Religion," in V. I. Lenin, *Marx: Engels: Marxism*, 4th English edn. (Moscow: Foreign Languages Publishing House, 1951), pp. 273-86.
[18] Jerzy J. Wiatr, *Czy zmierzch ery ideologii? Problemy polityki i ideologii w świecie współczesnym* (Warsaw: Książka i Wiedza, 1966), p. 233.

ing sides, especially in a crisis situation, it will not fail. He writes: "Should the socialist system or the integrity of the Fatherland become endangered by an external force then certainly the traditional (known to previous generations) type of ideological involvement would emerge again among the postwar generation as it did among its predecessors."[19]

But would this involvement demonstrate acceptance of the new values or merely adherence to the traditional and often romanticized value of honor and service on the field of battle? And, in the face of external threat, how would it be possible to differentiate between the motives for action, whether loyalty to the system or traditional, old-fashioned patriotism? It is precisely in anticipation of such threats and crisis situations that the system would like to identify itself and its ideology with the concept of Poland and the loyalties that concept commands. But to achieve this kind of identification the Party, as the Church before it, must itself assimilate some of the traditional values, condone and compromise with some of the traditional norms, styles, and prejudices, and, in the process, lose some of its purity.

In the meantime the ideologically compromising Party, the Party grown tolerant of traditional national norms, styles, and prejudices, serves as a comfortable umbrella for many upward bound youth who have themselves undergone a process of compromise through adjustment to the realities of the system. The Party has become a mass party and, as such, has further assimilated the elements of social compromise and the remnants of the old value system they have carried along. During the first quarter of 1966 alone, the Party admitted nearly 46,500 candidate members, 40 percent of whom were 25 years of age or younger.[20]

[19] *Ibid.*, p. 236.
[20] *Polityka*, Warsaw (May 28, 1966).

Chapter 6: Secondary School Teachers and the Internalization of the System's Values: the Socialization of the Socializers

The Cultural Paradox

NEGOTIATED matrimony is seen, in terms of Socialist morality, as a by-product of a system of exploitation. Instead of love and free choice on the part of two compatible adults, it involves the elements of barter and economic advantage. In traditional lore negotiated matrimony entails the trading off of a young maiden to an old but wealthy man or a young man to an old but wealthy matron. In either case the poor are seen as the objects of the trade (chattel, in this kind of transaction). Nevertheless, a part of the Polish press still features matrimonial advertisements—a residue of the traditional culture. Among the advertisements for negotiated marriage in *Kurier Polski*, organ of the economic middle-class oriented Democratic Alliance, are many placed by teachers. One example which represents the accepted style for such advertisements, reads as follows: "A maiden, age 39, without a past, of great spiritual virtues, with pedagogic education, owns house—would like to meet a cultured gentleman without bad habits, up to age 50 (divorcees are excluded from consideration). Serious offers are to be addressed to Box No. 7650, *Kurier Polski*, Warsaw, Szpitalna Street 8."[1]

Other advertisements are placed by middle-aged males seeking a spouse "without a past," who does not drink or smoke, but who possesses cultural refinement and culinary talents, preferably a female teacher. Still others are by

[1] *Kurier Polski*, official organ of Democratic Alliance, Warsaw (June 22, 1966).

184

The Socialization of the Socializers

young males or females seeking some measure of economic security through marriage. Generally these advertisements reflect still prevalent social values: piety, traditional morals, stress on economic well being, culture and refinement. Because of the traditional opposition of the Church to divorce, many of the advertisements clearly specify the undesirability of divorced males or females.

The great proportion of teachers searching for spouses through the traditional means of negotiated matrimony or being sought as spouses by others is still more evidence that the traditional moral code remains rather strong among persons in their profession, or that their economic plight is such that negotiated matrimony, despite the Socialist moral stigma attached to it, constitutes a convenient means of economic betterment not to be frowned upon.

Another reason for seeking marriage through the classified advertisement columns of the press is loneliness. In a study of 435 Polish teachers conducted by Józef Kozłowski, many described themselves as lonely. While most did not feel that this affected their job performance, Kozłowski contends that loneliness may have some impact. Among other things, it may be difficult for the lonely teacher to maintain the "proper moral posture."[2] In his loneliness, the teacher may not care about the negative attitude toward negotiated matrimony growing out of the Socialist moral code.

Whether prompted by the need for economic security or by loneliness, marriage (and the manner in which it is transacted) may not only tend to reinforce the teacher's low level of ideological commitment but also further diminishes his or her ability to serve as an efficient agent of cultural diffusion. This seems to be especially so in the case of female teachers, particularly in small towns and villages. Józef Sosnowski reports on research on the marriage patterns among young female teachers:

[2] Józef Kozłowski, *Nauczyciel a zawód* (Warsaw: Nasza Księgarnia, 1966), pp. 187-95.

The Socialization of the Socializers

The road to marriage for the young female teacher in the big city usually stems from a casual acquaintanceship. (Of) 100 young female teachers working in large cities . . . 84 met their future husbands quite accidentally, in 12 cases the future husband was a colleague from the school bench or a childhood sweetheart, and in 2 cases a colleague working in the same school and in one instance a colleague from the SN courses.

Among the 84 husbands casually met, 64 had an education inferior to that of the wife (usually vocational) and only in 20 cases did the husband have an education either equal or superior to that of his wife, the teacher. It appears, therefore, that generally husbands of young teachers tend to have an education inferior to their own and are thus unlikely to positively affect their wives' further intellectual growth.

Even worse is the situation of young female teachers working in villages. Quite often they enter into marriage with young farmers whose education is hardly of an elementary level.[3]

These then are the kinds of contingencies which often work to counter commitment to the new way of life or ability to meet some of the other expectations associated with the teacher's role. Despite his lower educational level the young peasant engaged in private farming (as most are) is indeed financially better off than the young elementary or secondary school teacher. The young teacher, especially one of lower-class background who sees her education and professional status as symbols of social advancement, may perhaps perceive marriage to a person of lesser education (especially to a member of the peasant class) as a step backward on the social ladder, a form of regression. As indicated previously, social snobbery is still very prevalent in this culture. The conditions which compel one to undertake such a move—whether economic, social, or of a private,

[3] Józef Sosnowski, "Przestoje na trasie kultury," *Kultura*, Warsaw, Vol. vii, No. 36 (326) (September 7, 1969), 8.

The Socialization of the Socializers

psychological nature—must indeed be severe and hard to bear. Thus although many SN students, especially among the female respondents, accepted, as demonstrated in the preceding chapter, the statement that "for harmonious family relations it is preferable that the wife have the same or lower level of education than the husband, that if employed she occupy a lower occupational level than her husband, and that she also earns less," the realities of life often produce quite opposite effects, and many women are compelled to compromise with their own views on propriety, particularly with respect to educational status requirements and expectations.

Teacher Commitment and Revolutionary Prospects

As in the case of the study among students of schools of teacher education, we were given access to (and, subsequently, became involved in all its phases) a study of Polish secondary teachers sponsored jointly by the Research Department of the Polish Teachers' Union and the Polish Secular School Association. The questionnaire utilized for this study contained questions taken from a questionnaire prepared by us and which I had hoped to be able to administer independently at the time, as well as items taken from research instruments used earlier in similar studies by Mikołaj Kozakiewicz (in 1959), Jan Woskowski (in 1963), and Józef Kozłowski (in 1964). The study included 276 secondary school teachers from communities varying in size and taken from scattered geographic areas.

The teachers in the largest group in the sample, 59 percent, are between the ages of 21 and 30; 20.7 percent are in the 31-40 age group. Only 7.9 percent are above the age of 50. The reason for the relatively small number of older teachers in Poland is probably due to the fact that during the Nazi occupation members of the Polish intelligentsia were particularly and brutally persecuted and many perished. What this means, however, is that most teachers in Poland have been entirely or primarily trained under the present sociopolitical system.

187

The Socialization of the Socializers

Although the teaching profession has the reputation of being feminized, this does not appear to be as true at the secondary as it is at the primary level. The number of males and females in the current sample was almost equal, with only a 14.1 percent edge in favor of the females (42.4 percent male, 56.5 percent female). The disparity would undoubtedly have been greater were elementary school teachers included. Unfortunately, official Polish statistics do not provide us with precise figures on sex distribution among teachers although the numerical superiority of females among SN students was evident in the previous study as well as in field observation. Officials of the Teachers' Union estimate that in the mid-sixties, over 75 percent of Polish elementary school teachers were females.

Although there is evidence of a high rate of attrition among teachers, especially during the first 10 years, 71.9 percent of the respondents indicated service in the occupation of a period from 6 to 20 years. Only 8.6 percent of the Polish teachers in the sample indicated service of a period exceeding 20 years which, of course, coincides with the relative youth of the profession and the general age level of the population—a phenomenon again attributable to the events of World War II. Current statistical data indicate that at the end of 1969, 47.8 percent of the country's population was born during the postwar period making the average Pole 27.5 years old.[4] However, only 18.4 percent among the teachers in the sample had been teaching for 5 years or less which may be a result of some of the hurdles encountered by those who wish secondary teaching immediately.

Teachers who have been in the profession a period of 10 years or less (64.7 percent or 178 persons) are assumed to have received all of their schooling under the conditions of the new order. They might be expected, therefore, to perform more effectively as agents of socialization into the new

[4] See "Poland's Area and Population: Statistical Data as of December 31, 1969," *Contemporary Poland*, Warsaw, Vol. v, No. 1 (January 1971), 26-29.

The Socialization of the Socializers

value system and to respond more favorably to the values officially espoused than would older teachers, especially those whose tenure predates the new order. Our previous investigation among SN students indicates though, that acceptance of the system's values does not necessarily coincide with lower age. Although all of the SN respondents were relatively young, and only a minority among them (those from Toruń) were working teachers, our other observations give some indication that adjustment to expectations and acceptance of the system's values increases with tenure. The secondary school study offered an opportunity for comparison and further exploration of this problem.

Only 22.3 percent of the sample spent most of their childhood and youth in a community with a population of over 50,000; 46.6 percent indicated village or small-town background. The greater part were born and raised in provincial towns of between 10,000 and 50,000. Persons of working-class background constitute the single largest group in the sample (40.5 percent), followed by teachers of peasant background (32.8 percent) and only then by intelligentsia (18.4 percent). This apparent anomaly in view of the over-representation of the intelligentsia in higher education may be explained in part by a high attrition rate after the minimum service period, and partly because persons of intelligentsia background simply opt for entry into other professions. Only 2.9 percent of the teachers in the sample (8 persons) indicated middle-class background (i.e., children of self-employed small business entrepreneurs or shopkeepers). The background of 5.4 percent is unknown. Children of provincial town workers constitute the most numerous group of teachers in Polish secondary education.

They, the sons and daughters of small-town proletarians, may indeed represent the "new intelligentsia" which, in Kwiatkowski's words, is singleminded, serious, ambitious, hard-working, concerned with income and security, career and authority oriented, loyal, but lacking in the social graces of the traditional intelligentsia. They may be likened to some middle class, relatively prosperous and educated American

The Socialization of the Socializers

Negroes who, having "made it" personally, absorb the values of their white counterparts and tend to be rather conservative in their thinking. Kwiatkowski describes the new intelligentsia in Poland as "churls with diplomas" who, however, in terms of the system's real goals and values are more functionally constructive than their colleagues of the "old intelligentsia." They are rather severe in judging those who do not quite come up to the standards of their own expectations. They may not be as adept at theorizing as members of the traditional intelligentsia but they look up to the Soviet Union as a model of order and technological achievement and they admire the strength of their Eastern neighbor. Their morals are puritanical and they are reminiscent of the nouveau riche in bourgeois society but with a major difference—they have bureaucratic minds. Yet, because of their lower class background, they continue to feel socially inferior to the traditional and largely gentry-rooted intelligentsia. The latter, according to Kwiatkowski, still dominate the exclusive literary and cultural clubs and circles, know how to enjoy life, leisure, and extramarital sex, and they do speak a more refined and literary language, without the accent of the "new intelligentsia" which betrays its plebeian heritage. The intelligentsia of proletarian or peasant background, for that matter, still must struggle for a place under the "social sun" although they are favored over the traditional intelligentsia in terms of organizational advancement and material rewards.[5]

In an earlier study by Józef Kozłowski, teachers indicated most frequently that the choice of profession was really a matter of accident. The choice of teaching was made, for example, because no other type of professional training institution was available, or because the prospective teacher experienced setbacks of various kinds while attending a lyceum of general education, thus precluding entry into a university, etc. This is particularly interesting in light of the stress on teaching as a high calling commanding individual

[5] Zbigniew Kwiatkowski, *Byłem niemilczącym świadkiem* (Warsaw: Iskry, 1965), pp. 272-74.

190

The Socialization of the Socializers

commitment. Warsaw based teachers, however, unlike their provincial colleagues, tended to make their professional choice less on the basis of economic or ideational considerations and more on the grounds of simple affinity for pedagogic work.[6]

Once in the profession, Polish teachers generally manifest a high level of satisfaction with their occupational choice. Thus, the current study indicates that of the secondary school teachers in the sample, 51.9 percent declared themselves as being "very satisfied" with their professional choice and another 32.5 percent as "satisfied." Only 8.4 percent of the teachers answered that they are "dissatisfied" with their professional choice and 7.2 percent indicated mixed feelings on this score. However, when asked "if presently given an opportunity to start anew, would you choose any other occupational-professional career," the commitment to the profession decreased slightly as one moves up the prestige level of education attained by the respondents (see Table 6-1).

TABLE 6-1

POLISH SECONDARY SCHOOL TEACHERS' RESPONSE TO QUESTION ON CHOICE OF TEACHING AS CAREER: BY EDUCATION

Education	N	Yes	No	Don't Know
University Completed	40	35.3%	58.6%	6.1%
University Not Completed	62	32.6	62.6	4.8
Higher School of Pedagogy Completed	85	32.5	62.7	4.8
Higher School of Pedagogy Not Completed	89	22.8	71.3	5.9
Other	37	15.0	83.4	1.6

Investigating the social position of teachers, Jan Woskowski also found that satisfaction varied with education, in similar manner. In his study, the higher the level of the teacher's own education the more he tended to be dissatisfied with the accomplishments of his pedagogic-educational labors. According to Woskowski the level of satisfaction was highest among teachers who completed only secondary

[6] Kozłowski, *op.cit.*, pp. 50-51.

191

The Socialization of the Socializers

pedagogic education, followed by SN graduates, and, lastly, teachers with higher education (i.e., higher schools of pedagogy and universities).[7]

When asked what factors they thought might influence a person to enter the teaching profession, respondents tended to stress considerations of an idealistic and altruistic nature (e.g., service to the people, intellectual satisfaction, etc.). These factors were often buttressed by material considerations (e.g., relatively easy entry into the profession and achievement of professional status, availability of long and free vacation time, relatively quick way of earning a living, etc.).

When asked what arguments they would use to persuade someone *not* to enter the profession, teachers in the sample pointed first to lack of proper work facilities. This was followed by complaints about lack of local cooperation, and lack of understanding among parents and students.

Judging from the sample, secondary teachers in Poland tend to perceive themselves as both educators and subject-matter specialists. They usually refer to their colleagues by their specialization—e.g., geographer, botanist, mathematician, Polonist, historian, etc. When asked the question, 31.6 percent viewed themselves as "primarily educators," 19.7 percent saw themselves as "primarily specialists," while 49.7 percent declared themselves as both. This emphasis on both education and specialization might be an outgrowth of the current stress on what Polish educators refer to as polytechnic education which combines subject-matter specialization, vocation, and character building. The obvious question which arises is whether a Polish teacher's self-perception might seriously affect his internalization of general educational goals and values. Since the specialist is presumably more oriented toward his occupational specialty, he might be expected to pay less attention to the general socio-

[7] Jan Woskowski, *O pozycji społecznej nauczyciela* (Lodz: Państwowe Wydawnictwo Naukowe on behalf of Center for Sociological Research, Institute of Philosophy and Sociology, Polish Academy of Sciences, 1964), p. 144.

The Socialization of the Socializers

political goals of the educational system than the teacher who considers himself primarily an educator.

Within the teachers' sample, almost all who identified themselves as specialists were teachers of mathematics, physics, and chemistry. The small number of shop teachers (12) also considered themselves specialists. Those who identified themselves as both specialists and educators were almost all in the humanities with only 30 in the exact sciences. Those who identified themselves as "primarily educators" were *all* in the humanities. Table 6-2 shows the response patterns on questions dealing with the sensitive and crucial problem of Church-state relations and the secular-religious dichotomy as given by teachers of varying self-perceptions with respect to specialization and/or educational generalism.

TABLE 6-2

PERCENT OF POLISH SECONDARY TEACHERS AGREEING WITH STATEMENTS ON STATE-CHURCH RELATIONS AND SECULAR-RELIGIOUS DICHOTOMY: BY SELF-PERCEPTION

Statement	Educators	Specialists	Educators & Specialists
1. Most advanced societies have separated, at least formally, institutions of religion from institutions of learning. This is a wise policy, benefiting learning, and should be affected regardless of social consequences.	77.7	69.3	78.9
2. The Church's concern should be exclusively with matters of faith, leaving politics in the hands of secular forces.	65.4	68.4	73.5
3. Religion is a legitimate subject of education in publicly supported schools if taught from a historical-philosophical perspective (rather than indoctrination).	34.6	48.1	45.2
4. If the community demands religious education such education should be included in the curriculum of the public schools.	17.5	26.9	19.0
	N=85	N=54	N=137

193

The Socialization of the Socializers

Generally Table 6-2 indicates that secondary school teachers in Poland appear to accept the general value premises of the political system concerning the role of religion in education and politics. However, there are some variations according to the self-perceptions of the respondents. The response patterns vary, especially among the specialists, with the severity of the antireligious tone of the statement. In their responses the specialists trail behind the specialist-educators in endorsing greater secularization, while exceeding the latter in rejection of statements reflective of an antireligious sentiment. Generally, educators' attitudes follow those of the specialist-educators, probably largely due to a similar educational tradition. Yet, the educators fall slightly behind the other categories in endorsing the notion that institutions of religion should be totally divorced from politics. Perhaps humanists who consider themselves primarily educators are more wary of rapid and radical changes in Church-state relations. They may fear the consequences of rapid secularization of Polish social and political life. It may be, too, that they are more affected by pressures emanating from the religious sector than specialists who are predominantly scientists. On the other hand, they do represent the disciplines which have undergone most radical changes as a result of the sociopolitical revolution and would, therefore, more than others be sensitive to signals emanating from the system. Those who consider themselves primarily educators would thus constitute a highly crosspressured group of people. Moreover, they, much more than teachers of scientific or technical subjects, are dependent on the educational enterprise as an employer.

Following Gomułka's return to power in 1956 and the short-lived silent alliance between Party and Church, religious instruction was for some time allowed on the premises of the public schools. When Mikołaj Kozakiewicz asked in 1959 whether instruction in the catechism should be removed from public schools, 73.5 percent of the humanists questioned answered yes; 68.4 percent of the teachers in the

The Socialization of the Socializers

physical sciences and mathematics agreed. In commenting on his findings, Kozakiewicz wrote:

> The religiously oriented teacher of physics is a materialist only as long as he concerns himself with the physical world. He is quite capable in the realm of his subject matter interests to defend a scientific world outlook. However, as concerns problems of cosmosophy or of metaphysical being, his materialism breaks down. Then such teacher reacts in terms of subjective feelings, and perceiving this as inadequate he resorts to a religious, idealistic, and cosmotheistic superstructure.[8]

The present survey contained a number of items exploring teachers' attitudes toward religion and the Church, on the one hand, and socialist secularism and Church-state relations, on the other. As mentioned earlier, there was the expectation that younger teachers would be more likely to assimilate the system's norms than their older colleagues. Since those who are 30 years of age or younger received their entire education under the new regime, it might be assumed that they would reflect the norms of the new political system in their own attitudes. The survey among SN students previously reported cast some initial doubts on this proposition. However, one who in 1966 was 30 years of age was only 9 years old when "Socialism arrived." Those 25 or younger, born during World War II, were, at most, 4 years old at the time of the establishment of the new regime. Even those between 31 and 40 years of age, given the interruption of the war, are likely to have received their professional training under the new regime and therefore might reasonably be expected to have absorbed the system's values themselves. It has also been shown already that the educators and educator-specialists generally manifest a greater propensity toward assimilation of systemic values and goals than specialists. Table 6-3 examines these groups with respect to their self-rated ties with the Church.

[8] Mikołaj Kozakiewicz, *Światopogląd 1,000 nauczycieli: Sprawozdanie z badań ankietowych* (Warsaw: Państwowe Zakłady Wydawnictw Szkolnych, 1961), p. 231.

The Socialization of the Socializers

TABLE 6-3

SELF-RATED TIES WITH CHURCH: BY SELF-PERCEPTION AND BY AGE
(percentages)

	Not at All	Very Strong /Strong	Moderate /Weak	Total Church Ties	N
I. *Self-Perceived Primacy of Professional Role*					
Primarily Educators	27.8	35.1	37.1	72.2	85
Primarily Specialists	24.5	42.3	33.2	75.5	54
Both Educators and Specialists	29.2	38.5	32.3	70.8	137
II. *Age*					
25 or less	19.8	58.4	21.8	80.2	82
26-30	33.9	43.4	22.7	66.1	83
31-40	26.9	36.2	36.9	73.1	57
41-50	31.5	30.5	38.0	68.5	29
Over 50	26.2	27.5	46.3	73.8	22

What is perhaps surprising and, from the point of view of the system particularly disturbing, is that whatever tendencies toward secularization exist, these seem to increase moderately with age. The survey on sex-related morality among SN students produced some hints to this effect and Table 6-3 corroborates those findings. That is, while only a minority within each age group indicates no ties whatever with the Church, the younger the teachers the stronger their religious or pro-Church sentiments.

When asked why they maintain ties with the Church, the most frequent response was tradition or habit (mentioned by 30.0 percent). This was followed by such motives as: "adjustment to environmental pressures" (22.6 percent), "spiritual need" and the "need for meaning in life" (20.1 percent), "worry for one's soul" and "salvation" (17.0 percent), "family pressure" (16.1 percent), "enjoyment of the liturgy, cultural or artistic experience" attendant on religious services (12.9 percent), "religious commitment" and "obedience" (6.2 percent), "political manifestation" or "defiance" (3.0 percent), other intellectual reasons (.5 percent). Significantly, however, reasons related to the needs for con-

The Socialization of the Socializers

formity to either family pressure or the pressure of tradition was most frequently enumerated by older teachers. Only 14.4 percent of those 25 years or younger gave pressure or conformity as reasons, compared to 17.1 percent of the 26-30 age groups, 20.0 percent for ages 31-40, 22.5 percent for ages 41-50, and 23.5 percent for those over 50. Many respondents did not answer the question or gave widely scattered responses.

Rather than conformity to pressures of family or tradition, the response of the younger teachers to the Church seems to be the result of some deeply felt needs or resentment against some aspects of the reality around them, and, in view of the fact that their own education was totally obtained under the new political system, indicative perhaps of some deep-rooted sociopolitical unrest as well as systemic failure. There may also be additional and unstated reasons why strong ties with the Church among Polish teachers are strongest among the young but show regression with age. One may be related to tenure in the profession which may produce conformity to official expectations (while age alone produces token conformity to community and family pressures). Another may be due to a lessening of feelings of self-assurance, self-reliance, rebellion, and spite along with a greater need for security which comes with age. The need for security might well result in a greater need to accept the realities of the system, and to make peace with existing conditions. At the same time one may pay slight tribute to informal, nonofficial pressures by the maintenance of some Church bonds. Still another reason why older teachers in Poland, especially those over 50, describe themselves as having only token ties with the Church could be related to the fact that prior to World War II the teaching profession, and the Teachers' Union in particular, experienced some severe difficulties with the Church. Teachers and their union were frequently the subject of criticism from the pulpit. Priests attached to both private and publicly supported secondary schools as instructors in catechism often came into sharp conflict with lay teachers working in the same schools, especially if the priests

197

The Socialization of the Socializers

suspected that these teachers taught in a manner or in a subject which might impinge upon the position of the Church and its teachings. In fact, several cases in which lay teachers felt unjustly persecuted or defamed came to court, pitting teachers against priests and vice versa, with conservative and Left-wing or liberal elements lining up in support of one or the other. Many teachers consequently found themselves allied, however vaguely, with the Left-wing and liberal forces thus accelerating, at least, a partial alienation of the teaching profession from the Church hierarchy. Moreover, the teacher who grew up in pre-World War II Poland where the Church exercised a strong formal influence, may have tended to sever his ties with the Church as part of a sociopolitical stance, a protest against conditions during his youth.

The situation has changed radically in the current era. Instead of being a strong and growing power, the Church is now, more often than not, on the defensive, identified with the general opposition. Although at certain periods, especially in times of governmental insecurity and uncertainty—as when a new leadership takes its post at the helm—the Church hierarchy is in a position to extract certain concessions from the government and thus stem, at least for a while, the official tide, the Church is generally perceived as being in disfavor. It is seen as the spokesman of traditional cultural and community values. Consequently, today's youth may very well look with sympathy toward the Church. The Left is now formally in power and the Party and the government can be blamed, in turn, for poverty and low standards of living as well as for any other economic, social or political misfortune. The Church, no longer sharing in the formal responsibilities for governing the country, is by the same token, absolved from blame.

The young may be prone to disenchantment and discontent partly because their own values of "modernity" are not fulfilled or met. Also, being new in the economic market their pay is proportionately lower and they feel most acutely the hardships and frustrations of the generally low standards of

198

The Socialization of the Socializers

living. Finally, being reared with the normative-idealistic visions of Socialism, they may be more sensitive to the discrepancy between these visions and the sociopolitical and economic reality surrounding them.

Yet, it is on the young that the system pins its greatest hopes. Those in charge of the educational enterprise in Poland could logically expect that the influx of young persons, fully educated by the "new school" into the ranks of the teaching profession, would accelerate the process of goal achievement. As early as in 1951 Władysław Ozga, then a department head at the Ministry of Education, optimistically predicted:

> The introduction of 100,000 new teachers into our schools during the period of the next six years will change radically the ideological and political character of the teaching profession in Poland. In 1955 we will have 60 percent of teachers brought up in the schools built on the new ideological conception of People's Poland and they will be conscious defenders of the new regime. These teachers, supported by the experienced older teachers who have accepted the Marxist-Leninist ideology, will create together a united Marxist army of educators of the new Socialist generation in Poland.[9]

These high hopes are apparently far from realization although close to 20 years have passed since Ozga made the above prediction. The present situation would indicate that quite the opposite has taken place within the time period—that the young teachers "brought up in the schools built on the new ideological conception" are, in fact, perhaps even less prepared to meet the system's challenges than are their elders.

In addition to the young teachers and those who perceive themselves as educators, the authorities might expect teachers brought up in urban areas, of working-class background, with a high level of education to be more receptive

[9] Gusta Singer. *Teacher Education in a Communist State: Poland 1956-1961* (New York: Bookman Associates, 1965), p. 190.

199

The Socialization of the Socializers

to the values and goals of the new system. Table 6-4 examines the teacher's ties with the Church by sex, the type of community in which he has spent most of his childhood and youth, socioeconomic background (i.e., occupation of his father), and education.

Since the sample consists of secondary school teachers, the field of their occupational activities is the medium-size

TABLE 6-4

SELF-RATED TIES WITH CHURCH: BY SEX, TYPE OF COMMUNITY WHERE REARED, SOCIOECONOMIC BACKGROUND, LEVEL OF EDUCATION
(percentages)

		Not At All	Very Strong /Strong	Moderate /Weak	Total Church Ties	N
I.	*Sex*					
	Male	29.9	30.0	40.1	70.1	117
	Female	24.9	48.7	26.4	75.1	156
	Unknown	–	–	–	–	3
II.	*Type of Community*[a]					
	Village/Small Town	15.4	58.9	25.7	84.6	78
	Town	31.7	36.6	31.7	68.3	129
	City	24.1	28.4	47.5	75.9	61
	Unknown	–	–	–	–	8
III.	*Socioeconomic Background*					
	Peasants/Farmers	15.9	49.6	34.5	84.1	91
	Workers	42.8	26.6	30.6	57.2	112
	Intelligentsia	26.0	34.0	40.0	74.0	50
	Other[b]	9.7	39.4	50.9	90.3	23
IV.	*Highest Education Attained*					
	University-Higher School of Pedagogy Completed	29.2	26.4	44.4	70.8	113
	University-Higher School of Pedagogy Not Completed	26.6	21.5	51.9	73.4	139
	Other[c]	29.2	45.1	25.7	70.8	24

[a] Village or small town—less than 10,000; town—between 10,000-50,000; city —more than 50,000.

[b] Private entrepreneurial (8 respondents) including self-employed artisans, shopkeepers, and others, excluding private farmers.

[c] Some *Sudium Nauczycielskie* (schools of teacher education) but primarily higher technical and art institutions as well as higher institutions for physical education training.

town or big city. As indicated, Polish secondary schools are centered in larger population centers. For this reason, we examined religious attitudes in terms of the size of community in which they spent most of their youth. Unfortunately, because the communities were broken down by size originally for comparative research purposes, some of the descriptions may not correspond to Polish reality. That is, Polish villages are small and a community approaching 10,000 population is not necessarily considered a small town, much less a village. Yet, neither could anything less than a settlement of 10,000 residents be considered a town. Consequently, the descriptions of the communities in Table 6-4 are more or less correct but it should be remembered that if an extra category had been added, e.g., a community of less than 3,000, the proportion of proreligious sentiments might well have shown an even greater increase among teachers brought up in such environment.

The Polish countryside is still dotted with roadside shrines and passersby faithfully take off their hats or kneel for short prayer. The traditional greeting on the road is "Jesus Christ be praised" to which the proper response is "For centuries and centuries." Although electricity and radio (at least in the form of a centrally located loudspeaker placed on a pole along the village street) has reached most villages, the water supply still is carried from a well, the toilet remains outdoors, and life goes on in traditional terms, especially as far as the village residents' relationships with the Church are concerned. The Church is still the center of the rural environment. Religion, often wrapped in superstitious beliefs, remains strong in the Polish village. Consequently, only 15.4 percent of the teachers brought up in communities of less than 10,000 claim no ties with the Church. While proreligious sentiments do not decrease in terms of total relationships to the Church with the increase of the size of the community, they do decrease in intensity.

The reason for the differences between big and medium-sized cities may be one of visibility. In the medium-sized provincial community the pressures for conformity, both by the secular political authority and by the Church and the traditional elements, would be greater than in the city. Faces and names are familiar to the residents. Observing one's neighbor is a favorite pastime. A person growing up in such a community—bound on a career or eager to enter a higher institution of learning—would want to behave in a manner that would not be displeasing to the secular authorities. At the same time family and traditional community bonds which are still strong may produce a pattern of fragmented behavior. It is significant to note that teachers brought up in towns of from 10,000 to 50,000 residents divide almost equally among those who rate their ties with the Church as "very strong" or "strong," those whose ties are more pro forma, and those who have no ties with the Church.

The hopes of the regime for the city's total secularization seem not to be realized and the village remains the fortress of Church strength. On the basis of his own study of 1,000 teachers (of all levels), Kozakiewicz states:

> While every second male teacher in the city within our sample is a nonbeliever, only every fourth male teacher in the villages is neither believing nor practicing. The lack of substantial differences in religious attitudes among male and female teachers in the villages may be explained primarily as a result of the fact that both male and female teachers working in the villages are constantly exposed to environmental pressures as well as to local tradition, and that both suffer from the lack of sufficiently strong cultural and intellectual incentives to affect a break from the pressures and from the tradition. Moreover, for both males and females open denial of faith or renunciation of religious practice would be an act of great civil courage which could alienate them from the environment.[10]

The percentage of respondents of peasant-farmer background with ties to the Church is, like those of village and

---

[10] Kozakiewicz, *op.cit.*, pp. 38-39.

small-town background, quite high. The larger number of teachers indicating peasant-farmer background (91) than a childhood and youth spent in the village or small town (78) may be due to migration from village to city and town. After the war many Polish residents (including farmers) from the territories annexed by the Soviet Union were resettled in the Western territories won from Germany. Persons of such fragmented background may have continued a peasant-farmer social class identification although residing in the city. In addition, it is both formally and politically advantageous, especially for adult career purposes, to be of working-class or peasant background. The claim to such formal background seems also to be fashionable, at least in certain circles, particularly among those who maintain a certain level of Socialist or Communist ideological identification. To have made good on the professional and social ladder while of lower class background would also reflect positively on the individual. All these factors may help explain the discrepancy between background and residence of youth on the part of some respondents.

Teachers of traditional intelligentsia background tend to maintain moderate bonds with the Church. It is the teacher of working-class background who comes closest to meeting the system's expectations regarding Church attitude. This coincides with the regime's expectations in terms of systemic ideology and hope for the future.

The working class, after all, is at least theoretically the most favored, and the government and the ruling Party purports to speak on its behalf. Working-class background, as indicated, is favored in consideration for career advancement and, formally at least, for admission to higher education. Within secondary schools, various allowances are made, both academically and in terms of economic accommodation, for students of working-class background. This is the class which is to eventually produce the cadres for the new intelligentsia since members of the older intelligentsia persist in perpetuating a cultural tradition which includes homage to traditional institutions. Moreover, while many members of the new political elite may feel personally envious of the genteel background of the old intelligentsia and try to imitate its style, they would feel politically more threatened by obvious discontent among the workers than by old intelligentsia grumbling. It is significant that while the workers' riots of December 1970 caused the Gomułka leadership to topple and the new leaders to rush to shipyards, factories, and mines in order to placate restless proletarians, the students' riots of two years earlier and the intellectual turmoil of that period only brought about, in response, a tightening of the reins. Since in ideological terms the working class is seen as the carrier of revolutionary upheaval this could conceivably also be the class that could be most threatening to the revolutionary regime in power. The fact, therefore, that 42.8 percent of the teachers of working-class background indicated no Church ties at all (as compared to 15.9 percent of teachers of peasant-farmer background, and 26.0 percent of intelligentsia background) would appear to be somewhat encouraging from the system's point of view. On the other hand, the evidence that even among the working-class teachers, a majority (57.2 percent) indicated some kind of ties with the Church must give the system's leadership cause for concern.

Level of education does not seem to have a critical impact on ties with the Church. But then, secondary school teachers in Poland all have a more or less similar educational background, given the requirements for teaching on this level. If elementary and preschool teachers had been included, the difference might well have been substantial. That the intensity of Church-related ties of secondary school teachers whose education has not yet been completed is slightly lower than for graduates may simply be a function of free time which, for the former, is more likely to be devoted to self-education, producing a dissertation, taking correspondence courses, or other activities to meet the requirements for a degree.

When questioned about the maintenance of ties with the Church, motivations borne out of a need to conform were mentioned more often by teachers of peasant-farmers, rural backgrounds than by any other group. Teachers of intelligentsia background especially tended to stress motives philosophical in nature, the need for psychological fulfillment, or esthetic enjoyment of the liturgy and the ceremony. Similarly, among the sexes, female teachers justified their Church ties in terms of some spiritual and philosophical needs as well as in terms of habit and tradition, while male teachers more often advanced reasons of conformity to environmental pressures.

Teachers declaring Church ties, of whatever strength, were asked about the frequency of their attendance at Church services, especially Sunday mass, confession, and communion, all of which are obligatory to varying extents from the Church's point of view (see Tables 6-5, 6-6, and 6-7). The practicing Catholic is expected to attend mass weekly, and to confess and receive communion at least once a year.

Of the teachers who declared ties with the Church, however, only among the youngest (25 years or less) do more than half conform to the requirement of attending mass. Patterns of laxity regarding this performance prevails in virtually all of the other categories. What is surprising is that teachers of working-class background who are believers are the most frequent in their attendance at mass even though, as a group, they declare the least overall attachment to the Church. The fact remains, however, that the majority of all teachers who professed ties to the Church (53.9 percent) attend service less than the required minimum of once a week, and many of them do not even bother to attend once a month. Despite self-proclaimed ties to the Church, commitment to religion is no better, perhaps, than their commitment to the values and goals of the political system which they also profess to uphold.

The discrepancy between professed Church ties and actual Church attendance manifested by teachers of peasant-farmer and working-class background is an interesting issue. Mikołaj Kozakiewicz, who noted similar discrepancies be-

TABLE 6-5

CHURCH ATTENDANCE OF POLISH SECONDARY SCHOOL TEACHERS DECLARING TIES TO THE CHURCH: BY AGE AND SEX
(percentages)

	N	Sunday Mass				Other Church Services	Confession and Communion		
		Weekly	Once a Month	Less Than Once a Month	Never	Less Than Once a Year	Annually or More Often	Less Than Annually	Never
I. Age									
25 or less	66	52.7	18.8	28.5	—	32.2	79.6	20.4	—
26-30	55	47.2	15.7	37.1	—	33.4	58.6	41.4	—
31-40	42	39.0	9.2	49.3	2.5	48.9	52.1	44.9	3.0
41-50	20	44.1	8.0	46.2	—	55.5	55.6	41.4	—
Over 50	16	45.5	11.9	35.3	6.3	75.1	56.4	43.6	—
II. Sex									
Male	82	43.7	7.3	46.0	3.0	54.4	50.3	46.7	3.0
Female	117	58.5	3.4	33.4	4.5	34.4	65.2	31.8	3.0

TABLE 6-6

CHURCH ATTENDANCE OF POLISH SECONDARY SCHOOL TEACHERS
DECLARING TIES TO THE CHURCH: BY SOCIOECONOMIC BACKGROUND
AND TYPE OF COMMUNITY WHERE REARED
(percentages)

	N	Sunday Mass				Other Church Services	Confession and Communion		
		Weekly	Once a Month	Less Than Once a Month	Never	Less Than Once a Year	Annually or More Often	Less Than Annually	Never
I. Socioeconomic Background									
Peasants-Farmers	77	40.5	17.5	42.0	—	43.3	59.8	40.2	—
Workers	64	54.4	7.8	37.8	—	47.4	63.0	37.0	—
Intelligentsia	37	46.0	13.7	40.3	—	44.8	61.0	39.0	—
Other	21	44.5	18.1	31.7	5.7	48.5	60.7	39.3	—
II. Type of Community									
Village-Small town	65	51.0	12.0	37.0	—	48.5	56.2	40.1	3.7
Town	88	47.5	20.0	32.5	—	48.4	57.9	39.1	3.0
City	46	51.2	12.1	36.7	—	42.8	53.5	39.5	7.0

TABLE 6-7

Church Attendance of Polish Secondary School Teachers Declaring Ties to the Church: By Primacy of Professional Role and Educational Level
(percentages)

	N	Sunday Mass				Other Church Services	Confession and Communion		
		Weekly	Once a Month	Less Than Once a Month	Never	Less Than Once a Year	Annually or More Often	Less Than Annually	Never
I. Primacy of Professional Role									
Primarily Educators	61	46.1	7.8	46.1	–	38.9	55.0	45.0	–
Primarily Specialists	41	56.6	9.6	30.2	3.6	54.0	66.7	33.0	.3
Both Educators and Specialists	97	49.1	6.6	40.5	3.8	46.4	57.0	37.0	6.0
II. Highest Education Attained									
University-Higher School of Pedagogy Completed	80	49.8	10.2	36.8	3.2	53.9	61.8	35.1	3.1
University-Higher School of Pedagogy Not Completed	102	44.3	14.4	40.3	1.0	46.2	58.2	41.7	.1
Other	17	41.4	14.7	41.4	–	45.8	62.0	38.0	–

The Socialization of the Socializers

tween verbal religious profession and actual Church attendance of teachers working in rural and metropolitan centers (with Church attendance of city teachers exceeding that of village teachers, although the latter professed to a higher degree of religiosity), suggests some possible reasons. Teachers of village background, although religiously devout, may shun Church attendance because of a desire to maintain a certain image and prestige. Many of them may feel threatened by the competing prestige and status claims of the priest, since in the village the teachers and the priest often represent different polarities, and the teacher may feel that by not going to Church, he is being loyal to his own organization, the secular authority. Moreover, some have personally experienced, or carry a memory of someone else's, conflict with a priest. Thus they often bear some grudge against the hierarchy while professing ties to the Church. Such experiences, on the other hand, would be unknown to the city teachers or the teachers of working-class background employed in an urban setting.

A simpler explanation, suggested by Kozakiewicz, may be distance from Church. A Church may be found only in a nearby town or another village some kilometers away. Many teachers of peasant or rural background have become inured to the idea that Church attendance is not necessarily a condition of piety, especially if distance interferes and transportation is not easily available.

Finally, Kozakiewicz points out, the village teacher or the teacher of peasant background, unlike the urban teacher or one of working-class background, would be more concerned with the undesirable effects of his visibility in Church.[11] The fear of becoming visible through Church attendance and being marked as not fully socialized into the values of the political system which employs him may follow the teacher of peasant or village background into the city and demand caution lest he betray himself.

As with Sunday mass, teachers of peasant-farmer background attend special Church services to a lesser extent

[11] *Ibid.*, pp. 62-63.

The Socialization of the Socializers

than teachers of working-class background. The attendance of working-class teachers at special services is only exceeded by teachers of traditional middle-class background (private entrepreneurs, etc.). However, as far as special services are concerned, the frequency of attendance is less among teachers of big-city background than it is among those of village and provincial town background. In fact, some teachers of village and small-town background or big-city background who frequent Sunday mass do not bother to attend the special services while few of medium-town background who attend the special services do not come to weekly mass.

As with mass, relatively few teachers attend confession and communion annually or more often. This would again indicate that although professing ties to the Church, the extent or intensity of commitment is quite low. Once again, it is the youngest teachers who exhibit the greatest depth of religious allegiance. Yet—and this cannot be stressed too often—it is they who are expected to be the conscious carriers of the values and ideas of the new order, on whose performance the greatest hopes are pinned. The young teachers, not only claimed the strongest ties to the Church, but nearly 80 percent of those with such ties claim attendance at confession and communion annually or more often—more than any other category of believing teachers. Kozakiewicz, on noting the proreligious and pro-Church tendencies among the youngest teachers, comments:

> This fact should give pause to those in charge of institutions of teacher education. It should also draw the attention of all concerned with the ideational conditions and the world outlook of the youngest teachers who will in the not too distant future fully replace older teachers and upon whose posture will hinge in the coming years the total posture of the teaching profession, and with it the entire ideological climate of our schools and of our educational system. . . . These findings must be treated as serious signals of alarm, calling for more intensive ideological

210

The Socialization of the Socializers

work on the world outlook of the future generations of teachers.[12]

The responses of the youngest teachers to religious issues raises the question of the future prospects of the present Polish school system in terms of officially stated goals. Specifically, some see a problem as to the suitability of these teachers to perform as agents of socialization into a materialistic-scientific world outlook and a Socialist consciousness. There are also questions of the ability of the Polish postwar school, as currently structured, and of which the younger teachers are the product, to bring up their students and pupils in a posture desired by the system. Even those who identify themselves as having "moderate-weak" ties to the Church and who seldom attend Church services are far removed from the system's ideal. With the younger teachers expressing a comparatively high level of attachment to the institution of religion it would seem that in time the ideal might become even more unattainable.

Few Poles are totally indifferent to religion and the Church. Even those who claim to be nonbelievers, or agnostics, or heretics profess their beliefs (or lack of beliefs) with a measure of passion. As pointed out earlier, Polish Catholicism, mingled with nationalism, has evolved into a phenomenon of great complexity which many Poles find hard to cope with or to treat dispassionately. While religious practice is officially frowned upon, commitment to the Church (identified with national traditions) has become almost a matter of principle, something to guard jealously and to pursue spitefully. Czesław Miłosz describes how his own conflict with a priest in a prewar Polish *gimnazjum* (middle school) has affected him:

> The priest took me for an atheist, but he was mistaken. I had, it is true, led him into error from jealousy: what we keep hidden is dearer to us than if we were to talk about it publicly. I noticed a similar tendency later in crypto-

[12] *Ibid.*, p. 70.

211

The Socialization of the Socializers

Catholics who had become part of the political apparatus of a Communist country. They were more ardently religious than those who practiced their faith openly.[13]

Both proreligious and antireligious pressures produce similar patterns of resistance. True feelings are often submerged and hidden by manifest behavior thus adding to the complexity of the religious-secular strain. The actual religious practices of the teachers of secondary education might indicate that they take Catholic orthodoxy rather lightly, or that they have reached some modus vivendi between their faith and the expectations of secular authority. However, the question of teacher reliability, in terms of the system's expectations, remains at issue.

In addition to possessing a materialistic-scientific world outlook, teachers in Poland are also expected to be politically active as well as politically conscious. For the purpose of determining the extent of sociopolitical activism among teachers, the following criteria were used initially: Party membership and leadership office in Party organizations; membership in a National Council (*Rada Norodowa*) regardless of level (since the NC is formally the basic local, district, or regional elected self-government body); and membership in non-Party social, cultural, civic, and patriotic organizations as well as leadership positions in them. Some of the non-Party organizations, however, are very much politicized. Often, as in the case of the Volunteer (Auxiliary) Citizens' Militia (ORMO), membership would indicate commitment to the system exceeding even that of membership in the Party, although among its 380,000 members about 123,000 lack formal ties with the dominant Polish United Workers' Party. The formally non-Party members of ORMO belong, instead, to the other organizations of the Front of National Unity as well as to the various youth as-

[13] Czesław Miłosz, *Native Realm: A Search for Self-Definition.* Catherine S. Leach, trans. (Garden City, N.Y.: Doubleday and Co., 1968), p. 85.

212

The Socialization of the Socializers

sociations.[14] On the other hand, a formally non-Party organization such as the Union of Fighters for Freedom and Democracy (*Związek Bojowników o Wolność i Demokrację*, ZBoWiD) serves as a rather politically mixed but effective and independent power base for certain people. This organization includes among its members veterans of the revolutionary underground, former soldiers of the International Brigade who fought in the Spanish Civil War, political prisoners of the interwar period and the Nazi occupation, veterans of partisan warfare and of past struggles for national independence as well as of the regular Polish armed forces—regardless of the political banner under which they once fought. It is a mass organization since special effort is made to attract to its ranks persons of varied past political associations (the stress being on patriotic service) and because its members enjoy certain privileges (e.g., domestic travel at reduced rates, special pension provisions, job and housing advantages, etc.). General and former Minister of Internal (Security) Affairs, Mieczysław Moczar, for example, serves as chairman of the Central Board of ZBoWiD, and it is generally believed that he was using it for the purpose of broadening his political influence both within and outside of the Party. Many members of the Union, former members of nationalistic underground organizations as well as officers of preregime military units, still adhere to their old values and beliefs. On the other hand, many of the veteran-members who reached the Union via prewar Communist Party activity resent the present laxity in discipline, style, and morals, especially among the young, although they themselves may have suffered from Stalinist arbitrariness. Still others, especially those among the old time Communists who belonged to the ethnic core group and were normally removed from the center of the prewar Party activities (in which Jewish intellectuals played a large role), but who have fought in the guerrilla units and the Commu-

[14] See *Przekrój*, Warsaw (February 28, 1971), 2. See also *Contemporary Poland*, Warsaw, Vol. v, No. 3 (March 1971), 43.

213

nist-dominated People's Army during the war, may feel a sense of loyalty to their comrades and commanders from the partisan days. Utilizing the accumulated hostilities and resentments, playing upon the combined forces of nationalism, puritanism (of traditional as well as Communist vintage), hardline Communist sentiments as well as personal and organizational loyalties, Moczar (using the Union and the internal security forces as a base) rose to challenge Gomułka's leadership following the student riots of March 1968. The adaptation of anti-Semitic personnel policies and stricter measures governing intellectual, academic, and artistic activities during the postriot period were, in a sense, Gomułka's response to General Moczar's challenge. He hoped thereby to steal the partisan general's thunder, further thwarting the latter's ambitions by blocking his election to the Politburo and diluting somewhat his authority over ZBoWiD. General Moczar, significantly, returned to temporary prominence only after Gomułka's fall (following the December 1970 riots) and after the new leadership under Edward Gierek needed all the support it could muster— that of the Church as well as that of Moczar and his followers.[15]

Table 6-8 dealing with the range of organizational membership of Polish secondary school teachers as well as with the "intensity" of such membership (determined by patterns of officeholding) indicates that the teachers in the sample are generally rather apathetic. Those who are "organized" tend to favor the ruling political Party, probably because the Party is central to the life of the community and its various agencies, and also because it is the group that offers the most practical rewards in return for membership and activity. If the current sample had included elementary school teachers as well, the percentage of those belong-

[15] For a more detailed description and analysis of the intra-Party struggles of the 1968 period, see Joseph R. Fiszman, "Poland—Continuity and Change" in *The Changing Face of Communism in Eastern Europe*, Peter A. Toma, ed. (Tucson: University of Arizona Press, 1970), especially pp. 76-78.

TABLE 6-8

MEMBERSHIP AND OFFICEHOLDING OF POLISH SECONDARY SCHOOL
TEACHERS IN POLITICAL PARTY ORGANIZATIONS, NATIONAL COUNCILS,
AND SOCIOCULTURAL AND CIVIC-PATRIOTIC ORGANIZATIONS: BY AGE
(percentages)

	25 or Less (N=82)	26 to 30 (N=83)	31 to 40 (N=57)	41 to 50 (N=29)	Over 50 (N=22)
I. Political Party Organizations					
Polish United Workers' Party (PZPR)	6.5	15.6	24.0	20.7	18.0
Other[a]	2.4	3.9	5.8	6.9	9.1
None	91.1	80.5	70.2	72.4	72.9
Officeholders in Political Party Organizations	1.2	7.5	15.9	14.0	9.1
II. National Councils (Rady Narodowe) of Various Levels	1.2	5.5	9.6	26.0	13.5
III. Sociocultural and Civic-Patriotic Organizations					
Artistic-Cultural[b]	3.6	3.6	3.5	3.4	4.5
Sporting	9.0	6.2	1.8	3.4	4.5
Youth Activity Organizations[c]	7.3	12.0	3.5	3.4	–
Professional (Other than Teachers' Union)[d]	6.0	1.2	3.5	3.4	9.1
Religious[e]	5.0	4.0	1.8	3.4	–
Civic and Patriotic[f]	1.2	1.2	7.0	7.0	20.0
Other[g]	2.4	2.4	3.5	10.0	–
Belong to more than one of above	–	5.0	5.0	6.9	–
Belong to none	75.0	71.0	81.0	83.0	80.0
Officeholders in Sociocultural and Civic-Patriotic Organizations[h]	4.0	10.6	5.0	24.0	36.0
Officeholders in more than one of above	–	–	5.0	10.0	–

[a] Other political party organizations: United People's (Peasant)—ZSL; Democratic Alliance—SD

[b] Artistic-cultural: literary circles (Mickiewicz, etc.); music, choral and drama groups; historical societies; Friends of Science; popular science clubs; etc.

[c] Youth organizations: Scouting—ZHP; Union of Socialist Youth—ZMS; Union of Rural Youth—ZMW; etc.

[d] Professional: specialized scientific-technical and professional associations

[e] Religious: Caritas; Pax; etc.

[f] Civic and patriotic: League for National Defense—LOK; Women's League—LK; Polish Red Cross; Liaison with Poles Abroad—Polonia; Friends of Children—TPD; Secular School Association—TSŚ; Veterans' and former political prisoners' associations

[g] Other: Polish-Soviet Friendship Society; Freethinkers and Atheists; Volunteer (Auxiliary) Citizens' Militia—ORMO; etc.

[h] Includes office in Polish Teachers' Union

ing to the other parties of the Front of National Unity, particularly the United People's (Peasant) Movement (ZSL), would probably have been somewhat higher. The latter organization uses the village as the base for its activities and many teachers working in rural schools belong to the ZSL. The absence of secondary schools, especially those of general education, in small towns and villages is reflected in the low percentage of membership in party organizations other than the dominant PZPR.

Teachers between the ages of 31 and 50 show a higher frequency of Party membership than teachers in other age categories. Teachers in this age group, especially between the ages of 40 and 50, seem to be the most adjusted to the system. It would seem that the system rests upon the activism of persons in this stage of life, i.e., when they have made peace with their environment, have become settled, and probably have reached the height of their professional and occupational career. The same situation prevails with respect to membership and activism in the National Councils. Since these Councils serve the larger community, however, and election to them takes place on a communitywide basis, the tendency is to recruit as candidates for membership older and, presumably, more respectable and prestigious persons. Similar principles probably apply in the elections of deputies to the national parliament (*Sejm*) where teachers, as pointed out earlier, constitute a substantial functional group. The result, however, is that a higher percentage of teachers above the age of 50 belong to National Councils than would be justified in terms of Party membership or Party leadership of persons of this age. Although 9.1 percent of the teachers over the age of 50 hold office in a Party organization, 13.5 percent of them enjoy membership in a National Council. On the other hand, although 15.9 percent of the teachers between the ages of 31 and 40 serve as Party functionaries, only 9.6 percent of teachers in this age group are recruited and elected to the National Councils. This is not a phenomenon unique to Poland or, for that matter, to Socialist countries. In the United

216

The Socialization of the Socializers

States, for example, one frequently hears allusions to a governmental gerontocracy. On the other hand, however, revolutionary regimes are traditionally led by persons of relatively young age, especially in the early stages of development.

The youngest teachers maintain the strongest ties with the Church, while showing the least interest in political or social activism. Older teachers, especially those over the age of 50, are disproportionately represented in civic and patriotic organizations. This is especially true of veterans and former political prisoners. The organization of the latter, as mentioned, provides tangible benefits and many teachers of this age group qualify for membership.

Teachers between the ages of 26 and 30 who hold office either in the Party or a National Council are usually placed in positions requiring daily routine work (e.g., that of secretary, recording secretary, treasurer, program chairman), rather than in positions of a more representative character. The latter are reserved for older persons of some stature in the community.

Whether politically active or not, teachers become involved in an ex-officio capacity in political and social activities which are either Party related or Party directed. Party membership ceases to be the major test for a Polish teacher's general politicization, as it were. By virtue of his position the teacher becomes an organizational cog in the machine of community action campaigns with various goals and objectives, e.g., to raise money for the Millennium School Fund, for the celebration of some patriotic event, etc. As Jan Woskowski writes:

> Membership in the teaching profession does not formally force one to take an active part in molding social reality through extra-school activity. However, the real situation developed in such ways that a teacher was often forced into becoming action oriented by the prevalent attitude toward the role of the teaching profession held by the central authorities, by the local authorities, and not in-

217

frequently by a direct order that he become involved. Such activity, more often than not, was not in the realm of the teacher's immediate interests nor in an area which he could even view as being legitimate inasmuch as it had no relationship to his primary tasks. Nevertheless, participation in such activities became necessary if he, the teacher, was to meet the official expectation with respect to the profession that he manifest and maintain a positive sociopolitical posture. As the authority of the people's government became strengthened, the number of "loyal and positive" teachers grew accordingly. It became increasingly difficult for a teacher to continue to be "apolitical" in a country in which basically all activities, regardless whether socioeconomic or educational-cultural, were given political significance.[16]

Dr. Woskowski speaks here of a situation which prevailed most sharply during the period from 1949 until 1956. The situation at the present, while lacking the pressures for mobilization and politicization characteristic of the Stalinist period in Poland, is nevertheless full of demands for teachers' time and involvement. The fear of punishment for non-involvement may be less now, but rewards for activism are perhaps more tangible than in the past. Terror is being replaced with positive inducements which the hard pressed teacher finds difficult to resist. Polish teachers, especially in the provinces, may welcome the distractions from monotony and loneliness which activism offers. Many teachers mentioned the importance of a television set, for example, to one working in a small provincial town—yet the cost of a television set is prohibitive in relation to a teacher's income. Activism is one of the few alternatives.

The pressure for extracurricular activities seems also to be greater in the provinces than in the large metropolitan centers. In fact, when the respondents were asked about the distribution of their time in terms of weekly activities, provincial teachers indicated that social work consumes

16 Woskowski, op.cit., p. 179.

The Socialization of the Socializers

more of their time than school work (see Table 6-9). The provincial teacher's lot is more geared to work, in and out of school, than that of his colleague in the big city. Conversely, activities related to private life (i.e., family, friends, private entertainment, etc.) are moved into the background. He does not even have time for his own education although many of the provincial teachers have indicated interrupted progress toward an advanced degree. Such interruption, for whatever reason, is, in fact, often instrumental in assigning a teacher to work in the provinces to begin with. At the same time, once there, he is denied proper facilities for completion of his own education and upgrading of his qualifications. It is one of the vicious circles from which many find it difficult to escape. The consequences are debilitating for both the individual and the school system.

When asked to rate the importance of their various roles, few teachers (8.9 percent) rated the citizen role as the most

TABLE 6-9

RANK-ORDER OF ACTIVITIES ENGAGED IN BY POLISH SECONDARY SCHOOL TEACHERS: BY LOCATION OF EMPLOYMENT AND HOURS ALLOTTED FOR EACH ACTIVITY[a]

Rank Order	Large Metropolitan City Type of Activity	Weekly Hours Allotted	Provincial Town Type of Activity	Rank Order
1	School Work	48 or more	Social Work	1
2	Immediate Family	41-47	School Work	2
3	Culture-Entertainment	30-40	Political Work	3
4	Social Life, Sports, Tourism	30-40		
5	Self-Education	20-29	Culture-Entertainment	4
		20-29	Immediate Family	5
6	Social Work	10-19		
7	Close Friends and Relatives	10-19		
8	Political Work	5-9	Administrative and Economic Activity	6
9	Administrative Work and Economic Activity	Less than 5	Social Life, Sports, Tourism	7

[a] Some of these activities overlap—e.g., entertainment and social life, political work and social work, etc.

219

important. Even the role related to their favorite leisure activity (i.e., amateur painter, writer, artist, sportsman, gardener, etc.) was rated by many more teachers (21.4 percent) as being more important than the role of citizen. This is in a country where the stress on citizenship and the sacrifice connected with that role has often been put to test in the past. To the teacher, however, this test currently seems to be a daily and unwelcome task to be disposed of routinely and without too much taxing emotional involvement. Yet, he seems to take his professional work seriously—so much so, in fact, that he rates his teaching role above family roles (see Table 6-10).

Perhaps rating the family role lower than his professional role and only slightly above that connected with his

TABLE 6-10

PRIMARY IMPORTANCE ATTACHED TO SELECTED ROLES BY POLISH SECONDARY SCHOOL TEACHERS: BY TENURE IN THE PROFESSION (percentages)

	Length of Tenure[a]				*Total Teachers*	
Role	*Less Than 6 Years (N=51)*	*6-10 Years (N=127)*	*11-20 Years (N=74)*	*Over 20 Years (N=24)*	*N*	*Percentage*
1. Teacher-Educator	31.4	36.3	51.3	45.9	111	39.9
2. Family-Related Role (i.e., mother, father, son, daughter, wife, husband, etc.)	33.3	30.7	20.3	50.0	83	29.8
3. Citizen-Related Role (sociopolitical and civic activity)	2.0	11.0	10.8	–	23	8.9
4. Leisure-Time Activity Related Role (e.g., angler, mountaineer, writer, musician, artist, gardener, etc.)	33.3	22.0	17.6	4.1	59	21.4
TOTALS	100.0	100.0	100.0	100.0	276	100.00

[a] Tenure in profession includes total tenure within the school system, including employment at other levels of education prior to entering secondary school teaching.

The Socialization of the Socializers

favorite pastime is a function, in part, of the traditionally hierarchical structure of the family. A substantial number of the respondents in the sample (42.4 percent) were male and thus were to be freed from the care of the family aside from the duty of providing for their material existence. Traditionally, even the married Polish male saw his going out with the boys or even the privilege of "chasing" girls as a prerogative of his manhood, not in conflict with his obligation to the family. His Catholicism does not serve as a barrier to this type of behavior since, as indicated, religion is perceived in collectivistic-social terms rather than as an imperative for personal conduct. It should be recalled here that a substantial number of male SN students (31.6 percent) and not a few female SN students (14.2 percent) subscribed to the traditional double standards with regard to marital fidelity, expecting less stringent norms from the male partner (see Table 5-6).

The overall high rating given to the role of professional teacher may result, in part, from the relative status and occupational permanence of secondary school teaching in Poland. In addition, the presence of a majority of women in that profession and the absence of occupational alternatives may buttress commitment. In the United States, for example, where males constitute a majority of teachers in some secondary school systems and where for a variety of reasons (primarily economic) they may consider teaching as transient, the commitment to the role of family member transcends that of a commitment to the professional role.[17]

The high rating given by many teachers in Poland (21.4 percent) to the leisure activity role may be the product of the persistence of one of the dominant Polish "character-types." Florian Znaniecki, Józef Chałasiński, and more recently, Jan Szczepański, have pointed out that the "playboy

[17] See, for example, Joseph R. Fiszman, "Occupational Group Values Vs. the System's Expectations: Teachers in East Europe and the United States," Unpublished paper delivered at the 63rd Annual Meeting of the American Political Science Association, Chicago, Illinois, September 7, 1967, pp. 43-45 (Mimeo.).

221

type of Pole" is well entrenched in traditional Polish culture and is currently counteracting the formation of a new Socialist type of Pole. The playboy, as the other traditional social types (Catholic, Economic Man, the Well-Mannered Gentleman, etc.), has a tradition to draw upon and to continue. The Socialist type, on the other hand, has no precedent in the Polish cultural past. A Polish Socialist subculture existed but only marginally and much less developed than, for example, in Germany prior to Hitler's coming to power, in Red Vienna prior to the *Anschluss*, or even within the Jewish minority in Poland itself. Such a subculture requires not only the existence of strong and well-organized political parties but also of a network of ancillary organizations in the form of movement related schools, clubs, social and cultural service facilities, particular welfare facilities, women and youth auxiliaries, etc. In prewar Poland, on the other hand, the Communist Party was both insignificant in numerical strength as well as illegal (and was formally liquidated by order of the Comintern in the mid-thirties) while the Polish Socialist Party although numerically strong and of a long-standing tradition suffered, as it were, from its own erstwhile nationalistic orientation—an orientation which it fostered along with its Socialist program but in which the former tended to cancel out the latter in the consciousness of a substantial segment of the Party's membership and leadership. This was, after all, the Party most associated with the struggle for Polish independence in the period immediately prior to World War I and which Józef Piłsudski used as his organizational base but which he also left once independence was attained in 1918. The new Socialist type, as a result of such cultural, historical and political developments, is yet to take root while traditional Polish social character types persist.[18]

Teachers in Poland, as elsewhere, are expected to be

[18] Jan Szczepański, "Osobowość ludzka w procesie powstania społeczeństwa socjalistycznego," *Kultura i Społeczeństwo*, Warsaw, Vol. VIII, No. 4 (1964), 3-25.

The Socialization of the Socializers

agents of cultural diffusion. The teacher must himself therefore be thoroughly cultured. The Poles place great stress on *kultura* and on the expectation that the teacher will be *kulturalny*. In fact, rather than an expectation, the Polish pedagogic literature takes the teacher's culture almost as a given. Culture is synonymous with teaching. There is an a priori assumption that the teacher is a person of culture.

In order to ascertain the cultural level, or at least the direction of cultural interests of Polish secondary school teachers, questions were asked about their book-reading patterns, tastes in films, etc. It appears that Polish teachers prefer the works of native writers, both classic and modern. Among the latter some interest is given to the interwar literature some of which (as the works by Maria Kuncewiczowa, Pola Gojawiczyńska, etc.) are appearing currently in reprint editions. They show a definite preference, however, for writers who attained literary fame prior to World War II but have remained in the country and write on themes derived from the recent Polish past, including the period of occupation, the struggle for liberation, and the immediate postwar period (e.g., Adolf Rudnicki, Maria Dąbrowska, Jarosław Iwaszkiewicz, Jerzy Andrzejewski, etc.). Poetry figures prominently among teachers' favorite reading material, along with books of such disparate nature as serious works on history, politics, and philosophy, humor and satire, detective novels set in a familiar locale, and works purportedly portraying social, moral, and erotic styles and mores (e.g., Dołęga-Mostowicz). Of foreign literature, among the most popular are translations from the French, Russian, and German.

The teachers mentioned domestic films as the most enjoyable. Some of these acquired international renown. Among the most frequently mentioned films of Polish production were *Ashes and Diamonds, Mother Joann of the Angels, Lotna, Knife in the Water, Eroica,* the epics *Farao* and *Grunwald, Canal, Squinting Luck (Zezowate Szczęście), The Base of the Dead (Baza Ludzi Umarłych),*

223

The Socialization of the Socializers

The Last Stop—with few exceptions, films dealing mainly with the Polish present or immediate past, or with chapters in the long history of Polish suffering and heroism. These were followed by films of Swedish (*Wild Strawberries*), Italian, French, and Russian production (*Ivan the Terrible* was repeatedly mentioned), as well as a Western based upon the novel by Main Reed (*Winnetou: The Red Gentleman*) of East German production. American Westerns were mentioned as popular but no particular film of that genre was cited by title. Instead, the film *Citizen Kane* was mentioned many times as "memorable." Japanese films were singled out by some teachers who particularly enjoyed *Rashomon* as well as the documentary on the Olympic Games in Tokyo in 1964.

In music, among the most frequently mentioned favorites were the symphonies of Beethoven, the concertos of Chopin and Liszt, the symphonies of Mahler, and especially *The Passion and Death of our Lord Jesu Christ According to St. Luke* by the young Polish composer Krzysztof Penderecki. Other works by Penderecki were also cited. Opera tastes leaned toward the native with *Halka* and *The Haunted Manor* (*Straszny Dwór*), both by Stanisław Moniuszko, most frequently cited as best known and liked, followed by Bizet's *Carmen*. George Gershwin's *Porgy and Bess* was known to a substantial number of respondents who have seen or heard it. Among the older teachers, however, the favorite music was either Polish folk tunes, patriotic (including soldier and guerrilla) songs, and the sentimental hits of the prewar period made popular again by such currently well-known Polish singers as Sława Przybylska and Irena Santor as well as by Mieczysław Fogg, a prewar nightclub singer whose fame has survived the years. They also enjoyed the semi-underworld or urban folk songs sung in Warsaw prior to World War II and mentioned several titles in this connection. Younger teachers, on the other hand, mentioned the music by Louis Armstrong, Dave Brubeck, some Czechoslovak and West European jazz productions, as well as the music produced by some native Polish ensembles, e.g., the "Red-Blacks" (*Czerwono-Czarni*), the "Blue-Blacks" (*Niebiesko-Czarni*), and others, and particularly the recordings of the Beatles and the Rolling Stones. None of the folk singers popular in the United States were mentioned by teachers. Students, on the other hand, indicated a familiarity with Pete Seeger, perhaps because he had visited the country and appeared frequently before young audiences.

Table 6-11 shows the pattern of reading other than books among the respondents. The daily press seems to be the most popular reading fare of Polish teachers, followed closely by the general professional press (such as the official Teachers' Union organ), and popular news and picture magazines (e.g., *Przekrój*, etc.). In addition, the teachers in the sample also show a great deal of interest in specialized and serious professional literature such as *Kwartalnik Pedagogiczny* (*Pedagogic Quarterly*), etc. Generally, if judged by the reading trends, Polish secondary school teachers seem to be both profession oriented and varied in their interests. Compared with teachers in a community in the United States, it would appear that the Poles are substantially more profession oriented. The tendency of the secondary school teachers in the American community is more toward the consumption of popular journals of opinion than toward the general professional educational press. The Poles appear to be avaricious readers of both periodicals and books and apparently consume large quantities of material in a variety of fields. While only 24.1 percent of U.S. teachers read the general professional press regularly, the comparative percentage for Poles was 59.9. While only 10.9 percent of the U.S. teachers read the specialized educational and professional press regularly, the percentage was 24.1 for the Poles; 29.1 percent among the U.S. teachers read popular news and picture magazines regularly while 57.2 percent of the Poles maintained a similarly high readership pattern in this area; 50 percent of the American teachers and 32 percent of the Poles read journals of opinion or literary journals. In the field of entertainment maga-

TABLE 6-11

POLISH SECONDARY SCHOOL TEACHERS' FAMILIARITY WITH VARIOUS TYPES OF PUBLICATIONS: BY AGE
(percentages)

	25 or Less (N=82)	26 to 30 (N=83)	31 to 40 (N=57)	41 to 50 (N=29)	Over Age 50 (N=22)	Unknown (N=3)	Total (N=276)
I. Daily Press							
Read Regularly	47.6	49.4	91.2	100.0	100.0	100.0	67.5
Read Occasionally	8.5	8.4	8.8	–	–	–	7.5
Never Read	43.9	42.2	–	–	–	–	25.0
II. General Professional Press							
Read Regularly	40.2	45.8	70.2	100.0	100.0	100.0	59.9
Read Occasionally	35.4	50.6	29.8	–	–	–	31.7
Never Read	22.0	1.2	–	–	–	–	6.9
N.A.	2.4	2.4	–	–	–	–	1.5
III. Specialized Educational-Professional Press							
Read Regularly	2.4	18.1	31.6	55.2	59.1	100.0	24.1
Read Occasionally	13.4	15.7	24.6	41.4	40.9	–	22.0
Never Read	84.2	66.2	43.8	3.4	–	–	53.9
IV. Popular News and Picture Magazines and Popular Digests							
Read Regularly	41.5	48.5	63.2	86.2	100.0	33.3	57.2
Read Occasionally	4.9	48.2	36.8	13.8	–	–	25.0
Never Read	53.6	3.6	–	–	–	–	17.2
N.A.	–	–	–	–	–	66.7	.6
V. Journals of Opinion and Literary							
Read Regularly	12.2	16.9	42.1	69.0	77.3	100.0	32.0
Read Occasionally	35.3	36.1	57.9	17.2	13.6	–	36.0
Never Read	52.5	47.0	–	13.8	9.1	–	32.0
VI. General Entertainment Magazines							
Read Regularly	36.6	28.9	31.6	51.8	31.8	33.3	34.9
Read Occasionally	35.6	25.3	35.1	24.1	21.0	22.2	23.2

zines, the regular readership was 19.5 percent for American teachers and 34.9 for the Poles.[19] Overall, however, while the Polish secondary school teachers seem to meet the cultural and professional interest expectations of the system rather well, significant differences emerge between the various age groups (see Table 6-11). Again, as in the previous tests of the teachers meeting the system's expectations, in this one too the younger teachers seem to fare less well than their older colleagues. In the areas of relevant readings the activity seems to increase with age. In fact, in the area of professionalization, as signified by reading of the rich Polish specialized educational and professional press, the interest increases dramatically with the older age groups until it reaches 59.1 percent among those over the age of 50. The downward sliding reading pattern—as one moves from the older teachers to the younger—is broken only in the area of reading magazines of the popular and general entertainment variety. Here the reading, or nonreading, pattern is not characterized by age with those between the ages of 41 and 50 manifesting the greatest enthusiasm while those between the ages of 31 and 40 and over 50 years of age maintain more or less similar levels of moderate interest in this type of material. What these findings suggest once again, is that tenure in the profession (in addition to age) induces the teacher to develop occupational, social, and general interests. Age, of course, helps in settling down to the sedate pursuit of reading. At the same time, however, these findings beg the serious question as to the preparedness of the younger teachers, those already fully educated under the new system, to meet the system's challenges and expectations. Since the teachers are expected, in addition to being cultured, to be sociopolitically conscious and aware, one cannot help but wonder from what sources a large number of younger secondary school teachers derive their knowledge about current events and the proper ideological and political interpretation of these events considering that

[19] Fiszman, "Occupational Group Values . . . ", pp. 49-50.

The Socialization of the Socializers

within the age group of 25 or younger, 43.9 percent never read the daily press and more than half never read popular news and picture magazines or popular digests, journals of opinion, nor even the general entertainment magazines which at least summarize regularly the most important events of the week.

It should be remembered that the hope was expressed by the leaders of the Polish educational enterprise that as younger cadres, brought up in People's Poland, fill the ranks of the teaching profession the task of socialization will become accelerated. Every test indicates, however, that quite the opposite takes place unless, of course, tenure in the profession as well as age do indeed exercise a socializing influence all their own. In general, the picture of the younger teacher conveys the impression that he is apathetic, almost alienated, disinterested, and merely marking time.

Assessing the effectiveness of the teacher in general as an agent of cultural diffusion, Józef Sosnowski maintains that:

> The results . . . unfortunately completely substantiate the casual observations about the minor role of teachers in the process of cultural diffusion. It appears that the teacher in the big city who has, after all, at his disposal very many sources of culture dissemination—spends only 30 minutes a day on their utilization. Such utilization is most often reduced to a hasty reading of a popular newspaper or to listening to a radio news broadcast . . . teachers in the city read very few novels, seldom go to the movies or to the theater. Even worse is the situation with teachers in small towns. These teachers assign only 15 minutes a day to their association with culture. . . . In this manner a vicious circle develops: The teachers who are supposed to strengthen culture not only among children and youth but also among adults cannot properly participate in culture themselves nor in its use.[20]

[20] Sosnowski, *op.cit.*, p. 8.

The Socialization of the Socializers

Sosnowski blames these conditions on lack of time and finances that would enable the teacher to make full use of whatever cultural facilities are available in the community. It would appear then that if the teachers indicated substantial time allocation (both in the metropolitan areas as in the provinces) to culture and entertainment (see Table 6-9), they most likely had in mind that type of entertainment which includes a gathering (*stypa*) with friends or colleagues over a favorite drink or perhaps a meeting or assembly which they attend in line of duty and which features a lecture or musical number performed by an amateur group. Sosnowski maintains further that the situation on the elementary school level (dominated overwhelmingly by women) is even more removed from the cultural expectations of the system.[21]

To many teachers the very goals of the school system, the purpose of their work, as it were, seem to be a considerable source of frustration. Secondary school teachers were asked to describe in their own words what they think the primary goals of education should be. Although they rated their own citizen role extremely low, they thought that the primary goals of education should be the development of good citizenship, a sense of social responsibility, and a well-rounded personality capable of contributing to the social and economic welfare of society. In their responses a considerable number of teachers stressed dissemination of knowledge and the development of proper work habits as a primary school objective. Fewer teachers mentioned the development of proper manners, good behavior (in the sense of obedient conduct), and the teaching of tolerance as major goals. The teachers were next asked whether they think the primary goals of the present educational system actually meet their expectations, i.e., if the actual goals are what they believe they should be.

Table 6-12 shows that a substantial proportion of the teachers in the sample (41.1 percent) think that the present

[21] *Ibid.*

goals of the educational system differ from the ideal they have in mind. A majority of teachers of intelligentsia background (56 percent) express outright dissatisfaction with the present Polish educational goals. Among the teachers of peasant-farmer background the difference between those satisfied with the goals and those dissatisfied is only 2.2 percent. As in the case of self-rated ties to the Church (see Table 6-4), the teachers of working-class background meet (as would be expected from an ideological point of view) the system's expectation regarding contentment with the system's goals. However, as in the area of the religious-secular dichotomy, the endorsement of teachers of working-class background of the system's goals is not without qualifications. Not only do 30.3 percent of working-class teachers

TABLE 6-12

AGREEMENT-DISAGREEMENT OF POLISH SECONDARY SCHOOL TEACHERS ON EXISTING PRIMARY GOALS OF EDUCATION IN POLAND: BY SOCIOECONOMIC BACKGROUND
(percentages)

	Peasants-Farmers (N=91)	Workers (N=112)	Intelligentsia (N=50)	Other (N=23)	Total (N=276)
Present goals *differ* from what they should be.	46.2	30.3	56.0	43.5	41.1
Present goals *do not differ* from what they should be.	48.4	49.2	38.0	30.4	45.3
Don't Know/No Answer	5.4	20.5	6.0	26.1	13.6

view the existing goals as departing from the ideal but 20.5 percent either did not know the answer or hesitated to give one. Only a minority of those questioned in all categories indicate general satisfaction. And as in previous tests, the position of the intelligentsia and of teachers of "mixed" (i.e., middle class and private entrepreneurial) background is the most dubious, from the system's point of view, as to "reliability," satisfaction, etc.

In his 1964 study Józef Kozłowski asked a similar goal

related question. Rather than asking the respondents to state the goals themselves, as they perceive them, and then proceeding to question them as to their satisfaction (in terms of their own stated ideals), he asked the teachers about their agreement with the goals which constitute their formal required educational objectives. He further asked his respondents to enumerate the goals and objectives which do satisfy them, and to state the reasons why. Conversely, he asked respondents to state the goals and objectives which do not satisfy them, and to state why not. The results of Kozłowski's inquiry are illustrated in Table 6-13. Rather than by socio-

TABLE 6-13

TEACHER APPROVAL-DISAPPROVAL OF EDUCATIONAL GOALS:
BY TYPE AND LOCATION OF SCHOOL
(percentages)

Type of School and Location in Which Employed	N	Approve Completely	Critical of Goals	Rejection of Present Goals	Don't Know
Special (Model) Schools	238	58.0	27.3	6.3	8.4
Warsaw Schools	95	41.0	40.0	5.3	13.7
Non-Warsaw Based Normal Schools	102	67.6	21.6	2.0	8.8
TOTAL	435	56.7	28.7	5.0	9.6

SOURCE: Based on Józef Kozłowski, *Nauczyciel a zawód*, Warsaw, Nasza Księgarnia, 1966, p. 68.

economic background, his responses are reported by type of school in which the teacher is employed and by location (primarily with respect to Warsaw schools and schools outside of the capital). It should be borne in mind that Kozłowski's research was undertaken about two years prior to the survey reported here. While some aspects of Polish sociopolitical and economic life have become relatively stabilized in the course of these two years, others have remained highly unsettled. The latter aspects of Polish life eventually led to the outbursts and leadership crises of 1968 and 1970-1971. However, even prior to these years

231

and despite the establishment of some kind of daily systemic routine and adjustment, the regime, apparently sensing and fearing an underlying restlessness and low level of satisfaction (primarily in the areas of the economy and intellectual expression), tightened the reins and moved away markedly from the libertarian slogans of 1956, the so-called "Polish October" which ostensibly broke away from the Stalinist tradition, asserted Polish independence from the Soviet Union, and returned Gomułka to power. In fact, it was not too long after the euphoria of October 1956, but particularly so by 1964, that the regime had grown increasingly conservative and security minded, that the powers of the Ministry of Internal Affairs (at a low ebb in 1956 and immediately thereafter) began to increase slowly but steadily, that popular attitudes toward the Eastern neighbor were again seen by the Polish leadership as manifestations of public confidence (or lack of it) in itself, and, finally, that the tensions between the state-Party, on the one hand, and the Church, on the other, have increased. In addition, it should be pointed out that Kozłowski's study includes teachers of all educational levels (elementary and secondary). These differences in the character of the two samples as well as in the time elapsed, however brief, during which the two surveys were conducted, may account for some of the discrepancies in the results obtained. Nevertheless, the differences in levels of satisfaction-dissatisfaction between the two studies are not as large as might be expected although, in Kozłowski's study, a clear majority (56.7 percent) approves the system's formal goals and objectives. Significantly, however, the levels of satisfaction-dissatisfaction in the Kozłowski study also differ with the occupational environment of the teacher. Thus, for example, the teachers in the sensitive and crucial Warsaw school system (which would employ teachers of intelligentsia and working-class background to a greater extent than non-Warsaw schools) approve of the stated goals and objectives much less readily than teachers employed elsewhere. If we add those who are critical of the goals to those who reject

The Socialization of the Socializers

them outright (in Warsaw schools), the dissatisfied out-number the satisfied by 4.3 percent. If we could further add to these the rather large number of Warsaw teachers (13 out of 95) who hesitated with a response, it would appear that a majority of Warsaw teachers have doubts, at least, as to the propriety of the system's educational goals and objectives. The extensive endorsement of the goals by non-Warsaw teachers (where those of intelligentsia background would be less prominently represented) confirms the findings of the present book with respect to the general behavior of teachers of varying background. The findings of both these studies highlight the essentially transitional nature of Polish society and the fact that the socioeconomic classes which are supposedly dominant in the official class pyramid and which are to provide the cadres for the "new intelligentsia," still manifest considerable socialization deficiencies.

In analyzing his data Kozłowski classifies the goals and objectives to which the teachers objected as follows: (a) goals of Socialist education; (b) goals that are formulated with such a degree of ambiguity that they invite varying interpretations; (c) goals rejected outright, other than those of Socialist education and regardless of formulation.

Among the rejected goals and objectives he differentiates three types: ideological, political, general educational. Interestingly enough, the teachers in the special (model) schools, a majority of whom (58 percent) approved of the stated goals and objectives related to ideology and "world outlook," generated the most opposition otherwise. Among the reasons given for opposition, he cites from some open-ended responses by teachers, e.g.: "Goals and objectives borne from ideological premises are transient, changeable, and therefore of little value to the student"; "Although I am an atheist I do not believe in ideology related educational goals because I believe in the freedom of conscience"; "I do not believe it proper to minimize the achievements of states of a different political system"; "I do not believe in condemning automatically everything that is capitalist," etc.

233

The Socialization of the Socializers

Other objections are more in the nature of reservations: "The goals of Socialist education are too lofty to be realizable"; "The slogan 'education of future builders of Socialism and in the spirit of Socialist morality' is too vague"; "This type of education does not prepare the pupils for their future vocational pursuits"; "It is important that the goals be in accord with the educator's own conviction"; "I have doubts as to the educational objectives because of two reasons: one, I myself do not understand it all and, second, I have doubts as to the propriety of the objectives; they create friction among colleagues and, as a result, diminish the teacher's authority."

Our own survey also asked the respondents to comment on the causes of their satisfaction or dissatisfaction with the perceived goals of the system. To cite a few as illustrations:

1. *Hostile Comments*

Rather than goals we ought to have more textbooks, supplies, and adequate school structures. There is too much talk of goals.

Intellectual growth depends on an atmosphere of free inquiry. Therefore, any kind of indoctrination only serves as a brake for such growth. The student ought to be schooled in such a way as to be able to arrive at his own conclusions.

Repression and propaganda only lead to opposite results and are therefore counterproductive.

While the mind accepts the rationale for the present goals of education, sentiments and tradition—hard to overcome—pull in the opposite direction.

It is proper to illuminate in class the foolishness of the dogma but religion as such grows from the inner needs of man. Both the Church and the state should be able to coexist in peace.

234

The Socialization of the Socializers

Only fools believe that a 1000 year-long tradition can be liquidated through administrative measures.

Religious education should be present in the school because it has served well our Fatherland and its citizens.

Religious training is useful in the formation of moral values.

Poland was powerful under the rule of believers—I wish that those in charge of People's Poland would join the Church.

2. *Comments favorable to perceived goals*

I am opposed to religion in public education. Religion is in the way of human progress in the area of science and technology and we need to advance in these areas.

The clergy has too long intimidated our population.

I am not so much opposed to religion as to the manipulation of the Church and since the Church has opted for a role in politics modern education must take a stand.

The dictate of the ideology must become the dictate of our conscience.

Although religious I endorse the principles of a materialist world outlook.

The school should be a training ground for materialist-scientific thinking patterns, free from superstition and dogma. The only trouble here is that much of our socialist education is in the hands of Party people who are themselves secret believers.

The materialist world outlook has really gained roots in People's Poland.

A blindly religious person is not teachable.

For the first time in our history we have loyal allies

235

and security on the borders. If our education can perpetuate these conditions I would be satisfied.

I think that religious matters are becoming increasingly
remote to the average Pole and the educational system
must adjust itself to the new conditions.

Separation of state and Church has merit. Religion is a
private affair.

The Church was traditionally openly hostile to public
education. Why should public education accommodate
the Church?

I am glad that the priest (*ksiądz katecheta*) was finally
removed from the school premises. He behaved in a
lordly way and applied corporal punishment toward children of nonbelievers.

I hope that soon the clergy will cease intimidating teachers, especially in the villages.

The school ought indeed be secular but I doubt whether
it really is.

The goals are good but the question is whether our teachers' training prepared the cadres to achieve these goals.

These remarks, culled from the responses, indicate once
more the depth of the schism between the contending
forces in modern Poland, especially on the religious issue.
As was shown previously, the majority of Polish teachers do
accept the principle of separation of school and Church,
but, at the same time, many also fear the social consequences of a radical rupture between the two with resultant severing of traditional moral bonds. The Church
is still a powerful force in the community, especially in
rural areas and small towns. Polish teachers, especially those
working in the villages, not infrequently only two or three per
school, may reflect the religious beliefs and attitudes of their
environment, but because of their professional work they

The Socialization of the Socializers

find themselves exposed on the front line of the Party-Church battle as representatives of the secular order. They find themselves pitted against the priest, often against their will, because the school is frequently perceived as a challenge to the local parish. If the school and the Church, the priest and the teacher, somehow reach a modus vivendi and opt for coexistence, then neither of them has really deeply internalized the values and norms of his particular order. In the course of interviews many teachers indicated that the priests they know are really good men, good patriots, and not harmful to the goals of Socialism, a position that would indicate either the priest has somehow accommodated himself to the political system or the teacher has accommodated himself to community reality. The fact is that in many provincial and rural localities such accommodations have indeed taken place. Where it did it was the secular authority which has given way and retreated before the religious authority rather than the reverse. Official exhortations, however, call for vigilance and posit the goals of education and the duties of teachers in very militant terms. The objectives of contemporary Polish education constitute a direct challenge to the Church. These objectives are based on the following premises and postulates:

1. That the school trains its pupils and students in a scientific world outlook
2. That the school treats instructional subject matter from a materialist point of view
3. That the school is an instrument for the promotion of secularization of Polish society
4. That the school is an active and sincere participant in the establishment of a Socialist order in People's Poland[22]

Assuming that these objectives were sincerely conceived and are meant to be implemented, how capable is the teacher, especially of religious orientation, of accomplishing

[22] Kozakiewicz, *op.cit.*, p. 223.

237

the tasks expected of him? Kozakiewicz asked this question of 1,000 Polish teachers (see Table 6-14).

Since many of Kozakiewicz's respondents identified themselves as both believing and practicing Catholics they were, in effect, asked about their own suitability to meet the goals of the system. Not surprisingly they found themselves suitable for meeting the educational goals and objectives of the system. One might brush off their responses as the result of a desire for group self-protection, or an attempt at soothing hostilities coupled with a natural desire for job security and, perhaps, even hypocrisy. However, the question must have been very awkward for them and difficult to answer. Significantly, however, while some had doubts about meeting the scientific, materialistic, or secular goals of education, none had any doubts about meeting the Socialist objectives. This is a position common to some Party ideologues who ascribe such ability to the Polish Catholics by assuming, first, that religion is not a formal ideology and, second, that it therefore should not hinder the religious person from embracing the ideology of Socialism. Polish Socialism, however, is formally of the Marxist variety and thus, while positing its vision of the future social order in ideational terms, bases the achievement of that order primarily upon materialist premises. Official Polish Socialism, in fact, rejects pre-Marxist or non-Marxist Socialism as either utopian or "bourgeois."

Religiously oriented teachers were also rated as suitable to promote secularization, although to a lesser degree than they were believed to be capable of building Socialism. Here the difficulty is apparently related to what is understood by the term "secularization." Obviously, the religious teacher can treat any subject in the physical sciences either by describing facts and phenomena or trying to reconcile the religious and scientific outlooks, or he may remain mute where reconciliation would seem impossible to him. But in the context of the Polish system the question of secularization does not relate merely to separation from Church but rather to secularism as a world outlook, a philosophical

238

OPINIONS OF POLISH TEACHERS AS TO THE SUITABILITY OF A RELIGIOUS TEACHER IN MEETING THE GOALS AND OBJECTIVES OF CONTEMPORARY POLISH EDUCATION: BY IDENTIFICATION WITH THE CHURCH AND RELIGION
(percentages)

Goals and Objectives	Believing and Practicing (N=337)	Believing Not Practicing (N=179)	Not Believing but Practicing (N=112)	Not Believing and Not Practicing (N=262)	Heretics, Agnostics, etc. (N=107)	Unknown (N=3)
I. Develop in students a scientific world outlook						
Suitable	44.2[a]	32.5	15.3	5.2	41.0	66.7
Not Suitable	4.4	20.8	25.9	59.8	10.8	–
II. Treat subject matter from a materialist point of view, often contradictory to religious premises						
Suitable	24.5	26.0	14.1	6.6	32.4	–
Not Suitable	3.4	13.0	30.6	45.9	12.2	–
III. Promote secularization						
Suitable	21.9	37.7	24.7	20.5	42.4	33.3
Not Suitable	1.9	13.0	28.2	40.6	6.5	–
IV. Participate in establishment of Socialist order in Poland						
Suitable	58.3	59.7	48.2	45.4	66.2	–
Not Suitable	–	3.9	16.5	21.4	6.5	–

SOURCE: Mikołaj Kozakiewicz, Światopogląd 1000 nauczycieli: Sprawozdanie z badań ankietowych, Warsaw, Państwowe Zakłady Wydawnictw Szkolnych, 1961, pp. 21-23, 228.
[a] The remaining balance in each case were "Don't Knows" or "Unknowns."

position contrary to that of religion. The meaning given secularism merely as separation from the institution of the Church is acceptable in systems where that separation is seen as organizationally and politically convenient, partially in order to accommodate various denominational approaches to religion. In People's Poland, however, Marxist Socialism is the official ideology, the formally accepted, endorsed, and propagated philosophical point of view, and it is this official creed which is placed in direct *contradiction* to religion.

What is also seen in Table 6-14 is that the further the respondent is removed from a proreligious attitude, the greater is his readiness to respond to the various questions, and his readiness to disqualify religious teachers as suitable in meeting the tasks of the current system. Heretics and agnostics may give the religious teacher the benefit of the doubt, but the respondent who is neither believing nor practicing is readiest to disqualify the believing teacher from most activities in the Socialist school.

Since the official position of the Party, the Front of National Unity, and of the government—taking into consideration the realities of a society in transition—is the religious teachers may indeed contribute to the establishment of a Socialist order, it is somewhat surprising that nevertheless 21.4 percent of those who are nonbelievers and nonpracticing and 16.5 percent of those who practice but do not believe, have challenged the suitability of religious teachers to meet this objective. These respondents may not be familiar with the Party position on the matter, or may take a position which is less politically accommodative and more Marxist doctrinaire. Kozakiewicz himself comments on this problem:

> One could and should realize all goals of socialist education with the aid of the teachers who are religious. But simultaneously we must considerably increase our ideological work among them so as to influence their world outlook, bring about a transformation in their outlook,

240

The Socialization of the Socializers

a broadening of their perspectives—not only for the good of education but for their own good as well because it will free them from the unpleasantness of contradiction, lack of intellectual consistency, painful moral scruples, from the necessity of having to maneuver constantly between idealistic religion and materialist practice in their professional and social activities.[23]

Although officially the contribution of the religious person is invited, and he may even be made welcome because of necessity, it is also realized that the teacher who has a commitment to Church and religion may find himself in a rather awkward position. Given the goals of the system (and provided that these are taken seriously) and the traditional deep-rooted influence of the Church, the possibility of a continuing long-range alliance between the system and teachers who have their feet in both camps is questionable. It is, after all, the future and thus the security of the system which depends on the work of conscious, loyal, dedicated, and committed teachers.

For reasons of economic survival in the modern age, for prestige, for security, as well as for reasons related to ideology and the developmental programs inspired by the ideology, great stress is placed on the need for the inculcation of the values of a scientific-technological culture, the development of industry and modern technology. As already pointed out, although great strides were made in that direction, the ingrained traditional values and norms serve as a counterforce to the goal of rapid industrial and technological change and its accompanying social styles. Thus, while the Pole takes great pride in newly established steel mills and industrial plants, much of the new industrial spirit remains in the realm of rhetoric and symbolic homage. There is talk about efficiency and well-functioning organization, but at the same time traditional attitudes toward time, work, and leisure still persist. While the Pole admires the gadgets of convenience associated with a technological culture, the

[23] *Ibid.*, p. 237.

good life to him is still one of leisure, drink, and retreat to the pastoral countryside. To change these patterns, to bring about greater receptiveness for the norms of an industrial society, the system relies heavily on the schools. Efforts are being made to develop a wider network of vocational training institutions and to encourage young people to learn a trade which has immediate economic and industrial relevance. Such encouragement is often boosted by promises of higher pay and appeals to patriotic pride. The idea of building Socialism is linked to the idea of industrial development, industrial work, and scientific-technological progress. Courses of vocational character have even been introduced to the secondary schools of general education which until not long ago were to a great extent the exclusive reserve of the humanities, and where knowledge of Latin was often emphasized more than physics and chemistry or even mathematics. How do secondary school teachers in Poland who were themselves brought up on a humanistic tradition, who were themselves educated in the classic tradition, react to the new emphasis on vocationalism? How can teachers steeped in Poland's romantic traditions become the champions of the nascent industrialism and the new technological and work-related values? Teaching of history, for example, has traditionally involved the glorification of heroic Polish cavalry charges against insurmountable odds; even the current historical accounts of the battles of September 1939 against the German invaders, while noting the sad state of unpreparedness and technological underdevelopment of the Polish forces, romanticize the encounters which pitted Polish horses and sabers against German motorized divisions and emphasize the point that the Pole, imbued with the spirit of patriotism and self-sacrifice, challenged and occasionally even overcame the impersonal machine.

In order to probe this issue teachers were asked to respond to the following statement: "One of the main tasks of the modern school system is to keep abreast of the ongoing technological and economic changes and to adjust itself to these." It was anticipated that older teachers, as well as

The Socialization of the Socializers

teachers trained primarily in the humanities, would react most negatively to the current drive for vocationalism, poly-technization, and scientificism. As it turned out, these expectations while correct in some respects were also wrong in many instances, and apparently did not take into consideration the specificity of Polish conditions. The results obtained (see Table 6-15) frequently show quite the opposite to be true: that acceptance of the technological-economic changes and the concomitant demands for vocationalism progresses with tenure in the profession up to a point, but slackens off with those employed for more than 20 years. It also progresses quite dramatically with age, but drops past 50. As expected, however, teachers who consider themselves primarily subject-matter specialists are more receptive to the idea of keeping abreast of technological advancements and economic changes than are those who consider themselves primarily educators and who, on other issues, accepted systemic expectations with greater readiness than have their specialist colleagues. Teachers who describe themselves as fitting the polytechnic scheme that stresses both character education and vocational skill training, the educator-specialists, lead in accepting the technology oriented goals of the system, perhaps because they see themselves in the role of synthesizers and bridge builders between the two cultures. Those identified primarily as educators, who are quite ready to reorient themselves in their world outlook on matters of religion and morality or to revise their views on Poland's past or future to fit the officially expressed line, appear resentful of the rapid changes brought about by technology and worried about its effects. While ready to accept the broad socially related goals of the system, they pause when it comes to accepting the values of a technical-industrial culture, especially as it impinges on their own immediate environment and work.

At the time this study was initially undertaken (1965), the problem of the "two cultures" was heatedly debated in the intellectual circles in Eastern Europe as it had been in the West several years before. Although very few of the

TABLE 6-15

POLISH SECONDARY SCHOOL TEACHERS' REACTIONS TO STATEMENT ON KEEPING ABREAST OF TECHNOLOGICAL AND ECONOMIC CHANGES AND NEED OF ADJUSTMENT TO THEM IN A MODERN SCHOOL SYSTEM: BY AGE, TENURE, AND SELF-PERCEPTION

(percentages)

	N	Agree Strongly	Agree	Total Agreement	Agree in Part	Disagree	Disagree Strongly	Total Disagreement	Don't Know/No Answer
I. Age									
25 or less	82	26.0	26.3	52.3	31.0	6.7	3.0	9.7	7.0
26-30	83	33.8	35.2	69.0	21.0	2.0	2.0	4.0	6.0
31-40	57	40.3	36.9	77.2	11.2	5.6	6.0	11.6	–
41-50	29	17.5	54.8	72.3	20.7	3.0	2.0	5.0	2.0
Over 50	22	20.0	29.9	49.9	23.1	20.0	5.0	25.0	2.0
Unknown	3	–	–	–	–	–	–	–	100.0
II. Length of Tenure in Profession									
Under 6 yrs.	51	25.7	25.5	51.2	40.4	4.1	1.0	5.1	3.3
6-10 yrs.	127	36.3	36.7	73.0	16.3	3.3	2.0	5.3	5.4
11-20 yrs.	74	22.2	52.6	74.8	20.2	3.2	1.8	5.0	–
Over 20 yrs.	24	30.2	37.4	67.6	6.3	11.7	8.0	19.7	6.4
III. By Self-Perceived Primacy of Professional role									
Primarily Educators	85	27.1	41.1	68.2	26.0	2.3	2.3	4.6	1.2
Primarily Specialists	54	40.3	37.9	78.2	12.3	2.5	3.0	5.5	4.0
Both Educators and Specialists	137	38.1	41.0	79.1	8.4	4.6	2.7	7.3	5.2

The Socialization of the Socializers

participants in the discussion were familiar with the book, C. P. Snow's *The Two Cultures*, the issues were the same as in the West when the book first appeared.[24] It seemed that both in the East and in the West the humanistically oriented advocates and ideologues of their respective world outlooks felt most threatened by the scientific revolution. On the other hand, the subject-matter specialist may have seen in such adjustment, an eventual escape from politics and purely political demands.

Older teachers (over 50 and/or over 20 years' tenure) may very well feel threatened by the unknown prospects of rapid scientific and technological change. They may, consequently, feel shaken in their security, both psychologically and professionally. In a country to which the full impact of the second industrial revolution has come late, the older teacher was a person of knowledge and esteem. Trained in the humanities, he may learn his Marxism at an even older age and adapt himself to the intellectual and sociopolitical demands of the system, but it may be harder for him to retool himself to fit the more exacting and skill oriented demands of a scientific technological revolution. He may have reservations about some of the new sociopolitical demands but at least he is able to understand the language in which these are posited and he can appreciate their functional utility; he finds, on the other hand, the demands of the scientific-technological revolution difficult to cope with, the language hard to understand, and he may feel threatened by the social effects of that revolution. The older teacher may indeed fear that as society becomes more technologically oriented and science minded, his knowledge will be obsolete and he will be relegated to an inferior status.

As in other tests, here too the youngest teachers (both in terms of age and in terms of professional tenure) are the

[24] Reference here is, of course, to C. P. Snow. *The Two Cultures* (Cambridge: Cambridge University Press, 1959). See rev. and expanded edn., *The Two Cultures: And a Second Look* (Cambridge: Cambridge University Press, 1965). Lord Snow refers in the *Second Look* to the Polish and East European debate, p. 54ff.

most disappointing from the system's point of view. One might reasonably expect, regarding the scientific-technological goals of the system, that they would be more receptive. They are, after all, children of the modern age and, as the scientists in the sample, they may see in the stress on science and technology hopes for apoliticization. Previous tests have also indicated that if the younger teachers have any intellectual commitments they would be to modernity, however shallowly conceived. To be sure, a majority of the younger teachers accept the scientific-technological goals of the new school, but it is a very slight majority. Several explanations suggest themselves: (1) many younger teachers automatically react negatively to whatever demands the system makes of them; (2) they are apathetic and cannot be aroused by any objectives; (3) they are skeptical about the system's abilities to achieve whatever goals it sets for itself with the result that they cannot get too aroused; (4) they, as the teachers over 50, do not really feel prepared to meet the challenge of an ongoing scientific and technological revolution, and while hungry for the material benefits brought about by technology and science, they feel professionally threatened by the social consequences of a full reign of science and technology. The reaction of the very old teachers and the very young is similar. It may be rooted in the same feelings of fear and inadequacy. If this is so, the reaction of the younger teachers would be the result of an education which, although espousing symbols of scientific and technological progress, has neither managed to instill in its charges the values of a scientific-technological culture, nor a deep-rooted intellectual commitment to its goals, nor, finally, the substantive know-how to cope with it. A glance at the performance of students in lyceums of general education in the next chapter may provide some clues in this area. If their own education is to blame for the lukewarm endorsement of the vocational and polytechnic goals of the system by the youngest teachers, then the wholehearted endorsement of these goals by the teachers of middle age and of 6 to 20 years tenure (whose educational experience

The Socialization of the Socializers

would either be the same as that of the younger teachers or less relevant to the scientific-technological changes) becomes more problematic. It might be attributed to a greater degree of conformity to systemic goals and objectives which comes with age and socialization into the profession rather than to deep internalization of the system's values. If so, perhaps such conformity can only be broken by a particular goal's threat to one's professional security and social status, as in the case of the oldest teachers and those of longest tenure in the profession.

As far as the polytechnic goals themselves are concerned, it is assumed that the general development of man hinges upon the development of a scientific and technical culture coupled with political, social, and economic progress in the direction of Socialism. In the narrower sense, as concerns the individual and the practical task of education for such development, the ideal is to inculcate both ideological commitment and scientific-technical expertise. As Professor Bohdan Suchodolski writes:

> An ever greater role is being played . . . by elements transcending narrow specialization. There is a growing tendency to expand the group of disciplines which is to constitute the scientific basis of particular professions. In many cases it becomes necessary to include in it disciplines very remote from the basic trend of professional studies. Thus, for instance, the education of a modern engineer must include some elements of social and psychological sciences; for he is now no longer just in charge of technological processes; he also stands at the head of a working team expected to show initiative, intelligence, to cooperate in the advance of technology.[25]

The tendency in practice might be, however, that while the engineer and physical scientist will become familiar with the language of the social sciences and the values of the political system, the humanist will remain immune to

[25] Bohdan Suchodolski, "Democratization," *Polish Perspectives*, Warsaw, English edn., Vol. IX, No. 12 (December 1966), 53.

The Socialization of the Socializers

the language of science and persist in seeing it as a threat. Moreover, if the humanist remains within the school system to educate the prospective engineer, given the former's reservations and fears, how successful can he really be in giving equal attention to promoting the scientific-technological and the Socialist culture?

Chapter 7: At the End of the Educational Effort: Schools and Students

Promises vs. Reality

AT THE Unity Congress, the grand conference called in 1948 to affect a formal merger between the hitherto separate Polish Workers' Party (*Polska Partia Robotnicza, PPR*—prewar Communists) and the Polish Socialist Party (*Polska Partia Socjalistyczna, PPS*), a resolution was adopted committing the major political forces of People's Poland to the achievement of the goal of universal education and of educational opportunities for all as a necessary precondition for the "creation of a Socialist culture."

In the course of discussing the long and often arduous road toward the education of a teacher (see Chapter 3), it became evident that the goal of providing equal educational opportunities for all citizens of People's Poland is still far from being realized. If various obstacles block the way of the would-be teacher, they are even more numerous and frequently insurmountable for those desiring a university education and a career in one of the traditionally prestigious and lucrative professions, other than teaching, e.g., law, medicine, architecture, etc. Despite special allowances given to children of the traditionally lower socioeconomic classes they remain, as in the past, outdistanced on the road to an educational career by the children of the intelligentsia and of traditional upper-class background. Advantages in terms of easier entrance to prestigious secondary schools of general education and to institutions of higher learning, especially to the universities, which accrue directly and indirectly, formally or informally, to the children of the already established political elite (including holders of medals and orders of merit) further contribute to existing inequities.

Schools and Students

Nor has the goal of universal education been fully realized and here, too, the burden of disadvantage falls on the traditionally lower classes and the traditionally underprivileged areas of the country. The school reform plans thus far have failed to address themselves to a realization of that goal, although statements were made about the need for greater dissemination of culture and education and although many prominent educators, as Professor Jan Szczepański, for example, predict the inevitable coming of universal secondary education, perhaps even within the next decade or so. In the meantime, universal education even on the elementary level is far from complete, especially in the rural areas. The school reform plans of 1966 did not even consider the possibility of busing as an alternative to a more expensive program of widespread school construction. Busing, despite its inherent shortcomings and much opposition to it, has been adopted in certain areas of the United States, for example, as a means of faciliting racial integration. In Poland, where distances between urban settlements are relatively small, busing could be a realistic alternative to the costly construction of secondary school dormitories for village and rural youth, and thus perhaps could bring universalization of secondary education closer to fulfillment. Yet it was not even considered.

One might assume that a system of centralized planning that prides itself as being both rational as well as socially and politically forwardlooking and that, at least in theory, acknowledges the relationship between education and the achievement of its own political, social, and economic objectives would arrange its priorities accordingly. It seems, however, that many of the goals and objectives become arrested in the quagmire of traditionalism, inefficiency, poverty, bureaucracy, and plain inertia. Carefully drawn plans become lost in the process of central decision-making—fraught as it is with conflicting pulls and hauls, pressures and counterpressures, vested interests putting forth their respective claims with urgency and muscle, political obligations at home and abroad that must be met, various policy exigencies as well as other elements built into the system itself.

In addition to the above there is, of course, the question of how well the teacher, given his own state of culture, expertise, and socialization, accomplishes the objectives of training future generations of thoroughly socialized, committed, and skilled citizens of the Socialist community. What indeed are the cultural, political, economic, organizational, as well as socioeducational factors which hinder or facilitate the stated goals and objectives both of the system as well as the educators? How are lofty aims translated into reality?

THE REALITY OF BUILDING THE SOCIALIST SCHOOL

The official literature makes frequent claims of big strides in the area of education when compared with the interwar period. The network of kindergartens, for example, has grown from 1,506 in 1938-1939 to 7,950 in 1966-1967. The number of institutions of higher learning has increased during the same period from 32 to 76. The number of lyceums of general education, however, has increased only by 77, from 789 in 1938-1939 to 866 in 1966-1967, and the total number of elementary schools has actually decreased, from 28,921 in 1938-1939 to 26,564 in 1966-1967.

The increase in kindergartens and the decline in elementary schools can be explained only in terms of the repercussions of the slaughter in World War II, boundary changes, urbanization, etc. Having given up the rural areas of the East and having gained instead the urbanized areas of the West that were under German administration before World War II, the Poles supposedly were able to cut back the number of elementary schools (especially rural) and replace them with more centrally located facilities in the urban centers. However, between 1938-1939 and 1966-1967 the elementary school population grew by 563,550 pupils (from 4,963,500 to 5,527,050) and the secondary school population by 88,506 (from 234,200 to 322,706). This growth took place despite a general decrease in total popu-

Schools and Students

lation size during the same period. The largest student body increase was registered by the vocational school system: from 227,632 in 1938-1939 to 1,629,180 in 1966-1967.[1] Children who survived the holocaust of the war are now the parents of elementary school pupils; whole segments of the population which in the past were prevented by socioeconomic circumstances from secondary schooling, now find such education, however difficult to obtain, not impossible; vocational education became to the system not only an economic necessity but a conscious educational policy.

At the end of the war, in 1945, Warsaw, the capital city, had only 25 serviceable school buildings. Most of its prewar school structures were destroyed during the month-long siege and the bombardments of 1939, the Jewish Ghetto uprising of 1943, the general Warsaw uprising of 1944, and the systematic, deliberate destruction by the German forces of what was left of the city after the rebellion was quelled. However, in 1970, 25 years later, the number of school buildings in Warsaw was increased to 263[2]—a considerable achievement, to be sure, but still not sufficient to fill the existing needs. It appears, however, that the initial postwar building fever, concentrated in great part on restoring the devastated capital as well as on rehabilitating historical shrines, monuments, churches, governmental administrative structures, has subsided substantially as the years passed and attention was diverted to the construction of industrial plants and factories and, to a lesser extent, to meeting the continuously pressing need for housing.

The Millennium celebrations of 1966 offered an occasion to mobilize extra resources for the expansion of the school network. Under the slogan "1,000 New Schools for the 1,000th Anniversary," a vigorous campaign was launched for constructing throughout Poland an additional 1,000 schools over and above those already planned for that year.

[1] Główny Urząd Statystyczny, *Rocznik Statystyczny Szkolnictwa 1944/45–1966/67* (Warsaw: GUS, 1967), pp. 19-20.
[2] *Polish Perspectives*, Warsaw, English edn., Vol. xiii, No. 12 (December 1970), 76.

Schools and Students

Funds were solicited from individuals as well as from organizations, groups (such as school children), and economic enterprises. September 1, the date of the 27th anniversary of the outbreak of World War II, was set as the target for completion. When the academic year 1966-1967 began, however, only a part of the ambitious plan was realized. By that time only 516 new elementary schools were ready for operation and among these only 148 were "Millennium Schools." By the end of March 1966, the construction enterprises managed to complete only 13 elementary school structures in various parts of the country, i.e., only 2.9 percent of the projected elementary school building program—and the building speed increased only slightly during the remainder of the year. However, at the beginning of the academic year 1966-1967, 49 new vocational school buildings and 40 new school workshops were ready, thus reaffirming the accelerated emphasis on that type of education. Also the dormitories (*internaty*) increased their capacity by 6,400 new places.[3]

As a result of the inability of the building enterprises to meet the plan for 1966, many school construction projects were postponed. Only 11 new school buildings were erected in Warsaw during 1967—7 elementary schools, 3 vocational schools, and 1 special school.[4] Nevertheless, construction continues to lag behind plans. The addition, as a result of the school reform, of grade 8 to the complete elementary schools placed a special burden on that educational level, taxing the existing plants and affecting the work of the teachers. Many schools lack adequate recreation facilities. In some school buildings the required physical exercises in the morning before classes begin and even regular physical education classes must be held in the corridors and hallways.[5]

As in the past, rural schools suffer the most. One provin-

[3] *Słowo Powszechne*, organ of PAX, Warsaw (May 19, 1966).
[4] *Stolica*, Warsaw, Vol. xxii, No. 53 (1047) (December 31, 1967), 10.
[5] *Głos Nauczycielski*, weekly organ of the Polish Teachers' Union, ZNP, Warsaw (April 25, 1971), 1.

cial school official pointed out that as a result of the school reform and the addition of an extra grade to each school at least 31 additional classrooms are needed in his county (*powiat*). This was at a time when each school suffered from a classroom deficit predating the reform. He said:

> We were told the situation can be improved only through the exercise of local initiative, that we should not look to the central authorities for help because in Warsaw they have their hands full. However, our district (*Województwo*) National Council did not plan for the need and did not appropriate the necessary funds. You see, Warsaw makes plans but these do not sift down to the local organs. Since 1961 the Education Department of our county (*powiat*) National Council has its own building crew since it was difficult to make any headway with the normal construction enterprises. Yet this building crew planned for 1966 only alterations, routine painting jobs, minor improvements in the existing facilities, but not the construction of new ones. And this in the Millennium Year when all the talk is about school construction.
>
> Q. What could be done?
> A. We are trying but, frankly, it is like beating your head against a wall. We hope to arouse people in the county, to generate public discussion on the problem—then maybe someone will move.

Part, but only part, of the difficulty is that the centrally based Fund for the Construction of School Buildings and Dormitories (*Społeczny Fundusz Budowy Szkół i Internatów*) will cover only 60 percent of the cost of constructing new school facilities. The remaining 40 percent of the cost must be derived from locally generated funds, to be obtained through special drives or from the income of local economic enterprises. It is also the responsibility of the local authorities, the local National Councils, to set the educational building goals for the areas within their respective jurisdiction and to create the funds to meet a substantial portion of the operating expenses. However, the sources

254

from which some local Councils could create the necessary funds are limited and, consequently, they turn to the Councils of higher administrative level, shifting the burden of responsibility upward. The problem is less acute in the wealthier regions such as Silesia, the political base of the present First Secretary Gierek, but in depressed areas the matter of providing 40 percent of the necessary funds takes on dramatic proportions with resultant ill effects on the teaching programs. Moreover, because of the inability of the various construction and maintenance enterprises to fulfill their job contracts on schedule, local authorities find themselves unable to draw up firm financing plans at the beginning of the fiscal year since they have to draw from the current budget for work undertaken in previous years but recently completed. Even within metropolitan Warsaw which is divided into city precincts (*dzielnice*) with corresponding *dzielnicowe* National Councils, certain precincts, more than others, must rely on the all-city Council which, in turn, finds it difficult to budget all the programs undertaken. However, Warsaw is in the fortunate position of having the central authorities located in the city and of having well established links with government ministries and the Party leadership. For 1967 the Warsaw National Council allocated one thousand million *złotys* for education, a sum which, even at the time of appropriation, was thought to be inadequate in meeting local needs in the field of education.[6]

Other localities within the Warsaw region are less fortunate however. For example, the county (*powiat*) of Grodzisk Mazowiecki within the Warsaw area has 53 elementary schools, of which only 47 were able to add the required grade 8 in 1966-1967 to bring them up to complete status. Of the 53 schools, 9 are located in towns and 44 in fair-sized villages. Most of the school buildings are in various states of disrepair. Seven need major alterations and additions, and 40 were listed as in need of routine repair work, i.e., roofing improvements, installation of water pipes, toi-

[6] *Życie Warszawy*, Warsaw (December 30, 1966), 8.

255

lets, heating facilities, etc. For 1966-1967 the county had 500,000 *złotys* allocated for capital school improvement and 220,000 for routine repair and maintenance work. The county authorities of Grodzisk Mazowiecki were thus more sympathetic to the needs of education than authorities elsewhere. However, in meeting their plans—for which funds were allocated—they met the seemingly usual difficulties: finding a building enterprise which would undertake the jobs and, once undertaken, be able to complete the work on schedule. In principle, municipal or state building enterprises should assume the responsibilities of constructing public structures (such as school buildings) and of capital improvements. But these enterprises must show a degree of economic self-sufficiency, and in order to keep a labor force on its rolls it must produce at the end of the year a bonus which can be shared by its employees. Consequently, the municipal and state construction enterprises would rather undertake the building of income-producing structures that yield a premium upon completion, i.e., apartment houses, industrial plants, etc. Apparently schools also have a lower priority with those responsible for drafting the work schedule than buildings for governmental administration or even health centers. The latter apparently court greater favor from the community, especially the traditionally lower classes which associate more immediate and tangible benefits with health facilities than with schools. As a result, those responsible for school construction and maintenance must turn to the independent construction cooperatives or private entrepreneurs that have lower priorities in securing building material than the municipally or state-run enterprises and that also have greater difficulties in attracting skilled labor (because of the various fringe benefits available to employees of the public economic sector). In order to obtain material, private contractors and even cooperative building enterprises must frequently rely on supplies from the free market which they can obtain only at a price that would raise the cost of the job beyond the point allowable. Yet most public building contracts carry the provision

Schools and Students

that the builder supply his own material. Moreover, since most of the work required by the schools involves repairs, the cooperatives and private contractors find these jobs less profitable than outright construction. Consequently they are reluctant to bid for them and would rather work on private jobs or, as with the municipal and state building enterprises, on industrial building sites. By hiring themselves out as subcontractors on industrial projects or by undertaking private home construction, the private construction entrepreneur or even the independent cooperative is in a position to set a more flexible price and have the total payment more realistically adjusted to the actual work cost.

For the opening of school year 1966-1967, the county of Grodzisk Mazowiecki was hoping to have 2 new school buildings of 6 rooms each, additional school office space, needed workshops, plus a teachers' apartment housing project. However, by the end of June 1966 none of the projected new structures, additions, or repairs were even near completion and the nervous school authorities were making plans to rent private homes and peasant dwellings as temporary living quarters for teachers and for holding classes. According to the Warsaw *Województwo* school *kuratorium*, a similar situation obtained in all counties of the Warsaw region and appropriate moral appeals were issued to municipal, state, and cooperative building enterprises, as well as to private entrepreneurs, in the hope that they might help complete the projected Millennium school plans.[7]

Yet although far from pleasing those in charge of the educational system, things are now improving and moving ahead, however slowly, even in the generally impoverished Warsaw area. Between 1945, the end of the war, and 1963, 94 schools opened in the towns of Warsaw *Województwo* (not including the schools within the capital city itself) and 1,244 schools were put in operation within the villages of that *Województwo*. Of these, 954 schools were located in new

[7] *Głos Nauczycielski*, Warsaw (June 26, 1966), 9.

257

buildings since the old ones were destroyed either by age or war damage. Within the same Warsaw region (outside of Warsaw proper), the number of secondary schools of general education has more than doubled since 1937-1938, from 32 to 66.

The *kuratorium* of the Warsaw City School District publicly advertises its new school construction and repair plans and, as required, invites competitive biddings from state enterprises, cooperatives, and licensed independent craftsmen. The successful bidder is, as indicated, expected to obtain his own material and supplies. However, as one *kuratorium* official pointed out with an air of resignation, while the construction of a new school building may attract some bids from various contracting enterprises (who, he said, "most certainly" would never complete the job within the specified time), the minor repair jobs will remain without bidding as they return very little profit.

A. Wiśniewski relates the following story involving the construction of a school building in a village located in the *Województwo* of Białystok: The 8-grade school was housed in a barracks which burned down. It will take at least two years to have a new structure built. Why so long? First, it takes time to adopt the decision to proceed with the construction. Second, the legal documentation required before an invitation for bids can be issued is involved and complicated. It means obtaining formal authorization, drawing up plans, finding the appropriate site, securing the necessary utilities, mollifying a variety of community interests and obtaining their written endorsements, etc. Once the first wave of documents is secured and approved, a second, more technical and specific than the first, is necessary. Various bureaucracies are involved in the process. Each pulls in its own direction and the approval and consent of each must be secured: the *powiat* education inspectorate, the Bureau of Projects, the *Województwo* National Council, the administration of building enterprises, the banks which offer the necessary building credits to cover the cost until the budget may be finally approved and set aside, etc. It takes almost a year from the time a project such as constructing a school is conceived until the time when the go-ahead order can be given. In official jargon, the first is known as the "Projective Plan" and the second as the "Directive Plan." But once the Directive Plan is in force, the already familiar difficulty of having a construction enterprise begin the actual work is encountered. Wiśniewski points out once more that the construction enterprises must "protect themselves" and, therefore, they are not too eager to undertake the building of schools which are less profitable to them than some other construction projects.[8]

That education must pay the price of economic failures and mistakes was admitted by Władysław Gomułka only shortly before his demise as First Secretary of the Central Committee of the Polish United Workers' Party. Speaking at a 1970 ceremony celebrating Teacher's Day, an occasion on which some distinguished educators were bestowed with high state decorations for meritorious service, Gomułka declared: "This year we are faced with extreme difficulties resulting from bad crops which struck our agriculture. It is imperative that we overcome now and in the future this failure of agriculture in meeting the country's demands . . . certain consequences are the price . . . to pay."[9]

Although Gomułka finished his address by assuring the teachers present that despite such and similar misfortunes "our country is progressing systematically, faster than capitalist countries,"[10] the optimism could have only a hollow ring to those concerned with the immediate problems facing the schools. It was such official optimism, coupled with a rather depressing economic reality, that brought about workers' discontent and riots on the Baltic Sea Coast and Gomułka's subsequent fall.

A poor economy, if caused by crop failures or by plain

[8] A. Wiśniewski, "Próba ognia," *Sztandar Młodych*, daily organ of Executive Committees of Union of Socialist Youth, ZMS, and the Union of Rural Youth, ZMW, Warsaw (April 20, 1966), 5.

[9] *Contemporary Poland*, Warsaw, Vol. iv, No. 12 (December 1970), 27.

[10] *Ibid.*

mismanagement and inefficiency, if due to natural disaster or poor planning, or if the result of pressures in meeting too extensive foreign obligations—whatever the reasons— must eventually affect the political-administrative decision-making process. A depressed economy will result in political in-fighting preceding the determination of priorities and the allocation of resources. The more limited the resources the sharper the contest. This seems to be a universal fact of political life, characteristic of all existing political systems, regardless of official ideology. What seems also well known although somewhat unexpected in a Socialist system—officially committed to the value of education and the fact that revolutionary regimes traditionally tend to launch ambitious educational plans amidst turmoil and hardship—is that education is able to wield far less muscle than some other interests in the contest for limited resources. Apparently even revolutionary regimes, once settled, tend to succumb much more readily to the pressures of industrial plant managers eager for expansion and to administrative bureaucrats, not to mention those who make demands on behalf of national defense and internal security, than they do to the soft and often complaining voices of those in education. Other interests too, along with education, particularly those related to social welfare or public service, seem to be perennial losers. Consumer service interests appear to be expendable and among the first to suffer from economic crisis in Socialist countries, and in this such countries differ from capitalist systems when facing economic difficulties. For example, in Poland, the Ministry of Communal Economy finds its own projects and programs continuously lagging behind schedule because of an inability to build or secure proper service and distribution centers.[11]

Central planners habitually seem to give greater priority to industrial development projects capable of producing immediate income than to services of any kind. Education rates a lower priority than industry although officially the

[11] Czesław Niewadzi, "Sprawa postępu technicznego." *Stolica,* Warsaw, Vol. xxiii, No. 20 (1067) (May 19, 1968), 3.

two are seen as interrelated. However, industrial investments have immediate and tangible payoff value while the payoff of investments in education is not immediately evident. The objective pressures for economic investments are also greater, they involve the immediate ability of Poland to compete in international markets, to attract hard currency, and the demands from Poland's trading partners in the East European bloc (organized in the Council for Mutual Economic Assistance, CMEA) to meet economic obligations, responsibilities, and targets. Consequently, demands from educational interests, as well as from service oriented interests, are warded off in the hope that the economic pressures will in time be lessened. In the meantime, while a school remains unbuilt, perhaps the education oriented interests will be placated and impressed by new steel mills and certainly by a general improvement in the economy which presumably will come about as a result of industrial expansion. In this respect, as indicated, the situation in Poland is not unlike the situation in systems of a free enterprise economy: despite the long-range benefits inherent in education, short-range projects promising immediate profit find it easier to generate community support. Even within the educational structure, the aspects of education most intimately related to tangible economic utility (applied research, etc.) receive greater support than educational projects whose immediate relationship to the marketplace is less apparent. In Poland, for example, research institutes receive greater official support than university based laboratories, and research scientists attached to industrial enterprises enjoy superior facilities and pay, albeit less prestige, than scientists associated with either the universities or the institutes.

Because of the difficulty in carrying out school building and repair plans, school authorities are faced annually with a situation where funds appropriated for this purpose cannot be used and must revert to the general fund of the appropriate agency of the National Council or the Ministry. They cannot be used for any other purpose. In 1965 alone 581,-000,000 *złotys* allocated for school construction projects were turned back despite the slogan "1,000 New Schools for the 1,000th Anniversary."[12] Thus, the principles of rational centralized planning notwithstanding, some plans are cancelled out by the hard facts of economic and political life that often follow rules all their own.

Ironically, when an independent entrepreneur in Raszyn in Warsaw *Województwo* who was disassembling dwellings came forth with a plan to construct a new school in his community from the materials salvaged from old houses, his project met with administrative opposition. Only with the intervention of the editors of *Kurier Polski*, the organ of the Democratic Alliance (*Stronnictwo Demokratyczne, SD*), did the Department of Education and Culture of the National Council in Piaseczno (the county seat) accept his offer. The existing school building had no sanitary facilities and was in a general state of collapse. But it still remained for the Administration of Apartment Buildings of Warsaw-Center to give its approval for the man to go ahead and use the salvaged material for the construction of a new school.

Once a school is operating the situation improves. Some economic enterprise in the neighborhood will take it under its wing, collect funds among its personnel for special school projects, and place its buses and trucks at the school's disposal so the students may enjoy an occasional excursion into the countryside.

THE PROBLEM OF ADEQUATE TOOLS FOR LEARNING

Less dramatic than the lack of adequate facilities, but no less annoying to the frustrated educator who feels left to his own devices, is the matter of scarcity and poor quality of instructional material. Little things, like the absence of pencils, chalk, notebooks, an adequate number of textbooks, stencils, typewriters, paper, can drive a teacher to despair. Geography teachers complained that regional maps had to be recalled because of errors and that, although the situation has improved in recent years, not every student is cer-

12 Wiśniewski, *op.cit.*, p. 5.

tain of owning his own world atlas, as required by the curriculum.

Up to the end of 1965, 2,282,000 new geographic atlases were issued. Among these, 1,638,000 were designed for grade 4 of the elementary school, 450,000 for elementary grades 6 through 8, and 194,000 more advanced atlases for use by lyceum students. In 1966, 200,000 atlases for grade 4 were added, 450,000 for grades 5 through 8, and 56,000 for lyceum use. In addition, the publication of 75,000 Polish geographic atlases, 100,000 small historical atlases, and 30,000 atlases illustrating the period of antiquity (all for use in the lyceum) were scheduled for 1966. An atlas dealing with the history of Poland was scheduled to appear in 1967. Impressive as these figures are, however, they do not meet the needs of a growing school population. Consequently, during the school year 1966-1967 only every third student in Polish elementary schools could boast the possession of a required atlas. On the secondary school level, although the situation appeared to be less desperate, it still was not good enough to assure every lyceum student his own geographic atlas.

Similarly, although new sets of textbooks were to appear for the newly established grade 8 of the elementary schools, these did not come out in time, nor were they issued in adequate numbers to fill the need. Many schools had to resort to dated textbooks, textbooks formally withdrawn from the market, or textbooks designed for other grade levels.

In order to keep up with the changes brought about by the ongoing sociopolitical revolution as well as with changes in science and technology, old texts become rapidly obsolete and new ones are commissioned for almost every school year. For example, for school year 1966-1967 a new text in arithmetic and another in the Polish language were to be introduced in grade 3 and a new nature study textbook (e.g., biology, botany, zoology) was earmarked for grade 4. The new sets for the new grade 8 included textbooks in mathematics, Polish and Russian languages and literature, and social studies (*Man in Society*). Secondary schools were to receive a new reader in Polish literature and a textbook on economic geography (for grade 10). Even the special schools for workers (evening schools) received new textbooks. In addition to the textbooks, new teaching aids were contemplated in citizenship education, mathematics, physics, and the history of Polish literature. Teacher training programs also called for new texts and aids for that academic year.[13]

Publishing houses, printers, and central distributing agencies cannot keep up with the demand. The lag is often so extensive that, as one principal pointed out in an interview, by the time a new text appears it is already obsolete either because of new knowledge in the field, or because of a changing political situation. For example, until 1966 geography, history, and international affairs texts dealt rather sympathetically with the state of Israel. Reasons of historical circumstance and of deep emotional complexity contributed toward such an attitude. The wholesale slaughter of Jews in Poland during World War II (perpetrated by the Nazis in the face of indifference, if not acquiescence, on the part of many Poles) left among some feelings of deep-rooted shame and guilt, sentiments whose existence is attested to by postwar Polish literature and film. Many Polish Jews, survivors of the holocaust, migrated to Israel where they joined the ranks of the economic, intellectual, and political elite. The new nation was portrayed as a country with a strong labor movement, successful collectivized farming which "made the desert bloom," and one that is sympathetic to the people's democracies, particularly Poland. Close cultural ties between the two countries indeed continued for a long time. Polish Jews, presently citizens of Israel, were bestowed with Polish medals and orders for their past revolutionary and patriotic activities, and Poles received medals from the Israeli government for their individual assistance to Jewish victims of Nazi persecution; on a mount in Jerusalem which houses the headquarters of Yad Vashem and a museum

13 *Express Wieczorny*, Warsaw (June 20, 1966).

264

dedicated to Jewish martyrdom in World War II, the Avenue of the Righteous bears plaques commemorating many a Polish name.

However, as already indicated (see Chapter 3), a relationship of almost intimate warmth came to an abrupt end in the summer of 1967 after Israel's surprise victory over the Arab states. Poland and the other people's democracies (except Rumania), following the lead of the Soviet Union, severed diplomatic relations with Israel. The picture of Israel as a friendly state suddenly changed to one of brutal aggressor emulating the old Nazi foe. The reversal—accompanied by official and semiofficial statements laden with anti-Semitic innuendos—generated a great deal of popular confusion and trauma, especially since the original Israeli victories were greeted by many with stunned disbelief as well as sympathy. These victories, in a sense, undermined the traditional Polish image of the Jew as a noncombatant, a "nonhero." The official explanations for the Israeli victories attempted to affirm the traditional Polish image of the Jew by attributing the successes to "treachery" (e.g., Israelis attacked an allegedly unsuspecting foe), as well as to supposed foreign assistance, primarily that of the United States whose "lackey" Israel was now portrayed to be. The anxieties of Jews in Poland lest the outcome of the conflict in the Middle East may spell the physical end of relatives and friends and of a large Jewish community, and their subsequent relief over the outcome of the war, was interpreted as a manifestation of "pro-Zionism." Pro-Israeli sympathies, on the other hand, among the population at large, especially within the intellectual community, were now officially frowned upon and interpreted as evidence of "pro-Western," "proimperialist," and thus, "anti-Socialist" attitudes. The new, sometimes not too well hidden anti-Jewish tone, was spearheaded by the various press organs of the PAX association, a lay Catholic group collaborating with the Party and the government, often in opposition to the formal Church hierarchy, and whose leadership belonged to the prewar, openly anti-Semitic and even profascist National-

Schools and Students

Radical Camp (ONR) and *Falanga*. In addition, the new course while playing up to traditional Polish Catholic sentiments hit upon fertile ground among ambitious and middle-level bureaucrats eager to advance into higher level positions occupied by Jews and also among some elements within the army and the internal security forces centered around General Moczar who were anxious to challenge the established leadership by using the traditional anti-Jewish argument.[14]

New textbooks dealing with or touching upon the problem not only of Israel and the Middle East but also with the role of the Jewish minority in the course of Polish history were called for. The assessment of the Jewish Ghetto uprising of 1943, and particularly of the role of the Polish underground during that tragedy, underwent revision. Polish Catholic assistance during the Nazi occupation to Jews in and out of the ghettos received stronger emphasis as did Jewish "ingratitude," expressed in the form of allegedly "Zionist" charges about anti-Semitism in Poland. Even the previously exalted portrayal of Dr. Janusz Korczak, a well-known Polish-Jewish educator who chose a martyr's death by accompanying the young children of the orphanage he headed to the extermination camp, although he had an opportunity to save his own life, was altered and his deed down-rated. A postage stamp issued in Korczak's memory was withdrawn from circulation and acts of heroism and martyrdom on the part of other educators, members of the Christian majority, were spotlighted instead.

[14] For a detailed discussion of the role and use of anti-Semitism in intra-Party and intragovernment factional struggles during the period immediately preceding and immediately following the Six Day War of 1967 see Anonymous, "USSR and the Politics of Polish Antisemitism 1956-68," *Soviet Jewish Affairs*, London, No. 1. (June 1971), 19-39. The author of the article maintains that it is "no secret" that Bolesław Piasecki, the chairman of PAX and prewar leader of the openly Fascist *Falanga*, is the Soviet "resident agent" in Poland and that Moscow is using him as a conduit for transmitting its wishes to the Polish leadership, especially where it desires to avoid the appearance of blatant pressure or when it is not quite certain how its wishes might be received.

266

Schools and Students

Every change, especially in the realm of politics, must be followed with an appropriately adjusted set of school aids that burdens the printing and distribution facilities. At a time when needed texts in standard subjects are in short supply, such changes create substantial problems for teachers as well as students. The letters to the editor columns of the popular Warsaw daily *Życie Warszawy* carried the following rather symptomatic letter by a secondary school student, followed by her name and home telephone number:

Dear little *Życie Warszawy*, help me. I am a student in a secondary medical school. I have enormous difficulties obtaining textbooks which I need for my studies. At the last test I received a "two" (*"dwójka"*) in Latin. [The Polish grading system is on a scale from 2 to 5. Number 2 connotes "inadequate" or "unsatisfactory" work; number 3, "adequate" or "satisfactory"; number 4, "good"; number 5, "very good."] I urgently need the following texts: (1) *Lingua Latina*—Latin for secondary medical schools; (2) *Anatomia i fizjologia człowieka* (*The Anatomy and Physiology of Men*), edited by Wojciechowski—State Institute of Medical Publications (Państwowy Zakład Wydawnictw Lekarskich); (3) *Duży atlas gospodarczy świata* (*The Great Economic Atlas of the World*); (4) *Duży atlas świata* (*The Great World Atlas*). I thank you in advance for your assistance and hope it will bring the much needed results. Your grateful student.[15]

Libraries which might help alleviate the situation although numerous and located all over the country are however poorly equipped, and the librarians are traditionally overworked and have a set of complaints all their own. For years now school libraries of whatever level have been able to apportion only the paltry sum of 16 *złotys* annually per student toward the purchase of books. The public libraries which are primarily designed for an adult clientele fare even less well in this respect: under the jurisdiction of the

[15] Letter to the Editor under title "Student Worries" ("Uczniowskie kłopoty"), *Życie Warszawy*, Warsaw (October 10, 1966), 10.

Ministry of Culture and Art, their annual expenditure on books is only 13 *złotys* per registered reader.[16] At the same time, however, select "model" schools or schools of special education are able to experiment with relatively expensive and sophisticated learning machines and much is written about these. By their very nature, however, these schools and their tools and equipment are capable of reaching only a limited audience.

The Weight of Educational Tradition and Heritage

In terms of providing the general population with the minimal tools of reading and writing, progress was indeed made (see Table 7-1). Illiteracy among older persons (age 50 and over), mostly peasants (peasant women in particular) is a residue of conditions prevailing during the interwar period. World War II prevented many others from obtaining even the bare minimum of education. The rate of illiteracy is subsequently still great among Poles of middle age and older, and attempts are being made to improve the situation through evening courses for adults, Workers' Universities, culture circles in the villages, "universities for parents," etc. Some of these are sponsored by the youth organizations, the Association for Promotion of Secular Culture, and other civic and sociopolitical organizations.

Beyond the level of simple literacy, however, conditions are far from perfect although improving with time. Thus, for example, the number of employees in the public sector of the economy (which *does not* include the bulk of the peasantry) in possession of only elementary or less than elementary education was reduced by 10 percent between the years 1958 and 1969. Yet, in 1969, a full 60 percent of the labor force in the public economic sector had *at best* an education which terminated at grade 7, the last grade of the prereform elementary school.[17]

[16] See Letters to the Editor, *Polityka*, Warsaw, Vol. xv, No. 2 (723) (January 9, 1971), 1.
[17] Danuta Zabłocka, "Wszystko nietak," *Argumenty*, weekly organ

Schools and Students

TABLE 7-1

ILLITERACY IN POLAND AMONG PERSONS AGE 7 AND OVER: BY AGE AND SEX
(Age in Percentages)

Sex	Year	Number of Illiterates	Percentage of Illiteracy in Relation to Total Population 7 and Over	7-13	14-17	18-29	25-49	50 and Over
		Total Number and Percentage		*Age Groups Percentage Within Age Groups*				
TOTAL	1921	7,552,900	34.6	24.7	8.8	10.4	30.7	25.4
	1931	5,945,900	22.6	9.3	6.9	9.2	39.0	35.6
	1950	1,144,600	5.5	3.6	1.9	3.8	22.3	68.4
	1960	644,000	2.7	1.2	.7	1.4	12.9	83.8
Male	1921	3,291,700	32.0	28.5	9.5	8.6	27.5	25.9
	1931	2,229,500	17.7	11.7	7.2	9.3	35.3	36.5
	1950	405,400	4.2	5.2	3.2	5.7	25.2	60.7
	1960	215,400	1.9	1.9	1.2	2.3	16.5	78.1
Female	1921	4,261,200	37.0	21.8	8.2	11.8	33.2	25.0
	1931	3,716,400	27.1	7.8	6.7	9.1	41.3	35.1
	1950	739,200	6.6	2.8	1.2	2.7	20.6	72.7
	1960	448,600	3.5	.8	.5	1.0	11.2	86.5

SOURCE: Główny Urząd Statystyczny, *Rocznik Statystyczny: 1966*, Warsaw, GUS, Vol. xxvi (1966), p. 34.

Moreover, a closer examination of the data contained in Table 7-1 shows that the regime of prewar "feudal-bourgeois and aristocratic" Poland was perhaps already well on the way toward liquidating illiteracy through its system of compulsory elementary education, however laxly enforced. Reestablished as an independent state in 1918, Poland had to cope with the effects of World War I and long years of foreign domination during which the controlling powers (Czarist Russia, Prussia, and Austria-Hungary, but especially the first two) pursued a deliberate policy of educational retardation, particularly in the rural areas and specifically

of Association for Promotion of Secular Culture, Warsaw, Vol. xv, No. 17 (672) (April 25, 1971), 1, 7.

with regard to the development of Polish language skills among the masses. It took a long time to overcome that heritage and the additional educational devastation wrought by World War I and occupation. Similarly, at present, more than 25 years after the end of World War II, the effect of that experience is still visible. One of the reminders of the war is the state of education and illiteracy among certain age groups.

The extent to which the impact of World War II is still in evidence (a war in which 6,000,000 Polish citizens, including the bulk, 3,000,000, of the country's Jews, perished) is to be seen by the fact that in 1965, 20 years after the war, Poland's population was still 3,298,000 less than it was in 1938 (31,551,000 as compared to 34,849,000). It is a country in which close to half of the population was born after World War II but in which the birthrate is steadily declining despite Catholic strictures against the use of contraceptives and against governmental birth control programs. Economic conditions compel large segments of the population to resort to birth control and abortion. Finally, Poland is a country in which females outnumber males (a heritage of the war years) by close to a million. Warsaw, the capital, had a smaller population in 1965 than it had in 1939 despite annexation of many outlying areas and suburbs.[18]

While the number of secondary schools of general education has, as mentioned earlier, more than doubled since the prewar period in Warsaw *Województwo* alone, the number of secondary students within the region (minus Warsaw proper) has increased twentyfold during that time. Although still restricted, secondary education has lost much of its earlier elitist and distinct economic class character. However, changing conditions have brought crowded classrooms and a lowering in the quality of education. The limited number of secondary school teachers, especially in the provinces, simply cannot give their students the same individualized attention as did their predecessors in the small

[18] Główny Urząd Statystyczny, *Rocznik Statystyczny: 1966*, Warsaw GUS, Vol. xxvi (1966), pp. 13, 28-29.

elitist secondary classroom before World War II. This, again, is a situation not unique to Poland or to Socialist countries in general but rather a characteristic of all modern societies pursuing a policy of mass education—whether such a policy is an expression of deliberate intent or merely in response to circumstances and social pressures.

If the student population in the lyceums of general education in Warsaw *Województwo* has increased twentyfold, the vocational school population in the same region has increased less than eightfold, from 7,000 during 1937-1938 to 50,000 in 1965. The comparatively lower increase in the vocational school population is, of course, a disappointment in the light of the regime's stress on such programs, and the fact that by 1962-1963 the authorities had opened 107 basic vocational schools and 96 *technikums* and vocational secondary schools in the Warsaw area in order to back up the official vocational push.[19] As in other fields, the plans and designs of the political system met head-on with ingrained cultural and community values and norms and, ultimately, had to give way.

Generally, however, in the process of obtaining an education and utilizing the educational opportunities available, the rural areas and economically poor provinces are being left behind, relatively, largely because much of the responsibility for providing educational facilities is left to local initiative and resources. These are simply not up to the task either in terms of the local economy or because of lack of an appropriate cultural and educational tradition. As a consequence, higher educational opportunities, and with them, better social and occupational opportunities, remain reserved to the citizens of the large metropolitan centers or to members of those social classes and groups that have always held education in high esteem.

Interestingly, although Warsaw *Województwo* contains within its geographic (but not administrative) boundaries

[19] Irena Nowak, "Przemiany społeczno-kulturalne województwa warszawskiego," *Kultura i Społeczeństwo*, Warsaw, Vol. x, No. 1 (January-March 1966), 169-70.

the capital of the country, the cultural, economic, and political center of the nation, it is among the poorest and least developing areas of Poland. The relative poverty of the communities of Warsaw *Województwo*, especially of its eastern part, is reflected in the area's comparatively lower secondary school population. They lack the type of publicly operated enterprises which would enable the community to invest substantially in education. While the country as a whole has a ratio of 51 secondary school students of *all* types (general education and vocational) per 1,000 population, the ratio for Warsaw *Województwo* is only 33.6 per thousand. Similarly, the number in schools of all types is below the national average. Yet, the communities in this region are within easy proximity of Warsaw, and Polish sociologists (e.g., Jerzy Wiatr and Jaroszewski) and planners have often pinned their hope on the influence of urbanization in upgrading cultural and educational levels.

Apparently, however, the cultural and educational pull of the capital has had a negative impact on nearby provincial towns. Precisely the reverse of what had been hoped is happening. Because of the proximity of the big city, the most talented, gifted, and ambitious provincial youth drift into Warsaw, leaving provincial towns to stagnate.

A few towns within Warsaw *Województwo*, however, Płock in the west and Ostrołęka to the north, are undergoing an educational boom. This is primarily because these towns were designated for urban expansion and new industries. Płock, for example, which suffered little damage during the last war became an oil refinery center and the Polish petrochemical capital. Distinctly industrial, with a rich agricultural area surrounding the town, Płock employs peasants from the countryside on a part or full-time basis in refineries and plants. Ostrołęka became the site in the late 1950's of the largest paper mill in Poland. Rather than urbanization as such, it is industrialization that seems to give an immediate and direct impetus to educational development.

One would think that the relationship between industrialization and education is due to the emergence of new employment possibilities generated by an expanding profit-making industry. No doubt such factors greatly affect the educational picture. Alongside the lure of industrial employment, however, is the pull of tradition and of traditional educational orientations. Thus, even in Płock and Ostrołęka the secondary schools of general education receive more applicants for admission than vocational schools of similar level and more prospective students are turned away from the former than from the latter.

The situation observed in Warsaw *Województwo* in terms of its relationship to the neighboring big city or in terms of popular educational predispositions relative to industrial needs, could be noted in other areas of the country as well. The youth of provincial towns are drawn not only to Warsaw but also to Cracow, Poznań, Lodz, and other metropolitan centers. The skill needs of the economy do not markedly affect popular educational choices. Thus, in the country as a whole there were 60,000 graduates from secondary vocational *technikums* as compared to 80,400 graduates of secondary schools of general education at the end of the 1965-1966 school year. There were, to be sure, in addition to the 60,000 *technikum* graduates, others who graduated from vocation oriented secondary institutions, e.g., 38,000 graduates from special agricultural schools, and 21,-000 graduates from pedagogic lyceums. The bulk of vocational students graduating that year were from night schools for workers (167,000) who come to upgrade their job qualifications. But among the regular student population, despite the entrance difficulties encountered, graduates of secondary schools of general education outnumbered the graduates of industry oriented vocational schools by 20,400 even though the latter were assured of immediate absorption into the employment market while the former, if unable to enter into institutions of higher learning, were facing a rather bleak employment future.

The organ of the Polish Teachers' Union, *Głos Nauczycielski*, estimated that of the 1966 crop of secondary school graduates of general education 27,000 will be admitted to higher education, 28,000 will enter various post-*matura* schools, 10,000 will seek clerical or other low skill white-collar employment, and 15,000 will begin some vocational education.[20] The economic lesson, however, has hardly an effect on popular educational choices. That same year, 1966, when 656,000 pupils of elementary schools graduated from grade 7 and faced the choice of going on to grade 8 (and hopefully to a lyceum of general education afterwards) or leaving elementary school at that point and transferring to a secondary vocational school, 60.5 percent decided to remain for grade 8, and to hope.

Effort vs. Result: The Matura-Holder
and the Test of Knowledge and Value Assimilation

The content of some courses has changed and, in some instances, where the content has remained substantially unaltered, the subject has received a new designation. Most changes were brought about by the school reform which formally went into force at the beginning of the academic year of 1967-1968. In addition to changes in titles, textbooks, supplemental aids, etc., the changes also involved, in some cases, revisions in the number of hours devoted to a subject. Thus, citizenship, to be offered in grade 4 of the new general education lyceum, was given 3 hours per week classroom time and military preparedness (*przysposobienie wojskowe*, PW) was officially renamed defense preparedness (*przysposobienie obronne*, PO). The reform also introduced vocational courses into the hitherto humanistic and classical curriculum of the lyceum of general education. These were grouped together under the heading of "technical education." Physics and astronomy, which had been subjects taught jointly by the same teacher, were separated. Foreign language training was given renewed emphasis and additional time. In the last year of secondary general education greater emphasis was placed on the student's independent study and self-education. The latter was de-

[20] Editorial, *Głos Nauczycielski*, Warsaw (June 26, 1966), 1, 3.

cided upon both for didactic and pedagogic purposes, as well as for the purpose of coping with the shortage of qualified instructors and adequate facilities. Classroom hours were increased in personal hygiene and course content was altered with greater emphasis given to mental health. Sex education and problems related to time budgeting and the rational organization of personal work patterns were included in the courses on hygiene.[21]

These courses, usually conducted by the homeroom teacher are intended to accomplish many tasks: to expedite the assimilation of the moral values which spring from the ideology and Socialist culture, to help the student overcome various life difficulties, and to facilitate adjustment to society's demands. Although students in Poland are quite eager to accept foreign, especially Western, fads and are curious about youth life abroad, they know very little about it. Youth indulgence in marijuana, hashish, or "hard" drugs which has reached epidemic proportions in the United States and certain West European countries beginning in the late sixties has not reached Poland as yet—in large measure due to a combination of economics, strict discipline, and harsh treatment of offenders. If anything, Polish youth, including those in schools of secondary education, engage in more traditional and "square" disciplinary vagaries: drink, sex, absenteeism, running away from home, political heresies. They are faced, however, with many of the same problems as youth in the West—difficulties of growing up, of facing a sometimes uncertain future, misunderstanding between generations, falling behind in studies, love pangs, and disappointment. The classes in hygiene that attempt to cover a number of diversified subjects within a relatively short time, conducted by a teacher not necessarily informed on or sympathetic to the problems confronting youth nor trained in psychology or psychiatry, obviously cannot satisfy the real needs of youth for counselling. Moreover, the school may not even be the proper vehicle to fill such needs. Although the problems are universal and many of

[21] *Sztandar Młodych*, Warsaw (April 20, 1966).

them have been of longstanding—facing, in fact, each succeeding generation—each youngster sees them from a very personal and intimate perspective. A large class may not be the appropriate forum for a frank airing of intimacies. The teacher may not be trusted (in fact, he may be feared or disliked for a variety of reasons), and students may be reluctant to discuss with him personal matters about which they may feel some guilt lest these be held against them some time in the future. There is a natural fear of repercussions from teachers, from youth organization leaders, and even from peers. The popularity of the Church among Polish youth may be due, in part, to the periodic need for confession, for counselling and hoped for absolution—functions which the priest traditionally fulfilled and for which the hushed atmosphere of the Church and the intimacy of the confession box would seem more hospitable than the large class and the teacher. Perhaps because even the Church could not adequately fill this need, or perhaps in an attempt to offer the Church and the priest some competition in this area also, confidential telephone services similar to the "hot lines" in drug infested cities of the United States sprang up in 1967. Agata Ursynowska maintains that the existence and relative popularity of these confidential counselling telephones is a result of failure on the part of parents, teachers, youth organizations, and adult counselling centers.[22] This obviously much needed service, however, provided by private initiative, is staffed by volunteer cadres and operates with limited funds. In Warsaw, for example, the telephone is located in a small room in the District Occupational-Educational Counselling Center on Szpitalna Street and, when first activated, was open only 4 hours a day (from 3:00 p.m. to 7:00 p.m.). The service was later extended by 2 hours—from 1:00 p.m. to 7:00 p.m. The telephone in Warsaw responds to an average of 10 calls per day. Most of the callers are girls between the ages

[22] Agata Ursynowska, "Telefon Zaufania," *Fakty i Myśli*, organ of the Association for the Promotion of Secular Culture, Bydgoszcz, Vol. xiv, No. 8 (306) (April 11-24, 1971), 3, 9.

of 13 and 17 and most of their problems concern conflicts in school, academic difficulties, general social or life adjustment, as well as sex. Sex appears to rank fifth in the problems broached over the confidential phone, exceeded by questions on how to cope with life and social demands—areas in which the teachers and the schools should be able to guide the young person but apparently find it beyond their capacity to do so successfully. The volunteer workers at the Center have at their disposal a very modest library on sexology, pedagogy, and psychology.[23]

The original intention of the reform was not to alter the total hours per week required for each lyceum grade but, as a result of the curriculum changes brought about by the reform, some adjustments in the total hour requirements had to be made. The required classroom hours for grade 1 of the secondary school of general education was set at 34, grade 2 at 34, grade 3 at 33, and grade 4 at 30.

In addition to periodic examinations, visitations from the *kuratorium* and inspectorate, and the final *matura* examination, annual communitywide, regional and national "knowledge competitions" take place amidst a festive atmosphere. These competitions, called "Educational Olympiads" or *Disce puer*, were first instituted in 1958 and involve subjects commonly taught in the various types of secondary schools during the first half of the school year at grade 10 (grade 2 of the reformed secondary school of general education, grade 4 of the pedagogic lyceums and vocational *technikums*). This limits the competitions generally to Polish language and literature, Russian language and literature, and mathematics. In addition, general education secondary school students compete in physics and chemistry, pedagogic lyceum students in chemistry and a subject drawn from their specialized curriculum, and *technikum* students in two vocational subjects designated at the last minute by a special commission.

The final test of their knowledge, however, and the most traumatic experience for the students, takes place in the

[23] *Ibid.*

month of May of the last year of their secondary education. For the student of the general education lyceum, passing this final series of tests means obtaining the much cherished "Certificate of Maturity," the *matura* which not only provides one with the key to possible entrance into institutions of higher learning and an esteemed profession but, if the student is a male, service in the armed forces with the rank of officer rather than private. In the immediate prewar years possession of a *matura* was the mark of social status and entitled the holder to vote for and be a possible candidate for the Senate. The gentleman-officer of the pre-World War II army was prohibited by military code from taking a spouse who lacked that official certification of education and good breeding. To the youngster of upper middle-class or upper-class background the day he received the *matura* meant traditionally that from this point on he would be treated as an adult—he could smoke in public, enjoy his vodka without being secretive about it, become engaged, frequent nightclubs, etc. This tradition still prevails and the male student, once in possession of the *matura*, is often addressed for the first time as "Mr." (*pan*).

Because so much hinges upon passing the *matura* examinations, parents of means engage special tutors, usually needy university students or moonlighting teachers. Polish television features special remedial and *matura*-preparation classes throughout the year but, as Professor Janusz Tymowski who served as a special television consultant to the former Ministry of Higher Education maintains, students avoid these television offerings until about the last two weeks before examinations.[24] For those who cannot afford private tutorial services, special pre-*matura* cram courses have sprung up in recent years. These courses apparently developed quite spontaneously, through private initiative, without any control from official educational authorities. Consequently, there is much discussion in the press as to

[24] As quoted Andrzej Świecki, "'A oni nie chcą się uczyć': Kto ma przygotować do studiów?," *Życie Warszawy*, Warsaw (September 5, 1969), 3.

their utility and their pedagogic, as well as social, effects. These courses have given rise to a virtual pre-*matura* educational black market with various sponsors vying for clients.

If failure in two subject matters in the course of any school year (and on any level of the educational system) means that the student must repeat all courses for the given grade (and only one repeat is normally allowed on the secondary level), subject matter failure during the last grade of the lyceum of general education prevents the student from taking the *matura* examinations during that year. In theory this provision is meant to maximize the student's chances of passing the examinations successfully—in practice, however, it is used by a lyceum administration and staff to maintain an image of academic excellence and professional competence by avoiding the possible embarrassment which may come about as a result of having placed a "high risk" student before a panel of outside examiners. Fear of future complications, in addition to punishment, may also be behind the practice of preventing students with severe disciplinary problems (severe enough to result in a failing grade for "conduct") from taking the examinations. "Bad conduct" is also sufficient cause for keeping a student on the same grade level at any time during his school career, or, alternately, for dismissal. Although the criteria for "good" or "bad" behavior are habitually vague, an attempt was made in recent years to define these criteria with greater specificity. They are: level of socialization, level of culture, level of diligence—criteria that obviously overlap various aspects of student behavior. The manner in which a student takes care, for example, of school equipment, or the quality of his relationship with teachers, school administrators, and peers could be judged in terms of all three criteria. Yet in 1970 use of these criteria in grading "conduct" was introduced experimentally into the schools of several *wojewódz-twos* in Poland.[25]

Having overcome the various obstacles, 140,000 secondary school students were ready to take the *matura* examinations

[25] *Głos Nauczycielski*, Warsaw (April 25, 1971), 1.

in 1966. They began on May 20 in all parts of the country except in the Poznań region where the initial tests were administered on May 16 and 17. The procedures for administering and taking the examinations were spelled out in detail in special regulations issued in 1965. They involved both written and oral tests. During the first examination day the students are required to take the written Polish language and literature tests. On the second day they take the written tests in mathematics. Then follows a pause of several days at the end of which the results of the written tests are made known and those who qualify (pass) proceed to take the oral examinations. The results of the oral examinations are made known on the same day they are taken. The same procedure is repeated with respect to the other subjects in which the student is examined and, usually, the last test takes place on June 10—a total examination period of twenty or more days.

Special examination commissions are appointed annually and, in addition to the regulations of 1965, new directives are issued almost every year at the beginning of the examination period. The aim of these new directives is to acquaint the commission members with their task and to ensure that the normal school operation will not be interrupted during the period. In 1966 the directives stipulated that only one oral examination be given in a day and that the final results be made known without undue delay so as to alleviate the apprehension of students and parents. There is considerable anxiety during the prolonged examination period with frequent reports of nervous breakdowns and suicide attempts among students.

During the course of the research, I was given access to some written examination questions and completed tests in several regions of the country. It appears that although the language of the questions differs from school district to school district, they are essentially the same since they are drawn from the same standard texts and curriculum. In the field of Polish language and literature, the students were given a choice in the written examinations from among three basic themes.

A subsequent reading of examinations reveals that the students generally prefer to stick to subjects covered in the texts or previously handled in class, and to treat the question in standard fashion (i.e., not to deviate from the treatment given the subject by the textbook author). They prefer specific questions to questions of a general theoretical and speculative character since the former make it easier for them to answer in specific terms, to pour out what they have previously learned or memorized. They avoid the choice of themes which would involve them in ideological discussion or the necessity to express an individual position, and they avoid passing judgment. Students skirted the question which asked "Which period in Polish literature, in your judgment, was the most creative both in terms of productivity and historical impact?" Finally, they avoid themes that would reflect individual initiative in the selection of reading matter.

In the Poznań school district the written examination questions in Polish language and literature read as follows:

1. Prove on the basis of freely chosen literary examples that the literature of People's Poland continues indeed the progressive tradition of the Polish Millennium.

2. On the basis of which values, as manifested in his writings, did Henryk Sieńkiewicz endear himself to all Poles?

3. Which of the contemporary novels you have read on your own would you consider most outstanding and why?

The students examined in the Poznań school district overwhelmingly chose to respond to the second question. It required a relatively specific and standard answer, was noncontroversial inasmuch as it dealt with a classic Polish writer, acceptable at present to all factions of the political spectrum because of his exposition of patriotic values and virtues, and because his works had a definite anti-Prussian and pro-Slavic orientation. This, however, was not always so.

281

Schools and Students

The outstanding prewar Polish Communist literary critic, Julian Brun (Bronowicz), who died during the war years while an emigré in the Soviet Union, referred to Sieńkiewicz as "the prophet of the Polish petty bourgeoisie" whose more modern novels served as an apology and "guiding post" for that class.[26] Suspect as a nationalist by intellectuals of the radical Left prior to the emergence of People's Poland, Sieńkiewicz has since become the literary symbol of Polonism and Polishness, of national unity. As such he is presently acceptable to the Left precisely because of their current vital interest in the propagation of the values of patriotism, national pride, and loyalty—traditional petty bourgeois values. Even the style of the old petty bourgeoisie, its esthetic tastes and life aspirations, became more palatable, it seems, since they stand for order, hard work, deference to authority—positive attributes to the Communist bureaucrat in power as it was to the non-Communist bureaucrat before.

The students in the Katowice school district were faced with the following questions during the written examination in Polish language and literature:

1. In your opinion, which literary period of the thousand-year long Polish history has contributed most vitally to the life of our nation and why?
2. What lasting values could contemporary youth discern in the ideological posture of the heroes of Polish romantic literature?
3. To what extent did the literature dealing with World

[26] See Andrzej Gass, "Całe życie jednej sprawie," *Kultura*. Warsaw, Vol. IX, No. 12 (406) (March 21, 1971), 3. Mr. Gass's article is devoted primarily to the life and work of Julian Brun (1886-1942) but analyzes in depth the latter's critical assessment of Żeromski and Sieńkiewicz, two literary contemporaries. In contrasting their respective literary outputs in Marxist terms, Brun, writing in jail in 1926, concluded that while Stefan Żeromski had the qualities of a "national prophet in the fullest sense of that romantic term," Sieńkiewicz merely served to reaffirm the values and aspirations of the dominant petty bourgeoisie. At the same time, however, Brun also criticized Żeromski for "idealism," and for rejecting class struggle as a factor of social progress.

Schools and Students

War II and the period of occupation enable you to answer the question: What is more worthy in men, the saving of one's own life or that of human dignity?

The students in Katowice (47 out of 101 taking the test in one school) preferred to answer the first question and in their responses most of them cited the works of Henryk Sieńkiewicz. In the Opole district the most favored examination question read very much like the most favored question in Katowice: "Which literary period in our thousand-year history is the closest to your heart and do you value the most? With which works of that period do you feel most intimately related?"

In the Lodz school district a total of 5,500 secondary general education school graduates took the *matura* examinations in 1966 and among the 3 choices the question favored, by a slight margin, read as follows: "How is the struggle of Poles against German aggression and brutality in the course of our thousand-year long history portrayed in the literature of the XIX and XX Century?" And, again, the most specific references dealt with the works of Sieńkiewicz.

In the Rzeszów school district the 3 choices were:

1. What was the significance of Sieńkiewicz to the Polish society of his time and what elements of his work have played a decisive role in determining his lasting position in our literature?
2. What contribution was made by the writers of the period of Renaissance and Enlightenment toward the development of secular culture in Poland?
3. Professor Sonnenbruch and Antoni Kossecki faced the Court charged with crimes against humanity—state the charges and attempt a defense.

As could be expected by now, most responses were to question No. 1. The questions and responses reviewed point to a rather limited range of literary knowledge and interest. The constant references to the "thousand-year history" were a function of the fact that 1966 was the year of the Millennium celebrations. It also marked the 50th anniversary of the death of Henryk Sieńkiewicz. One *kuratorium* official, however, tried to put the blame for the limited literary knowledge and interests of the *matura* students on the restricted range of readings to which they are exposed in the course of their lyceum studies. In an interview he said:

> You cannot really blame the students although the natural tendency is, of course, to put the blame on their shoulders. Take, for example, the textbook from which they are taught. It is titled *Contemporary Literature* (*Literatura współczesna*). You open the chapter dealing with the literature of People's Poland and what do you get, really? Only snatches of selections, chosen for no apparent reason, a little bit of this and a little bit of that. Some of our most prominent writers, such as Iwaszkiewicz, Jastruń, Przyboś, Różewicz, Putramant, Czeszko, Brandys, Breza, Słonimski are represented by fragments without explanations.

Q. What about foreign literature?

A. Well, open the chapter entitled "Foreign Literature." You have there again only profiles: a little bit from Mayakovsky, a little bit from Yesenin, Svetlov, and from contemporary Western literature a little bit from Apollinaire, Paul Eluard, Louis Aragon, Bertolt Brecht, and that's all—all writers more or less of the Left. Apollinaire perhaps because he was of Polish origin and we take special pride in him. Not a word about or from Hemingway, Steinbeck or Sartre. When I visit a literature class in a school I can sense the sterility although the teacher usually tries hard to make a good impression. It is normally easy for them to deal with excerpts of literary works, including excerpts from novels (contemporary novels such as those by Andrzejewski) assigned outside of the official text.

Q. Would this be the only explanation of why students tend to pick the kind of topics they do?

A. Hell, no. The questions invited stereotyped responses. And you know what? I took my own *matura* examinations one year before the war, in 1938, and the questions asked now —except for slight variations—do not differ from the type of questions asked then. What we are dealing with here is tradition and educational inertia. There is a whole set of unchanging standard questions, a steady repertoire: the origins of Polish literature, the works of specific classic au-

284

thors, romantic literature and, of course, Mickiewicz's "Ode to Youth" (*Oda do młodości*), something about contemporary literature.

Q. You would say then that the difficulties begin in the classroom, with the curriculum?

A. Definitely. There is fear of innovation and this is so on all levels. Some among us are not too certain as to the validity of innovative ideas and are afraid to experiment. The student can go through lyceum, pass all his examinations and never have read anything by such contemporary poets as Tuwin or Broniewski although they happen to be otherwise very popular. Partially it is because we are trying to fit too much diversity into a limited program schedule and we must leave out the treatment in depth of many worthwhile areas. I could, if I want, defend the results although it pains me personally. The student faced with required readings has little time left for independent exploration. Personally, I believe that we have placed too much emphasis already on the so-called wartime literature. We are now in the end of the second decade of Socialist construction and we have an appropriate literature but precious little of it has sifted down to the classroom.

Sentiments similar to the above were expressed by various other persons in the course of interviews, as well as in commentaries appearing periodically in the press, especially literary journals. But both teachers and school administrators seem reluctant to exercise bold initiative or to engage in innovative experiments. They often feel caught in a web of rules, regulations, and educational tradition and let it go at that, taking the path of least resistance. One senses a fear, an uncertainty related to attempts to break out and away from the established pattern. As a result, much in the curriculum remains unchanged despite formal reform measures. The latter aim at the general and administrative-organizational alteration of the educational structure, but seldom challenge the substance of the educational process. Many recognize the need for substantive curriculum revisions. Many realize that from the point of view of the system such revisions must be made. At the same time, however, it seems as if the system itself inhibits attempts at substantive reform.

Schools and Students

Some observers blame the sterility of the secondary school curriculum on the lack of close, intimate contacts between the institutions of higher learning and those working in the secondary school system. Unless specifically invited or approached, a university professor would scarcely think of visiting a secondary school or talking on a basis of equality with a secondary school teacher. Before World War II there were many young academicians in the large metropolitan centers, brilliant young university "docents" and assistants who were, however, of the "wrong" ethnic, religious, or social background. For such reasons, they had limited chances for advancement within the then existing academic personnel structure and were forced to seek supplementary employment in secondary schools. By so doing they served as a direct link between the intellectual environment of the universities and the hardworking secondary school teachers. There are no similar links at the present and, moreover, there is a formal rule—selectively applied to be sure—against the maintenance by a single individual of parallel employment.

Caught in such working conditions and circumstances, 5 percent of secondary general education teachers with university education resigned from their posts within the last few years. They are aided in their decisions by a remuneration system which allows teachers in vocational schools a monetary premium of somewhere between 10 and 15 percent above the base salary for rank and tenure but denies the same to those working in the more prestigious general education lyceums. Reacting to the ongoing press discussion on educational problems, one reader was led to write: "In our school system a new learning program is often introduced only to discover that there is no one capable of undertaking that program's realization."[27]

The gap between educational plans and their realization is, in part, due to a strict division of labor which separates the planner from the program executor, the classroom teacher. As one secondary school teacher said in an interview:

[27] As cited, Świecki, op.cit., p. 3.

Schools and Students

The educational authorities tend to ignore the opinions and suggestions of practicing, working teachers. The teacher is faced with programs and curricula changes in the shaping of which he had no part. The general press is usually poorly informed about educational problems or approaches these rather reluctantly.

Q. What about the teachers themselves?

A. Within the Teachers' Union there is some discussion and one frequently can hear complaints. One can also read about it in the educational press. The problem is that much of the debate takes place on a very specialized plane and in an obscure professional jargon, and thus leaves the general public cold.

Q. How would you explain then the public discussion following the *matura* examinations?

A. Such discussion takes place almost every year at this time. Following *matura* examinations many people on the educational sidelines suddenly discover what everybody actively engaged in teaching has known all along. That is, the examination topics and questions are ill chosen, and the way they are phrased and formulated invite superficial and shallow responses. Our youth simply is unfamiliar with the basic facts of our own literary history, is ignorant of contemporary literature—oh, you come across some student now and then who has a lively, natural interest of his own and not infrequently such interest will be stifled by the weight of the existing curriculum requirements. Usually, students are not trained to think independently. In addition, in the provincial schools there is provincialism in language and style, and they don't know how to spell.

Q. Isn't this the usual complaint, heard from every generation of educators, everywhere?

A. I don't know. One would expect from a secondary school student some ability for independent thinking, an ability to draw conclusions, handle effectively a variety of opposing opinions. We theoretically abhor cramming, memorization. We stress intelligence and condemn what we popularly call "*kujonie*," hammering in. However, what this results in is that the student gets the idea that one does not necessarily have to read a particular novel in order to be able to bluff about it, that glittering phrases somehow can take the place of daily hard work and application. The examination questions themselves, as you have seen, invite empty phrases rather than a show of honest, earnest learning and knowledge. I think that the examinations favor the weakest and most shallow among the students but do not do justice to the good students and their teachers. And, of course, it is the complaints from the weak students that you hear most frequently. As a teacher of Polish literature I feel terrible about it all.

Many complain of a lack of solid preparation, a lack of good study habits and industry among the present generation of secondary school students. Some observers even draw the perhaps exaggerated conclusion that "*matura*-holders display in their entrance examinations to institutions of higher learning an inability to handle problems—an inability unworthy even of a good elementary school student."[28]

The tendency among the young to avoid topics dealing with the current scene, modern history, or ideology may be a reaction to the overdose they receive of these topics. The continuous flow of ideological strictures, of patriotic speeches, narratives of war, suffering, and heroism may turn counterproductive in its effects on the audience for whom it is designed, the youth. A young girl from Zakopane complained to the editors of *Polityka* shortly after having taken and passed her *matura* examinations:

> To judge by the program, what is a secondary school student expected to know from contemporary literature? He is expected to know *Ashes and Diamonds (Popiół i diament)*, *The Germans (Niemców)*, *Medallions (Medaliony)* and a few other works dealing with the war. . . . Let's have a glance at contemporary Polish literature. The literature written after the war is concerned overwhelmingly with the war and war-related human experiences. . . . Even young writers write about the war. Why?[29]

The answer to the question "Why?" rests, of course, with the quality of the particular experience. The war has left lasting, overpowering impressions and effects on all those

[28] *Ibid.*
[29] Barbara Iwa, "Matura z polskiego," Letter to the Editor, *Polityka*, Warsaw, Vol. x, No. 31 (491) (July 1966), 1.

who suffered through it, however young they were at the time. There is a constant inner need to refer to that experience. To those who lived through the war, the years 1939-1945 are still fresh in their memories, but to the secondary student in the last half of the 1960's, born after the war's end, those years are "old hat" and boring if referred to over and over again. Many show fatigue from overexposure to war-related literature, films, speeches, memoirs, celebrations, commemorations, and the like. Consequently, the young may feel a need to retreat, escape into the less gory, less complicated, more tranquil and romantic times of the heroes populating Sieńkiewicz's swashbuckling novels.

It is not only escape into the literature of a more distant past that youth seeks. Colonel Janusz Przymanowski complained that the average young Pole sometimes knows more of the history of antiquity than he does of his own nation's recent past, that he is more interested in the events which took place on the shores of the Mediterranean many centuries back (events such as portrayed in Sieńkiewicz's famous *Quo Vadis?*) than he is in the events which happened not long ago on the shores of the Baltic Sea.[30]

It would almost appear though as if, to many of the current crop of secondary school students, the history of Poland itself began only with the emergence of People's Poland. In a gathering of graduating lyceum students which I attended, only 2 (out of 20 present) indicated any significant knowledge of the history of pre-World War II Poland. One of the 2 had returned relatively recently with his family from exile in the West and the other indicated a family history of close ties with the prewar regime (i.e., the father was a colonel in the prewar army who was killed during the war while commanding a guerrilla unit of the anti-Communist Home Army, *Armia Krajowa*, A.K., and the mother served a jail sentence during the Stalinist period). When questioned, the group of students also betrayed an ignorance of the history of the Polish labor movement, the Socialist

[30] Col. Janusz Przymanowski, "Ściśle jawne: Parę taktów takyki," *Życie Warszawy* (November 13-14, 1966), 3.

movement, or that of Polish Communism. Although the Polish Socialist Party (*Polska Partia Socjalistyczna*, PPS) constituted one of the two major components establishing the Polish United Workers' Party at the Unity Congress of 1948, none of the 20 students present had ever heard of the PPS and none knew that Józef Cyrankiewicz, the long-time Prime Minister (and for a time after the 1971 leadership re-shuffle, Chairman of the Council of State—equivalent to the post of ceremonial president), was one of the prewar leaders of that Party. Nor did they hear of the prewar cooperative housing developments in the Żoliborz suburb of Warsaw, es-tablished by the Socialists and named after the writer Stefan Żeromski's visionary novel, *Glass Houses*. Intellectually close to the Socialists, frequently attacked by the Right-wing and the clergy, Żeromski's *Glass Houses* came to symbolize the dream of a bright Polish future, in contrast to the "leproid provincial towns and musty little villages." Yet the graduat-ing lyceum students not only did not know of the prewar cooperative houses in Żoliborz but also indicated some in-difference to Żeromski as a writer and to the whole web of emotional and intellectual images conjured up by his name and associated symbols. These symbols, however, the titles of Żeromski's novels (*Glass Houses, Spring's Eve*), are often referred to as part of the intellectual, spiritual, and native-progressive tradition to which the present system fell heir. This is not to say that the students I talked with were not familiar with Żeromski or his works—only that there was no indication that they lend the subject any special emotional significance, that his name attached to school buildings and streets has or should have any special meaning in a Socialist Poland. In fact, these students showed much greater ani-mation when we later switched the discussion to the "Beatles."

Similarly, names of prewar Communist Party leaders drew blanks as did other details of the history of the prewar Polish Communist Party.

In a prize winning book on citizenship and modern war-fare, army Majors Marian Jurek and Edward Skrzypkowski

290

join in the complaint that, in character education, the street, rather than the school, exercises a greater impact on the formation of youth:

> They impress one another with desires which are shockingly private in nature. They emulate models and life styles which are related to the consumption of material goods; they want money, a car, clothing, a place of their own. A "regular fellow" is one who can impress his peers with a new pair of shoes and a new tie—especially those within the age group of 14-18, students of secondary schools, and especially those attending lyceums of general education.[31]

At the height of the celebrations commemorating the 20th anniversary of the founding of the Polish People's Army, i.e., at a time when the exploits of the army were extolled and publicized, a research team sponsored by the Public Opinion Research Center of Polish Radio found, after administering a questionnaire (in 1963) to a national sample of young *matura*-holders, that they rate the significance of the battle at Monte Cassino in Italy higher than the participation of the Polish Army, alongside the Soviet Army, in the capture of Berlin. From the system's point of view, the latter is far more important since it underlines the historical and political meaning of the battles and victories on the Eastern Front and the alliance with the Soviet Union, factors which led to the eventual establishment of People's Poland. On the other hand, the Polish army units engaged in the capture of the monastery atop Monte Cassino were under the command of the Polish Government-in-Exile in London which fought alongside the Western Allies. It is only recently that the exploits of Polish troops fighting in the West (e.g., in the air defense of Great Britain, at Tobruk, in the suburbs of Falaise, etc.) as well as the exploits of the London-directed underground Home Army (*Armia*

[31] Marian Jurek and Edward Skrzypkowski, *Konfrontacje: Tradycjonalizm a współczesność w wychowaniu wojskowym* (Warsaw: Ministry of National Defense, MON, 1965), pp. 63-64.

Krajowa, A.K.) are given honorable mention. Only relatively recently has the 1944 battle of Monte Cassino, which opened the road to Rome, received homage in articles and song. But in 1963, at the time when the survey mentioned was conducted, strong emphasis was still given primarily to the Polish People's Army which was formed on Soviet soil in 1943 and which fought in the battles of Lenino, the Warsaw suburb of Praga, the crossing of the Nysa River, the Pomeranian Line, as well as Berlin. Instead of emphasizing the activities of the A.K.—which continued illegally for some time after People's Poland was established—official stress was given to the activities of the Left-wing underground forces, and primarily those of the A.L. (The People's Army, *Armia Ludowa*). The choice of Monte Cassino over Berlin is therefore of enormous significance. Yet, in 1963, 60.7 percent of the *matura*-holders gave greater importance to the former. Only 14.8 percent thought that the capture of the German capital was of greater importance in the history of Polish warfare. Similarly, when the respondents were asked to rate the importance of various Polish combat heroes, most, while choosing the most celebrated military figure of the Polish People's Army, the late General Karol Świerczewski ("Walter")—after whom many schools, including the Army's General Staff Academy, factories, and city streets are presently named[32]—could not name a single

[32] Karol Świerczewski, a young Warsaw metal factory apprentice during World War I, was evacuated with the other workers of the plant when the Czarist armies retreated from Poland. Caught in the revolutionary upheaval, he joined the Red Guards and the Communist Party. Having graduated from the Frunze Military Academy in Moscow in 1927, he went on to pursue an apparently successful military career, at the same time serving as a Comintern operative. Under the alias of "Walter" and with the rank of general, Świerczewski was active in the Spanish Civil War, in command, first, of a French-Belgian Volunteer Brigade and, later, of "Division A" which included among other international volunteer units the XIII Polish International Brigade, named after the hero of the Paris Commune, Jarosław Dąbrowski. Following the defeat of the loyalists, Świerczewski returned to Moscow where he joined his *alma mater*, the Frunze Academy, as a Senior Lecturer. After the German invasion of the USSR, he was assigned to a variety of command posts, both at the front and in the

292

other military personage, living or dead, of current Polish history. Instead, following the name of General Świerczewski, the respondents mentioned fighting men of Poland's distant past or fictional heroes from Henryk Sieńkiewicz's

---

rear. Among the latter assignments was that of commander of an Infantry Officers' Training School in the Siberian Military District. When the original Polish army units in the USSR, under the leadership of General Anders, left the Soviet Union to fight at the side of the Western Allies, the Soviet government, in 1943, decided to organize on Soviet soil Polish military units, presumably "loyal" to *its* cause, from among the Polish war refugees and prisoners of war (of the September 1939 campaign) left behind by Anders. General Świerczewski was given the task of assisting in the formation of these units, and, eventually, took command of the now celebrated Second Polish Army in the USSR which fought at the side of the Soviet Red Army and participated in the liberation of part of Czechoslovakia from the Germans. At the same time he was also active in organizing the political organizations which were to form the future cadre base of the Communist regime in Poland. While most of the Polish Communists who found themselves in the USSR were there as a result of the war, others had been there earlier. For many, the Soviet decision to "activate" these elements meant release from prison or camp where they had been interned as suspected and "unreliable" foreigners. Świerczewski was among the founders of the Central Bureau of Polish Communists in the USSR and after joining the reconstituted Polish Communist Party (now officially renamed Polish Workers' Party—*Polska Partia Robotnicza*, PPR, since the original CP was liquidated by order of the Comintern in the thirties), he became a member of its Central Committee and of the Land National Council, the forerunner of the first postwar *Sejm*. After the war, Świerczewski remained in Poland and in uniform, serving consecutively as Inspector of the Polish People's Army, as commander of the Poznań Military District, as head of the Polish military delegation to the International Control Commission in Berlin, and in 1946 as Deputy Minister of Defense. That year he also visited the Western Hemisphere, including the United States and Canada, where he tried to mobilize Polish ethnic support for the cause of People's Poland. A deputy to the first postwar parliament (the so-called Constitutional *Sejm*, since it adopted the basic laws of People's Poland), he served on its Military Affairs Committee. During an inspection tour of border garrisons on behalf of the Committee, Świerczewski was ambushed and killed on March 28, 1947, by Ukrainian nationalist partisans. Posthumously decorated with the highest order of People's Poland he is interned in an imposing mausoleum along the Avenue of the Meritorious at the Powązki Cemetery in Warsaw. His book on the Spanish Civil War (*In the Battles for Spain's Freedom*), originally written in Russian, appeared in Warsaw in 1970 in a Polish trans. See *Za Wolność i Lud,* organ of the Union of Fight-

historical novels, e.g., Zybszko from Bogdańc, Wołodyjow-ski, Skrzetuski, etc.[33]

Lest the high rating given the battle of Monte Cassino be interpreted as an expression of a political view in favor of the opposition among the secondary school graduates, it should be pointed out that many bemoan modern youth's ignorance of other exploits of the Polish armed forces in the West and of the battles marking the campaign of September 1939 (except for the defense of Westerplatte of which a dramatized film account was recently released, the Hel Peninsula, the battle on the Bzura River, or the defense of Warsaw). The names of military commanders who distinguished themselves in the uneven battles of September 1939 are completely unknown to the young.[34] Nor are they familiar with the exploits of the underground forces other than those of the People's Army, the People's Guard (Socialists), the Peasant Battalions (Peasants' Alliance). Some of this ignorance is due, no doubt, to the past efforts on the part of the regime, particularly during the Stalinist period, which either frowned upon or else delegated into a "memory hole" the activities of the old opposition. Only a few acts by the Home Army, for example the assassination of the German SS General Kutschera, received the publicity given the exploits of the Left during the occupation. The Warsaw Uprising of August 1944, although staged by the A.K., is portrayed as a joint popular effort involving the entire political spectrum and all underground forces. But even in accounts of that uprising special emphasis is given the deeds of the relatively few People's Army (A.L.) units as well as to the futile attempts of isolated small detachments of the regular Polish People's Army—at that time already in control, with the Soviet Red Army, of the eastern banks of the Vistula River (across from Warsaw in the Praga suburb)—to cross

---

ers for Freedom and Democracy, ZBoWiD, Warsaw, No. 6 (290) (March 16-31, 1967), 1, 10-11, for details of Świerczewski's ("Walter's") life.

[33] Jurek and Skrzypkowski, *op.cit.*, p. 80.

[34] Przymanowski, *op.cit.*, p. 3.

the river in order to aid the embattled underground forces. Why the regular Soviet army units themselves did not force the river until the uprising was over, the rebels and the civilian population evacuated into camps, and the city systematically destroyed by the German troops is never explained nor is the fact even mentioned.

Under the new reform programs the students, especially of senior secondary school grades, were to be given greater initiative for individual study. Junior grade students were to be relieved from the hitherto heavy burden of homework and become involved in group projects under the guidance of a teacher. However, often the students were given tasks to solve without being told how to solve them, nor the underlying theoretical principles of a given assignment.

Teachers, as we have seen, are not too anxious to introduce experiments and innovations of their own even though the quality of the work in the classroom often depends on the teacher's willingness to use imagination, initiative, or simply extra effort. However, many teachers in their enthusiasm to prove successful implementation of "polytechnization" and the introduction of vocationally oriented courses in schools of general education, assigned to the students work projects which the latter found hard to complete on their own. As a result, some parents of means turned to professional help so that their daughters might produce assignments on time: needlework, sweaters, skirts, and dresses. The final product of these projects turned out to be of such high quality that the *kuratorium* in Lublin arranged a permanent exhibit of what it assumed to be the students' own accomplishments in the area of vocational education.[35] Parents whose sons and daughters had more traditionally oriented teachers, or teachers less eager to meet the goals of "polytechnization," found the school year less expensive, but their children's names were not featured as exhibitors at the *kuratorium* display.

Despite the new emphasis on the physical sciences and

[35] BAR, "Koniec roku," *Kamena*, Lublin, Vol. xxxiii, No. 12 (345) (June 30, 1966), 10.

mathematics, the final examination results in these fields turned out to be far from satisfactory. In fact, according to knowledgeable informants, the lowest examination scores were obtained in such subjects as physics, chemistry, and mathematics. In one oral examination in chemistry it developed that students did not know that such symbols as alpha and beta, for example, were derived from the Greek alphabet.

Courses in civics and defense preparedness (formerly known as military preparedness) are supposed to fill the gap in the "patriotic knowledge" of the secondary school student of general education. Similarly, the stress on polytechnization is supposed to provide the student with some skills and a general appreciation for the values of labor. However, Majors Jurek and Skrzypkowski agree with the statement they cite from *Man and the Technique of Warfare* by T. Nowacki and T. Pióro: "We could not in all honesty and with a full sense of responsibility entrust to the graduate of today's secondary school even the smallest line of defense. These graduates, equipped as they are with theoretical knowledge, are incapable of building even the most primitive things. . . . We would even doubt their capability of erecting a decent pig sty."[36]

The student of the secondary school of general education may not have learned how to erect a pig sty, but his skill in this direction is not tested when he comes up for his *matura*. However, many fail in the areas in which they are tested, and most failures occur, as indicated, in the exact and physical sciences. Failure in a single subject disqualifies a student from the *matura*. However, he may request a make-up examination in the area in which he did not pass the first time. Any such reexamination must take place within a 3-year period following regular school attendance.

The student who fails in his attempt to obtain a *matura* the first time may opt for one more year of regular school attendance. However, a student who failed only one subject (e.g., mathematics) would seldom choose this avenue since

[36] Jurek and Skrzypkowski, *op.cit.*, p. 85.

it would necessitate repetition of the complete course load. But without a *matura* he is prevented from even applying to any institution of higher learning. Consequently, most students who fail any portion of a *matura* examination join the labor force hoping somehow to remedy their scholastic deficiency through tutorials, evening cram courses, or some other remedial process. Many students who fail at the first try are absorbed into the labor market, however, and never attempt reexamination or renew their interest after the 3-year deadline. In the latter case, reexamination involves special pleading and intervention with the appropriate school authorities, including the Ministry of Education and Higher Learning, and is rarely, if ever, successful.

For those who have succeeded in all tests and have been granted the *matura*, the period immediately following June 20 is one of excitement and exhilaration. In certain localities the presentation of the *matura*-certificates acquires the dimensions of communitywide festivities. In Warsaw since 1966, the graduates of the city's lyceums, *technikums*, and those who complete the terminal grades of the various vocational schools (in 1966 there was a total of over 30,000) gather at the central Theater Square, facing the imposing Grand Theater, at the base of "The Nike," the monument erected to honor the Heroes of Warsaw. Usually the occasion is set for June 23 with the participation of representatives of the Warsaw military garrison, the Polish United Workers' Party (PZPR), the Warsaw National Council, the Front of National Unity (FJN), the *kuratorium*. Amidst speeches and song and music and the recitation of poetry, the outstanding 80 lyceum graduates are presented with their Certificates of Maturity (the cherished *matura*), and special medals for good work and social activism are awarded to some of the graduates. In 1966 the medals were specially cast Youth Millennium Medals.[37]

Even before the *maturas* are formally handed out, as soon as the last examination is over, a seemingly unending series of "*matura* balls" and parties begins for the graduates. Some

[37] *Express Wieczorny*, Warsaw (June 20, 1966).

of these are formal, others informal. Teachers are usually required to attend the former and for most students this is the first (and last) occasion on which they meet socially with their mentors. This is also the first time they are allowed on the school premises (where the formal balls take place, usually in the gymnastic hall) in "civilian" attire (the girls in evening gowns, the boys in dark suits, white shirt and tie) rather than in the obligatory school uniform—navy blue (white collars for the girls) with the number of the respective lyceum on a shield sewn to the left sleeve. These uniforms and shields were instituted for the secondary school system during the 1930's to enable the authorities to better police the students during off-school hours. Students caught out of uniform or minus the identifying lyceum number are subject to disciplinary punishment. Since tradition and administrative measures die hard, the uniforms and numbers were never rescinded under the new political system although students resent them and parents complain of the cost they must bear (for uniforms, shields, special caps, etc.).

I attended the ball which took place in 1966 in one of the oldest and most prestigious lyceums in Warsaw, No. 27 (named after Czacki). It was a very chic affair indeed, the young celebrants addressed each other formally, the young boys bowed and kissed the young ladies' hands before and after each dance—in traditional Polish fashion, indicating gratitude and chivalry. Some boys not only bowed and kissed hands but also clicked their heels when bowing. The music was loud and "big beat" and the couples danced with a great deal of enthusiasm and energy. Among the dances was a foxtrot-type arrangement to the tune of *Ave Maria* and one that began with the sounding of taps—both popular at the time among the young on the European continent. Many of those in attendance smoked cigarettes and some vodka was consumed in corners, hallways, and on the stairs.

Possession of the *matura* does not mean that the graduate is informed of the specific scores he has obtained during

298

the examinations. These are revealed only upon request and at the discretion of the lyceum director. However, these scores play a certain role in admitting a lyceum graduate, provided he has passed all entrance examinations and other requirements, to an institution of higher learning, especially one of prestige. It is often not until October that some *matura*-holders learn whether they were admitted to the institution of higher learning of their choice. As a rule, only every third lyceum graduate is fortunate enough to be admitted to the institution of higher learning of first preference. The ratio is even less favorable with respect to admissions to the University of Warsaw or the Jagiellonian University of Cracow.

In any event, following the postexamination celebrations and the awarding of the certificates, many begin to worry in earnest about the future. The entrance examinations to institutions of higher learning follow immediately on the heels of the *matura* examinations. Those who failed the entrance examinations or passed but for some reasons are denied admission to the postsecondary educational establishment to which they have applied, have a second chance during the month of August when they may compete for the remaining vacancies following the June examinations. In 1966-1967 even the low-prestige *Studium Nauczycielskie* (SN type of schools of teachers' education) found themselves with more applicants than they could physically handle. As a consequence, many students—*matura* certificates in hand—faced the prospect of entering the job market, most often against their will, to compete for jobs in industry or in administration. In competing for the former they are likely to lose out to the graduates of the vocational *technikums* or even to the graduates of the *basic* vocational schools (who are also younger). In seeking employment in administration, not infrequently they face the tough competition of university trained applicants. Many of them, therefore, settle for low-paying jobs in the service industries or for clerical positions in offices. The able-bodied male *matura-*

holder who is unsuccessful in gaining entrance to an institution of higher learning faces the prospect of service in the armed forces.

The summer of graduation from a secondary school of general education is not, in the final analysis, one of the most pleasant in the life of the Pole who has just been formally certified as a member of the new intelligentsia. It is a trying period indeed. Many, no doubt, carry psychological scars derived from this experience throughout their lives and are bitter. Some feel cheated of often undefined benefits they had expected. If, in the end, they have not really internalized the values that the system wants to implant, the post-*matura* experience of some further serves to prevent their involvement in the system's lofty hopes, goals, and values, or even identification with it.

Some graduates who did not gain entrance to an institution of higher learning will try again in the following years but with diminishing chances. If lucky, some of those left out at the first try eventually will gain admission to a teachers' training college—if not as a regular student, because of the restriction on age, perhaps as an enrollee in one of the latter's numerous extension divisions. The older entrant, with a bit more experience, and perhaps a bit more toned down or resigned, is also grateful for the new chance of obtaining professional status. It is perhaps this factor which makes the older person entering the teaching profession more accommodative to the system's demands.

Change and Education: Expectations and Reality

Despite the emphasis on polytechnization and vocationalism, some economic planners and managers in major industrial enterprises maintain that the school system does not prepare its graduates for the new industrial economy. On the other hand, the charge is often heard that the economy and those in charge fail to utilize fully the existing educational and scientific potential.[38]

[38] Bogdan Gotowski, "Nauka i potrzeby kraju," *Życie Warszawy*, Warsaw (September 26, 1966), 3.

Schools and Students

It is quite possible, even likely, that the educational system, despite periodic reforms, lags behind the new industrial and technological tempo. In the immediate post-World War II years, the task facing the educational system was to replenish the ranks of the educated lost or destroyed during the war. The school system thus became inured to a task geared to established educational traditions. Schools now find it difficult to shift gears. In many instances existing school systems are simply not equipped in terms of physical facilities, personnel, or educational tradition to meet new socioeconomic and political expectations. The secondary schools have a surplus of teachers trained in philosophy and the humanities (disciplines of traditional prestige) and not enough in the physical sciences or in vocational subjects.[39]

In spite of their inadequacies, teachers feel compelled to meet the system's demands. Often they try to cover up their own lack of preparation by falling back on "empty talk," slogans. Such protective devices are used especially in classes designed to transmit the sociopolitical and ideological outlook of the new system. Not having an answer of his own to the many questions raised, or not sure as to the righteousness of the cause he is called upon to promulgate, the teacher often allows student-activists to take over. He may start a discussion in citizenship by tossing out a question such as "What is a People's Government?" and then sit back and see how and in what direction the discussion develops, interfering only now and then in the process.

Wincenty Okoń contends that "talk is grossly abused and misused" and that it frequently "has little value as far as the transmission of actual knowledge is concerned."[40] The student is quick to sense the teacher's lack of preparation or subject-matter knowledge, or his lack of commitment. To

[39] Relative to the surplus of philosophy teachers at the secondary school level, see letter to the editor by Wit Drapich, Director of the Department of University and Economic Studies, in *Polityka*, Warsaw, Vol. x, No. 31 (491) (July 30, 1966). 5.

[40] Wincenty Okoń, *Proces nauczania* (Warsaw: Państwowe Zakłady Wydawnictw Szkolnych for the Institute of Pedagogy, 5th edn., 1965), pp. 105-06.

compensate for their own deficiencies teachers frequently fall back on the traditional instructional device of reading from a textbook, the required text or some other, supposedly unknown to the students, or use "prefabricated lessons" prepared by the *kuratoria* as samples, or lecture from old notes accumulated from their own student days or from casually attended lectures. These devices, however, tend to induce in the student audience a state of "mental laziness," as Okoń points out, or sheer intellectual apathy. Not infrequently, as Kozakiewicz has shown, the modern student knows more about a certain subject than his teacher and such student superiority has a demoralizing effect on the instructor's self-esteem.[41]

"Character education," including "political-ideological education," suffers most in the process because the tendency is to resort to propaganda and sloganeering rather than to undertake serious attempts toward in-depth education and the remolding of the student's personality. As Dr. Kozakiewicz writes elsewhere:

> The aim of Socialist education is to create a new positive personality. . . . Whereas propaganda attempts to dictate to the person what he is to think about a given subject without basically altering his personality, political education ought to teach him how to think. . . . Socialist political education aims at forming the young person's mind, his will and his moral style so that he may become aware of the true and real destiny of his epoch and his own life—so that he may live and act according to that awareness.[42]

The above, however, assumes ideal conditions and expresses hopes. The teacher himself is left without concrete guidelines as to how to proceed with his character molding

[41] Mikołaj Kozakiewicz, "Alergia nauczycielskiego zawodu," *Fakty i Myśli*, organ of Executive Board of the Association of Freethinkers and Atheists, Bydgoszcz, Vol. ix, No. 21 (193) (November 1-15, 1966), 1, 6-7.

[42] Mikołaj Kozakiewicz, *Niezbadane ścieżki wychowania* (Warsaw: Nasza Księgarnia, 1964), pp. 263-65.

tasks. Moreover, he is himself not always fully socialized into the values and norms of the ideal Socialist personality and character type. The tendency, therefore, is to mark educational time, e.g., to follow routine instructions from above, as well as educational tradition.

Similarly, the major thrust of the reform debate concerned technical and administrative innovations, e.g., whether to adopt a 12-grade public school system with the "breaking point" in the direction of secondary education or of work at the 9th grade, as advocated by Professor Marian Falski,[43] or to follow the recommendation by the Polish Teachers' Union which called for a 9-grade elementary school with an additional 3-grade educational superstructure, or assimilate the East German model of 10-year compulsory education with a parallel system of 12-grade schools for those aiming for higher education. The debate came to a halt when the 7th Plenum of the Central Committee of the Polish United Workers' Party adopted the reform program which was subsequently accepted by the *Sejm* (parliament) and introduced (partially, to be sure) during academic year 1966-1967. This was the system of 8-grade elementary education and 4-grade general secondary education. Seldom did the reform debate indicate a real concern for substantive radical reformation of the school system aside from vague and general statements on the needs to adjust the educational system to the new sociopolitical system or the changing economy. As Wincenty Okoń points out: "The reform . . . did not relatively change much in the basic Polish school model."[44]

Too late to have any effect on the educational reforms which were already being instituted at the time, but implying criticism of the reform and dissatisfaction with educational plans which avoid tackling some of the basic problems, were some of the statements voiced on the second day of the Congress of Polish Culture in the fall of 1966.

[43] See Marian Falski, *Aktualne zagadnienia ustrojowo-organizacyjne szkolnictwa polskiego.* (Wrocław: Zakład im. Ossolińskich, 1957).
[44] Okoń, *op.cit.*, p. 38.

Some of the statements aimed at the need to radically rethink and transform some of the basic philosophical and organizational assumptions of the Polish educational system. Other statements concerned pleas for special disciplinary and academic interests. Most, to be sure, were general and rhetorical rather than specific in nature.

The boldest statements were made by the eminent Polish sociologist, Professor Jan Szczepański, the historian of Polish literature, Professor Jan Zygmunt Jakubowski, and the archeologist, Professor Zdzisław Rajewski. Dr. Szczepański, a member of the Polish Academy of Sciences, former *Rektor* of the University at Lodz, former *Sejm* deputy (non-Party), and, at the time, head of the Basic Sociological Research Section of the Academy's Institute of Philosophy and Sociology,[45] argued:

(1) Gifted students at all levels of the educational system ought to be surrounded with special care and conditions should be created so that such students may become involved, to a greater extent than presently practiced, in independent study and research facilitating intellectual growth; this would mean that some of the traditionally accepted teaching tools must be reexamined and new ones, if necessary, adopted.

(2) Secondary education must become universal in People's Poland rather than continue to be elitist; this means that serious attention must be given to the economic, educational, and personnel problems of the educational enterprise.

[45] Professor Jan Szczepański became director of the Institute of Philosophy and Sociology of the Polish Academy of Sciences following the upheaval of spring 1968 and the ensuing major personnel changes in various institutions of the system. The post of director had been previously occupied by Professor Adam Schaff, at the time also a member of the Central Committee of the Polish United Workers' Party. Professor Szczepański, the last living student of Florian Znaniecki, was elected to the presidency of the International Sociological Association at the annual Congress in Evian, France, in 1966 and he served in that post until 1970. The post-Gomułka leadership appointed him to direct a "Committee of Experts" whose task it is to analyze critically the state of Polish education.

(3) There should be greater coordination than presently exists between the results obtained from social science research efforts and the cultural policies adopted and promulgated by the authorities responsible for the activities in the areas of culture and education.

(4) Since language forms the basis of national culture, greater care should be given to the development of language skills and greater care to the uses of language not only in the schools but also in the media of mass communication.[46]

Professor Jan Zygmunt Jakubowski, chairman of the Department for the History of Polish Literature at Warsaw University, repeated the call for closer links between institutions of higher learning, especially the universities, and the lower level educational institutions, particularly secondary schools of general education. He also came forth with a specific proposal that secondary school teachers be given academic and scientific status (which would, of course, involve a commensurate pay scale) and that personnel exchange programs be established so that university personnel, especially of junior rank, could teach on the secondary level and, in return, secondary school teachers could be drawn into academic activities, including scholarly research.[47]

Professor Zdzisław Rajewski, an archeologist of the Institute for the History of Material Culture of the Polish Academy of Sciences, and director of the State Archeological Museum in Warsaw, advocated the organization of educational cadres for the actual penetration of the provinces and rural areas, the small towns and villages which presently are in a state of educational and cultural deficiency.[48]

Other statements at the same session of the Congress, though routine in character, were nevertheless interesting and revealing. Thus, for example, the *Rektor* of Warsaw

[46] As reported in *Polityka*, Warsaw, Vol. x, No. 45 (505) (November 5, 1966), 1.
[47] *Ibid.*   [48] *Ibid.*

University, the mathematician Professor Stanisław Turski, spoke of the closer links between the universities and society at large in the past and asked for the reestablishment of the system of popular public university lectures open to all. The *Pro-Rektor* of the Higher State School for Theater and Film Arts (the "Leon Schiller School"), Professor Stanisław Wohl, proposed the formation of a special interdepartmental and interministerial commission for wider and more efficient use of audiovisual aids in the fields of science, education, and the propagation of culture. Professor Kazimiera Zawistowicz-Adamska of Lodz University, ethnologist, complained that members of her profession are poorly used and asked for a revision of the system of recruitment for higher education, particularly in the field of ethnography. The *Pro-Rektor* of the Higher Music School in Warsaw, Professor Teodor Zalewski, spoke of the "blank" spots in the country's culture map, areas void of artists and cultural activities, and asked for a program for the employment of art and music school graduates and assistance in efforts to "distribute" them over the country. Finally, Professor Henryk Markiewicz of the Jagiellonian University in Cracow, a member of the Academy, demanded better textbooks on the secondary school level, especially in the areas of literature and foreign language.[49]

The above statements most certainly pointed to at least some of the problems marring the contemporary Polish educational picture, and impairing the chances for achievement of the system's stated goals and objectives. The problems are:

1. Adherence to traditional forms of instruction and reluctance to experiment with new and innovative programs in the area of teacher-student relations
2. Lack of equality in educational opportunities—despite the oratory about "democratization"—especially affecting certain socioeconomic groups, particularly in the rural areas and provincial small towns

[49] *Ibid.*

306

3. Inability or reluctance to mobilize adequate economic, social, and organizational resources to bring about genuine universalization of secondary education (both general and vocational)

4. Absence of efficient use by policy makers of the findings derived from scholarly and intersubjective research, particularly in the areas of the social sciences and educational methodology

5. Continuation of the elitist, hierarchical, and traditional patterns of educational organization causing status differentiation between various levels and types of educational institutions. These prevent, consequently, the establishment of closer links of communication and cooperation between the various levels and educational types, with concomitant feelings of superiority among some and feelings of inferiority and alienation among others

6. Alienation of the educational enterprise, especially of higher levels, from the total life of the community

7. Deficiency in the appropriate use of existing professional cadres with respect to training and skill, on the one hand, and sociocultural and educational needs on the other.

There does not, therefore, seem to be a lack of awareness as to the existing problems among certain members of the elite. There is even sufficient open discussion about these problems, but those most aware of the problems are seldom in decision-making positions. Some of those most aware and concerned may even find themselves on periodically formed committees or commissions (similar to the "Committee of Experts" which Professor Jan Szczepański was asked to chair in 1971 by the post-Gomułka leadership and whose task is to analyze critically the state of Polish education and present recommendations) but the ultimate decisions affecting education are not theirs. Nor are such decisions ever made, it seems, primarily with educational or even ideological and socialization-related considerations in mind. Factors of economy, organizational and group interests, and

307

political realities, invariably infringe upon the decision-making process. The result is that the road between awareness of what has to be done and actually doing it is as long and cumbersome in People's Poland as elsewhere.

Chapter 8: Conclusions

AT THE beginning of this study five related hypotheses were posited. Some were fully verified, others only with qualifications. In one case the data on hand were not sufficient to warrant conclusions.

The first hypothesis assumed that commitment to professional group norms (including specialization) would tend to reduce the teacher's ability to internalize the system's ideological values, subsequently rendering him less efficient as a transmitter of such values to students.

This hypothesis was confirmed only in part. Secondary school teachers who consider themselves subject-matter specialists, in the main mathematicians or physical scientists, reflected a position on religious issues which was substantially at odds with official ideology. Their position on questions of moral and ethical valuation, as well as certain aspects of educational policy, tended to reflect tradition and to favor the position of the Church rather than that of the Party. On the other hand, these teachers were more sympathetic than their nonspecialist colleagues to the scientific-technological goals of the system. The meaning of this support, however, is ambiguous. While the regime sees scientific and technological progress as part and parcel of its ideological objectives and premises, specialists may tend to see such progress as favoring development of pluralism and diminishing politicization. This does not, however, suggest that the scientific community can reasonably be considered to oppose the regime. What the findings suggest is that the Polish scientific community, at least at the level with which we are dealing, reflects the same kind of apolitical posture which is often found in the United States. To the extent that this is the case, it may well be easier for these specialists to maintain their allegiance to the Church since the political implications of such an act may not be obvious or particularly relevant to their major interests. Furthermore, it is im-

Conclusions

portant to recognize that in their crucial capacity as teachers of science they support the goals of the revolutionary regime. In this respect it may be said that they fulfill the expectations of the system in their most significant sphere of activity. Their "counterrevolutionary" religious attitudes may be of little consequence as long as their professional behavior meets the system's expectations.

Unlike the specialists, those who conceive of themselves as primarily professional educators are more attuned to the system in their attitudes toward religion. This finding is not particularly surprising in the light of similar findings in this country. Like their counterparts in the United States, Polish educators tend to support the political status quo. Moreover, the primary difference between the educators and the specialists in this context may well be nothing more than a sensitivity to the political implications of a variety of religious issues. In this case, the greater sensitivity to the implications of religious issues is countered by a reversal among the groups when it comes to support for scientific and technological goals. Here, the educator, whose own position is threatened by these goals, assumes a position less supportive of the system.

The second hypothesis suggested that older teachers with long tenure in the profession would show greater acceptance of systemic demands, values, and expectations than younger teachers or teachers of shorter tenure in the profession. It was argued that this would hold even though the younger teacher would have been educated wholly under the new system while the older group would have been educated primarily or in large part in the prewar era. On the whole, this hypothesis was substantiated and, from the system's point of view, this might appear to be a worrisome conclusion. It may indicate that the socialization efforts to which younger teachers were exposed in the course of their own education turned out to be, in the final analysis, counterproductive. Age and tenure do influence a teacher's attitude toward greater accommodation and acceptance of the sys-

310

tem's demands, values, and goals. What is not quite certain is whether *presystem* sociopolitical experiences and the *presystem* type of education to which most older teachers were exposed, at least in part, during their professional training and career are additional contributing factors toward such acceptance.

Relations between the Church, on the one hand, and the state and Party, on the other, are subject to fluctuations, to periodic ups and downs. These fluctuations hinge upon the extent of mutual interdependence the normally opposing forces have upon each other. In times of severe economic crisis, or when threatened by some common external danger, or when a new political leadership assumes charge of the system, Church-state tensions are generally at a low ebb, and the Church hierarchy is in a position to extract meaningful concessions. Nevertheless, as a rule, among the indicators showing a failure to socialize the younger teacher into the system's values and goals, is his continuing greater commitment to the Church with its *fundamental* moral, political, and philosophical opposition to the new regime. It may also be, however, that this particular phenomenon is simply a function of age and family ties and all that these entail. The various crosspressures to which young persons are exposed, coupled with the usual difficulties of growing up, may lead them to seek some anchor of security within the fold of religion and the Church. Having been brought up under the new system and introduced from an early age to that system's normative aims, the young are more sensitive to the gap between what was promised and what the regime was actually able to deliver. Older persons, on the other hand, seasoned by experience, wise in the battle for survival, perhaps a bit cynical as well, may have learned how to cope better with reality. The gap between the normative order and reality may very well be at the root of youth discontent everywhere. Bitterness over the reality of their own youth in prewar Poland may also help explain the relative ease with which the oldest teachers have adapted

311

themselves to the demands and expectations of the postwar regime which they may have perceived as an improvement over the past.

As time passes, the relationship of the current generation of young teachers to the Church may well become more distant. The evidence reviewed suggests that even though the young teachers' ties with the Church may appear formidable, they are probably weaker on the whole than in the generation immediately preceding it at a similar stage. It may well be that the next generation of teachers will be even less attached to the Church. The country, after all, is in a transitional phase. One cannot reasonably expect to overturn the accumulated tradition of a thousand years in the course of a single generation. In this regard, the transition to a secular state among succeeding generations may well be facilitated as the pace of industrialization and development accelerates. However, secularism and the fostering of a materialist world outlook, while major systemic goals, are not synonymous with Socialism, related as they may be. The latter entails, in addition, the internalization of a whole set of positive moral attitudes. Resistance among the young to these places in jeopardy the complete realization of the Socialist revolution. Instead, young Poles seem to have assimilated values and styles that they associate with "modernity" which, while secularizing (inasmuch as these are frowned upon by the traditionalist Church), are also quite removed from Socialist ideals.

One must also be cautious in interpreting the greater commitment of older teachers. It should be remembered that shortly after the establishment of People's Poland, the country experienced (as did most other East European countries and the USSR at the time) a severe period of Stalinist terror. Although the terror in Poland was of somewhat lesser proportions than, for example, in Czechoslovakia, Rumania, Hungary, or East Germany, its repercussions are felt to this day. One of the repercussions is an undercurrent of extreme caution, particularly in the area of frank political criticism. The Stalinist era oriented itself,

312

Conclusions

among other things, toward purging professional ranks of alleged counterrevolutionary elements, particularly in fields of sociopolitical and economic sensitivity. In this respect what we may be getting now is a residue of those who were indeed committed to the new regime, or sufficiently intimidated to feign commitment, rather than a true cross-section of those teachers educated in the prewar era. Seen from this perspective, the apparent danger to the future of the regime implied by the lesser dedication of younger teachers may be softened by the fact that the relaxation of political rigidity in the post-Stalinist period may simply give a more accurate picture of the *general state* of commitment to the regime.

The third hypothesis deals with the effects of social background. Factors of social background (including class origin, urban or rural residence, Church affiliation, etc.) were expected to impede or facilitate the teachers' internalization of ideological values and the efficiency of their transmission to students. Teachers of provincial, small-town, working-class background seem to be the most amenable to the system's ideological appeals, especially as these relate to the sensitive area of state-Church relations. Teachers of traditional middle-class and (private) entrepreneurial background seem to be the most resistant, followed by teachers of peasant-farmer and rural background. This despite the fact that youth of peasant-farmer background, along with working-class youth, are accorded, at least in theory, various allowances upon entering secondary and higher education and, once there, enjoy certain tangible privileges, and despite the fact that on the whole the economic and social status of the peasantry has undergone improvement under the new system. It is generally assumed that peasant background is a definite formal asset for the young and ambitious seeking a career within the Party or governmental bureaucracy.

On the issue of religion, teachers of intelligentsia and big-city background maintain a position somewhere between those of small-town working-class background and the

313

teachers of peasant-farmer and rural origin. On the whole, however, a *majority* of teachers within each social background category still maintains some ties with the Church. Moreover, although fewer teachers of working-class background maintain ties with the Church, those among them who do have such ties exceed in the intensity of their religious orientation the intensity of teachers of other class backgrounds. This might be a distressing finding from the system's viewpoint inasmuch as one would logically assume that teachers who are themselves not fully socialized into the system's values would not be able to perform at an optimum as socializers of others.

Among teachers of comparably advanced age (46 years and over), it was assumed that those trained after World War II would manifest a higher commitment to the official educational values than those trained prior to World War II. The underlying assumption was that older teachers fully trained under the new system would feel a sense of gratitude toward it for having enabled them to enter a profession at a rather advanced stage in life. Presumably such teachers would be recruited from among activists of working-class or peasant background whose chances under the preceding system were minimal or whose education would have been interrupted by war and occupation. However, the number of persons within the 41-50 age category was only 29 and those over the age of 50 numbered 22—a total of 51 persons in the advanced age groups. The actual number of those in the sample over the age of 46 and educated after World War II was so insignificant as to preclude any meaningful conclusions for that group. In the course of depth interviews, however, teachers who fell into this category gave the general impression of having a higher level of commitment than teachers of similar age who received their education during a more or less "normal" period of life, and most definitely higher than the commitment encountered among younger teachers who received all of their education under the present system.

Finally, it was predicted that among teachers trained after

314

Conclusions

World War II, the younger teachers would be less committed to the official educational values than are the older teachers. In effect, we dealt with this issue earlier. This hypothesis was borne out in repeated tests in a variety of value areas (secularism, scientificism, sexual morality, etc.). Commitment to official systemic values and goals, as a rule, does increase with age. Even among the students in the schools of teacher education, those younger in age showed lower levels of commitment than those of somewhat older age. This recurring failure to involve the very youngest of the teachers (and student-teachers) in the complex of systemic values, norms, and goals may call into question the ability of the system to affect a greater degree of socialization in the future which would enable it to achieve its goals more effectively.

People's Poland faces the dilemma of most other political systems, but it is particularly acute where official emphasis is on a single ideological belief: i.e., whether superior weight should be given to expertise or to political loyalty. Ideally, the system would prefer the experts to be politically loyal and vice versa. However, experts, even in times of normalcy, develop functional group interests which may bring them into conflict with systemic demands and expectations. Generally, as much as the system needs the expert, political (not necessarily ideological) considerations usually win out in confrontation. Such political considerations may be due to tactical, administrative, or economic exigencies, including foreign obligations and domestic needs. This is probably less true at the current period than in the immediate post-revolutionary phase. The post-Gomułka leadership under Edward Gierek, seeking its allies from among the technocratic elements and identification with the new industrial managers, may even be able to accelerate the process further. Władysław Gomułka who dominated the political scene from October 1956 until the end of 1970 was very much the guardian of Party orthodoxy and discipline and, as such, mistrustful of the young, the technically educated, of all those who did not share the experiences of the "old guard" before, during, and after the war. He, consequently, lost touch with reality and with the various deep-running social undercurrents and pressures—a condition which ultimately contributed to the dissatisfaction of the workers and to the riots that subsequently toppled his regime. The new Gierek leadership speaks, in fact, of a "division of labor" which would more accurately match expertise with decision-making competence. In this respect, the educational organization might be expected to improve as time passes and to develop its own sets of priorities and guidelines, relatively free from external interference, as it were. Whether or not the analysis and recommendations of Professor Jan Szczepański's Committee of Experts (appointed by the post-Gomułka command) concerning the state of education will be taken seriously may indeed be one of the major tests of the extent to which expertise (and, in this case, sociological and educational expertise) is to take precedence over demands, sometimes borne of narrow Party or even factional considerations which, however, have little in common with the interests of education as the educators themselves perceive them to be. There will remain, of course, the crucial problem of central allocation of continuously meager economic resources—a function which could hardly be expected to be free from the realm of political decision-making. Such decisions remain within the realm of politics in most modern political systems—regardless of ideology, commitment to education, and regardless of how well attuned the system is to the voice of the experts. Even in systems governed by functional experts the voice of the educational expert must compete for limited resources with the expert speaking on behalf of national security, industry, agriculture, management, and the ultimate decision has to be a political one. Moreover, even if the educational enterprise could be expected to fare better (and more smoothly) under conditions more amenable to the "loyal expert," the ability of that enterprise to forge genuine commitment to the system may continue to remain problematic.

Moving further beyond the limited confines of the five hypotheses, it is clear that during the entire revolutionary period, the schools have been considered a key element in the development of a stabilized and committed Socialist constituency. As we have seen, however, the success of the schools in realizing their charge has been less than overwhelming, but no less so probably than the ability of the other institutions of the system to meet the respective expectations placed upon them. The existing gap between promise and delivery, between the normative and the empirical order, already discussed here, is perhaps best reflected in one of the many wry witticisms making the rounds in People's Poland: this one asserts that whereas a traditional fairy tale begins with the phrase "once upon a time there was," a modern Polish one begins "once upon a time there will be."

One of the chief barriers in the schools' realization of their stated goals has been, of course, the persistence among faculty of those same traditions that have prevented the larger society from embracing wholeheartedly the new Socialist ideology and the radical cultural, social, and political changes which accompany it. More important than the ties with the past, however, may be the lack of positive commitment by educators. In the context of the current system, they see themselves as a deprived group in terms both of prestige and of compensation although, as far as prestige is concerned, the teaching profession appears to enjoy, at least theoretically, the same high esteem traditional for teachers in this political culture. However, considering the incredible demands which the system imposes upon them, perceptions by the teachers of their actual status and future may not be unrealistic. It would be easy, of course, to discount the dissatisfaction with prestige in the light of existing empirical evidence and survey results, but such arguments are irrelevant if teachers' own perceptions run counter to them. In this regard, it is clear that the status hierarchy within the teaching profession itself is such that the potential satisfaction to be derived from the teacher's position in the larger community is very likely countered by the relatively low esteem, *within the profes-*

Conclusions

sion, of elementary school teachers, or those who have not graduated from the prestige institutions of higher learning. A substantial proportion of those employed on the secondary school level, not to mention the elementary level, are either graduates of lower prestige institutions or persons still striving to complete their degree requirements at a university or higher school of pedagogy. It may very well be then that the reference group which is critical in the formation of the teacher's perceptions of himself is the professional community and not the public. That is, the bulk of the teachers in Poland, while enjoying relatively high esteem in the community, are, in a very real sense, professional failures since they do not possess the credentials which lead to greater professional recognition. Although within the larger Polish society prestige and income are not directly related to each other, such a relationship does exist within the general field of education. Those among the educators who enjoy the highest esteem (i.e., university professors) also enjoy the highest income levels, and income as well as prestige slide downward as one moves down the educational ladder. In this regard, the system's failure to exact a change in the traditional professional status system may be a crucial barrier to teacher satisfaction and potential commitment. The failure is further underscored by the persistence of traditional gentry prestige models and styles within society—models and styles from which even the new political elite cannot quite free itself, even if it wants to (which seems doubtful for a large segment within it).

Compounding the prestige problem then is the extremely low salary of teachers, especially at the lower levels. Although teachers undoubtedly are sensitive to the esteem that the profession enjoys in the larger community, it may indeed ring hollow in the face of an unwillingness to provide commensurate rewards. There is an admonition in this country, not unknown elsewhere, that "status won't buy groceries." It is appropriate to keep this in mind when evaluating the overall satisfaction of the teacher. To the

Conclusions

extent that the present discrepancies between general community status and rewards continue to exist, one can expect dissatisfaction to grow. In this case, one might also reasonably expect a concomitant reduction in commitment to the system. It must be added too, that there is only one way to resolve the problem satisfactorily from the point of view of the teacher, and that is to improve substantially material benefits.[1] A reduction in the prestige of the profession would also eliminate the existing discrepancy but, obviously, that will not solve the problem. From the teachers' viewpoint, however, such a reduction in status is what is perceived as happening, especially as industrialization and technological progress move forward, as education, despite difficulties, becomes more widespread, and the teacher is losing his traditional "knowledge monopoly."

Indeed, adding to the problem of positive commitment are the difficulties introduced by the necessity for rapid industrialization. To the extent that they are forced to, planners in Poland, as elsewhere for that matter, are apparently inclined to invest national resources in those areas where a payoff can be demonstrated relatively quickly. The result is that industrial growth and development, along with other interests, take priority over education. Investment in education is expected from those sectors of the population and from those sections of the country least able to do so. The result is that the cause of education is losing ground, in relative terms, as the nation moves forward on some other fronts. However, the gap between educational needs and requirements, and the development of the educational sys-

---

[1] A plan to upgrade teachers' and university faculty salaries was under serious, although informal, discussion during Fall 1971. According to the plan, teachers' salaries are to be increased by an average of 40 percent over the next five years, starting in May 1972, with highest pay increases going to lower-ranking personnel. The new plan would also abolish the system of bonuses and premiums given periodically to individual teaching collectivities. It was indicated that the new salary scheme was being advanced prior to the convening of the 6th Party Congress scheduled for December 1971 thus signifying a move on the part of the Gierek leadership to appeal to an important and hitherto underpaid segment of the intelligentsia. *New York Times*, October 10, 1971.

Conclusions

tem nationwide, continues to grow as a result. Worse yet, it widens fastest in precisely those areas which have always been educationally deprived: the poor, nonindustrialized, rural regions. As this pattern continues, existing patterns of stratification, based in large part on education, are strengthened rather than reduced—the vision of a classless society, inherent in the ideology, notwithstanding.

The existing wide network of adult education facilities can only serve to remedy, in part, some of the past inequities but it could not affect substantially the entrenched social structure nor the prospects of radically altering that structure in the future as the introduction of at least universal secondary schooling would. In terms of both the normative goals of the sociopolitical revolution and of industrialization, education rather than some other attributes should increasingly serve as the major legitimate stepping-stone toward individual advancement. To the extent that the educational system becomes vitally linked with the individual's future yet frustrates his hopes and fails him, it is transformed into an object of animosity, contributing only to the general dissatisfaction. Yet, introduction of universal secondary education remains a distant hope—the distance somewhat "sweetened" and rationalized in the eyes of Polish educators by the fact that the Soviet Union, more than 50 years after the revolution and much more advanced industrially and technologically than Poland, still is without universal secondary education but anticipates achieving this goal during the second half of the 1970's, at the earliest. In addition to the failure to meet adequately the rising educational expectations of all social strata, whetted as these are by the promises conjured up by ideologically inspired visions, the educational enterprise, being as closely identified with the existing political system as it is in Poland, frequently serves as that system's lightning rod for accumulated frustrations, disappointments, and grievances, and subsequently suffers by proxy.

Coupled with the failure to provide adequately for educational needs throughout the country, the education of

320

Conclusions

teachers themselves is seriously retarded in the face of the system's lack of extensive support to educational development. There is evidence to indicate that teachers are not only ill prepared, but that they recognize this fact and are not happy about it. The need for improvement in the preparation of teachers is as critical as the needs for educational development in other areas and at other levels. While there is formal adherence to the goal of improvement, here too rhetoric has far outpaced action. The demand for teachers grows faster than the capacity for training them. Even the low status schools of teacher education (SNs), marked for phasing out, continue to operate at full capacity. The mobilization of resources to education at this level is no more substantial than at any other, and the prognosis for the future is none too bright.

Given the substantial dissatisfaction and the poor preparation of teachers, it is no surprise to find that students do not appear to reach the Socialist ideal any more successfully than their mentors. This may not be the cause for alarm, however, that some Polish critics seem to think it to be. After all, there is substantial evidence which suggests that ideological dedication is simply not a part of the cultural repertoire of secondary school students anywhere. One may extract superficial commitment if the proper conditioning mechanisms are introduced. However, it may be that such commitment is unlikely except in the vaguest and most general sense. If forced to, they would probably defend their country or pay lip service to its ideological foundations (as long as they do not have to identify them). To expect much beyond that, however, may be delusion.

The point where commitment becomes more critical is later, when the student will begin to exercise the prerogatives of a citizen, whatever these may be. A general lack of commitment among the mature may be a far more ominous sign than the apparent apathy of students.

But even the apathy of the mature, including the teacher, may not be a sign of imminent danger. While it may, in the case of a revolutionary situation, indicate a failure of

321

spirit it may also signal a growing concession to the legitimacy of the system, if not an outright satisfaction with it. In this respect, the lack of active support of the system may, in the long run, be less important in the Polish experience than the fact that there is not a significant active opposition among teachers. While there are ties with the Church which might be interpreted as opposition, these might also be interpreted as pro forma, a convenient way of avoiding the largely informal social difficulties which may ensue with a clean break, in addition to personal habit. It is only among the youngest teachers that one discerns a commitment to religion and to the Church which transcends mere conformity to community or family pressures or which is a result of factors extraneous to a religious belief system but is, instead, the product of a deeply felt need or of a particular political stance in opposition to the existing order. On the whole, however, there is little evidence to indicate that ties with the Church have a critical impact on the classroom. While they may reduce the effectiveness of the teacher in transmitting the values of the political system in that his own commitment is not substantial, there is little evidence that competing values are introduced into the classroom. The net result is that while the teacher is much less a factor in the success of the revolution than the regime would like, he does not actively retard it. Indeed, although the system counts on the sociopolitical activism of the teacher, it appears much more concerned over its failure to reach and to commit to its goals the masses of industrial workers. Perennial teachers' complaints did not, for example, bring about an increase in the rate of their collective income nor did it secure better homes for schools or teachers. On the other hand, workers' discontent may lead to strikes and riots (as it did in 1956 and in 1970) and, eventually, result in altered socioeconomic plans as well as a changed leadership. While restlessness among students and intellectuals (like that of March 1968) brings in its wake sterner disciplinary measures, restlessness among workers produces attempts in persuasion, in finding some measure of accommodation to mass demands, even after coercion was tried. An explanation for such differentiated treatment of workers, on the one hand, and intellectuals, on the other, may perhaps be found in the canons of the ideology from which the leadership itself deviates from time to time. That is, while a revolution needs its intellectual cadres to fill various functional leadership roles, it is the working class which, ultimately, can spell the revolution's success or defeat.

Yet, in the final analysis, it is probably true that the process of transition is not proceeding as quickly as it might if those charged with the socialization of the young were, themselves, more adequately socialized. But the teachers, like their charges, have been brought up in a system whose programs and ideals have only been realized in small part. In this regard, they too were taught by individuals only partially committed to the new system. Despite the fact that their enthusiasm for the new ideology and all that it entails is not overwhelming, it is probably greater than among those from whom they learned. Undoubtedly the same will be true of the next generation of Polish teachers, and the next, until, possibly, the celebration of the second millennium. The future of Poland now appears to consist of a prolonged period of transition. Contending forces, representing competing values, norms, and behavioral styles, will probably move alternately between combat and coexistence, tension and relative quiescence, until some form of extended modus vivendi is reached. There are clear indications that in the cohabitation of the new system with the old, some of the forces of the new culture give way to the traditional. Regardless of this fact, however, Poland is a nation transformed. Whereas in the past young boys and girls, members of the illegal Communist youth organization, furtively and in the middle of the night swung tiny red flags across overhanging streetcar wires, the red banner is now the symbol of the new order and is officially displayed alongside the traditional national colors. The Party, surfaced from the underground, is now in power and, as such, an attractive base for the upwardly mobile, the authority oriented, and the ambitious. The new power, moreover, is becoming increasingly acknowledged as a reality, at least in the legal (if not in the Socialist) consciousness of the masses. Key facets of the revolution have become a part of the everyday life of the country, and people have accepted them and made peace with it. In part such acceptance is, no doubt, due to a lack of alternatives and national choice.

If the revolutionary forces have been compelled to compromise with prevailing community values and styles, there is every indication that they have done so willingly, as long as their authority and power are preserved in the process. Such accommodation is likely to be the format for Poland's future and will include greater sensitivity to the existing traditional institutions, including the Church, as well as the still persisting norms of the traditional culture. Consequently, the leadership of the system may be increasingly compelled to appear in the mantle of "good Poles" rather than of "good Communists," or to attempt, at least, to emphasize the former aspect of its character rather than the latter—an emphasis it does not appear to mind and one which the Soviet Union probably would not mind either as long as the existing patterns of bonds, ties, and alliances remain intact, and as long as the formal organization of power, centered around the Party, continues to exist within an atmosphere of relative productivity and order. The events following the workers' riots of December 1970 seem to bear out this prognosis.

Many of the young Communists who furtively unfurled little red flags or painted slogans on city walls in the depth of the night during the times of the Party's illegality, have not survived the years of underground and war to see the emergence of People's Poland. Some of those who have survived are now veterans of the movement or well advanced into middle age, in positions of authority, satisfied and comfortable. Others have removed themselves or were removed because they somehow did not fit the new roles

Conclusions

and changing needs. As the ideologues of the hitherto competing value systems, both the new as well as the traditional, pass from the scene, the symbols of the revolution, now canonized, come to be used (in conjunction with some of the symbols of the traditional culture) as mere legitimizers of the existing sociopolitical and economic reality or as prodders for greater popular efforts, rather than as embodiments of goals and ideals yet to be met. These goals and ideals become less relevant in daily practice or in the formulation of policy. Consequently, those in charge of the system's daily operation may begin to view the educational enterprise not as an organ of socialization into a given set of norms and beliefs but rather as an agency of support for an existing power structure. The existing arrangement of authority and organization supersedes in importance the system of revolutionary beliefs, norms, or even styles. The educational establishment in Poland is traditionally well-suited to serve the former, and indeed performs much better for this purpose than it does in meeting the normative goals.

Bibliography and Index

Bibliography

NOTE: The Bibliography is divided into major topical categories each of which concerns a certain aspect of this book. To avoid repetition some entries which could fit under two or more classifications are listed only under the one which appears most appropriate under the circumstances. Foreign language titles are followed by English translations. In the case of Polish language sources, only books, monographs, pamphlets, and major journal articles are listed. Polish language periodicals and dailies of particular interest or importance to the subject matter are listed at the end, with appropriate English translations.

I. The Political System, Culture and Society: Stability and Change

GENERAL

Almond, Gabriel A. *Political Development: Essays in Heuristic Theory.* Boston: Little, Brown and Co., 1970.

————. "Political Systems and Political Change." *American Behavioral Scientist*, VI, 6 (June 1963), 3-10.

————, and Powell, G. Bingham, Jr. *Comparative Politics: A Developmental Approach.* Boston: Little, Brown and Co., 1966.

————, and Verba, Sidney. *The Civic Culture.* Princeton: Princeton University Press, 1963.

Aristotle. *The Politics of Aristotle.* Ernest Barker, trans. New York: Oxford University Press, 1958.

Bagehot, Walter. *Physics and Politics: Or Thoughts on the Application of the Principles of "Natural Selection" and "Inheritance" to Political Society.* Boston: Beacon Press, 1956.

Barber, Bernard, and Inkeles, Alex, eds. *Stability and Social Change.* Boston: Little, Brown and Co., 1971.

Bendix, Reinhard, and Lipset, Seymour Martin, eds. *Class,*

Bibliography

Status and Power: A Reader in Social Stratification. Glencoe, Ill.: The Free Press, 1953.

Black, C. E. *The Dynamics of Modernization: A Study in Comparative History.* New York: Harper and Row, 1966.

Bottomore, T. B. *Classes in Modern Society.* New York: Pantheon Books, 1966.

Brinton, Crane. *The Anatomy of Revolution.* New York: Random House, Vintage, 1957.

Cantril, Hadley. *The Patterns of Human Concern.* New Brunswick, N.J.: Rutgers University Press, 1965.

Centers, Richard. *The Psychology of Social Classes.* Princeton: Princeton University Press, 1949.

Connor, James, ed. *Lenin on Politics and Revolution.* New York: Pegasus, 1968.

Dahrendorf, Ralf. *Class and Class Conflict in Industrial Society.* Stanford: Stanford University Press, 1959.

Davies, James C. *Human Nature in Politics: The Dynamics of Political Behavior.* New York: John Wiley and Sons, 1963.

————. "Toward a Theory of Revolution." *American Sociological Review,* xxvII, 1 (February 1962), 5-19.

Durkheim, Emile. *The Division of Labor in Society.* George Simpson, trans. Glencoe, Ill.: The Free Press, 1933.

Easton, David. *A Systems Analysis of Political Life.* New York: John Wiley and Sons, 1965.

Edgerton, Robert B. "'Cultural' vs. 'Ecological' Factors in the Expression of Values, Attitudes, and Personality Characteristics." *American Anthropologist,* Vol. 67 (April 1965), 442-47.

Eisenstadt, S. N. *Modernization: Protest and Change.* Englewood Cliffs, N.J.: Prentice-Hall, 1966.

Eliot, T. S. *Notes Towards the Definition of Culture.* New York: Harcourt, Brace and Co., 1949.

Elizur, D., *Adapting to Innovation.* Jerusalem: Academic Press, 1970.

Fromm, Erich. *Escape from Freedom.* New York: Rinehart, 1941.

Bibliography

Gerth, H. H., and Mills, C. Wright, eds. and trans. *From Max Weber: Essays in Sociology.* London: Routledge and Kegan Paul, 1952.

Goldhamer, Herbert, and Shils, Edward A. "Types of Power and Status." *American Journal of Sociology,* Vol. 45 (September 1939), 171-82.

Goldschmidt, Walter. "Theory and Strategy in the Study of Cultural Adaptability." *American Anthropologist,* Vol. 67 (April 1965), 402-08.

Heilbroner, Robert L. *The Great Ascent: The Struggle for Economic Development in Our Time.* New York: Harper and Row, 1963.

Jacob, Philip E., and Toscano, James V., eds. *The Integration of Political Communities.* Philadelphia: J. B. Lippincott, 1965.

Johnson, Chalmers. *Revolutionary Change.* Boston: Little, Brown and Co., 1966.

Kerr, Clark et al. *Industrialism and Industrial Man: The Problems of Labor and Management in Economic Growth.* Cambridge: Harvard University Press, 1960.

Kłosowska, Antonina. *Kultura masowa: Krytyka i obrona* (Mass Culture: Critique and Defense). Warsaw: Państwowe Wydawnictwo Naukowe, 1964.

Kon, I. S. *Socjologia litchnostii* (The Sociology of Personality). Moscow: Izdatelstvo polititcheskoi literatury, 1967.

Kotarbiński, Tadeusz. *Traktat o dobrej robocie* (A Treatise on Good Work). 3rd rev. and enlarged edn. Wrocław: Ossolińskich, 1965.

Landtman, Gunnar. *The Origin of the Inequality of the Social Classes.* Chicago: Chicago University Press, 1938.

Lane, Robert E. *Political Life.* New York: The Free Press, 1959.

LaPalombara, Joseph, ed. *Bureaucracy and Political Development.* Princeton: Princeton University Press, 1963.

Lasswell, Harold D. *Politics: Who Gets What, When, How: With Postscript (1958).* New York: Meridian Books, 1960.

Bibliography

Lasswell, Harold D. *The World Revolution of Our Time.* Stanford: Stanford University Press, 1951.

Lenski, Gerhard E. *Power and Prestige: A Theory of Social Stratification.* New York: McGraw-Hill, 1966.

————. "Status Crystallization: A Non-Vertical Dimension of Social Status." *American Sociological Review,* xix (August 1954), 405-13.

Lerner, Daniel. *The Passing of Traditional Society: Modernizing the Middle East.* Paperback. New York: The Free Press, 1964.

Lipset, Seymour Martin. *Political Man: The Social Bases of Politics.* Garden City, N.Y.: Doubleday and Co., 1960.

————. *Revolution and Counterrevolution: Change and Persistence in Social Structures.* Revised edn. Garden City, N.Y.: Doubleday and Co., 1970.

————, and Bendix, Reinhard. *Social Mobility in Industrial Society.* Berkeley-Los Angeles: University of California Press, 1960.

————, and Smelser, Neil J., eds. *Sociology: The Progress of a Decade.* Englewood Cliffs, N.J.: Prentice-Hall, 1961.

Maisel, Y. A. "Razvitie litchnostii ee sovremennaya nauka" ("Personality Development and Modern Science"). *Filozofskyie ee Sociologitcheskyie Isledovania* (Social Science Faculty, Leningrad University), vii, 1965, 101-11.

Malinowski, Bronisław. *A Scientific Theory of Culture and Other Essays.* Chapel Hill: University of North Carolina Press, 1944.

Marshall, T. H. *Citizenship and Social Class.* London: Cambridge University Press, 1950.

Marx, Karl. *Writings of the Young Marx on Philosophy and Society.* Loyd D. Easton and Kurt H. Guddat, eds. and trans. Garden City, N.Y.: Doubleday and Co., 1967.

Mayer, Kurt B., and Buckley, Walter. *Class and Society.* Third edn. New York: Random House, 1970.

Merton, Robert K. *Social Theory and Social Structure.* Revised edn. Glencoe, Ill.: The Free Press, 1957.

Michels, Robert. *Political Parties: A Sociological Study of the Oligarchical Tendencies of Modern Democracy.* Eden

332

Bibliography

and Cedar Paul, trans. Glencoe, Ill.: The Free Press, 1958.

Mosca, Gaetano. *The Ruling Class*. Hannah D. Kahn, trans. London: McGraw-Hill, 1939.

Ossowski, Stanisław. "Old Notions and New Problems: Interpretations of Social Structure in Modern Society." *Transactions of the Third World Congress of Sociology*, III, London, 1956.

Parsons, Talcott. *The Social System*. Glencoe, Ill.: The Free Press, 1951.

———. *The Structure of Social Action*. Glencoe, Ill.: The Free Press, 1949.

Plato. *The Republic of Plato*. Francis MacDonald Cornford, trans. New York: Oxford University Press, 1945.

Presthus, Robert. *The Organizational Society: An Analysis and a Theory*. New York: Alfred A. Knopf, 1962.

Pye, Lucian W., and Verba, Sidney, eds. *Political Culture and Political Development*. Princeton: Princeton University Press, 1963.

Rokeach, Milton, ed. *The Open Mind and Closed Mind*. New York: Basic Books, 1960.

Rostow, W. W. *Politics and the Stages of Growth*. Cambridge: The University Press, 1971.

Rousseau, Jean Jacques. *The Social Contract and Discourses*. G.D.H. Cole, trans. New York: E. F. Dutton and Co., 1950.

Runciman, W. C. *Social Science and Political Theory*. Cambridge: The University Press, 1963.

Sheldon, Eleanor, and Moore, Wilbert E., eds. *Indicators of Social Change*. New York: Russell Sage Foundation, 1968.

Simmel, Georg. *Conflict and the Web of Group Affiliations*. Glencoe, Ill.: The Free Press, 1956.

Smelser, Neil J. *Social Change in the Industrial Revolution*. Chicago: University of Chicago Press, 1959.

Snow, C. P. *The Two Cultures: And a Second Look: An Expanded Version of the Two Cultures and the Scientific Revolution*. Cambridge: The University Press, 1965.

Somers, Gerald G., et al., eds. *Adjusting to Technological*

Bibliography

Change. Industrial Relations Research Association, No. 29. New York: Harper and Row, 1963.

Titmuss, Morris. *Income Distribution and Social Change*. Toronto: University of Toronto Press, 1962.

Tucker, Robert C. *The Marxian Revolutionary Idea*. New York: W. W. Norton and Co., 1969.

Veblen, Thorstein. *The Theory of the Leisure Class: An Economic Study of Institutions*. New York: Macmillan Co., 1912.

Weber, Max. *The Theory of Social and Economic Organization*. A. M. Henderson and Talcott Parsons, trans. Glencoe, Ill.: The Free Press, 1947.

Weiner, Myron, ed. *Modernization*. New York: Basic Books, 1966.

Wiener, Norbert. *The Human Use of Human Beings: Cybernetics and Society*. Garden City, N.Y.: Doubleday and Co., 1954.

Yglesias, Jose. *The Fist of the Revolution*. New York: Random House, 1969.

Znaniecki, Florian. *Modern Nationalities: A Sociological Study*. Urbana, Ill.: University of Illinois Press, 1952.

EASTERN EUROPE

Bryski, Zbigniew. "The Communist 'Middle Class' in the USSR and Poland," *Survey* (London), 73 (Autumn 1969), 80-90.

Brzeziński, Zbigniew K. *The Soviet Bloc: Unity and Conflict*. Cambridge: Harvard University Press, 1960.

Djilas, Milovan. *The New Class: An Analysis of the Communist System*. New York: Frederick A. Praeger, 1957.

Farrell, R. Barry, ed. *Political Leadership in Eastern Europe and the Soviet Union*. Chicago: Aldine, 1970.

Fischer-Galati, Stephen, ed. *Eastern Europe in the Sixties*. New York: Frederick A. Praeger, 1963.

Grossman, Gregory, ed. *Value and Plan: Economic Calculation and Organization in Eastern Europe*. Russian and East European Studies. Berkeley-Los Angeles: University of California Press, 1960.

Bibliography

Ionescu, Ghita. *The Politics of the European Communist States.* New York: Frederick A. Praeger, 1967.

Janos, Andrew C. "The One-Party State and Social Mobilization: East Europe Between the Wars." *Authoritarian Politics in Modern Society: The Dynamics of Established One-Party Systems.* New York: Basic Books, 1970, 204-36.

Johnson, Chalmers, ed. *Change in Communist Systems,* Stanford: Stanford University Press, 1970.

Lednicki, Wacław. *Russia, Poland and the West: Essays in Literary and Cultural History.* New York: Roy, 1954.

London, Kurt, ed. *Eastern Europe in Transition.* Baltimore: Johns Hopkins Press, 1966.

Richta, Radovan et al. *Civilization at the Crossroads: Social and Human Implications of the Scientific and Technological Revolution.* Marian Šlingová, trans. Prague: International Arts and Sciences Press, 1969.

Seton-Watson, Hugh. *The East European Revolution.* New York: Frederick A. Praeger, 1951.

Skilling, H. Gordon. *The Governments of Communist East Europe.* New York: Thomas Y. Crowell, 1966.

Toma, Peter A., ed. *The Changing Face of Communism in Eastern Europe.* Tucson: University of Arizona Press, 1970.

Tucker, Robert C. "Communism and Political Culture." *Newsletter on Comparative Studies of Communism,* IV, 3 (May 1971), 3-12.

U.S. Congress, Joint Economic Committee. *Economic Developments in Countries of Eastern Europe: A Compendium of Papers Submitted to the Subcommittee on Foreign Economic Policy of the Joint Economic Committee.* 91st Cong., 2nd Sess., 1970.

U.S. Department of Commerce, Bureau of the Census. *Projections of the Population of the Communist Countries of Eastern Europe, By Age and Sex: 1969 to 1990.* Series P-91, No. 18, Washington, D.C., 1969.

V *borbye za tekhnitcheskii progres: Sbornik statyeii* (In Struggle for Technological Progress: Collection of Es-

Bibliography

says). Leningrad: Leningradskii Polytekhnitcheskii Institut im. M.I. Kalinina, 1965.

Wolfe, Thomas W. *Soviet Power and Europe: 1945-1970.* Baltimore: Johns Hopkins Press, 1970.

POLAND

Anonymous. "USSR and the Politics of Polish Antisemitism 1956-68." *Soviet Jewish Affairs,* London, No. 1 (June 1971), 19-39.

Barnett, Clifford R. *Poland: Its People, Its Society, Its Culture.* New York: Grove Press, 1958.

Benes, Vaclav, and Pounds, Norman J. G. *Poland.* New York: Praeger, 1970.

Bethell, Nicholas. *Gomułka: His Poland, His Communism.* New York: Holt, Rinehart and Winston, 1969.

Bieńkowski, Władysław. *Problemy teorii rozwoju społecznego* (Problems of Theory of Social Development). Warsaw: Państwowe Wydawnictwo Naukowe, 1966.

Blit, Lucjan. *The Anti-Jewish Campaign in Present-Day Poland: Facts, Documents, Press Reports.* London: Institute for Jewish Affairs, 1968.

Brant, Irving. *The New Poland.* New York: Universe, 1946.

Brzeski, Andrzej. "Poland as a Catalyst of Change in the Communist Economic System." *The Polish Review,* xvi, 2 (Spring 1971), 3-24.

Chałasiński, Józef. *Kultura i naród* (Culture and Nation). Warsaw: Książka i Wiedza, 1968.

Dziewanowski, M. K. "The Limits and Problems of Decompression: The Case of Poland," in *The Satellites in Eastern Europe.* Henry L. Roberts, ed. *The Annals of the American Academy of Political and Social Science,* Vol. 317 (May 1958), 88-96.

Feiwel, George R. *Industrialization and Planning Under Polish Socialism.* 2 vols. New York: Praeger, 1971.

———. *The Economics of a Socialist Enterprise.* New York: Praeger, 1966.

Fiszman, Joseph R. "Education and Social Mobility in People's Poland." Paper presented at Annual Meeting of

Bibliography

American Association for the Advancement of Slavic Studies, Denver, Colo., March 25-27, 1971. Under the same title, also in *The Polish Review*, xvi, 3 (Summer 1971), 5-31.

———. *Education and Sociopolitical, Cultural and Economic Change*. UNESCO Conference on Adult Education, Involvement and Social Change, Ljubljana. Yugoslavia, May 5-7, 1970. Monograph No. 2. Ljubljana: Institute of Sociology and Philosophy at the University of Ljubljana, 1970.

———. "Poland—Continuity and Change," in *The Changing Face of Communism in Eastern Europe*. Peter A. Toma, ed. Tucson: University of Arizona Press, 1970, pp. 40-88, 353-54.

Gałaj, Dyzma. "Działalność i perspektywy badań rejonów uprzemysławianych" ("Activity and Perspectives on Research in Industrializing Regions"). Paper presented at meeting of Scientific Secretariat of Section I, Polish Academy of Sciences, May 26, 1965. *Sprawozdania z prac naukowych wydziału nauk społecznych*, iii, 4 (39) (1965), 1-20.

Gamarnikow, Michael. "Poland: Political Pluralism in a One-Party State." *Problems of Communism*, xvi, 4 (July-August 1967), 1-14.

———. "The Polish Economy in Transition." *Problems of Communism*, xix, 1 (January-February 1970), 40-47.

Gella, Aleksander. "The Life and Death of the Old Polish Intelligentsia." *Slavic Review*, xxx, 1 (March 1971), 1-27.

Institute of Philosophy and Sociology, Polish Academy of Sciences. *Empirical Sociology in Poland*. Warsaw: Państwowe Wydawnictwo Naukowe, 1966.

Johnson, A. Ross. "The Polish Riots and Gomułka's Fall." Mimeographed paper. Santa Monica: RAND Corp. (March 1971).

Kowalski, Józef. *Zarys historii polskiego ruchu robotniczego w latach 1918-1939* (Outline History of the Polish Labor Movement, 1918-1939). Vol. i, 1918-1928; Vol. ii, 1929-1939. Warsaw: Książka i Wiedza, 1959.

Bibliography

Kozakiewicz, Mikołaj. *Kariery płockie: Szkolnicwo a uprzemysłowienie* (Płock Careers: Education and Industrialization). Warsaw: Nasza Księgarnia, 1971.

―――. "Wpływ uprzemysłowienia na życiowe szanse młodzieży: W świetle badań w płockim rejonie uprzemysławianym" ("The Impact of Industrialization on the Life Chances of Youth: In the Light of Research in the Płock Industrialized Region"). *Kultura i Społeczeństwo*, XIII, 2 (1969), 199-212.

―――. "Young Poles A.D. 1970." *Polish Perspectives*, XIII, 7-8 (July-August 1970), 31-42.

Kruszewski, Z. Anthony. *The Oder-Neisse Boundary and Poland's Modernization*. New York: Praeger, 1972.

Kulski, W. W. "Classes in the Classless State." *Problems of Communism*, IV, 1 (January-February 1955), 20-28.

Kuncewicz, Maria, ed. *The Modern Polish Mind: An Anthology*. Boston: Little, Brown and Co., 1962.

Kwiatkowski, Zbigniew. *Byłem niemilczącym świadkiem* (I was a Nonsilent Witness). Warsaw: Iskry, 1965.

Malanowski, Jan. *Stosunki klasowe i różnice społeczne w mieście* (Class Relations and Social Distinctions in the City). Warsaw: Państwowe Wydawnictwo Naukowe, 1967.

Matejko, Aleksander. "Świadomość inteligencka" ("Intelligentsia Consciousness"). *Kultura*, Paris, 7/286-8/287 (July-August 1971), 126-37.

―――. "The Executive in Present Day Poland." *The Polish Review*, XVI, 3 (Summer 1971), 32-58.

Miłosz, Czesław. *Native Realm: A Search for Self-Definition*. Catherine S. Leach, trans. Garden City, N.Y.: Doubleday and Co., 1968.

―――. *The Captive Mind*. Jane Zielonko, trans. New York: Alfred A. Knopf, 1953.

Morrison, James F. *The Polish People's Republic*. Baltimore: Johns Hopkins Press, 1968.

Nowak, Irena. "Przemiany społeczno-kulturalne województwa warszawskiego" ("Sociocultural Changes in the War-

Bibliography

saw District"). *Kultura i Społeczeństwo*, x, 1 (January-March 1966), 163-78.

Poland's Millennium of Catholicism. Lublin: Société des Lettres et des Sciences de l'Université Catholique de Lublin, 1969.

Polska Ludowa: Słownik encyklopedyczny (People's Poland: An Encyclopedic Dictionary). Warsaw: Wiedza Powszechna, 1965.

Prochazka, Zora, and Combs, Jerry W., Jr. *The Labor Force in Poland.* International Population Statistics Reports Series P-90, No. 20. Foreign Demographic Analysis Division, Bureau of the Census, U.S. Department of Commerce. Washington, 1964.

Przecławski, Krzysztof. "Niektóre aspekty procesów urbanizacji" (Some Aspects of Urbanization Processes"). *Studia Socjologiczne*, No. 4 (1965), 37-55.

Sarapata, Adam. "Social Mobility." *Polish Perspectives*, IX, 1 (January 1966), 18-27.

Seidler, Grzegorz Leopold. "Marxist Legal Thought in Poland." *Slavic Review*, 26, 3 (1967) 382-94.

Sellier, François. *Salaires et sécurité sociale en Pologne* (Salaries and Social Security in Poland). Centre d'étude de Pays de l'Est Institut de Sociologie Solvay. Brussels: Université Libre, 1959.

Siciński, Andrzej, ed. *Społeczeństwo polskie w badaniach ankietowych Ośrodka Badania Opinii Publicznej przy Polskim Radiu i TV: Lata 1958-1964: Przegląd zebranych materiałów* (Polish Society in Light of Questionnaire Surveys Conducted by the Center for Public Opinion Research of Polish Radio and TV: Years 1958-1964: A Review of Collected Material). Warsaw: Państwowe Wydawnictwo Naukowe, 1966.

Skórzyński, Zygmunt. *Między pracą wypoczynkiem: Czas "zajęty" i czas "wolny" mieszkańców miast w świetle badań empirycznych* (Between Work and Rest: "Busy" Time and "Leisure" Time of City Dwellers in the Light of Empirical Research). Research Workshop on Mass

339

Bibliography

Culture, Institute of Philosophy and Sociology, Polish Academy of Sciences. Wrocław: Ossolińskich, 1965.

―――, and Ziemilski, Andrzej, eds. *Wzory społeczne wakacji w Polsce: Studia i materiały z badań socjologicznych* (Social Models of Polish Vacations: Studies and Materials from Sociological Research). 2 vols. Warsaw: Instytut Naukowy Kultury Fizycznej, 1971.

Smolinski, Leon. "Economics and Politics: IV Reforms in Poland." *Problems of Communism*, xv, 4 (July-August 1966), 8-13.

Sturmthal, Adolf. "The Workers' Councils in Poland." *Industrial and Labor Relations Review*, xiv, 3 (April 1961), 380-96.

Szczepański, Jan, ed. *Wykształcenie a pozycja społeczna inteligencji* (Education and the Social Position of the Intelligentsia). Lodz: 1960.

―――. "Inteligencja a pracownicy umysłowi" ("The Intelligentsia and White Collar Workers"). *Przegląd Socjologiczny*, xii, 2, n.d., 7-23.

―――. *Odmiany czasu teraźniejszego* (Variations on the Present Tense). Warsaw: Książka i Wiedza, 1971.

―――. *Polish Society*. New York: Random House, 1970.

―――. "Refleksje nad planowaniem życia społecznego." ("Reflections on the Planning of Social Life"). *Wieś Współczesna*, n.d., pp. 54-63.

―――. "Sociology 1968." *Polish Perspectives*, xii, 3 (March 1969), 27-33.

―――. "Społeczne aspekty industrializacji w Polsce Ludowej" ("Social Aspects of Industrialization in People's Poland"). *Studia Socjologiczne*, No. 3(18) (1965), 19-41.

―――. "The Polish Intelligentsia: Past and Present." *World Politics*, xiv, 3 (April 1962), 406-20.

―――. "Założenia i zagadnienia badań nad klasą robotniczą" ("Assumptions and Problems of Research on the Working Class"). *Studia Socjologiczne*, No. 1 (12) (1964), 5-18.

―――. "Zmiany w strukturze klasowej społeczeństwa polskiego" ("Changes in the Class Structure of Polish So-

340

Bibliography

ciety"). *Przemiany Społeczne* (Social Changes), reprint, n.d., n.p.

Tejkowski, Bernard. "Społeczność małego miasteczka Pomorza Zachodniego" ("Small-town Society in Western Pomerania"). *Studia Socjologiczne*, 4 (1965), 103-17.

Tyszka, Andrzej. *Uczestnictwo w kulturze: O różnorodności stylów życia* (Participation in Culture: Life-Style Differentiations). Warsaw: Państwowe Wydawnictwo Naukowe, 1971.

Wesołowski, Włodzimierz, ed. *Zróżnicowanie społeczne* (Social Differentiation). Institute of Philosophy and Sociology, Polish Academy of Sciences and Institute of Sociology, Warsaw University. Wrocław: Ossolińskich, 1970.

Wiatr, Jerzy J. *Polska—nowy naród: Proces formowania się socjalistycznego narodu polskiego* (Poland—A New Nation: The Process of Formation of the Polish Socialist Nation). Warsaw: Wiedza Powszechna, 1971.

————, ed. *Studies in Polish Political System.* Department of Political Sociology, Institute of Philosophy and Sociology, Polish Academy of Sciences. Wrocław: Ossolineum, 1967.

————. *Społeczeństwo: Wstęp do socjologii systematycznej* (Society: An Introduction to Systematic Sociology). Warsaw: Państwowe Wydawnictwo Naukowe, 1965.

Żarnowski, Janusz. *O inteligencji polskiej lat międzywojennych* (On the Polish Intelligentsia of the Interwar Period). Warsaw: Wiedza Powszechna, 1965.

Zielinski, Janusz G. "On the Effectiveness of the Polish Economic Reforms." *Soviet Studies*, xxii, 3 (1971), 406-32.

II. Religion, Ideology and Ethics

Aiken, Henry D. *The Age of Ideology.* New York: Mentor, New American Library, 1956.

Almond, Gabriel A. *The Appeals of Communism.* Princeton: Princeton University Press, 1954.

Bibliography

Apter, David, ed. *Ideology and Discontent.* New York: The Free Press, 1964.

Bell, Daniel. *The End of Ideology: On the Exhaustion of Political Ideas in the Fifties.* Glencoe, Ill.: The Free Press, 1960.

Berdayev, Nicolas. *Christianity and Anti-Semitism.* Alan A. Spears and Victor B. Kanter, trans. New York: Philosophical Library, 1954.

Berger, Peter L. *The Sacred Canopy: Elements of a Sociological Theory of Religion.* Garden City, N.Y.: Doubleday and Co., 1967.

Blit, Lucjan. *The Origins of Polish Socialism.* Cambridge: Cambridge University Press, 1971.

Durkheim, Emile. *Elementary Forms of the Religious Life.* Joseph W. Swain, trans. Glencoe, Ill.: The Free Press, 1954.

Engels, Friedrich. *Anti-Duehring: Herr Eugen Duehring's Revolution in Science.* Moscow: Foreign Languages Publishing House, 1962.

———. *Dialectics of Nature.* Moscow: Foreign Languages Publishing House, 1962.

Hegel, G. *Reason in History: A General Introduction to the Philosophy of History.* R. S. Hartman, trans. New York: Bobbs-Merrill, 1953.

Hersch, Jeanne. *Idéologies et Réalité: Essai d'orientation politique* (Ideologies and Reality: Essay on Political Orientations). Paris: Gallimard, 1957.

Jaroszewski, Tadeusz M. "Dynamika praktyk religijnych i podstaw światopoglądowych w Polsce w świetle badań socjologicznych" ("The Dynamics of Religious Practices and World Outlook Postures in Poland in the Light of Sociological Research"). *Kultura i Społeczeństwo,* x, 1 (January-March 1966), 133-49.

Kamenka, Eugene. *The Ethical Foundations of Marxism.* London: Routledge, 1962.

Kautsky, Karl. *The Dictatorship of the Proletariat.* Ann Arbor: University of Michigan Press, 1964.

342

Bibliography

Kelsen, Hans. "Democracy and Socialism." *Conference on Jurisprudence and Politics*, No. 15 (1954), 63-87.

Kerschner, Lee R. "Cybernetics and Dialectical-Historical Materialism in the Soviet Union." Paper presented at the Far Western Slavic Conference, Claremont Colleges, Calif., April 10-11, 1965.

Kłoczowski, Jerzy, ed. *Kościół w Polsce* (The Church in Poland). 2 vols. Cracow: ZNAK Publishing House. Vol. ɪ, 1966; Vol. ɪɪ, 1970.

Kołakowski, Leszek. "Tezy o nadziei i beznadziejnośći" ("Theses on Hope and Hopelessness"). *Kultura*, Paris, No. 6/285 (June 1971), 3-21.

————. *The Alienation of Reason: A History of Positivist Thought*. Norbert Guterman, trans. Garden City, N.Y.: Doubleday and Co., 1968.

————. "The Fate of Marxism in Eastern Europe." With comments by Cyril E. Black and Aleksander Gella. *Slavic Review*, 29, 2 (June 1970), 175-202.

————. *Toward a Marxist Humanism*. Jane Zielonko Peel, trans. New York: Grove Press, 1968.

Kuusinen, O. V. *Fundamentals of Marxism-Leninism*. C. Dutt, trans. Moscow: Foreign Languages Publishing House, 1963.

Lane, Robert E. *Political Ideology*. New York: The Free Press, 1962.

Lenin, V. I. *Marx: Engels: Marxism*. 4th English edn. Moscow: Foreign Languages Publishing House, 1951.

Lichtheim, George. "Class and Hierarchy: A Critique of Marx?" *European Journal of Sociology*, v, 1 (1964), 101-11.

Lukács, Georg. *Geschichte und Klassenbewustsein* (History and Class Consciousness). Berlin: 1923.

————. *Studies in Marxist Dialectics*. Rodney Livingstone, trans. Cambridge: M.I.T. Press, 1971.

Luxemburg, Rosa. *The Russian Revolution and Leninism or Marxism*. Ann Arbor: University of Michigan Press, 1962.

Bibliography

Malinowski, Bronisław. *Magic, Science, and Religion.* Glencoe, Ill.: Free Press, 1948.

Mannheim, Karl. *Ideology and Utopia.* Louis Wirth and Edward Shils, trans. New York: International Library of Psychology, Philosophy, and Scientific Method, 1936.

Marx, Karl. *Early Writings.* T. B. Bottomore, trans. and ed. New York: McGraw-Hill, 1964.

————. *Selected Writings in Sociology and Social Philosophy.* T. B. Bottomore, trans., Bottomore and Maximilian Rubel, eds. New York: McGraw-Hill, 1956.

————, and Engels, Friedrich. *Basic Writings on Politics and Philosophy.* Lewis S. Feuer, ed. Garden City, N.Y.: Anchor, Doubleday and Co., 1959.

————. *Manifesto of the Communist Party.* New York: International Publishers, 1934.

————. *Selected Correspondence: 1846-1895.* New York: International Publishers, 1942.

————. *Selected Works.* Moscow: Foreign Languages Publishing House, Vol. ɪ, 1958; Vol. ɪɪ, 1951.

Mendel, Arthur P., ed. *Essential Works of Marxism.* New York: Bantam Books, 1965.

Meyer, Alfred G. *Leninism.* Cambridge: Harvard University Press, 1957.

Moore, Barrington. *Political Power and Social Theory.* New York: Harper and Row, 1962.

Muszyński, Heliodor. *Teoretyczne problemy wychowania moralnego* (Theoretical Problems Concerning Moral Education). Warsaw: Państwowe Zakłady Wydawnictw Szkolnych, 1965.

Nemira, K. "Sovest" ("Conscience"). *Kategorii Marksistko-Leninskoy Etiki* (Categories of Marxist-Leninist Ethics). Higher Party School of Novosibirsk. Moscow: Misl, 1965, 7-93.

Novosibirskaya Vyzshaya Partiina Shkola (Higher Party School of Novosibirsk). *Kategorii Marksistko-Leninskoy Etiki* (Categories of Marxist-Leninist Ethics). Moscow: Misl, 1965.

Orędzie biskupów polskich do biskupów niemieckich:

Bibliography

Materiały i dokumenty (Proclamation of Polish Bishops to German Bishops: Materials and Documents). Warsaw: Polonia, 1966.

Parsons, Talcott, ed. "Religion and Social Structure," in *Theories of Society*, Vol. I. New York: The Free Press, 1966, pp. 645-82.

Rokeach, Milton. "Political and Religious Dogmatism: An Alternative to the Authoritarian Personality." *Psychological Monographs*, LXX, 18 (1956), 1-43.

Schaff, Adam. *A Philosophy of Man*. New York: Monthly Review Press, 1963.

———. *Marksizm a jednostka ludzka: Przyczynek do marksistowskiej filozofii człowieka* (Marxism and the Human Individual: A Note to the Marxist Philosophy of Man). Warsaw: Państwowe Wydawnictwo Naukowe, 1965. Available in English trans. by Olgierd Wojtasiewicz as *Marxism and the Human Individual*. New York: McGraw-Hill, 1970.

Schumpeter, Joseph A. *Capitalism, Socialism, and Democracy*. 3rd edn. New York: Harper and Brothers, 1950.

Singer, Milton. *The Scientific Study of Religion*. New York: Macmillan, 1970.

Smith, Donald Eugene. *Religion and Political Development*. Boston: Little, Brown and Co., 1970.

Stiehler, G. *Die Dialektik in Hegels "Phänomenologie des Geistes"* (The Dialectic of Hegel's "Phenomenology of the Spirit"). Berlin: Akademie, 1964.

Tawney, R. H. *Religion and the Rise of Capitalism*. New York: Harcourt, Brace and Co., 1926.

Troeltsch, Ernst. *The Social Teachings of the Christian Churches*. Olive Wyon, trans. London: Allen and Unwin, 1911.

Tucker, Robert C. "The Deradicalization of Marxist Movements." *American Political Science Review*, LXI, 2, June 1967, pp. 343-58.

Ulam, Adam. *The Unfinished Revolution: An Essay on the Sources of Marxism and Communism*. New York: Random House, 1960.

Bibliography

Wiatr, Jerzy J. *Czy zmierzch ery ideologii? Problemy polityki i ideologii w świecie współczesnym* (Is it the End of Ideology? Problems of Politics and Ideology in the Contemporary World). Warsaw: Książka i Wiedza, 1966.

———. *Socjologia zaangażowana: Szkice o socjologii i polityce* (Sociology Engaged: Sketches on Sociology and Politics). Warsaw: Książka i Wiedza, 1965.

III. The Sociology and Politics of Professional-Occupational Groups

GENERAL

Burnstein, Eugene et al. "Prestige vs. Excellence as Determinants of Role Attractiveness." *American Sociological Review*, xxviii, 2 (April 1963), 212-19.

Goblot, Edmond, "Class and Occupation." Jesse Pitts, trans. *Theories of Society*, Vol. i, Talcott Parsons et al., eds. New York: The Free Press, 1961, pp. 525-40.

Goode, William J. "Community within a Community: The Professions." *American Sociological Review*, xxii (April 1957), 194-200.

———, and Cornish, Mary Jean. *The Professions in Modern Society*. New York: Russell Sage Foundation, n.d.

Hall, J. R., and Jones, D. C. "The Social Grading of Occupations." *British Journal of Sociology*, i (1950).

Hughes, Everett C. *Men and Their Work*. New York: The Free Press, 1958.

Hulin, Charles L. "Effects of Community Characteristics on Measures of Job Satisfaction." *Journal of Applied Psychology*, l, 2 (1966), 185-92.

———, and Smith, Patricia Cain. "Sex Differences in Job Satisfaction." *Journal of Applied Psychology*, xlviii, 2 (April 1964), 88-92.

Inkeles, Alex. "Industrial Man: The Relation of Status to Experience, Perception, and Value." *American Journal of Sociology*, lxvi (July 1960). Also Bobbs-Merrill Reprint Series in the Social Sciences, No. 131.

———, and Rossi, Peter H. "National Comparisons of Oc-

Bibliography

cupational Prestige." *American Journal of Sociology*, LXI (1956), 329-39. Also in *Sociology: The Progress of a Decade*, Seymour Martin Lipset and Neil J. Smelser, eds. Englewood Cliffs, N.J.: Prentice-Hall, 1961, pp. 506-16.

Krause, Elliott A. *The Sociology of Occupations*. Boston: Little, Brown and Co., 1971.

Miller, D. C., and Form, William H. *Industrial Sociology*. New York: Harper and Brothers, 1951.

Parsons, Talcott. *Essays in Sociological Theory*. 2nd edn. Glencoe, Ill.: The Free Press, 1954.

Robinson, John P. *Measures of Occupational Attitudes and Occupational Characteristics*. Ann Arbor: Survey Research Center, Institute for Social Research, University of Michigan, 1969.

Rosenberg, Morris. *Occupations and Values*. Glencoe, Ill.: The Free Press, 1957.

TEACHERS

Fiszman, Joseph R. "Occupational Group Values vs. the System's Expectations: Teachers in East Europe and the United States." Paper presented at the 63rd Annual Meeting of the American Political Science Association, Chicago, Ill., September 7, 1967.

———. "Teachers: Agents of Socialization: The Case of Poland, Yugoslavia and the United States." Paper presented at Far Western Slavic Conference, Palo Alto, Calif., April 1969.

———. *Teachers in Poland as Transmitters of Socio-Political Values*. Report, Project S-417. Washington: Office of Education, U.S. Department of Health, Education, and Welfare, 1969.

Gołębiowski, Bronisław. *Nauczyciele i uczniowie: Młode pokolenie wsi Polski Ludowej* (Teachers and Pupils: The Young Village Generation of People's Poland). 6 vols. Warsaw: Ludowa Współdzielnia Wydawnicza, 1969.

Korab. "Western." *Kultura*, Paris, 5/261 (June 1969), 35-74.

Kozakiewicz, Mikołaj. "Co myślą kończąc Studium Nauczycielskie?" ("What They Think Upon Graduation from

Bibliography

School of Teachers' Education?"). Cadre Material for Internal Use. Discussion Material Series. Warsaw: Secular School Association, 1968 (Mimeo.).

——. "Kilka słów o środowisku nauczycielskim" ("A Few Words About the Teachers' Milieu"). *Wieś Współczesna*, No. 6 (1967), 73-82.

——. "Rural Teachers' Marriages as a Reflection of Transformations in Płock Industrialized Region." *Wieś Współczesna*, No. 3 (157) (March 1970), 70-82. English language *Summaries*, pp. 8-10.

——. *Światopogląd 1000 nauczycieli: Sprawozdanie z badań ankietowych* (The World Outlook of 1,000 Teachers: A Report of a Questionnaire Survey). Warsaw: Państwowe Zakłady Wydawnictw Szkolnych, 1961.

Kozłowski, Józef. *Nauczyciel a zawód* (The Teacher and the Profession). Warsaw: Nasza Księgarnia, 1966.

Krawcewicz, Stanisław. *Zawód nauczyciela: Z badań nad doskonaleniem i samokształceniem* (The Teaching Profession: From Research on Continuous Improvement and Self-Education). Warsaw: Książka i Wiedza, 1970.

Riesman, David. "The Teacher Amid Changing Expectations." *Harvard Educational Review*, xxiv, 2 (1954) 106-17.

Rosenthal, Alan. *Pedagogues and Power: Teacher Groups in School Politics*. Syracuse: Syracuse University Press, 1969.

Sadaj, B. *Społeczne problemy zawodu nauczyciela* (Social Problems of the Teaching Profession). Warsaw: Państwowe Zakłady Wydawnictw Szkolnych, 1967.

Szymański, Józef. *Rola kierownika w doskonaleniu pracy szkoły podstawowej* (The Principal's Role in Perfecting the Work of the Elementary School). Warsaw: Państwowe Zakłady Wydawnictw Szkolnych, 1965.

Waller, Willard. *The Sociology of Teaching*. New York: John Wiley & Sons, 1965.

Woskowski, Jan. *Nauczyciele szkół podstawowych z wyższym wykształceniem w szkole i poza szkołą* (Elemen-

Bibliography

tary School Teachers with Higher Education In and Out of School). Inter-Institute Center for Research on Higher Education. Warsaw: Państwowe Wydawnictwo Naukowe, 1965.

———. *O pozycji społecznej nauczyciela* (On the Social Position of the Teacher). Center for Sociological Research, Institute of Philosophy and Sociology, Polish Academy of Sciences. Warsaw: Państwowe Wydawnictwo Naukowe, 1965.

———. *Z badań nad nauczycielami zawodu* (From Research on Vocational Teachers). Center for Work Culture, Institute of Philosophy and Sociology, Polish Academy of Sciences. Wrocław: Ossolińskich, 1966.

Zeigler, Harmon. *The Political Life of American Teachers.* Englewood Cliffs, N.J.: Prentice-Hall, 1967.

———. *The Political World of the High School Teacher.* Eugene, Oregon: Center for the Advanced Study of Educational Administration, 1966.

IV. Education and Socialization

GENERAL

Alternative Futures and Educational Policy. Stanford Research Institute Report prepared for Bureau of Research, U.S. Office of Education. OEC-1-7-071013-4274. Washington, D.C., 1970.

Beck, Robert H. *Change and Harmonization in European Education.* Minneapolis: University of Minnesota Press, 1971.

Becker, H. S. "Social-Class Variations in the Teacher-Pupil Relationship." *Journal of Educational Sociology,* xxv (April 1952), 451-65.

Bender, Gerald J. "Political Socialization and Political Change." *Western Political Quarterly,* xx, 2, Part 1 (June 1967), 390-407.

Bendix, Reinhard. "Compliant Behavior and Individual Personality." *American Journal of Sociology,* lviii, 3 (1952), 292-303.

Bibliography

Berenda, R. W. *The Influence of the Group on the Judgment of Peers.* New York: King's Crown, 1950.

Clark, Burton R. *Educating the Expert Society.* San Francisco: Chandler, 1962.

Coleman, James S., ed. *Education and Political Development.* Princeton: Princeton University Press, 1965.

Conant, James Bryant. *The Comprehensive High School: A Second Report to Interested Citizens.* New York: Mc-Graw-Hill, 1967.

Curti, Merle. *The Social Ideas of American Educators— With New Chapter on the Last Twenty-Five Years.* American Historical Association Commission on the Social Studies. Totowa, N.J.: Littlefield, Adams and Co., 1968.

Dahrendorf, Ralf. "Die soziale Funktion der Erziehung in der industriellen Gesellschaft" ("The Social Function of Education in Industrial Society"). *Speculum: Saarländische Studentenzeitschrift,* I, 7 (1956).

Davis, A. *Social Class Influences Upon Learning.* Cambridge: Harvard University Press, 1948.

Dawson, Richard E., and Prewitt, Kenneth. *Political Socialization.* Boston: Little, Brown and Co., 1969.

Dewey, John. *Democracy and Education: An Introduction to the Philosophy of Education.* New York: The Free Press, 1966.

Durkheim, Emile. *L'Education Morale* (Moral Education). Paris: Felix Alcan, 1925.

Easton, David, and Dennis, Jack. *Children in the Political System: Origins of Political Legitimacy.* New York: Mc-Graw-Hill, 1969.

————. "The Child's Acquisition of Regime Norms: Political Efficacy." *American Political Science Review,* LXI, 1 (March 1967), 25-38.

Elkin, Frederick. *The Child and Society: The Process of Socialization.* New York: Random House, 1960.

Erikson, Erik H. *Childhood and Society.* New York: Norton, 1950.

Fichter, Joseph H.S.J. *Parochial School: A Sociological Study.* Garden City, N.Y.: Doubleday and Co., 1964.

Bibliography

Goldrich, Daniel. *Sons of the Establishment: Elite Youth in Panama and Costa Rica.* Chicago: Rand McNally, 1966.

Greenstein, Fred. *Children and Politics.* New Haven: Yale University Press, 1965.

Hahn, Robert G., and Bidna, David B., eds. *Secondary Education: Origins and Directions.* New York: Macmillan Co., 1965.

Hess, Robert D. "The Socialization of Attitudes Toward Political Authority: Some Cross-National Comparisons." *International Social Science Journal,* xv (1963), 542-59.

Kafoury, Gregory. "Moral Incentives in the Cuban Revolution." Unpublished M.A. Thesis. Department of Political Science, University of Oregon, 1971.

Kluckhohn, C., and Murray, H. A., eds. *Personality in Nature, Society, and Culture.* 2nd edn. New York: Alfred A. Knopf, 1953.

Kozakiewicz, Mikołaj. "O szerszy rozwój postaw zaangażowanych" ("About Broader Development of Involvement Postures"). *Wieś Współczesna,* xiv, 7 (161) (July 1970), 105-09.

Langton, Kenneth P. *Political Socialization.* New York: Oxford University Press, 1969.

Litt, Edgar. "Civic Education Norms and Political Indoctrination." *American Sociological Review,* xxviii (February 1963), 69-75.

———, ed. *The Political Imagination.* Glenview, Ill.: Scott, Foresman, 1966.

Massialas, Byron G., and Kazamias, Andreas M., eds. *Crucial Issues in the Teaching of Social Studies: A Book of Readings.* Englewood Cliffs, N.J.: Prentice-Hall, 1964.

Piaget, Jean. *The Moral Judgment of the Child.* Glencoe, Ill.: The Free Press, 1948.

Pitts, Jesse R., ed. "Processes of Socialization." *Theories of Society,* Vol. ii. New York: The Free Press, 1961, pp. 821-65.

Postman, Neil, and Weingartner, Charles. *Teaching as a Subversive Activity.* New York: Delacorte Press, 1969.

Bibliography

Rokeach, Milton. *Beliefs, Attitudes and Values.* Berkeley: Josey-Bass, 1968.

————. "On the Unity of Thought and Belief." *Journal of Personality,* xxv, 2 (1956), 224-50.

Rousseau, Jean Jacques. *Emile or Treatise on Education.* William H. Payne, trans. New York: D. A. Appleton and Co., 1908.

Sewell, William H., and Ellenbogen, B. F. "Social Status and the Measured Intelligence of Small City and Rural Children." *American Sociological Review,* xvii (October 1952), 612-16.

————, and Haller, A. O. "Social Status and the Personality Adjustment of the Child." *Sociometry,* xix (June 1956), 114-25.

Sigel, Roberta S., ed. *Learning about Politics.* New York: Random House, 1970.

————. *Political Socialization: Its Role in the Political Process.* Philadelphia: Special Issue, *The Annals of the American Academy of Political and Social Science,* Vol. 361 (September 1965).

Spencer, Herbert. *Essays on Education, Etc.* London: J. M. Dent and Sons, 1911.

Spinley, Betty M. *The Deprived and the Privileged.* London: Routledge and Kegan Paul, 1953.

Tapp, June L., ed. *Socialization, the Law, and Society.* Special issue, *Journal of Social Issues,* xxvii, 2 (1971).

Warner, W. S. et al. *Who Shall Be Educated?* New York: Harper and Brothers, 1944.

Wirt, Frederick M., and Kirst, Michael W. *The Political Web of American Schools.* Boston: Little, Brown and Company, 1972.

Wolfenstein, Martha, and Kliman, Gilbert, eds. *Children and the Death of a President: Multi-Disciplinary Studies.* Garden City, N.Y.: Anchor, Doubleday and Co., 1966.

EASTERN EUROPE

Academy of Social Sciences, Central Committee of the Communist Party (b) of the USSR. *Die Grundlagen der kom-*

Bibliography

munistischen Erziehung (Principles of Communist Education). Berlin: Volk und Wissen, 1964.

Administration of Teaching in Social Sciences, Ministry of Higher Education of the USSR. *Program of the Course in Dialectical and Historical Materialism for Institutions of Higher Learning (140 Hours).* Moscow: Political Literature, 1957. Reproduced in full in *Administration of Teaching in Social Sciences in the USSR: Syllabi for Three Required Courses.* Ann Arbor: University of Michigan Press, 1960.

Bereday, George Z. F. "Education and Youth." *The Annals of the American Academy of Political and Social Science,* Vol. 317 (May 1958), 63-70.

Bowen, James. *Soviet Education: Anton Makarenko and the Years of Experiment.* Madison: University of Wisconsin Press, 1962.

Cary, Charles D. "A Program for *Vospitanie* (Upbringing) in the Schools: An Approach to the Study of Political Socialization of Youth in the USSR." Paper presented at Meeting of Far Western Slavic Conference, Palo Alto, Calif., April 25-26, 1969.

Central Committee, Communist Party of Slovakia. *O výbere a výchove kadrov: Bibliografická pomôcka k spisom V. I. Lenina* (On the Selection and Education of Cadres: Bibliographical Aid to the Writings of V. I. Lenin). Bratislava: Slovenské Vydavatelstvo Politickiej Literatúry, 1961.

DeWitt, Nicholas. *Education and Professional Employment in the USSR.* 61-40. Washington: National Science Foundation, 1961.

Fischer-Galati, Stephen A. "Communist Indoctrination in Rumanian Elementary Schools." *Harvard Educational Review,* xxii (1952), 191-202.

Hanhardt, Arthur M., Jr. "Political Socialization in the German Democratic Republic." *Societas,* i, 2 (Spring 1971), 101-21.

Korol, Alexander G. *Soviet Education for Science and Technology.* New York: Technology Press, M.I.T.—John Wiley & Sons, 1957.

Bibliography

Kossakowski, A. *Zur Psychologie der Schuljugend* (Toward the Psychology of School Youth). Berlin: Volk und Wissen-Volkseigener Verlag, 1969.

Krupska, Nadieżda. *Wybór pism pedagogicznych* (Selection of Pedagogic Writings). M. Szulkin, trans. from Russian into Polish. Warsaw: Państwowe Zakłady Wydawnictw Szkolnych, 1951.

Kurdybacha, Łukasz. *Idee oświatowe i wychowawcze W. I. Lenina* (The Educational and Pedagogical Ideas of V. I. Lenin). Warsaw: Państwowe Wydawnictwo Naukowe, 1970.

Lilge, Frederic. "Lenin and the Politics of Education." *Slavic Review,* 27, 2 (June 1968), 230-57.

Meyer, Frank S. *The Molding of Communists: The Training of the Communist Cadre.* New York: Harcourt, Brace and World, 1961.

Ognyov, N. *The Diary of a Communist Schoolboy.* Alexander Werth, trans. New York: Brewer and Warren, 1930.

Pennar, Jaan, et al. *Modernization and Diversity in Soviet Education.* New York: Praeger, 1971.

Pundeff, Marin V. "Education for Communism." *Eastern Europe in the Sixties.* Stephen Fischer-Galati, ed. New York: Frederick A. Praeger, 1963, pp. 26-51.

Shimoniak, Wasyl. *Communist Education: Its History, Philosophy, and Politics.* Chicago: Rand McNally, 1970.

Zdravomislov, A. G., and Yadov, V. A., ed. *Trud ee razvitye litchnostii* (Labor and Personality Development). Leningrad: Lenizdat, 1965.

POLAND

Bandura, Ludwik. *Trudności w procesie uczenia się* (Difficulties in the Process of Learning). Warsaw: Państwowe Zakłady Wydawnictw Szkolnych, 1968.

Chałasiński, Józef. "Universities and Nationality." *Poland* (May 1969), 33-34.

Commission of Pedagogic Sciences, Polish Academy of Sciences. *Rocznik Komisji Nauk Pedagogicznych* (Commission Yearbook).

Bibliography

Cyrankiewicz, Józef. "Szkoła socjalistycznego wychowania młodego pokolenia" ("The School of Socialist Education of the Young Generation"). *Ruch Pedagogiczny*, IX (XLI), 4 (April 1967), 409-15.

Czerwiński, Franciszek. "W sprawie wychowania patriotyczno-internacjonalistycznego" ("On the Subject of Patriotic-Internationalist Education"). *Życie Szkoły*, XXIV, 4 (264) (April 1969), 8-9.

Dąbrowski, Kazimierz, ed. *Selected Bibliography of Polish Educational Materials*. Prepared for the Office of Education, U.S. Department of Health, Education and Welfare. Lodz: Polish Scientific Publishers PWN, 1968.

Dziduszko, Karol. *Uniwersyteckie kształcenie nauczycieli* (University Education of Teachers). Warsaw: Państwowe Zakłady Wydawnictw Szkolnych, 1963.

Falski, Marian. *Aktualne zagadnienia ustrojowo-organizacyjne szkolnictwa polskiego* (Contemporary Systemic and Organizational Problems of Polish Schools). Wrocław: Ossolińskich, 1957.

Główny Urząd Statystyczny (Main Statistical Bureau). *Rocznik statystyczny szkolnictwa 1944/45-1966/67* (Statistical Yearbook of Education 1944/45-1966/67). Warsaw: GUS, 1967.

Golański, Henryk. "Planning for the Future." *Polish Perspectives*, IX, 12 (December 1966), 21-31.

Grynberg, Henryk. "Pochodzenie społeczne czyli Łapa" ("Social Background or Łapa"). *Kultura*, Paris. 4/259 (1969), 45-57.

Grzybowski, Konstanty. "Place in Society." *Polish Perspectives*, IX, 12 (December 1966), 43-49.

Gurycka, Antonina. "Dzieci bierne społecznie" ("Socially Apathetic Children"). *Psychologia Wychowawcza*, X (XXIV), 4 (April 1967), 298-411.

Hamm-Brücher, Hildegard, "Bildungsreise durch Polen: Ein Land der Lernenden" ("Educational Tour Over Poland: A Land of Learners"). *Die Zeit*, Hamburg (June 27, 1967), 10.

Han-Ilgiewicz, Natalia. *W poszukiwaniu dróg resocjalizacji:*

Bibliography

Retrospektywna analiza experymentu pedagogicznego z grupą chłopców wykolejonych (In Quest of Ways Toward Resocialization: A Retrospective Analysis of a Pedagogic Experiment with a Group of Delinquent Boys). Warsaw: Państwowe Wydawnictwo Naukowe, 1967.

Jurek, Marian, and Skrzypkowski, Edward. *Konfrontacje: Tradycjonalizm a współczesność w wychowaniu wojskowym* (Confrontations: Traditionalism and Modernity in Military Education). Warsaw: MON, 1965.

Kamiński, Aleksander. "Wychowanie nowoczesne, to także wychowanie do wczasów" ("Modern Education Is also Education for Leisure"). *Nowa Szkoła*, No. 5 (1961), 2-5.

Kliszko, Zenon. "Participation and Co-Responsibility—Main Direction in Ideological Shaping of Younger Generation." Excerpts from speech at Plenum of Gdańsk PUWP Voivodship Committee. *Contemporary Poland: Supplement-Documents*, n.d., pp. 5-9.

Kłuczyński, Jan. "Oświata a rozwój gospodarki" ("Education and Economic Development"). *Nowa Szkoła*, No. 6 (1967), 47-51.

Kołabińska, Maria, ed. *Praca dydaktyczno-wychowawcza w szkole dla pracujących: Z doświadczeń nauczycieli* (Didactic-Educational Effort in Schools for Workers: From the Experience of Teachers). Main Methodological Center, Ministry of Education. Warsaw: Państwowe Zakłady Wydawnictw Szkolnych, 1965.

Kowalewska, Salomea. *Przysposobienie do pracy w przemyśle: Z zagadnień kultury pracy* (Preparation for Work in Industry: Problems of Work Culture). Center for Work Culture, Institute of Philosophy and Sociology, Polish Academy of Sciences. Wrocław: Ossolińskich, 1966. Also available in English edn. as *Some Aspects of Preparation for Work in Industry*. Wrocław: Ossolineum, 1966.

Kozakiewicz, Mikołaj. "Dyskusja nad reformą szkolną: O reformie kształcenia nauczycieli dyskusynie" ("Discussion on School Reform: About the Education of Teachers, Debate"). *Kwartalnik Pedagogiczny*, x, 3 (1965), 171-75.

Bibliography

————. *Halo, młody przyjacielu* (Hallo, Young Friend). Warsaw: Ludowa Spółdzielnia Wydawnicza, 1967.

————. "Higher Education: Quantity into Quality." *Polish Perspectives*, xv, 2 (February 1972), 14-20.

————. "Industrialisation et promotion de la jeunesse: Théorie et pratique" ("Industrialization and Youth Advancement: Theory and Practice"). *Revue de l'institut de sociologie* (Brussels), cxcvii, 3 (1970), 417-26.

————. "Nie agitować, ale organizować przeżycie" ("Not to Propagandize but to Organize Experience"). *Życie Szkoły*, xxiv, 4 (264) (April 1969), 5-7.

————. *Niezbadane ścieżki wychowania* (Unexplored Paths of Education). Warsaw: Nasza Księgarnia, 1964.

————. *O światopoglądzie i wychowaniu* (On World Outlook and Education). Warsaw: Państwowe Zakłady Wydawnictw Szkolnych, 1965.

————. *Paradoksy młodzieżowe* (Youth Paradoxes). Warsaw: Książka i Wiedza, 1970.

Krzysztoszek, Zofia. "Kilka uwag o wychowaniu patriotycznym i internacjonalistycznym" ("A Few Remarks on Patriotic and Internationalist Education"). *Życie Szkoły*, xxiv, 4 (264) (April 1969), 13-15.

Kuligowska, Krystyna. "Kilka uwag i propozycji w sprawie zwiększenia efektywności szkół" ("A Few Remarks and Suggestions on Ways to Increase School Effectiveness"). *Nowa Szkoła*, No. 9 (1967), 2-9.

————. "O współzależności między wynikami nauczania a przygotowaniem nauczyciela" ("On the Interdependence Between Learning Results and Teacher Preparation"). *Nowa Szkoła*, No. 7-8 (1967), 10-18.

Kupisiewicz, Czesław, ed. *Metody i przykłady programowania dydaktycznego* (Methods and Examples of Programmed Learning). Warsaw: Państwowe Wydawnictwo Naukowe, 1970.

————. "Seeking a New Program." *Poland*, No. 5 (177), (May 1969), 6-7, 21.

Matejko, Alexander. "Planning and Tradition in Polish

Bibliography

Higher Education." *Minerva*, VII, 4 (Summer 1969), 621-48.

Ministerstwo Szkolnictwa Wyższego (Ministry of Higher Education). *Informator dla kandydatów do szkół wyższych i średnich szkół zawodowych dla maturzystów* (Guide for Candidates to Higher Education and to Secondary Professional-Vocational Schools for Matura-Holders). Warsaw: Państwowe Wydawnictwo Naukowe (annual publication).

Muszyński, Heliodor. *Wstęp do metodologii pedagogiki* (Introduction to Pedagogical Methodology). Warsaw: Państwowe Wydawnictwo Naukowe, 1971.

Okoń, Wincenty. *Process nauczania* (The Teaching Process). Fifth edn. Institute of Pedagogy. Warsaw: Państwowe Zakłady Wydawnictw Szkolnych, 1965.

Podoski, Kazimierz. "Koszty kształcenia i wykształcenia w Polsce" ("Costs of Training and Education in Poland"). *Nowa Szkoła*, No. 7-8 (1967), 4-9.

Polak, Wojciech. *Organizacja pracy domowej ucznia: Zagadnienia obciążania* (Organization of a Pupil's Homework: The Problem of Overloading). Warsaw: Nasza Księgarnia, 1965.

Pomykało, Wojciech, ed. *Ideologia i światopoglad w wychowaniu* (Ideology and World Outlook in Education). Warsaw: Państwowe Zakłady Wydawnictw Szkolnych, 1968.

Przecławski, Krzysztof. *Instytucje wychowania w wielkim mieście: Wybrane problemy socjologii wychowania* (Educational Institutions in the Big City: Select Problems from the Sociology of Education). Warsaw: Państwowe Wydawnictwo Naukowe, 1971.

Ratuszniak, Zygmunt. "The System." *Polish Perspectives*, IX, 12 (December 1966), 5-14.

Searing, Marjory E. *Estimates of Educational Attainment in Poland: 1950-1969*. International Population Reports Series P-95, No. 68. Washington: Bureau of the Census, U.S. Dept. of Commerce, 1970.

Singer, Gusta. *Teacher Education in a Communist State: Poland 1956-1961*. New York: Bookman Associates, 1965.

Bibliography

Suchodolski, Bohdan. "Democratization." *Polish Perspectives*, IX, 12 (December 1966), 50-56.

―――. *Edukacja narodu: 1918-1968* (The Education of a Nation: 1918-1968). Omega Series. Warsaw: Wiedza Powszechna, 1970.

―――. *Społeczeństwo i kultura doby współczesnej a wychowanie: Zarys pedagogiki* (Society and Culture in the Present Era and Education: A Pedagogic Outline). Vol. I. Warsaw: Państwowe Zakłady Wydawnictw Szkolnych, 1958.

Sulewski, Wojciech. *Z frontu tajnego nauczania* (From the Front of Secret Teaching). Warsaw: Czytelnik, 1966.

Szaniawski, Ignacy. *Humanizacja pracy a funkcja społeczna szkoły: Antynomie wykształcenia ogólnego, politechnicznego i zawodowego oraz drogi ich przezwyciężenia* (Humanization of Work and the Social Function of the School: Obstacles in General, Polytechnic and Vocational Education, and Ways of Surmounting Them). 2nd rev. edn. Warsaw: Książka i Wiedza. 1967.

Szczepański, Jan. "Osobowość ludzka w procesie powstania społeczeństwa socjalistycznego" ("The Human Personality During the Process of Emergence of the Socialist Society"). *Kultura i Społeczeństwo*, VIII, 4 (1964), 3-25.

―――. *Sociological Aspects of Higher Education in Poland.* Reprint, n.p., n.d.

―――. "The State and the Planning of Higher Education." *Poland* (January 1969), 32-33, 50-51.

Sztumski, Janusz, ed. *Uniwersytety dla rodziców TSŚ w świetle badań* (Secular School Association Universities for Parents in the Light of Research). Warsaw: Nasza Księgarnia, 1969.

Tatara-Hoszowska, Władysława. *Problemy kształcenia dziewcząt w Polsce Ludowej* (Problems Connected with the Education of Girls in People's Poland). Warsaw: Państwowe Zakłady Wydawnictw Szkolnych, 1970.

Teachers' Symposium. "Kształtowanie patriotyzmu i internacjonalizmu w mojej codziennej pracy" ("The Molding

Bibliography

of Patriotism and Internationalism in My Daily Work").
Nasza Szkoła, xxiv, 4 (264) (April 1969), 25-33.

———. "Nasze środowisko dawniej i dzisiaj" ("Our Environment: Past and Present"). *Nasza Szkoła*, xxiv, 4 (264) (April 1969), 33-45.

Walczyna, Jadwiga. "O nowe elementy knocepcji wychowania patriotycznego i internacjonalistycznego" ("New Elements of the Concepts of Patriotic and Internationalist Education"). *Życie Szokły*, xxiv, 4 (264) (April 1969), 10-13.

Żytomirska, Maria, and Radwan, Zbigniew. *Praca dydaktyczna w Studium Nauczycielskim* (Didactic Work in Schools of Teachers' Education). Warsaw: Państwowe Zakłady Wydawnictw Szkolnych, 1965.

V. Sex Education and Sex Morality

Bardis, Panos D. *The Family in Changing Civilization*. 2nd edn. New York: Associated Educational Services, 1969.

Baruch, Walter Dorothy. *New Ways in Sex Education*. New York: McGraw-Hill, 1959.

Beigel, Hugo G. *Sex from A to Z*. New York: Stephen Daye Press, Frederick Ungar, 1961.

Breasted, Mary. *Oh! Sex Education*. New York: Frederick A. Praeger, 1970.

Cagnon, John H., and Simon, William, eds. *Sexual Deviance*. New York: Harper and Row, 1967.

Colton, Helen. *How to Talk Sex with Our Children*. Los Angeles: Family Forum, 1970.

Cox, Frank D. *Youth, Marriage and the Seductive Society*. Dubuque: William C. Brown, 1968.

Górecki, Jan. *Rozwód: Studium socjologiczno-prawne* (Divorce: A Sociological-Legal Study). Warsaw: Państwowe Wydawnictwo Naukowe, 1965.

Holmes, Urban T. *The Sexual Person: The Church's Role in Human Sexual Development*. New York: Seabury Press, 1970.

Bibliography

Johnson, Eric W. *Sex: Telling it Straight.* Philadelphia: J. B. Lippincott, 1970.

——, and Johnson, Corinne B. *Love and Sex and Growing Up.* Philadelphia: J. B. Lippincott, 1970.

Kelley, Robert K. *Courtship, Marriage and the Family.* New York: Harcourt, Brace Jovanovich, 1969.

Kozakiewicz, Mikołaj. *U podstaw wychowania seksualnego* (At the Base of Sex Education). Society for Planned Motherhood, TSM. Warsaw: Państwowy Zakład Wydawnictw Lekarskich, 1969.

Lederer, William J., and Jackson, Don D. *The Mirages of Marriage.* New York: W. W. Norton and Co., 1968.

Lewin, S. A., and Gilmore, Joan. *Sex without Fear.* New York: Medical Research Press, 1969.

Lifton, Robert Jay, ed. *The Woman in America.* American Academy of Arts and Sciences. Boston: Beacon Press, 1965.

Ligon, Ernest, and Smith, Leona. *The Marriage Climate.* St. Louis: Bethany Press, 1963.

Malewska, Hanna. *Zachowania seksualne u ludzkiej samicy* (The Sexual Behavior of the Human Female). Warsaw: Państwowe Wydawnictwo Naukowe, 1967.

Marshall, Donald, S., and Suggs, Robert C., eds. *Human Sexual Behavior: Variations in the Ethnographic Spectrum.* New York: Basic Books, 1971.

Millet, Kate. *Sexual Politics.* New York: Doubleday and Co., 1970.

Neubeck, Gerhard, ed. *Extra-Marital Relations.* Englewood Cliffs, N.J.: Prentice-Hall, 1969.

Nimkoff, M. F., ed. *Comparative Family Systems.* New York: Houghton Mifflin, 1965.

Potter, Jessie. *Education for Human Sexuality: Reading and Resources.* Oak Lawn, Ill.: Potter, 1970.

Rubin, Isadore, ed. *Sexual Freedom in Marriage.* New York: Signet, New American Library, 1969.

Taylor, Donald L., ed. *Human Sexual Development.* Philadelphia: F. A. Davis Co., 1970.

Bibliography

Toffler, Alvin. *Future Shock*. New York: Random House, 1970.

VI. *Polish Dailies and Periodicals; Yearbooks and Other Official Sources*

Argumenty (Arguments). Weekly organ of Association for Promotion of Secular Culture. Warsaw.

Contemporary Poland. Monthly bulletin of Polish Interpress Agency. Warsaw.

Dookoła Świata (Around the World). Weekly organ of Union of Socialist Youth. Warsaw.

Dziennik Komitetu Pracy i Płac (Committee on Labor and Wages Bulletin). Official daily record of labor and wage regulations. Warsaw.

Dziennik Ludowy (People's Daily). Organ of Executive Committee of United Peoples-Peasant Alliance, ZSL. Warsaw.

Dziennik Urzędowy Ministerstwa Oświaty i Szkolnictwa Wyższego (Official Bulletin of Ministry of Education and Higher Learning). Warsaw.

Dziennik Ustaw (Statutes' Daily). Official record of laws and statutes. Warsaw.

Express Wieczorny (Evening Express). Popular daily. Warsaw.

Fakty i Myśli (Facts and Thoughts). Biweekly organ of Executive Board of Association of Atheists and Free-thinkers. Bydgoszcz.

Gazeta Pomorska (Pomeranian Gazette). Daily organ of Województwo Committee of Polish United Workers' Party, PZPR. Grudziądz.

Gazeta Robotnicza (Workers' Gazette). Daily organ of Województwo Committee of Polish United Workers' Party, PZPR. Wrocław.

Głos Nauczycielski (Teachers' Voice). Weekly organ of Polish Teachers' Union. Warsaw.

Głos Robotniczy (Workers' Voice). Joint daily organ of Województwo and Lodz City Committees of Polish United Workers' Party, PZPR. Lodz.

362

Bibliography

Informator Nauki Polskiej (Polish Science Informant). Annual guide to scientific institutes, institutions of higher education, archives, museums, libraries and scientific societies. Includes personnel roster and addresses. Warsaw: Państwowe Wydawnictwo Naukowe (Polish Scientific Publishers).

Rocznik Statystyczny (Statistical Yearbook). Annual compilation of statistical data issued by Main Statistical Office (*Główny Urząd Statystyczny*, GUS). Available also in abridged pocket-size edn. GUS also publishes quarterly statistical bulletins as well as specialized statistical data. Warsaw.

I.t.d. (Etc.). Weekly organ of Polish Student Association. Warsaw.

Kamena. Literary-cultural biweekly. Lublin.

Kulisy (Behind the Scenes). Illustrated popular weekly. Warsaw.

Kultura (Culture). Monthly. Leading sociocultural, political, and literary emigré publication. Paris.

Kultura (Culture). Weekly. Warsaw.

Kultura i Społeczeństwo (Culture and Society). Quarterly publication of Committee for Research on Contemporary Culture, Polish Academy of Sciences. Warsaw.

Kurier Polski (The Polish Courier). Daily organ of Democratic Alliance, S.D. Warsaw.

Kwartalnik Pedagogiczny (Pedagogic Quarterly). Theoretical journal. Warsaw.

Magazyn Polski (Polish Magazine). Monthly. Warsaw.

Nowa Szkoła (The New School). Monthly organ of Ministry of Education and Higher Learning. Warsaw.

Nowe Drogi (New Roads). Monthly theoretical organ of Central Committee of Polish United Workers' Party, PZPR. Warsaw.

Panorama. Illustrated weekly. Warsaw.

Poland. Monthly illustrated publication designed for foreign distribution. Available in English as well as in other foreign languages. Warsaw.

Polish Perspectives. Monthly sociopolitical and cultural-lit-

Bibliography

erary publication designed for foreign consumption. Available in English as well as in other foreign languages. Warsaw.

Polish Review. Quarterly scholarly publication of Polish Institute of Arts and Sciences in America. New York.

Polityka (Politics). Sociocultural and political weekly. Warsaw.

Przegląd Socjologiczny (Sociological Review). Quarterly publication of Sociological Institute, Lodz University. Lodz.

Przekrój (Crosscut). Popular illustrated weekly. Warsaw.

Radar. Youth monthly. Warsaw.

Rocznik Socjologii Wsi (Rural Sociology Yearbook). Organ (since 1962) of Center for Rural Sociology, Institute of Philosophy and Sociology, Polish Academy of Sciences. Warsaw.

Rodzina i Szkoła (Family and School). Monthly journal for parents and teachers. Warsaw.

Ruch Pedagogiczny (Pedagogic Movement). Biweekly. Warsaw.

Quarterly Review of Scientific Publications. Annotated bibliographies issued by Polish Academy of Sciences' Distribution Center for Scientific Publications. Warsaw.

Słowo Powszechne (Universal Word). Daily organ of Catholic lay group PAX. Warsaw.

Sprawozdania z prac naukowych wydziału nauk społecznych (Reports on Scientific Works of Social Science Section). Monthly publication of Polish Academy of Sciences.

Stolica (Capital). Illustrated weekly. Warsaw.

Studia Socjologiczne (Sociological Studies). Quarterly publication of Institute of Philosophy and Sociology, Polish Academy of Sciences. Warsaw.

Studia Socjologiczno-Polityczne (Studies in Political Sociology). Quarterly publication of Warsaw University. Warsaw.

Sztandar Młodych (Youth Banner). Joint daily organ of Executive Committees of Union of Socialist Youth (ZMS) and Union of Rural Youth (ZMW). Warsaw.

Bibliography

Trybuna Ludu (People's Platform). Official daily organ of Central Committee of Polish United Workers' Party, PZPR. Warsaw.

Twórczość (Creativity). Literary monthly. Warsaw.

Walka Młodych (Youth Battle). Weekly organ of Union of Socialist Youth, ZMS. Warsaw.

Wieś Współczesna (Contemporary Village). Monthly theoretical organ of United People's-Peasant Alliance, ZSL. Warsaw.

Wychowanie (Upbringing). Biweekly. Warsaw.

Zagadnienia i Materiały (Problems and Materials). Semimonthly cadre guide. Organ of Central Committee of Polish United Workers' Party, PZPR. Warsaw.

Zarzewie (Embers). Weekly organ of Union of Rural Youth, ZMW. Warsaw.

Za Wolność i Lud (For Freedom and the People). Biweekly organ of Union of Fighters for Freedom and Democracy, ZBoWiD. Warsaw.

Życie Literackie (Literary Life). Sociocultural and literary weekly. Cracow.

Życie Szkoły (School Life). Monthly (except for July-August) organ of Ministry of Education and Higher Learning. Warsaw.

Życie Szkoły Wyższej (Higher Education Life). Monthly organ of Ministry of Education and Higher Learning. Warsaw.

Życie Warszawy (Warsaw Life). Formally non-Party daily. Warsaw.

Index

activism, 37, 38-41, 61ff
Administration of Apartment
  Buildings, 262
agnostics, 211, 239-40. *See also*
  heretics, secularism
agriculture, 5, 28-29, 46, 49,
  67, 78, 95, 102, 140, 179, 186,
  202-09, 230, 259, 264, 316;
  agricultural circles, 112;
  agricultural engineering, 53;
  agricultural schools, 48, 53,
  65-67, 97-98, 109, 112, 273;
  agricultural workers, 53, 91;
  collectivization, 179; land
  reform, 179; Minister of
  Agriculture, 79; state farms
  PGR), 48-49, 78; village
  cooperatives, 125. *See also*
  peasantry
alcoholism, 14, 25, 116, 126,
  184, 229, 242, 275, 278, 298
American Association for Health,
  Physical Education, and
  Recreation, 154n
American College of Obstetricians and Gynecologists, 153n
American Medical Association,
  154n
American Social Health
  Association, 154n
Anders, General, 293
Andrzejewski, Jerzy, 223, 284
Apollinaire, Guillaume, 284
Aragon, Louis, 284
archeologists, 304-05
architecture, 249
Aristotle, 3
Armstrong, Louis, 224
arts, 14-17, 51, 53, 58-60, 66-70,
  74, 80, 95, 110, 126, 159-60,
  200, 214-15, 223-25, 228-29,
  264, 268, 289-90, 294,
  297-98, 306; art education,
  51, 53, 58-60, 66, 69-70, 95,
  200, 215, 306; film, 15-16, 70,
  223-24, 228, 264, 289, 294,

306; film arts, 59, 70; Higher
  State School for Theater and
  Film Arts ("Leon Schiller
  School"), 306; institutes, 70;
  Ministry of Culture and Arts,
  70, 268; plastic arts, 59;
  theater, 70, 74, 80, 110, 215,
  228, 297, 306. *See also*
  culture, dance, music
Association of Self-Employed
  Artisans, 93
astronomy, 274
Augustyn, Maria, 98
Austria-Hungary, 269. *See also*
  Hungary
authority, 5, 17, 33, 35, 37,
  40-41, 51, 58, 71-72ff;
  educational, 5, 17, 33, 51, 72,
  83, 100, 120, 130, 132, 134,
  257, 261, 271, 278, 287;
  political, 74, 84, 101-04, 107,
  109, 133-34, 149, 159, 180,
  199, 202, 212, 217-18, 254-56,
  298; religious, 237; symbols,
  35, 37, 40-41, 58, 71, 105,
  131-35, 141-43, 145, 148-49,
  159, 175, 178-80, 189, 209,
  215, 234, 282, 323-25. *See
  also* bureaucracy, leadership
awards, decorations, 39, 103,
  137, 249, 259, 264, 293, 297;
  material benefits, 95-96, 131,
  139, 178-79, 190, 214, 217-18,
  286, 318-19; titles, 39, 128-29

BAR, 295
Bardis, Panos D., 153n
Baruch, Dorothy Walter, 153n
Beethoven, Ludwig Van, 224
Beigel, Hugo G., 153n
Białystok, 48, 258; *Województwo*,
  109-10, 130
Bidna, David B., 21n
Bielsk, 130
biology, 62, 67, 122, 263
Bizet, Georges, 224

367

Index

Bloch, Ernst, 147n
Błażej, 48n
Bońkowicz-Sittauer, Jerzy, 48n
Borowska, Janina, 51n
boundaries, 5, 12, 18-20, 28, 155, 251
Brandys, Kazimierz, 284
Breasted, Mary, 153n
Brecht, Bertolt, 284
Breza, Tadeusz, 284
Broniewski, Władysław, 285
Brubeck, Dave, 224
Brun (Bronowicz), Julian, 282
building, 95, 98, 252-59; administration, 256; enterprises, 253-59, 262; housing, 56, 74, 80-83, 95-98, 109-10, 129, 131, 133, 140-41, 148, 184, 213, 252, 256-57, 262, 290, 322; industrial, 257; schools, 37-38, 82, 98, 119, 234, 250-62, 322
bureaucracy, administrative, 30-31, 40-44, 47, 57, 61, 64, 77, 84, 95-96, 108ff; educational, 36, 41-42, 48, 51, 55-56, 61, 64, 96, 109-10, 121-26ff; industrial-managerial, 72, 81, 90-91, 130, 139, 254, 260, 300, 315-16; Party, 81, 120-21, 139, 216, 282, 324; personnel key, 136. *See also* authority, leadership, planners
Bureau of Projects, 258
Bydgoszcz, 130

Canada, 293
Castro, Fidel, 171
censorship, 74
Chałasiński, Józef, 221
chemistry, 22, 62, 67, 88, 135, 193, 242, 277, 296
child care, 46-47, 61, 66-67, 147, 204, 251; Children's Day, 112
Chmielnicki, Bohdan, 77
Chopin, Frederic Francois, 224
Chorzów, 130
Church-Party relations, 17, 311. *See also* state-Church relations
Ciechanów, 65-66

Cieszyn, 130
citizenship, 3, 220, 229, 274, 290, 301
class structure/stratification, 3, 10, 250, 320
coercion (terror), 61, 77-80, 178-79, 218, 289, 293, 312, 323; correctional institutions, 61; prisons, 61, 293. *See also* education, repercussions, socialization, Stalinism
commitment-loyalty, 7-10, 22-28, 34, 40-44, 47, 84, 106ff
Communism, 4, 22-26, 44, 54, 72, 78, 104, 110, 142, 171, 203, 212-14, 290, 293, 323-24, *see also* ideology, Socialism; Third International (Comintern), 78, 222, 292-93; Communist Party, 78, 181, 213, 222, 290, 292, 323; Polish Workers' Party, 104, 249, 293. *See also* Jews, Polish United Workers' Party
community, 9, 19, 39-41, 55-56, 74-75, 79-81, 101ff. *See also* national councils
competitiveness, 138, 140, 144-45, 151, 167, 277
complaints, 29-30, 47, 66, 82, 104, 123-25, 131-32, 136, 192, 260, 267, 287-88, 291, 298, 306, 322
compromise, patterns of, 17, 143, 179-83, 187, 234, 236-38, 240, 310-11, 323-24. *See also* conformity, demands, pressures
conformity, 8-9, 82, 145, 149, 158, 178-79, 182, 196-97, 201, 205, 212, 216, 247, 300, 310, 322. *See also* compromise, demands, pressures
constitution, prewar, 45, 103-04
Council for Mutual Economic Assistance (CMEA), 261
Council of Ministers, 27; status of member, 90-91, 102
Council of State, 27, 141, 290
Cox, Frank D., 153n

Index

Cracow (Kraków), 14, 49, 59, 62, 130, 273, 299, 306; university, 59, 299, 306
Cuba, 171
culture, 6, 10, 12, 14-17, 31, 35, 43, 59, 61ff; Congress of Polish Culture, 31, 303-06; houses of, 14, 61; institutes and organizations, 64, 70, 222; Ministry of Culture and Art, 70, 268; night clubs, 126, 159-60, 224, 278; political culture, 93, 182ff; technological-industrial, 138-39, 241-48ff; traditional, 6, 146, 158, 201, 222, 271. *See also* arts, dance, media, music, teachers' reading pattern, traditionalism
Cyrankiewicz, Józef, 27, 290
Czechoslovakia, 79-80, 142, 159, 224, 293, 312
Częstochowa, 130
Czeszko, Bohdan, 284

dance, 15, 70, 126, 159-60, 298; Mazowsze, 15. *See also* arts, culture, music
Dąbrowski, Jarosław, 292n
Dąbrowska, Maria, 223
demands, 6, 8, 24, 34, 45, 58, 71, 77, 87, 125, 131, 144-45, 148, 150-51, 159, 178, 243ff. *See also* coercion, pressures
Democratic Alliance (SD), 56, 73, 78, 104, 119, 137, 184, 215, 262
Dewey, John, 31
diplomas, *magister*, 99-100; *matura*, 45, 68, 76, 86, 274, 277-79, 283-84, 287-88, 291-92, 296-300. *See also* education, intelligentsia, professions, schools
discipline, 28, 71-73, 134, 150, 213, 275, 279, 298, 315, 322
Dołęga-Mostowicz, Tadeusz, 223
Drapich, Wit, 301n
drug use, 275
Dubček, Aleksander, 80
Dziduszko, Karol, 62n, 85n

Easton, Lloyd D., 4n, 145n
economy, 4-6, 259-62, 273, 307; adaptation to change, 242-43; banks, 258; consumer service, 260; enterprises, 30, 56, 72, 123, 130, 132, 139, 154, 253-54, 256-57, 262, 272; failures, 259; foreign obligations, 260-61; investments, 131, 261; Ministry of Communal Economy, 260; PEKAO, 135, private sector, 14, 49-53, 71, 73, 93-94, 97, 101-02, 200, 210, 230, 256-58, 262, 278, 279, 313; public sector, 14, 93-96, 140, 256, 268, 272; reform, 179-80. *See also* agriculture, building, education, expertise, industrialization, planning, schools, science, technological development
education, adult, 61, 63, 69, 128, 137, 204, 268, 320; artistic-cultural, 53, 58-60, 66, 69-70, 95, 215; budget, 132ff; bureaucracy, *see* bureaucracy; classroom atmosphere, 85, 141, 270, 284-85, 322; coeducation, 172-75; Committee of Experts, 304, 307, 316; correspondence, 63, 69, 137, 204; curriculum, 58, 60, 77, 119, 122, 138, 174, 176, 193, 218, 263, 274, 277, 281, 285-88; development, 272; economic, 53, 59, 63; elementary, 49, 60, 95, 185, 263, 268-69, 303; experimentation-innovation, 285, 295, 303, 306; facilities, 48, 219, 262, 271, 275, 298, 301; general, 10, 22, 27, 30, 32-33, 40, 45-47, 49, 54, 56, 61-62, 64, 68-70, 79, 87, 95-96, 105, 180, 268; goals, 3-4, 7, 122-23, 130, 182, 193, 223, 230-31, 237-40, 249-51, 291, 302, 306, 310; grading

Index

Index

371

Index

372

Index

Index

materialism (*cont.*)
195, 211, 212, 235-40, 312.
See also Marxism,
modernization, planning,
rationalism, Socialism
mathematics, 48, 52, 62-63, 67,
122, 193, 195, 242, 263-64,
277, 280, 296, 309
Mayakovsky, Vladimir, 284
Mazowsze region, 98
Mazury Lake area, 154-55
media, 150; journalists, 90, 102;
press, 16, 40, 61, 88, 99, 116,
123, 132, 150, 160, 184-85,
225-28, 262, 265, 278, 285-87;
radio-television, 15, 86,
109-10, 150, 201, 218, 228,
278. *See also* culture
Meyer, Alfred G., 4n, 54n
Mickiewicz, Adam, 80, 215n, 285
middle class, 13-15, 24, 39,
50, 73, 184, 200, 210, 230,
313
Middle East, 80, 265-66; Arab
states, 265; Six Day War,
265-66. *See also* Israel
military, 28, 32, 45, 63, 68, 72,
76-79, 83, 89-91, 102, 105,
123, 142, 183, 213-15, 224,
242, 260, 266, 274, 278, 289,
290-97, 300, 316; Army
General Staff Academy, 292;
(Auxiliary) League for
National Defense (LOK), 215;
discipline, 28; district
command, 76, 293; Ministry
of National Defense (MON),
28n, 293n; officers, 32, 45,
76-77, 79, 89-92, 102, 105,
278, 289; Polish Peoples' Army
(regular), 28, 76-79, 89, 142,
291-94, 297; pre-regime units
(regular), 89, 142, 213, 242,
289, 291-92, 294; Second
Army, 293; social background
of, 76, 89; training, 63, 68,
72, 76-78, 274, 296. *See also*
education, internal security,
parliament, Soviet Union,
Spanish Civil War, warfare
Millennium celebrations, 26-27,

112, 148, 217, 252-54, 257,
262, 281-84, 297, 323;
Millennium School Fund, 112,
217, 253-54, 257. *See also*
school finances
Millet, Kate, 153n
Miłosz, Czesław, 211-12n
minorities, 76; Belo-Russians, 5,
77; Germans, 5, 141;
Lithuanians, 5, 77; Ukrainians,
5, 77. *See also* Jews
mobilization, 218, 307, 321
Moczar, Mieczysław, 79, 213-14,
266
modernization (modernity), 10,
153, 159-66, 175-77, 182,
198, 246, 312. *See also*
materialism, planning,
rationalism, Socialism
Moniuszko, Stanisław, 224
moral attitudes and styles, 15,
32-35, 43-44, 50, 69, 79,
106-07, 123, 143-44, 148, 153,
157-77, 182, 184-85, 190, 213,
234-36, 243, 274-75, 302,
309, 311-12. *See also* family,
health care, sex
music, 15-17, 51, 66-67, 69, 74,
110, 215, 224-25, 229, 297-98,
306; education, 51, 66-67, 69,
306; folk, 15, 224-25, 297;
Higher Music School
(Warsaw), 306; jazz, 224;
Mazowsze, 15; opera, 224;
rock-and-roll, 15, 225, 290.
See also arts, culture, dance
Muszalówna, Kazimiera, 30n
Muszyński, Heliodor, 44

National Council on Family
Relations (U.S.), 153n
national councils, 36, 38, 103,
112, 120, 132, 212, 215-17,
254-58, 261-62, 297;
departments of culture and
education, 36, 120, 254, 262.
See also community
nationalism, 7, 13-17, 24, 74,
79-80, 94, 106, 180-83, 211-14,
222, 282

Index

National-Radical Camp (ONR),
265-66
nature study, 263
New Zealand, 90, 92-93
Niewadzi, Czesław, 260n
Nowacki, T., 296
Nowa Huta, 14
Nowak, Irena, 271n
Nowy Sącz, 130

occupations, 9, 19, 89-95, 102-03,
121, 132, 165-67, 314; group
norms, 121; ranking, 90-92, 95,
102, 167. *See also* expertise,
professions
O'Connor, Lynn, 167n
Okoń, Wincenty, 301-03
Opole, 62, 283
opposition, 198, 294, 322. *See
also* sociopolitical deviation
Ostrołęka, 272-73
Ozga, Władysław, 199

parliament (*Sejm*), 27, 86, 98,
103-04, 119, 180, 216, 293,
303; Christian-Catholic
representation, 104n, 215;
Commission for Education and
Science, 86, 98; Constitutional
Sejm, 293n; Land National
Council, 104n, 293n; Military
Affairs Committee, 293n;
nonparty bloc, 119; prewar
Senate, 45, 103n-04n, 278. *See
also* parties, sociopolitical and
civic organizations
patriotism, 17, 26-27, 34, 89,
141, 148, 237, 242, 264,
281-82, 288
PAX, 104, 215, 253, 265-66
peasantry, 9, 12, 24, 37-39,
42-44, 48-57, 73, 77, 81, 89,
93, 102, 142, 149, 179, 186,
189-90, 200-09, 230, 257, 268,
294, 313-14; background, 43,
49-50; status, 90-92, 313. *See
also* agriculture, youth
Pejović, Danilo, 147n
Penderecki, Krzysztof, 224
pharmacology, 85

philosophy, 59, 68, 78, 85, 223,
301
physics, 22, 62-63, 67, 122, 193,
195, 242, 264, 274, 296
Piasecki, Bolesław, 266n
Piaseczno, 262
pilfering, 94
Piłsudski, Józef, 141-42, 222
Pióro, T., 296
Pius XI, 21n
planners, 6, 30, 122, 260, 272,
286, 305-07, 319; planning, 11,
139, 147, 252-62, 286, 303,
322. *See also* bureaucracy
Plato, 3
Płock, 272-73
Podlasie, 109
Polak, Wojciech, 32n
policy-making, 7, 179, 264-65,
307-08, 316, 325
Polish Academy of Sciences
(PAN), 13, 30, 90-92, 94, 108,
112, 152, 154, 192, 304-05.
See also research institutes
Polish Government-in-Exile, 20,
291
Polish Red Cross, 215
Polish-Soviet Friendship Society,
215
Polish United Workers' Party
(PZPR), 17-18, 21, 23, 26-27,
36, 39, 43-44, 51, 54-56, 64,
72-73, 81, 98, 103-04, 110,
119-22, 130, 134-35, 139-43,
148, 180ff; Central Committee,
26, 51, 56, 64, 141, 180-81,
259, 303-04; Politburo, 27, 43,
214; science and education
(culture) departments, 36,
119, 130, 180. *See also*
Communist Party, Polish
Socialist Party
Pomerania region, 130
population, 5, 23-25, 28, 57, 93,
142, 144, 151, 178-79, 188-89,
201, 251-52, 268, 270-72, 295,
319
Poznań, 49, 59, 148, 273, 280-81;
university, 59
prejudice, 170, 177, 183, 266.
See also Jews

375

Index

Index

23, 28-29, 45, 78, 106-07,
141-43, 147, 157, 168, 171,
181, 187, 194, 204, 213, 217,
245, 260, 263, 310-17, 320-25
Rickover, H. G., 30n
riots, October 1956 ("Polish
October"), 17, 21, 79, 232,
322; students' (Spring 1968),
17, 79-80, 84, 88, 93-94,
180, 231-32, 304, 322;
workers' (December, 1970),
21, 81, 119, 139, 143, 179-80,
204, 214, 231-32, 259, 316,
322-24. *See also* students,
working class
roles, 40, 44, 47, 73, 106, 122,
139, 148, 194, 208, 217-21,
228, 247, 266, 283, 324
Rolicki, Janusz, 65n, 70
Romańska, Agnieszka, 152n
Rossi, Peter H., 90n, 92
Rousseau, Jean Jacques, 3, 19
royalty, 18-19
Różewicz, Tadeusz, 284
Rudnicki, Adolf, 223
Rumania, 265, 312
Russia, 19, 77-78, 80, 141, 144,
181, 269; Czarist Army, 292;
orthodoxy, 19, 144; revolution,
54, 78, 292. *See also* languages
and literature, Soviet Union
Rzeszów, 49, 62, 283

San Juan, 24
Santor, Irena, 224
Sarapata, Adam, 90-92, 102
Sartre, Jean-Paul, 284
satisfaction, 104, 152, 191-92,
230-34, 296, 303, 316-24
Schaff, Adam, 147n, 304n
schools, construction, 37-38, 46,
82, 98, 111, 119, 234, 250-58,
261-62, 290, 322; facilities,
131, 192, 254, 322; finances,
75, 98, 217, 253-54, *see also*
Millennium celebrations;
grades, 172, 174ff, *see also*
education-reforms; inspections,
122-23, 136, 139; kuratorium
(curatoria), 36, 69, 122, 126,
139, 258, 284, 295-97, 302;

network of, 251-52ff; nonteaching staff, 132; parents'
committees, 124; pedagogic
councils, 36, 96, 124; role of,
122, 147-48; hygiene, 68
level and types:
agriculture: 53, 61, 66,
97, 273
economics: 58-59; higher
schools of, 59-60; Main
School for Planning and
Statistics, 59
elementary: 33, 39, 45-49,
60-70, 76, 83-88, 95-98,
108-10, 121-24, 131,
155-59, 174-77, 204, 229,
232, 251-55, 263, 274, 288,
303, 318
extension: 63, 66, 69,
204, 300
higher schools of
pedagogy: 46-49, 52-53,
58-65, 68-71, 83, 86, 191-92,
200, 208, 318; Higher
School of Pedagogy
(Gdańsk), 62; Higher
School of Pedagogy
(Opole), 62; State Institute
of Special Pedagogy (Maria
Grzegorzewska), 62
medical academies: 53,
57, 76
music: 51, 306; Higher
Music School (Warsaw),
306
night schools for workers:
264, 273
preschools (*kinder-
gartens*): 46-47, 66-67, 147,
204, 251
professional: 190, 249,
see also librarians, religion,
individual school entries
secondary: 63-66, 69-70,
73, 76-77, 83, 86, 95, 111,
131-36, 160, 172-76,
184-86, 189-93, 197,
200-05, 216, 221, 225-29,
232, 251-52, 258, 262, 267,
270-73, 277-79, 286-91,
294-305, 309, 318-21;

377

Index

Index

325. *See also* coercion, education, repercussions, values
social sciences, 10, 25, 31, 77, 88, 96, 247, 305-07; studies, 61, 263; sociology, 31, 68, 89, 152, 272, 304, 316. *See also* research institutes
sociopolitical deviation, 77-82, 126, 167ff. *See also* opposition, psychiatry, psychology, sex
Sopot, 58
Sosnowce, 130
Sosnowski, Józef, 185-86n, 228-29
Soviet Union (USSR), 5, 7, 16, 20-21, 80, 91-92, 133, 141-42, 190, 203, 232, 265-66, 282, 291-95, 312, 320, 324; Frunze Military Academy, 292n; Moscow, 80, 266, 292n; Red Army, 142, 291-95. *See also* languages and literature, Russia
Spanish Civil War, 142, 213, 292n-93n; International Brigade, 213, 292n. *See also* military, Soviet Union, warfare
Spychalski, Marian, 27n
Stalinism, 17, 133-34, 213, 231-32, 289, 293-94, 312-13. *See also* coercion
Staszic, Stanisław, 147
State Archeological Museum, 305
state-Church relations, 17-19, 21, 131, 144-45, 147-48, 193-95, 209, 234, 236-37, 311. *See also* Church-Party relations, religion
status, 14-15, 32, 40-41, 47-49, 57-58, 70, 81, 88-89, 93, 100-05, 108, 121, 131, 148, 186-87, 192, 209, 221, 245, 247, 300, 305-07, 313, 317-21. *See also* prestige, individual occupations-professions
Statute on the Employment of Graduates of Higher Institutions of Learning, 82
Steinbeck, John, 284
Strzelecki, Ryszard, 27n, 43
students, 8, 22-23, 26, 33-35,

40-56, 60-61, 63-82, 85-87, 123, 147ff; associations, 56, 72-75, 79, 215; Association of Polish Students (ZSP), 72-75, 79; cabarets, 74; choral groups, 74; classroom behavior, 149; clubs, 68, 74, 122; counseling, 66, 74, 275-77; dance ensembles, 74; discipline, 71, 73, 279; discussion circles, 72; dormitories, 67, 71, 111, 135-36, 250, 253-54; education majors, 60ff; employment market, 273, 297, 299; financial assistance, 56-57, 74, 80, 84, 99, 203; reading patterns, 281, 284-85; recreation, 64, 72, 74, 78-79, 122, 253; repercussions, 70, 84, 276, 279, 298, 322-23; selection, 33, 51-57, 68-71, 249-50, 252, 271, 273-74, 306-07, 313; social background, 42, 49-56, 189, 249-50, 300; sports, 74, 78; status, 47, 49, 57, 70; student government, 71, 122; student house, 71; pledge, 71; suicide, 280; summer camps, 64, 78; unrest and riots, 43, 77, 79-82, 93-94, 159, 180, 214, 322; vacations, 78. *See also* youth
Suchodolski, Bohdan, 26, 31n, 247
Suggs, Robert C., 153n
Svetlov, Mikhail, 284
symbols, of authority, 35, 37, 40-41, 58, 71, 105, 131-35, 141-43, 145, 148-49, 159, 175, 178-80, 189, 209, 215, 234, 282, 323-25; cultural and literary, 138, 186, 241, 246, 282, 290; political-ideological, 17, 20-21, 23, 29, 134, 141, 148, 163, 182-83, 323; of progress, 16, 246, 296; traditional and religious, 13, 16, 19, 148, 182, 325
Szczepański, Jan, 25n, 31, 117n, 221-22n, 250, 304, 307, 316
Szymański, Józef, 122n, 124
Świecki, Andrzej, 278n, 286n

379

Index

Świerczewski, Karol ("Walter"), 292-94n

Tarnów, 130
Taylor, Donald L., 153n
teachers, 7-10, 32-35, 39-41, 43-44, 46-47, 55-58, 60ff; activism of, 61, 64, 73-74, 96, 111-12, 129, 212, 214-16, 219; age and tenure, 8, 98, 129, 188-89, 197, 220-21, 227-28, 243-47, 286, 310; awards and rewards, 39, 103, 129, 131, 259, 286; charter and statutes, 128; classroom behavior, 34-36, 41, 77, 85, 112, 125-27, 149-50, 285, 295, 301-03, 306, 322; conferences with parents, 125; conflicts, 124-25, 132, 151, 209, 211; elementary, 132, 188, 214; expectations, 33-34, 36, 38, 44, 67; guidelines, 122, 302; housing cooperative, 83, 97-98, see also building-housing; humanists, 87, 96, 193-94, 243, 245, 247-48, 301; job assignments, 82-84ff; loyalty, 64ff; material conditions, 99ff; perceptions, 41, 192-93, 196, 219-20, 229, 244, 317-19; professional duties of, 33, 121; professional morality of, 33-34; professional press, 226; reading patterns, 223-28; recreation and culture orientation, 96, 109-10, 130, 214-15, 218-21, 224-29; repercussions-fears, 41, 55, 133, 150-51, 285; retirement, 135-36; role of, 40, 47, 106, 147-48, 208, 217-21, 228-29; satisfaction of and with, 104, 191-92, 230-34, 317-19, 321; scientists, 9, 194, 246; secondary, 132, 187-88, 194, 206ff; social background, 8-9, 35, 39, 151, 189-90, 199-200, 203-07, 210, 230-33, 313-14; sociopolitical behavior, 39, 125-26ff; specialists, 60, 193-96, 208, 244-47; status of,

40-41, 47, 57-58, 88-89, 90-93, 100-01, 104-05, 108, 121, 131, 186-87, 192, 209, 221, 245, 247, 300, 305, 317-19; union of, 39n-40n, 46n, 97-98, 120-23, 129-36, 187-88, 197, 215, 225, 253, 273, 287, 303; time allocation of, 229; training of, 43, 49, 52, 60, 62, 68-70, 85-87, 95, 200, 264, 299-301; vocational, 96, 194, 286
    teaching: 9, 34-35, 39, 46-47, 55, 61ff; load, 121; methodology, 59-61, 64, 68; practice, 60-64, 68, 78, 129, 287; profession, 9, 35, 95, 132, 158, 188, 197; quality of, 95ff; theory, 63. *See also* education, schools, science, sex, socialization, technological development
technological development, 6, 9-10, 12-14, 28-31, 43-45, 79, 87, 92, 137, 168, 182, 190, 235, 241-47, 263, 301, 315, 319-20; engineering, 62, 67, 90-92, 102, 247-48; telecommunications, 67; textiles, 67. *See also* economy, education, expertise, industrialization, schools, science
Tejkowski, Bernard, 37n, 107-08n
Tobruk, 291
Toma, Peter A., 214n
Toruń, 58-59, 130, 154-55, 170, 173-74, 189; university, 59, 88, 155
tourism, 15, 219
trade unionism, 24, 30, 40, 56, 81, 83, 130-36, 140, 253
traditionalism, 3, 6-7, 10ff; in education, 6, 122, 173, 194, 268, 273
transport, 16, 67, 81, 93, 109, 142, 209; automobile as status symbol, 93, 142; education in, 67; state of motorization, 16, 109, 209; traffic, 81
Turkey, 28; Turks, 18

Index

Tułodziecki, Wacław, 121
Turski, Stanisław, 306
Tuwim, Julian, 285
Tymowski, Janusz, 278

Ukraine, 155
Union of Polish Scouting (ZHP), 215
Union of Rural Youth (ZMW), 72-74, 79, 104, 112, 215
Union of Socialist Youth (ZMS), 72-75, 78, 104, 215
Union of Soviet Socialist Republics, *see* Soviet Union
United People's (Peasant) Movement (ZSL), 72-73, 104, 119, 137, 215-16; prewar people's-peasants party organizations, 73, 104, 294
United States of America, 17, 23-24, 29, 31, 33, 35, 39, 52, 63, 68, 73, 75, 81, 89, 91-92, 113, 153-55, 167, 172, 189, 216-17, 221, 224-25, 227, 250, 265, 275-76, 293, 309-10; communes in the, 167-68; drug use, 275; Harvard Report, 30n; high schools, 172; Negroes, 189-90; New York, 23; Puerto Ricans, 23-24; Reserve Officers' Training, 68; teachers, 33-34, 92, 154, 221, 225, 227
Unity Congress, 249, 290. *See also* Communism-Polish Workers' Party, Polish United Workers' Party (PZPR), Socialism-Polish Socialist Party (PPS)
universities, 14, 43-47, 52-53, 55, 58-65, 68-73, 83-94, 102, 117, 121, 132, 135-38, 178, 190-91, 249, 261, 286, 299, 304-06, 318-19; Adam Mickiewicz University, 59; Catholic University, 58; Gdańsk University, 58; graduates, 117ff; Jagiellonian University, 59, 299, 306; Lodz University, 58-59, 304, 306; Maria Curie-Skłodowska University, 58-59,

178; Mikołaj Kopernik University, 59, 88, 155; for parents, 268; personnel of (professors, etc.), 89-94, 102, 132, 138, 286, 318; *rector*, 71, 121, 306; Warsaw University, 55, 59, 62, 299, 305; Wayne State University (USA), 154n; for workers, 72, 268; Wrocław University (Bolesław Bierut), 58-59, 135. *See also* economy, education, expertise, planning, prestige, science, schools
urbanization, 4-5, 8-12, 25, 28, 73, 151, 202-03, 209-10, 218, 251-52, 271, 273
Ursynowska, Agata, 276
U.S. Department of Health, Education, and Welfare, 153n

vacations, 78, 192
values, 3-4, 8-10, 13-15, 21ff; educational, 8-9, 15ff; efficiency in transmission of 313. *See also* education, socialization
Varna, 18
veterans, 139, 141, 213-17, 324; Union of Fighters for Freedom and Democracy (ZBoWiD), 213-17, 293
Vienna, 222
Vietnam, 17
Vranicki, Predrag, 147n

Waller, Willard, 33
warfare, 290, 292; battles, 18, 142, 291-92, 294; guerrilla (partisan) and underground, 79, 213-14, 224, 252, 289, 291-92, 294-95, 297; September 1939 campaign, 252, 293-94; war of 1920, 142; war with Turkey, 18; World War I, 269-70, 292; World War II, 5, 12-13, 15-16, 24-25, 28, 57, 79, 135, 141-42, 151-52, 155, 195, 203, 214, 223-24, 242, 251-53, 258, 264-65, 268, 270-72, 283, 285,

381

Index